STOKES
FIELD GUIDE
TO BIRDS

Eastern Region

Donald and Lillian Stokes

D0011384

Little, Brown and Company

Boston New York Toronto London

First Edition

Library of Congress Cataloging-in-Publication Data
Stokes, Donald W.
      Stokes field guide to birds: eastern region / by
   Donald and Lillian Stokes. — 1st ed.
         p.   cm.
      Includes index.
      ISBN 0-316-81809-7
      1. Birds — East (U.S.) — Identification. I. Stokes,
   Lillian Q. II. Title. III. Series: Stokes, Donald W. Stokes
   field guides.
      QL683.E27S76 1995
      598.2974 — dc20   95-6611

10 9 8 7 6 5 4 3 2 1

RRD-IN

Designed by Barbara Werden

Published simultaneously in Canada by Little, Brown & Company (Canada) Limited

Printed in the United States of America

Color Tab Index to Bird Groups

Quick Guide to the Most Common Birds

Seabirds — Loons, Grebes, Shearwaters, Pelicans, Cormorants

Heronlike Birds — Bitterns, Herons, Egrets, Ibises

Swans, Geese, Ducks — Whistling-Ducks, Swans, Geese, Ducks

Hawklike Birds — Osprey, Kites, Eagles, Hawks, Falcons

Chickenlike Birds — Pheasant, Grouse, Turkey, Quail

Marsh Birds — Rails, Gallinule, Moorhen, Coot, plus Cranes

Shorebirds — Plovers, Stilt, Avocet, Sandpipers, Dowitchers, Phalaropes

Gull-like Birds — Jaegers, Gulls, Terns, Skimmer, plus Alcids

Pigeonlike Birds — Pigeon, Doves

Owls and Other Nocturnal Birds — Owls, Nighthawks, Whip-poor-will

Swift, Hummingbirds — Swift, Hummingbirds, plus Kingfishers

Woodpeckers — Woodpeckers, Sapsucker, Flicker

Flycatchers — Flycatchers, Phoebes, Kingbirds

Shrikes, Vireos — Shrikes, Vireos

Jays, Crows — Jays, Crows, Ravens

Swallows — Martin, Swallows

Chickadees, Nuthatches, Wrens — Chickadees, Titmice, Nuthatches, Wrens

Thrushes, Mimics — Bluebird, Thrushes, Robin, Catbird, Mockingbird, Thrashers

Warblers — Warblers, Parula, Redstart, Ovenbird, Waterthrushes, Chat

Tanagers, Grosbeaks, Buntings — Tanagers, Cardinal, Grosbeaks, Buntings

Sparrows — Towhees, Sparrows, Junco, Longspurs

Blackbirds, Orioles — Blackbirds, Grackles, Cowbirds, Orioles

Finches — Finches, Crossbills, Redpolls, Goldfinches

Stokes Nature Guides

by Donald Stokes

A Guide to Nature in Winter
A Guide to Observing Insect Lives
A Guide to Bird Behavior, Volume I

by Donald and Lillian Stokes

A Guide to Bird Behavior, Volume II
A Guide to Bird Behavior, Volume III
A Guide to Enjoying Wildflowers
A Guide to Animal Tracking and Behavior

by Thomas F. Tyning

A Guide to Amphibians and Reptiles

Stokes Backyard Nature Books

by Donald and Lillian Stokes

The Bird Feeder Book
The Hummingbird Book
The Complete Birdhouse Book
The Bluebird Book
The Wildflower Book — East of the Rockies
The Wildflower Book — From the Rockies West

by Donald and Lillian Stokes/Ernest Williams

The Butterfly Book

Stokes Field Guides

by Donald and Lillian Stokes

Stokes Field Guide to Birds: Eastern Region
Stokes Field Guide to Birds: Western Region

By Donald Stokes

The Natural History of Wild Shrubs and Vines

Contents

A Bird Guide for the 21st Century

More people than ever are watching birds. In addition to having fun, they want their birding to be a meaningful experience that results in a closer relationship to birds. To help people accomplish this, we have produced the *Stokes Field Guide to Birds*. What led us to this project was a desire to improve upon existing guides and to make a useful tool that would help people become better bird watchers and gain a new appreciation and understanding of birds. That is why our book not only provides fast and easy access to all the birds you might want to look up, it also presents important information on breeding biology, vocalizations, behavior, and conservation — information we believe will be more relevant than ever in the years to come and that will enrich your experience of the birds you see.

THREE-DIMENSIONAL BIRDING: IDENTIFICATION, BEHAVIOR, AND CONSERVATION

The preservation of the environment depends on those who love it, watch it, and know about it. Bird watchers have a key role to play in the coming century. They are among the dedicated people actually observing the natural world closely. They experience firsthand the changes that are occurring in bird populations in their own yards, their states or provinces, and even nationally.

The 21st century needs bird watchers who can accurately identify a bird, who know its needs for survival and reproduction, and who are aware of its population status.

These are all aspects of what we call three-dimensional birding — identification, behavior, and conservation. A knowledge of all three is needed for the public to begin making well-informed decisions that will help preserve bird populations. And since birds are excellent indicators of the general health of the environment, if we work to preserve their populations we will also be helping the environment as a whole.

It is our hope that through this guide more people will be able to identify birds and will become aware of the habitat needs and conservation status of the species they watch. We hope all bird watchers will become three-dimensional birders — avid and informed enthusiasts of birds and advocates for the environment.

HOW TO BECOME MORE INVOLVED

It is up to those of us who know the importance of the natural world to take an active role in protecting it. In bird-watching, this can result in more fun and a more meaningful experience. Here are some ways that you can become more involved with helping birds:

- Learn to identify more birds.

- Learn more about the biology of the species you watch through reading and your own observations.

- Become aware of the population trends of the birds you see.

- Keep a notebook of your observations as a record of all that you learn.

- Share your love for and knowledge of birds with others, both young and old.

- Participate in bird surveys and censuses.

- Join birding organizations and bird clubs in your area.

- Join local, national, and international conservation organizations.

- Create good bird habitats in your own backyard by providing bird feeders, birdhouses, and plantings that attract birds.

- Help your local conservation commission acquire and manage town lands so that they support more birds.

All of these activities add up to an involved bird-watching public. This is what three-dimensional birding is all about.

Acknowledgments

Undertaking a task as huge as field guides to North American birds requires the help and hard work of many people. We would like to thank those who had a major part in the writing and producing of these guides.

First and foremost we would like to thank the photographers who have devoted so much of their time and energy to capturing these birds on film. Their names are listed in the photo credits.

Second, we want to thank the various experts who read early drafts and helped make them better. Four people read the entire manuscript and made extensive comments. They were Wayne Petersen, David Wolf, Paul Roberts, and Allen Baldridge. We also had others read special sections: Debra Shearwater reviewed seabirds; Bill Clark reviewed vultures, hawks, eagles, falcons; Claudia Wilds reviewed gulls and terns; Joseph Jehl, Jr., reviewed shorebirds; and Trevor Lloyd-Evans reviewed warblers. Of course, we take full responsibility for the accuracy of the final work.

We would also like to thank Paul Roberts for enjoyable initial discussions on the scope and format of the guides, Wayne Petersen for discussions on the Learning Pages and the careful review of all slides, and our son, Justin Brown, for help in researching some of the breeding and behavior accounts.

The conservation data were gathered from a variety of sources. We want to give special thanks to Bruce Peterjohn and Sam Droege for their assistance in getting the data of the Breeding Bird Survey and the Christmas Bird Count and John Sauer for his guidance in interpreting the data. We were also fortunate to have the Network of Natural Heritage Programs and Conservation Data Centers and the Nature Conservancy arrange for us to use their superb database on the conservation status of North American birds.

We had a wonderful production staff at Little, Brown and Company, and we worked closely with them in all aspects of production in order to make the best possible guides. We especially want to thank Donna Peterson in production, Barbara Werden in design, and Peggy Leith Anderson in copyediting, who knows the book, word for word, better than anybody but ourselves. We also want to thank John Kramer for his help in setting up our Power Macintoshes so that the material was essentially typeset during writing, and in such a way that we could draw our range maps more efficiently. In addition, we want to thank our hard drive, Merlin, for not letting us down.

We also want to share our appreciation of our editors, Jordan Pavlin and, especially, Bill Phillips, editor in chief, vice president, and associate publisher of Little, Brown, for his longstanding support of our writing, from the very first book to these field guides, and for his warm friendship.

The Basics of the Guide

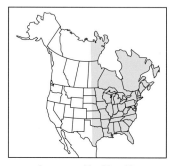
Area covered by this guide

SPECIAL SECTIONS

This guide offers a number of useful tools for bird watchers at all levels of skill and interest. Spending a few minutes now to familiarize yourself with these features will help you take full advantage of them whether you are using the guide at home or in the field.

Quick Alphabetical Index

Right inside the front and back covers is a concise alphabetical index to the birds. If you know the kind of bird you want to look up, this is a fast way to find it.

Color Tab Index

Facing the front and back covers is the **Color Tab Index to Bird Groups.** This provides access to the birds by groups — heronlike birds, shorebirds, woodpeckers, sparrows, and so forth. The color tabs are a fast way to automatically turn to the right portion of the guide. In addition, this index and the Species Accounts are arranged in phylogenetic order, that is, according to their believed evolutionary relationships, thus familiarizing all users with the only order of birds generally agreed upon by

scientists and birders in North America.

Quick Guide to the Most Common Birds

Immediately preceding the Species Accounts is the **Quick Guide to the Most Common Birds.** These are help pages designed especially for beginners. Here, the species of birds most commonly seen at bird feeders and in backyards are shown in a special format for quick reference and easy comparisons.

These pages will help beginners successfully master the identification of common birds so that they can then go on to learn others. Next to each picture is the number of the page where a detailed description of the bird may be found.

Learning Pages

Interspersed with the Species Accounts are other special sections called **Learning Pages.** These provide beginning and intermediate bird watchers with a basic orientation to the more complex and challenging groups of birds: hawks, shorebirds, gulls, flycatchers, warblers, and sparrows.

Learning Pages occur at the start of each of these bird groups. They provide an overall introduction to identification of the group, helpful organizing concepts or tips, and pictures of the most commonly seen species within each group.

SPECIES ACCOUNTS

The main body of the field guide is composed of full-page accounts for each species. Photographs, text, and range map are all on the same page, along with other new, informative features.

Species, Names, Order

All regularly occurring species within the range of the guide are included. Their scientific and common names and order are in accordance with the July 1995 supplement to the 6th edition of the American Ornithological Union Checklist of North American Birds.

In a few cases, two species are placed on the same page. This is done when one species follows the other in the phylogenetic order and looks extremely similar, making the comparison helpful. It is also done to keep the guide slightly shorter and reduce the weight of the final book.

Bird Feeder and Birdhouse Symbols

Identifying symbols have been included next to the names of birds that use bird feeders and birdhouses. This will help you recognize the species you may see at feeders or birdhouses, and may also encourage you to provide appropriate food and housing for these species. In the section called **Feeding** we have listed the feeder foods these birds prefer. The symbols are generalized and not meant to show the specific type of feeder or house used by that species.

Bird feeder   Birdhouse

Range Maps

Up-to-date range maps show whether a bird is likely to be found in a particular area. The maps have 1–3 colors. Blue indicates winter range; yellow indicates summer range, which includes both breeding range and areas moved into in summer after breeding; green is year-round range.

There are several things to remember when using any range map. Ranges of birds are always changing in response to the environment and population of the species. At the edge of a range the bird is not seen in substantial numbers, but there are always some individual birds outside this edge, stretching the limits of the range. Also, maps may show a continuous range, but birds may live only locally within that range. This is particularly true of species that live in specialized habitats.

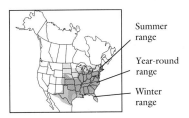

Summer range

Year-round range

Winter range

Photographs

Hundreds of color photographs have been carefully selected to show male, female, immature, and seasonal plumages of each species. For species in which male and female look almost identical, only one sex is shown. In many cases, such as hawks, gulls, and terns, we have also shown birds in flight, since this is often the most common way these birds are encountered. Photos for species that have only one adult plumage throughout the year have no identifying caption. All other photos are clearly captioned to identify age, sex, and season of the plumage shown.

Identification Section

The first information in the identification section is the average length of the species, measured in inches, from tip of beak to tip of tail. This allows rough comparisons of size between species.

In the identification clues for adult birds, some clues are in **bold-face type.** These are the main clues to the identification of the species and, in most cases, are sufficient to distinguish this species from all others in the area. Additional clues in normal typeface provide further distinguishing marks that have proven helpful.

All descriptions of plumages refer to adult birds unless otherwise noted. There are separate headings for **MALE** and **FEMALE** when their plumages differ. If these headings are not included in a species account, then the sexes are alike.

Seasonal plumages are indicated by the headings **SUMMER** and **WINTER.** Summer is roughly from March through August and includes the breeding period; winter is roughly from September through February and coincides with the nonbreeding period. We vary from this approach only in describing the warblers, because traditionally their summer plumage is referred to as spring and their winter plumage as fall.

In preparing this guide, we had to choose what terminology to use to describe the various plumages of birds. Although there is general agreement among the scientific community to use the system of plumage terminology proposed by Humphrey and Parkes in 1959,

this system is still too complex for the lay public, more detailed than most bird watchers need, and not used in field guides.

Understanding any plumage terminology requires a basic knowledge of how and when birds acquire their various feathers. When a bird first hatches, it is covered with fine feathers called **natal down.** This is soon replaced by the first full set of feathers, which is called the **juvenal plumage.** In most North American birds, juvenal plumage is molted and replaced by new feathers in late summer. This new plumage may be like adult plumage or may be different. When it differs from that of the adults, we call it **immature plumage.** We continue to call it immature until it is like adult plumage.

In summary, we use the term **immature** to refer to any plumage between juvenal and adult plumages.

It is important to remember that sexual maturity and plumage maturity do not always coincide. Some birds can breed while still in immature plumage, and some birds may be in adult plumage but still not sexually mature.

In this guide, juvenal plumages kept only in summer are not described. This is because, in most species, they are only briefly held. Also, juveniles in summer are often still being attended by their parents and can thus be recognized by identifying the adults.

Any juvenal plumage kept into fall, and all immature plumages, are included in this guide. In most cases, we tell how long the bird stays in immature plumages; for example, "Imm. plumage kept until spring," or "Imm. plumage kept 1 year." This timing starts from the bird's first fall.

In a few instances, such as shorebirds, juveniles keep their plumage into fall and we see them gradually molting out of it as they migrate south. We have given them the heading FALL JUV.

In one case, we have varied from our system; this is in the hawks. Nonadult hawks in fall are technically in their juvenal plumage. We have called them immatures because there is such a strong tradition of referring to them in this way.

Feeding

This section describes the feeding location, method of getting food, and the foods eaten. Foods listed are the items that make up the bulk of the bird's diet. Most birds eat a wide variety of incidental foods and the complete list would be too long to include. When birds come to feeders, we mention the foods they prefer.

Nesting

Nesting and breeding information starts with a description of the nest, its materials, and placement. Many birds use a wide variety of nesting materials, and we have listed only the major items.

Under **Eggs** we have included a range of numbers for the clutch size. The majority of birds will lay the average of this range. Incubation period (marked by the letter **I**) is the time from the laying of the last egg until the first egg hatches. The fledgling phase (marked by the letter **F**) is the time from hatching to first flight (in precocial birds) or the time from hatching to leaving the nest (in altricial birds).

Following the time of fledging, there is the term **altricial** or **precocial.** These terms refer to the development of the young. Upon hatching, altricial young are dependent on the parents for food and warmth, for they cannot move well and are generally at first naked; they stay in the nest. Precocial young, upon hatching, are feathered and can generally feed themselves; they often leave the nest within a day or two of hatching.

The last information in the nesting and breeding section is the number of broods a bird has in a season. It is marked by a **B.** Shown is the number of successful broods a species will attempt in a normal season. It does not include cases of renestings after failed broods.

A question mark after one of the letters means that aspect of the bird's breeding biology, to the best of our knowledge, is not known and needs more study.

Other Behavior

This section deals with behaviors of the bird that you are likely to see or that are particularly interesting, such as flight displays, courtship activities, territory formation, and migration behavior, as well as other intriguing features about the bird's life. We hope you take time to watch and enjoy these aspects of birds.

Habitat

The major ecological habitats that the bird uses when within the United States and Canada are summarized in this section.

Voice

This section describes the main vocalizations of the bird. The term **song** refers to a partially learned, generally complex vocalization. The term **call** refers to short, instinctively given vocalizations.

Conservation

In the conservation section we share with you some of what is known about the population status and conservation of North American birds.

One way we do this is to say whether the bird is classified as federally endangered in the United States and/or Canada. Species or subspecies so designated are in danger of extinction in part or all of their range. Once a species is listed as federally endangered, the federal Fish and Wildlife Service may get funds and legislation to help protect it from further harm and foster its recovery.

We also tell you the bird's population trend (whether it is increasing or declining) and other pertinent information. Below is an example of the population trend information and a brief explanation of its symbols.

In cases where there are not enough data to suggest any population trend, you will see the phrase TREND UNKNOWN.

BBS: E ↑ C ⇓ CBC: ↑

BBS stands for the Breeding Bird Survey (see text). **E** and **C** stand for eastern and central regions of the continent.

CBC stands for Christmas Bird Count (see text).

Arrows indicate increasing (up) or decreasing (down) populations. Single arrows (↑) indicate smaller changes; double arrows (⇓) indicate larger changes. Horizontal arrows (→) indicate stable population.

Because this information is a key component of what we call three-dimensional birding, we want to explain it in some detail.

AN IN-DEPTH EXPLANATION OF THE CONSERVATION INFORMATION

There are two main programs used in North America to determine population trends of birds: the Breeding Bird Survey and the Christmas Bird Count.

The **Breeding Bird Survey** (BBS) was started in the United States and Canada in 1966 and was run by the U.S. Fish and Wildlife Service and the Canadian Wildlife Service; it is now administered by the National Biological Survey and the Canadian Wildlife Service. The survey is done by volunteers who drive a 24.5-mile route, stopping every half mile for 3 minutes during which they record all birds seen or heard. The route is fixed and driven only once, on a day during the height of the breeding season. There are over 3,000 routes all across the United States and Canada. In 1993, routes were also started in Mexico. The data from the survey are broken down into three regions of the continent: western (from the Rocky Mountains west), central (from the Rocky Mountains to the Mississippi River), and eastern (from the Mississippi River east). In this guide, BBS data have been reported for the eastern and central regions.

The **Christmas Bird Count** (CBC) was started in 1900 and is run by the National Audubon Society. It is the largest survey of birds in the world, with more than 45,000 volunteer participants. There are over 1,500 designated count areas in the United States and Canada, each 15 miles in diameter. Within a week or two of Christmas, each designated area is censused for one day, with participants seeking out and counting all birds in that area. CBC data are not broken down by region; they reflect population trends throughout Canada and the United States. CBC does not cover birds that winter south of the United States.

Other Surveys

Many species of birds are not covered well by either the Breeding Bird Survey or the Christmas Bird Count. To gather population trend information on these species, we have relied on other information and research that we believe is the best available. These sources are referred to in the text with different initials, which are listed below along with the organizations and people for which they stand.

CWS   Canadian Wildlife Service. The Canadian Wildlife Service, Ottawa ON K1A 0H3, publishes a regular report entitled *Bird Trends.* We used much of their information on shorebirds.

HWI   Hawkwatch International, personal communication, Steve Hoffmann. Hawkwatch International, Salt Lake City, is a nonprofit organization that concentrates on raptor conservation.

ICN   Ian C. T. Nisbet, unpublished manuscript.

The Meaning of the Arrows

The arrows used in the conservation information indicate increases or declines in the species' population; up arrows mean an increase, down arrows mean a decline, horizontal arrows mean a stable population. Arrows are based on the estimated average per-year change in the species' population for the period of the data analyzed. Single arrows ($\downarrow$) indicate a trend of less than 2% per year. Double arrows ($\Downarrow$) indicate a trend of 2% or greater per year. BBS data used are for the years 1966–1993; CBC data are for 1965–1989; CWS data are for 1974–1991; other data are for approximately the last 25 years.

We have used the double arrows to try to highlight those birds whose populations have gone through major changes in the last 2–3 decades.

If no arrow appears, the bird does not breed in that region or data are insufficient to indicate a trend.

Interpreting the Data

The data from the BBS and CBC provide us with a unique opportunity to track the populations of birds in the United States and Canada. The studies are the broadest of their kind in North America and are the ones most often relied on for population information.

However, they are not perfect. There are inherent problems with the collection and analysis of data. For example, habitats in count areas or along survey routes may change over time and affect the numbers and species of birds seen. Coverage has improved with more routes and census areas and more participants; in addition, observers are getting better and seeing more birds. In the CBC, census areas are not evenly spaced across the continent; also weather, such as stormy or sunny days, can affect the counts in the short run.

Other factors affect the analysis of the data. If the trend is based on the whole country, it may mask a change in one or more smaller regions. We are reporting the regional breakdown of the BBS data and the continent-wide analysis of the CBC data so that you can compare the two.

Another critical factor is the number of years from which data are taken. We have chosen to look at long-term changes by using the entire length of the study for which the data are adequately analyzed. If we had reported a recent 5–10 year span, the data might look different.

The information presented in this guide is the best available on bird populations and has not yet been made readily accessible to bird watchers or the public. Many organizations are working hard to pull together population data, for it is essential that we know the status of birds around us. We hope that more and better ways of censusing and tracking birds will be developed in the future and that many of you will be participants in gathering the data.

For More Information

More detailed information on BBS data can be obtained by writing:

BBS Coordinator
Patuxent Environmental
    Science Center
12100 Beech Forest Road
Laurel, MD 20708

More detailed information on CBC data can be obtained by writing:

National Audubon Society
Christmas Bird Count
700 Broadway
New York, NY 10003

Parts of a Bird

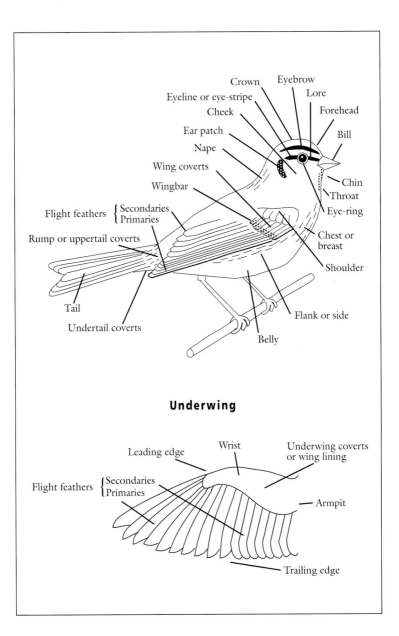

Crown Eyebrow
Eyeline or eye-stripe Lore
Cheek Forehead
Ear patch Bill
Nape
Wing coverts
Wingbar Chin
Throat
Flight feathers { Secondaries Eye-ring
Primaries
Rump or uppertail coverts Chest or breast
Shoulder
Tail Flank or side
Undertail coverts Belly

Underwing

Leading edge Wrist Underwing coverts or wing lining
Flight feathers { Secondaries Armpit
Primaries
Trailing edge

Quick Guide to the Most Common Birds

Backyard and Feeder Birds Grouped by Color

Scan these pages for the bird you have seen. If you find it here, go to the page shown for more information. If you don't see it here but have an idea as to the type of bird it is, turn to the Color Tab Index or the Quick Alphabetical Index and look for the group of birds that seems closest to your bird, then turn to that section and look through the pictures.

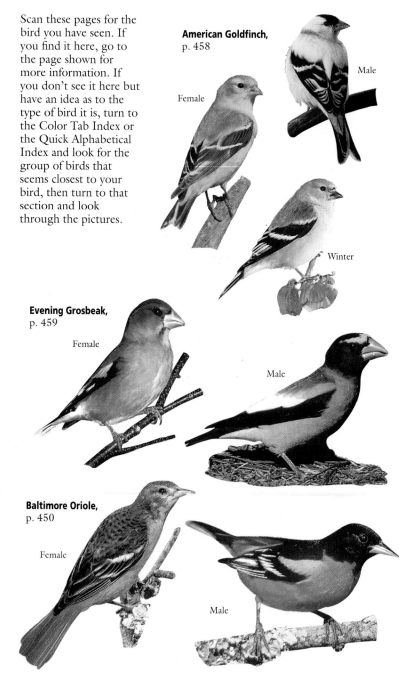

American Goldfinch, p. 458

Male

Female

Winter

Evening Grosbeak, p. 459

Female

Male

Baltimore Oriole, p. 450

Female

Male

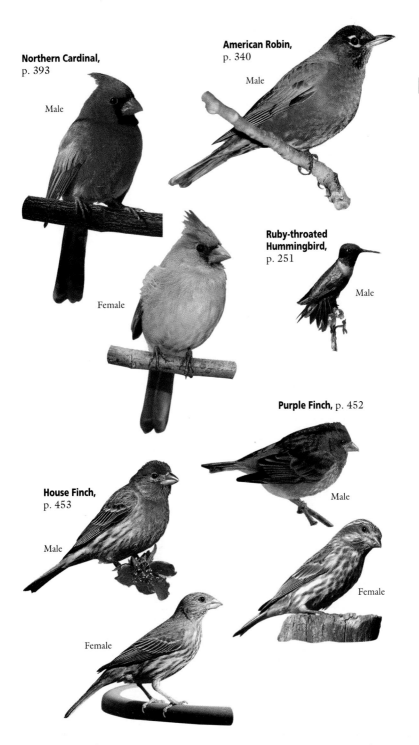

Northern Cardinal, p. 393

Male

Female

American Robin, p. 340

Male

Ruby-throated Hummingbird, p. 251

Male

Purple Finch, p. 452

Male

Female

House Finch, p. 453

Male

Female

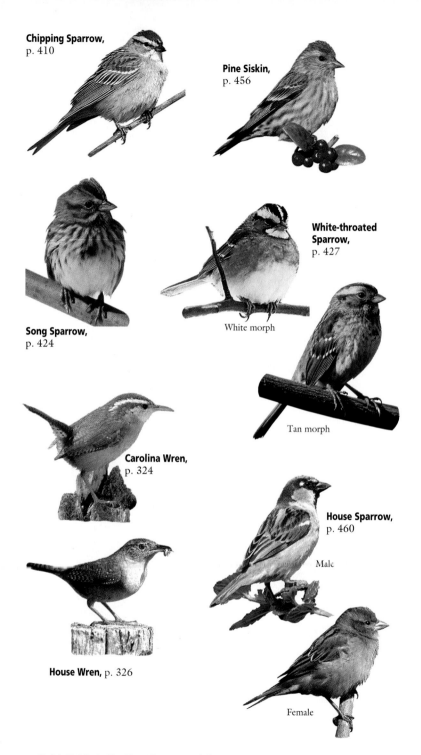

Chipping Sparrow, p. 410

Pine Siskin, p. 456

White-throated Sparrow, p. 427

White morph

Song Sparrow, p. 424

Tan morph

Carolina Wren, p. 324

House Sparrow, p. 460

Male

House Wren, p. 326

Female

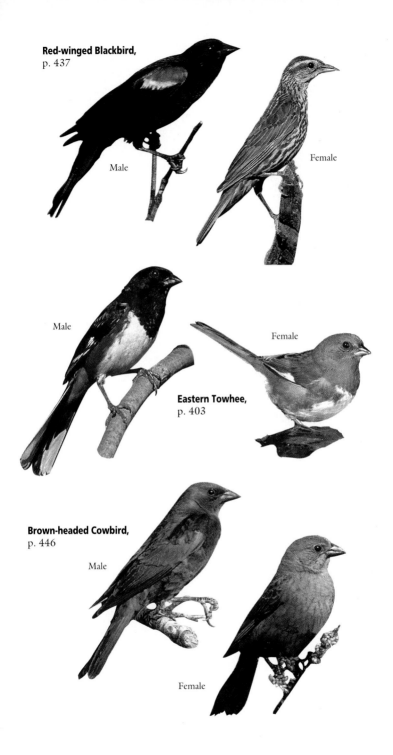

Red-winged Blackbird,
p. 437

Male

Female

Male

Female

Eastern Towhee,
p. 403

Brown-headed Cowbird,
p. 446

Male

Female

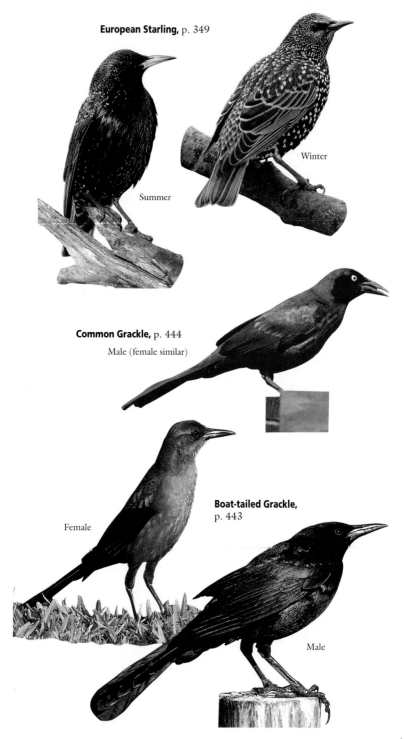

European Starling, p. 349

Winter

Summer

Common Grackle, p. 444

Male (female similar)

Female

Boat-tailed Grackle, p. 443

Male

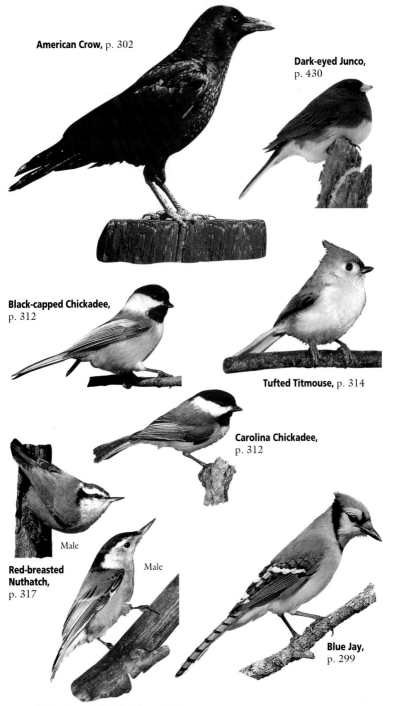

American Crow, p. 302

Dark-eyed Junco, p. 430

Black-capped Chickadee, p. 312

Tufted Titmouse, p. 314

Carolina Chickadee, p. 312

Male

Red-breasted Nuthatch, p. 317

Male

Blue Jay, p. 299

White-breasted Nuthatch, p. 318

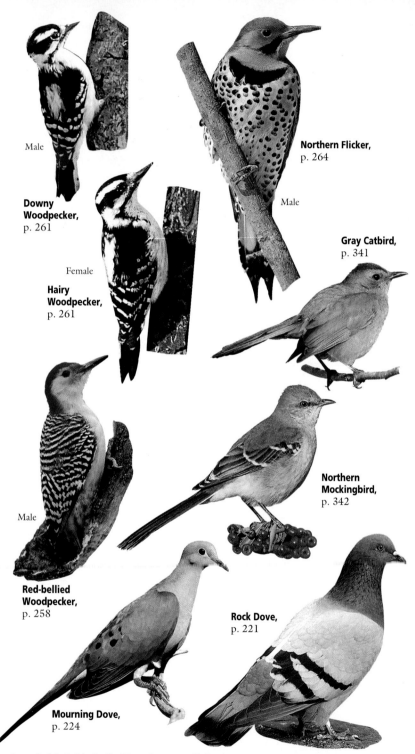

Male

Downy
Woodpecker,
p. 261

Northern Flicker,
p. 264

Male

Female

Hairy
Woodpecker,
p. 261

Gray Catbird,
p. 341

Male

Northern
Mockingbird,
p. 342

Red-bellied
Woodpecker,
p. 258

Mourning Dove,
p. 224

Rock Dove,
p. 221

SPECIES
ACCOUNTS

Red-throated Loon

Gavia stellata

Summer

Winter

Identification: 25" **SUMMER: Gray face and dark red throat;** nape striped with black and white lines. **WINTER:** Note **gradual blending between white front and gray back of the neck.** (Border between light and dark areas is straight and lacks white triangular indentation seen in Common Loon.) **Thin bill** appears upturned; fine white spots on back may be visible. **IMM:** Similar to winter adult, but with grayish flecking on cheek. Imm. plumage kept 1 year.

Feeding: Feeds by diving underwater and pursuing fish. In winter, sometimes seen feeding in small flocks.

Nesting: Platform nest of grasses, twigs, and mud lined with finer materials, placed at the water's edge. Eggs: 1–3, olive-brown with dark marks; I: 24–29 days; F: 48–50 days, precocial; B: 1.

Other Behavior: Most loons need a running start of about 20 yd. on the water to take flight. This species can take off in less distance and is the only loon known to be able to take flight from land. During migration, flocks of hundreds may gather on the Great Lakes to feed. The birds migrate during the day in loose flocks.

Habitat: Summers on tundra lakes and arctic coasts; winters along coasts and in Great Lakes.

Voice: At start and end of winter gives short wailing call; otherwise quiet. Uses a variety of calls on the breeding ground.

Conservation: CBC: ↓

Pacific Loon
Gavia pacifica

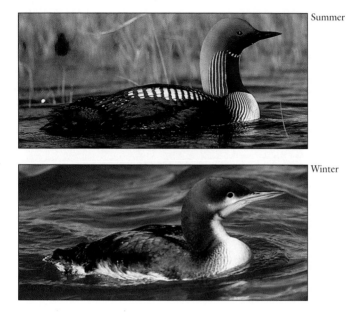
Summer

Winter

Identification: 26" **SUMMER: Pale gray crown and nape;** black-and-white checkered back; iridescent throat patch can appear purple, green, or black. **WINTER: Straight sharp border between the light and dark areas of the neck;** thin dark bill is held horizontal; eye is in the black cap. Some individuals have a thin dark line under the chin. **IMM:** Similar to winter adult, but with whitish scaling on back. Imm. plumage kept 1 year, ►The rare Arctic Loon, *G. arctica*, is similar but larger and breeds in western Alaska.

Feeding: Feeds by diving underwater and pursuing prey such as fish, crustaceans, and frogs.

Nesting: Platform nest of stems, roots, and mud, placed near the water's edge. Eggs: 1–2, brown with dark marks; I: 23–25 days; F: 60–65 days, precocial; B: 1.

Other Behavior: One of the most numerous loons off the Pacific Coast, often feeding in flocks of hundreds or thousands along the coastline. The most commonly seen loon on winter pelagic trips in the West. It is rare, but regularly occurring, off the East Coast.

Habitat: Summers on tundra lakes; winters along coast.

Voice: Generally quiet in winter; summer calls include a sharp call like "kwao" and a wail that rises in pitch.

Conservation: CBC: ⇑

4

Common Loon

Gavia immer

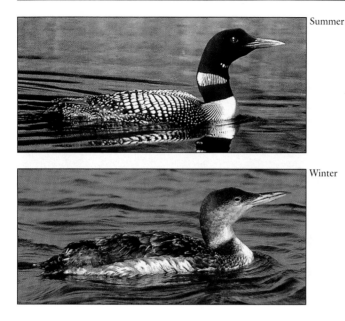

Summer

Winter

Identification: 32" The most commonly seen loon. **SUMMER: Black head and black bill;** black-and-white barred neck-ring; checkered back. **WINTER: The border between the white front and black back of the neck is irregular, with a white, triangular indentation at midneck.** Holds **thick bill** horizontal. **IN FLIGHT:** Feet trail behind tail and are larger than in other loons. **IMM:** Similar to winter adult. Imm. plumage kept 1 year. Immatures spend 1st year along coast.

Feeding: Feeds by diving underwater and pursuing fish. Feeding dives average 45 seconds long.

Nesting: Platform nest of aquatic vegetation, placed on the ground on an island or at the water's edge. Eggs: 2, olive-brown; I: 29 days; F: 2–3 months, precocial; B: 1.

Other Behavior: Listening to loon sounds can tell you about their behavior. The yodel-call is used for territory advertisement and defense; the tremelo-call is used during moments of alarm; and the wail-call is often used to help the pair keep in contact with each other. Loons may dive to escape danger and can remain underwater for up to 3 minutes.

Habitat: Summers on lakes; winters mostly along coast.

Voice: Wail-call: a drawn-out wail. Tremelo-call: a short tremulous call. Yodel-call: a wail followed by a long undulating call.

Conservation:
BBS: E ⇑ C ⇑ CBC: ↑ Boats on lakes can disturb breeding birds.

Least Grebe

Tachybaptus dominicus

Summer

Identification: 10" Limited to S. Tex. The smallest of the grebes. SUMMER: **Dark gray head and body; thin dark bill; yellow-orange eye.** WINTER: Differs from summer plumage only in having a **white chin.** All year the bird has white fluffy feathers at the rear, which can be shown or hidden.

Feeding: Eats primarily aquatic insects by diving and catching them underwater or taking them from the water surface.

Nesting: Platform nest built of reeds and other water plants, tied to vegetation in shallow water. Eggs: 4–6, whitish; I: 21 days; F: ?, precocial; B: 2–3.

Other Behavior: These birds may nest in any month of the year, if conditions are right and water levels are high. They often stay hidden among the reeds at the edges of small ponds, and the exposing of the white feathers at their rear may be a display.

Habitat: Shallow ponds.

Voice: Sounds not well known. An alarm note like "teek" and a short trill sometimes done as a duet have been heard.

Conservation: CBC: ↑

Pied-billed Grebe
Podilymbus podiceps

Summer

Winter

Identification: 12″ A small, stocky, brown grebe with a short stout bill. **SUMMER:** Obvious **black ring around white bill;** the chin is black. **WINTER:** The **bill has a faint ring or no ring,** and the chin is light.

Feeding: Feeds by diving underwater and catching fish, aquatic insects, frogs, and crayfish.

Nesting: A platform nest of decaying vegetation, attached to growing vegetation in shallow water. Eggs: 4–7, bluish green; I: 23 days; F: ?, precocial; B: 1–2.

Other Behavior: One of the earliest migrants among the grebes, often arriving on ponds before the ice is all melted. In territorial skirmishes males come together and tilt heads up while calling. Parents may do a distraction display of flapping their wings between dives when their young are in danger. Their white rear feathers may be flashed in times of alarm.

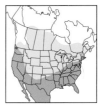

Habitat: Summers on lakes and ponds; winters also in sheltered saltwater bays.

Voice: During breeding, calls include a "cow cow cow cow cow," a loud "keck keck" in alarm, and a softer "cuk cuk cuk." It is generally quiet in winter.

Conservation:
BBS: E ↑ C ↓ CBC: ↑

7

Horned Grebe

Podiceps auritus

Summer

Winter

Identification: 14" **SUMMER: Golden ear tufts; reddish-brown neck. WINTER: White cheek patch is level with eye and extends almost all the way around the back of the head.** Also has white front to neck and whitish streaks along flanks.

Feeding: Feeds by diving underwater, eating small fish, crayfish, shrimp, and aquatic insects. Also eats land insects, frogs, and salamanders.

Nesting: Floating platform nest of plants and mud, anchored to vegetation. Eggs: 3–7, bluish white; I: 22–25 days; F: 44–60 days, precocial; B: 1.

Other Behavior: Like other grebes, this species can lower its body as it swims so that just its head shows; at other times it rides high on the water. In winter, often seen alone or in small flocks just outside the breaking waves, where it feeds. Tends to jump forward before diving down into the water.

Habitat: Summers on marshy ponds and lakes; winters mostly along the coast and on some inland lakes.

Voice: Makes a variety of loud croaks, chatters, and shrieks on the breeding ground; otherwise silent.

Conservation:
BBS: E C ⇓ CBC: ↓ Vulnerable to oil spills.

8

Red-necked Grebe

Podiceps grisegena

Summer

Winter

Identification: 19" SUMMER: Large grebe; long reddish foreneck; whitish chin and cheek; black cap. WINTER: Large and dusky, without sharp contrasts in plumage. The **long yellowish bill** helps distinguish it from the similar winter Horned and Eared Grebes. The **white on the chin extends up behind the grayish cheek.** IMM: Similar to winter adult, but without white mark behind cheek. Imm. plumage kept at least through winter.

Feeding: Feeds by diving underwater, eating fish, aquatic insects, marine worms, crustaceans, and mollusks. Also eats land insects and some vegetation.

Nesting: Floating platform nest of fresh and decayed reeds, rushes, and grasses, anchored to nearby vegetation. Eggs: 2–6, bluish white; I: 22–23 days; F: 50–70 days, precocial; B: 1.

Other Behavior: Adults eat their own molted feathers and even feed them to their young, as do some other grebes. All grebes avoid danger by diving underwater. Adults can dive underwater with young riding on their back — the young just hold on.

Habitat: Summers on lakes, ponds; winters mostly along coast.

Voice: Sounds include long wails, short vibrating wails, and chattering trills. Generally silent in winter.

Conservation:
BBS: E C ⇓ CBC: ↑
May be subject to thinning eggshells and infertile eggs due to pesticides.

Eared Grebe

Podiceps nigricollis

Summer

Winter

Identification: 12″ SUMMER: **Golden ear tufts** and **black neck.** WINTER: **Small thin bill appears uptilted; grayish neck and cheek** with a whitish ear patch; **triangularly shaped head** due to elevated crest. Occasionally the cheek is whitish. In water, usually rides high in rear, low in front.

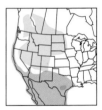

Feeding: Feeds by diving underwater, eating small fish, crustaceans, mollusks, aquatic insects, and the eggs of leeches.

Nesting: Floating platform nest of fresh and decayed vegetation, anchored to surrounding plants. Eggs: 3–9, dull bluish white; I: 20–22 days; F: 20–21 days, precocial; B: 1.

Other Behavior: Eared Grebes may nest singly or in colonies of several hundred pairs. Usually remain as flocks in wintering areas as well. On the breeding grounds they may be heard calling at dusk. Up to 1 million birds stage and molt at Mono Lake, Calif., and somewhat smaller numbers at other large saline lakes in the arid West. These large concentrations in small areas make them vulnerable to environmental changes.

Habitat: Summers on lakes and marshes; winters along the coast and on some inland lakes.

Voice: Breeding calls include a soft "pooeep" and a louder "hikarikup, hikarikup." Generally quiet in winter.

Conservation: BBS: E C ⇑ CBC: ↓

Western Grebe
Clark's Grebe

Aechmophorus occidentalis   Aechmophorus clarkii

Western

Clark's

Identification: 25″ Large long-necked grebes with sharp contrast between black above and white below. **WESTERN: Black cap extends below the eye; greenish-yellow bill. CLARK'S: Black cap stops just above eye; orange-yellow bill;** in winter, eye may have some light gray above and behind it.

Feeding: Feed by diving underwater, eating fish, mollusks, crustaceans, and aquatic insects.

Nesting: May nest in colonies containing hundreds of pairs; floating platform nest of decayed and fresh plants, placed in shallow water. Eggs: 2–7, pale blue-white; I: 23 days; F: 62–75 days, precocial; B: 1.

Other Behavior: As with all grebes, these species lack a long tail and use their lobed feet to help steer them underwater and in the air. During breeding the young may ride on parents' backs when in the water. Spectacular courtship displays occur on water and include running together over the water surface and presenting aquatic vegetation to each other. The 2 species winter in large flocks. Their ranges overlap and are not well known. Clark's is the less numerous of the 2.

Range for both species

Habitat: Summers on lakes and marshes; winters on coastal waters and some inland lakes.

Voice: Western's call is a 2-part "creek-creek"; Clark's call is an ascending "creek."

Conservation: Western: BBS: E C ⇧ Clark's: TREND UNKNOWN. Hurt by oil spills.

11

Northern Fulmar

Fulmarus glacialis

Light morph

Light morph

Dark morph

Identification: 19" A large gull-like bird generally seen only at sea. **Thick neck; stocky yellow bill; prominent rounded forehead;** pale "window" shows on upper outer wing. Varies in color from uniformly dark smoky gray (mostly in Pacific Ocean) to a white body with gray upperwings (mostly in Atlantic Ocean). IN FLIGHT: **Alternates flapping with gliding on stiff wings.**

Feeding: Feeds on the surface of the water, eating fish, jellyfish, shrimp, and other animal matter. Will occasionally dive as much as 6 ft. underwater in pursuit of food.

Nesting: Breeds colonially. Saucerlike nest on the shelf of a cliff or scraped in the ground, usually lined with fine material, and near or above the ocean; can also nest in holes or burrows. Eggs: 1, white with dark marks; I: 50–60 days; F: 46–51 days, altricial; B: 1.

Other Behavior: Often seen near fishing or seabirding boats. During breeding it feeds mostly at night. As a defense, both young and adults can vomit an oily substance on predators.

Habitat: Open sea; breeds along the far northern coasts. Occasionally blown to shore or found in harbors.

Voice: Usually silent at sea, but when competing for food may give a loud call like a low-pitched quack of a duck.

Conservation: ICN: ↑ CBC: ⇓

Black-capped Petrel

Pterodroma hasitata

Identification: 16" **Black cap; white forehead; white collar; white band at the base of the tail.** Similar to the Greater Shearwater, except for the white forehead, body shape, and flight style. **IN FLIGHT: Quickly rises high with rapid wingbeats and then glides down,** roller-coaster fashion.

Feeding: Feeds by picking squid and small fish from the water surface with its bill.

Nesting: Breeds colonially. Shallow nest of bare earth in rock crevice or cliff shelf up to 1,500 ft. above water. Eggs: 1, white; I: 51–54 days; F: 90–100 days, altricial; B: ?

Other Behavior: Breeds on steep cliffs in Hispaniola from Nov. to May and then comes north along the Gulf Stream during our summer.

Habitat: Open sea.

Voice: Generally quiet when out at sea.

Conservation: TREND UNKNOWN. Was thought to be extinct, but now seen regularly off Atlantic Coast. Breeding sites are few and subject to human disturbance.

Cory's Shearwater

Calonectris diomedea

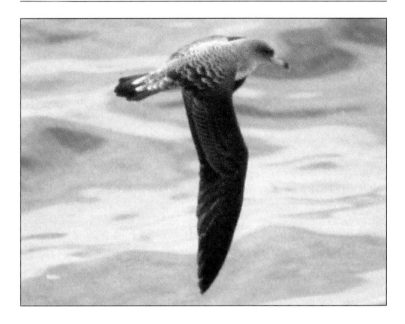

Identification: 20" The largest eastern shearwater. **White underparts; grayish-brown upperparts; yellowish bill. IN FLIGHT:** Deep slow wingbeats, and wings bent at the wrist, making them look bowed from head-on. Glides close to the water, but can bank quite high in windy weather.

Feeding: Feeds on the surface of the ocean or through shallow dives, eating large squid, fish, and crustaceans.

Nesting: Colonial nester. Saucerlike nest in burrow or rock crevice. Eggs: 1, white; I: ?; F: ?, altricial; B: ?

Other Behavior: Cory's Shearwaters breed in the Northern Hemisphere on islands in the Mediterranean Sea and eastern Atlantic Ocean. Following breeding (May–Aug.), they appear on the Atlantic and Gulf Coasts from late summer into fall. They seldom follow ships and may form large flocks at sea.

Habitat: Open sea.

Voice: Generally quiet when out on the open sea.

Conservation: TREND UNKNOWN. Island nesting sites threatened by introduced predators and by direct human disturbance.

Greater Shearwater
Puffinus gravis

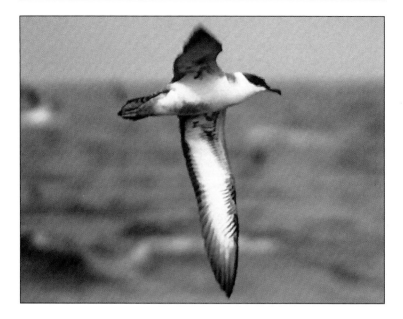

Identification: 20" One of the 2 large "white-bellied" shearwaters in the East. Rare in the West. **White below; grayish above with scaled look; black cap; white collar;** gray smudge in center of belly; speckled wing linings; narrow white band at base of tail. **IN FLIGHT:** More gliding and slower wingbeats than other eastern shearwaters. Glides into wind to gain height, then soars downwind.

Feeding: Feeds on the surface of the water and by diving and swimming underwater, eating small fish, squid, and crustaceans.

Nesting: Colonial nester. Shallow nest of grasses at the end of a burrow. Eggs: 1, white; I: 55 days; F: 84 days, altricial; B: 1.

Other Behavior: May scavenge behind ships, especially if oily fish parts are thrown overboard.

Habitat: Open sea.

Voice: Makes squealing noises when fighting over food at sea.

Conservation: TREND UNKNOWN. Breeds on only a few S. Atlantic islands. It is vulnerable to introduced predators, such as cats and rats.

Sooty Shearwater
Puffinus griseus

Identification: 17″ Only "dark-bellied" shearwater in the East. **Dark overall; dark bill and legs; silvery underwing linings,** which look like a flash of white as the bird lifts its wings in flight. **IN FLIGHT:** Quick wingbeats; some soaring and gliding.

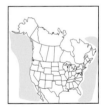

Feeding: Feeds on the surface of the water, eating fish and squid. When floating, may dip its head underwater to look for food. May dive for food and use its wings to help it swim underwater.

Nesting: Colonial breeder. Saucerlike nest of dead leaves and twigs, placed at the end of a 3–4 ft. burrow. Eggs: 1, white; I: 56 days; F: 100 days, altricial; B: ?

Other Behavior: Gathers in flocks of thousands during summer. Occasionally seen from land. Follows birding boats.

Habitat: From coastal waters to open sea.

Voice: May make a variety of bleating sounds when fighting for food out at sea.

Conservation: CBC: ⇑

Manx Shearwater

Puffinus puffinus

Identification: 14" This shearwater is **small** with **black upperparts, bright white underparts,** and **white undertail coverts.** Black on head extends down well below eye. Very similar to Audubon's Shearwater. **IN FLIGHT:** Flies with bursts of rapid wingbeats followed by long glides.

Feeding: Feeds on the surface of the ocean and also dives and swims underwater to eat small fish, crustaceans, and squid.

Nesting: Breeds colonially on islands. Shallow nest of dry grass and leaves at the end of a 4–6 ft. burrow in rocky soil. Eggs: 1, white; I: 50–54 days; F: 70–75 days, altricial; B: 1.

Other Behavior: Generally does not follow ships. This is the only eastern shearwater that breeds in N. America. Recent sightings on the West Coast suggest that there may be a new, undiscovered nesting colony there.

Habitat: Coastal islands and open sea.

Voice: Generally quiet in open sea.

Conservation:
ICN: ⇑ CBC: ⇑

Audubon's Shearwater

Puffinus lherminieri

Identification: 12" This is the smallest eastern shearwater. **Dark brown upperparts; white belly; underwings white with wide dark border; dark undertail coverts.** Dark cap extends to just below the eye. Very similar to the rarer Manx Shearwater. **IN FLIGHT:** Note long tail and more fluttery wingbeat (than Manx Shearwater) followed by short glides.

Feeding: Feeds on the surface of the ocean and also makes shallow dives into the water, eating small fish, squid, and crustaceans.

Nesting: Colonial nester. Shallow nest of twigs or dried grass under thick vegetation or in rock crevice. Eggs: 1, white; I: 51 days; F: 72 days, altricial; B: ?

Other Behavior: This shearwater does not usually follow ships. When diving it may remain underwater up to 20 seconds.

Habitat: Open sea; Gulf Stream.

Voice: Generally quiet when out at sea.

Conservation: TREND UNKNOWN.

Wilson's Storm-Petrel

Oceanites oceanicus

Identification: 7″ One of 3 storm-petrels regularly seen in the East. **Small; blackish; wide U-shaped rump patch; short tail square or slightly rounded. IN FLIGHT: Direct flight with continuous fluttery wingbeats and few glides; wings short, straight, and rounded at tip.**
➤The similar Band-rumped Storm-Petrel, *O. castro*, is larger, has a square or slightly forked tail, and flies like a shearwater, alternating flaps with glides.

Feeding: Feeds on the surface of the water by hovering as it grabs plankton, small fish, and squid with its bill.

Nesting: Breeds colonially. Shallow nest of loose twigs at the end of a burrow, in a rock crevice, or on a rock ledge up to 300 ft. above water. Eggs: 1, white with dark marks; I: 39–48 days; F: ?, altricial; B: 1.

Other Behavior: When feeding, it may patter its feet on the water surface as it hovers. Follows ships at sea if food is available. Breeds in the far south of the S. Hemisphere in colonies of millions of birds; may be one of the most abundant species of bird in the world. Rare, but annual in fall off central Calif.

Habitat: Open sea, but occasionally may be seen from the coast.

Voice: Soft peeping sounds when feeding at sea.

Conservation:
TREND UNKNOWN.

Leach's Storm-Petrel
Oceanodroma leucorhoa

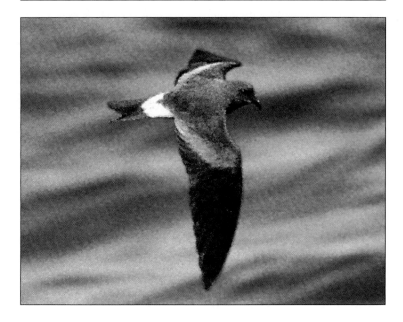

Identification: 8″ Triangular off-white rump patch (sometimes narrowly divided in the center); **long forked tail.** Off S. Calif., some birds may have dark rumps; they are then distinguished from other dark storm-petrels by their flight behavior. **In Flight: Distinctive zigzag flight; alternates flaps with glides; wings narrow, pointed, and bent at the wrist.**

Feeding: Feeds by hovering just above the surface of the water, eating plankton, small fish, and squid.

Nesting: Colonial nester. Shallow nest of dry grasses and weed stems at the end of a 1–3 ft. burrow in a field or among rocks. Eggs: 1, white; I: 38–46 days; F: 63–70 days, altricial; B: 1.

Other Behavior: Does not usually follow ships and does not regularly patter its feet on the water when feeding. Nests on coastal islands and goes to and from the nest at night. This may help protect it from gulls, which rest at night. Feeds farther offshore than other storm-petrels. As in all storm-petrels, nestlings are fed a regurgitant of stomach oil. Introduced cats and rats put island colonies at risk.

Habitat: Coastal islands and far offshore; occasionally near shore during storms.

Voice: High purring and clucking notes given on breeding grounds at night; generally quiet out at sea.

Conservation:
ICN: ↓

Masked Booby

Sula dactylatra

Immature

Adults

Identification: 34" A large white seabird; dark mask surrounds eyes and chin; yellowish bill. IN FLIGHT: Note **black tail** and **black trailing half of wings**. IMM: Dark color of head and neck is separated from that of the back by a white patch or collar; belly white. Imm. plumage kept 2 years.

Feeding: Dives vertically from up to 40 ft. above water, eating fish and squid.

Nesting: Breeds colonially. Nest a shallow scrape in sand anywhere from sea level to 500 ft. above sea. Eggs: 2, light blue; I: 42 days; F: 115 days, altricial; B: 1.

Other Behavior: May try to catch flying fish it has seen leap out of the water. May be attacked in flight by Magnificent Frigatebirds that attempt to make them disgorge their prey. Most sightings of Masked Booby are from Gulf of Mexico. It is resident around the Dry Tortugas since 1970s and nesting there since 1984. Vagrant off Calif.

Habitat: Open sea.

Voice: Generally quiet when out at sea.

Conservation: TREND UNKNOWN.

21

Brown Booby

Sula leucogaster

Immature

Adult

Identification: 27" Noticeably smaller bird than the related Northern Gannet and Masked Booby. **Dark brown except for bright white belly and wing linings; yellowish bill and feet.** IMM: Dark brown with lighter brown belly and wing linings. Imm. plumage kept 2 or more years.

Feeding: Dives into water from 30–50 ft. high to catch fish, often flying fish. Can stay underwater over 30 seconds.

Nesting: Nests colonially. Nest is a scrape in the sand near water level or much higher. Eggs: 1–3, pale blue; I: 40–43 days; F: 105 days, altricial; B: 1.

Other Behavior: Tends to feed near shore and make dives for prey at an acute angle. Usually seen in small flocks but can gather in large numbers when food is plentiful. They fly typically in loose line formation low over the water. Most often seen off the coast in the Southeast, especially the Gulf of Mexico and Dry Tortugas.

Habitat: Open sea.

Voice: Generally quiet out on open sea.

Conservation: TREND UNKNOWN.

Northern Gannet

Morus bassanus

Adult

Immature

Identification: 37″ A **large** seabird that is **all white except for black wing tips and golden buff on head.** Tail and wings are long and pointed. **IMM:** At first, wings and upper body are all dark, belly and chin lighter, sometimes separated by a darker breast band. Over the next 2 years, the head and belly whiten, followed by the back, wings, and tail. Imm. plumage kept for up to 3 years.

Feeding: Feeds by diving into the water from up to 100 ft., eating schooling fish such as mackerel and herring.

Nesting: Colonial nester. A shallow nest of seaweed and grass on the ground or the edge of a cliff. Eggs: 1, pale blue; I: 42–44 days; F: 95–107 days, altricial; B: 1.

Other Behavior: Seen in large flocks during spring and fall migration, often flying in line formations. Sometimes seen near shore during storms. On their breeding grounds they walk from their nest to an open spot with wings raised and bill pointed up, possibly helping them get by other nests without inviting aggression. They take off from the cliffs, running and flapping their wings over a short distance.

Habitat: Summers on coastal cliffs and islands; winters at sea.

Voice: Generally quiet at sea, but on the breeding ground gives loud harsh "keruk keruk" calls.

Conservation: ICN: ↑ CBC: ⇑ Overfishing could affect their food supplies and populations.

American White Pelican

Pelecanus erythrorhynchos

Adult

Adult

Identification: 62" Large white bird; large orange-yellow bill; orange-yellow throat pouch. Keellike growth occurs on middle of upper bill during breeding. **In Flight:** Trailing half of wings is black; soars gracefully. **Imm:** Similar to adult, but bill and throat pouch are gray and dark areas of wings brown. Imm. plumage kept 3–4 years.

Feeding: Feeds while swimming, dipping bill into the water to catch fish in its pouch. Usually feeds in small groups that may cooperatively herd fish toward shallow water where they are easier to catch.

Nesting: Nests colonially on large inland lakes. Nest a slight depression on bare ground, or a more elaborate mound of earth, brush stems, and debris. Eggs:1–3, white; I: 29–36 days; F: 21–28 days; B: 1.

Other Behavior: One of the largest birds in N. America; can soar for long distances and often flies in line or V formations. Over breeding grounds may do conspicuous flights involving soaring and diving.

Habitat: Summers on large inland lakes; winters along coast

Voice: Generally quiet away from breeding grounds; young at nest can give loud whines or grunts.

Conservation: BBS: E ⇑ C ⇑ CBC: ⇑ Populations at some inland lakes are vulnerable to local drought.

Brown Pelican
Pelecanus occidentalis

Adult

Immature

Nonbreeding adult (l.), breeding adult (r.)

Identification: 45″ A large coastal bird; gray-brown body and wings; large dark bill; dark throat pouch. Neck all white in nonbreeding adult; nape is brown in breeding adult. IMM: All dark with increasing amounts of white on head. Imm. plumage kept 3–4 years.

Feeding: Feeds by diving from the air into the water and catching fish in its throat pouch. This distinguishes it from the American White Pelican, which feeds while floating on the water. Imm. Brown Pelicans occasionally feed while swimming on the water.

Nesting: Nests colonially on coastal islands. Nest a rim of soil and debris 4–10 in. high on ground, or a saucerlike nest of sticks, grass, and reeds in the top of a mangrove tree. Eggs: 2–4, white; I: 28–30 days; F: 71–88 days, altricial; B: 1.

Other Behavior: Breeds, roosts, and feeds in flocks. Often flies in line formations high in the air or low over the water surface. When catching fish, scoops up fish and water, then surfaces and drains water out of pouch before swallowing fish.

Habitat: Coastal.

Voice: Adults usually quiet; at nest give a soft "check check." Young at nest can give loud barks and screams as they compete for food.

Conservation:
BBS: E ⇑ C CBC: ⇑ Loss of nesting habitat on coastal islands can threaten pop. Federally endangered in West.

25

Great Cormorant
Phalacrocorax carbo

Adult

Immature

Identification: 36" The largest cormorant in N. America. Seen mostly in winter since it breeds quite far north. **All dark; broad white band of feathers on cheeks and chin.** In late winter, tops of legs have white patches that remain through breeding. **IMM:** All dark with a streaked light brown throat and a white belly. Imm. plumage kept 2–3 years.

Feeding: Feeds by diving and swimming underwater to catch fish; can stay submerged for up to 70 seconds.

Nesting: Breeds colonially on coastal cliffs and islands. Platform nest of sticks and twigs lined with finer materials, placed on ledge of cliff. Eggs: 5–6, pale blue-green; I: 29–31 days; F: 50 days, altricial; B: 1.

Other Behavior: All cormorants use their feet to propel them underwater, and when they surface, they can float low with just their neck and head showing, or higher with their whole body showing. These cormorants were domesticated in Asia and used to catch fish, which they then regurgitated to their owners.

Habitat: Coastal.

Voice: Silent away from nest; at nest can give a variety of deep croaks and grunts.

Conservation:
ICN: ⇑ CBC: ↑

Double-crested Cormorant

Phalacrocorax auritus

Adult

Immature

Identification: 33" Most commonly seen cormorant in the East and usually the only one seen well inland. **All black** with a **broad orange throat pouch.** "Double-crested" in name refers to crests that grow during breeding; they are hard to see. **IN FLIGHT: Neck is crooked** rather than straight as in other cormorants. **IMM:** Dark brown with light brown belly, light throat, and orange throat pouch. Imm. plumage kept 2–3 years.

Feeding: Feeds by diving and swimming underwater, eating mostly fish. May hold wings out to dry after diving in water.

Nesting: Nests colonially. Platform nest of sticks and seaweed lined with leafy twigs and grass, placed in a tree or on the ground. Eggs: 2–7, pale blue; I: 24–29 days; F: 35–42 days, altricial; B: 1.

Other Behavior: Can be seen soaring high, using rising thermals of air to gain altitude and then coasting on a long glide. May have trouble taking off from land and water, often needing to run along the water to gain speed. After fishing, often stands with wings outstretched to dry. Flocks often fly in line or V formations.

Habitat: Coasts, inland rivers, and lakes.

Voice: Silent away from nest; at nest can give a variety of deep croaks and grunts.

Conservation: BBS: E ⇑ C ⇑ CBC: ⇑ Populations rapidly recovering from pesticide-caused declines.

Neotropic Cormorant

Phalacrocorax brasilianus

Adult

Immature

Identification: 26" Distinguished from the Double-crested Cormorant by its **smaller size, long tail,** and **narrow, sharp-pointed, yellowish throat pouch with a white border.** Imm: At first all dark brown, then lighter on belly and throat. Has sharp-pointed throat pouch like adult, but without white border. Imm. plumage kept 2–3 years.

Feeding: Feeds by diving into water and swimming after fish. Occasionally joins others of its species and beats wings over water, driving fish ahead so they can be more easily caught.

Nesting: Colonial nester. Platform nest of small twigs, placed on forking branches 3–20 ft. above water. Eggs: 2–6, pale blue; I: ?; F: ?, altricial; B: ?

Other Behavior: Like other cormorants, it may float with its head dipped down under the water as it looks for fish to pursue.

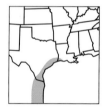

Habitat: Freshwater marshes and ponds and coastal areas.

Voice: Little is known about its vocal behavior.

Conservation:
BBS: E C ⇑ CBC: ⇑

Anhinga
Anhinga anhinga

Male

Female

Identification: 34″ **Large black waterbird; long thin neck; long pointed yellow bill; long tail.** Wings have silvery streaks and spots on the shoulders, and body is glossed with green. **MALE:** All-dark neck. **FEMALE:** Light brown neck and breast. **IMM:** Like female, but brown on the body. Imm. plumage kept 1–2 years.

Feeding: Feeds by diving from the surface of the water, spearing prey with its pointed bill. It eats fish, aquatic insects, frogs, and just-hatched alligators.

Nesting: Nests in small colonies, often with herons. Platform nest of sticks and twigs lined with finer material, placed in tree. Eggs: 1–5, pale blue-green; I: 25–29 days; F: ?, altricial; B: 1.

Other Behavior: Like cormorants, Anhingas hold their wings out to dry after swimming. When swimming, often just the head and neck appear above water, which is one reason they are called the snakebird. When nesting, they may use the old nests of herons. Flight is a series of flaps followed by a glide. They often soar high in the air and migrate by day in large flocks.

Habitat: Freshwater swamps, marshes, lakes, and rivers.

Voice: Generally quiet, but during breeding may give guttural calls and grunts during pair interactions on the ground, or a series of high whistles like "eek eek eek" while flying.

Conservation: BBS: E ⇑ C ⇓ CBC: ↑

Magnificent Frigatebird
Fregata magnificens

Immature (top), adult male (bott.)

Adult male

Identification: 41" Large, black, soaring seabird with unique silhouette; short neck; long narrow wings; deeply forked tail. MALE: Black with a bright red throat pouch. FEMALE: Black with a broad white band across her chest. IMM: Varied, with more white than adult female, such as on head, or belly *and* chest. Period of imm. plumage unknown, most likely 4–6 years.

Feeding: Feeds from aerial dives to pick fish, jellyfish, and crustaceans from the water surface. Also eats carrion fish and steals eggs and chicks from seabird nesting colonies.

Nesting: Nests colonially on ocean islands. Shallow nest of sticks and twigs lined with grass, placed in the top of a low tree. Eggs: 1, white; I: 50 days; F: ?, altricial; B: 1; breeds every other year.

Other Behavior: In courtship display, male inflates red throat pouch and sways from side to side in presence of female. Also called man-o'-war bird because it frequently steals food from other birds such as boobies. Wonderful flier, being able to soar for long periods and dive straight down after food.

Habitat: Ocean, coasts.

Voice: Generally quiet out at sea.

Conservation:
BBS: E ⇑ C CBC: ↓

American Bittern
Botaurus lentiginosus

Identification: 25˝ A stocky bird with **brown streaking underneath** and a sometimes visible **black streak extending down neck from base of bill. In Flight:** Brown back and dark outer wings. **Imm:** Similar to adult, but lacks black streak. Imm. plumage kept into winter.

Feeding: Solitary feeder. Stands or walks extremely slowly, then strikes prey with lightning stab. Diet includes lots of fish; also reptiles, amphibians, insects, and small mammals.

Nesting: Nests singly, but nests have been found within 40 yd. of each other. Platform nest composed of cattails, sticks, grasses, placed in dense marsh vegetation a few inches above water. Eggs: 2–7, buffy olive-brown; I: 28–29 days; F: leave nest at 14 days, time of first flight unknown, altricial; B: 1.

Other Behavior: When standing or when alarmed, bitterns often assume a posture with neck elongated and bill pointed straight up so that they appear camouflaged, blending into the vegetation around them. Sometimes they gently sway while holding this position. Males may be polygamous. Secretive birds.

Habitat: Freshwater or brackish marshes with tall vegetation.

Voice: During breeding male gives a booming "pumper-lunk" call. Sounds like an old-fashioned hand pump. Alarm call is "kok-kok-kok."

Conservation:
BBS: E ↓ C ⇓ CBC: ↓ Loss of wetlands is causing declining populations.

Least Bittern

Ixobrychus exilis

Male

Identification: 13" Our smallest heron. **Dark crown and back; rich buff underparts. Male:** Crown and back are black. **Female:** Crown and back are rich brown. **In Flight:** Note **buffy inner wing patches**. Flies weakly with quick wingbeats.

Feeding: Stalks through the reeds in crouched posture or stands in place, and sometimes sways neck. Eats small fish, frogs, insects, small mammals, and sometimes bird eggs and chicks.

Nesting: Small platform of sticks and live or dead vegetation, placed in cattails, bulrushes, or bushes 8–14 in. above water. Eggs: 2–7, pale blue or greenish white; I: 19–20 days; F: up to 25 days, altricial; B: 2.

Other Behavior: This is a secretive bird. Will flutter briefly above reeds. Climbs in and even runs through reeds 2–3 feet above water. Alarm posture with bill pointing skyward like that of American Bittern. In courtship, males give cooing sounds.

Habitat: Marshes that include dense vegetation, like sedges and cattails; salt marshes.

Voice: Male gives guttural "uh-uh-uh-oo-oo-oo-ooah," female makes ticking sound. Both give "tut-tut."

Conservation: BBS: E ↓ C ⇓ CBC: ⇑ Declining due to loss of wetlands.

Great Blue Heron
Ardea herodias

Dark morph

White morph

Identification: 50″ Our largest and most widespread heron. **Grayish-blue body; white head; black stripe over the eye. Imm:** Similar to adult, except head has solid black cap, which gradually changes to white. Imm. plumage kept 2 years. ►Rare white morph of Great Blue Heron, the "Great White Heron," is entirely white with legs and bill orangy yellow; it is limited to S. Fla.

Feeding: Feeds in shallow water by standing or walking slowly, then grabbing small fish, frogs, birds, and aquatic insects with its bill. Can feed in deeper water by plunging or swimming. Also hunts on land for small mammals. Individuals may form temporary feeding territories up to several hundred yd. in diameter which they defend.

Nesting: Breeds in generally small colonies in isolated areas or singly. Large platform nest of sticks lined with finer twigs and vegetation, placed in trees or shrubs 30–70 ft. above ground. Eggs: 3–7, pale bluish green; I: 28 days; F: 55–60 days, altricial; B: 1.

Other Behavior: Males display from nest sites with neck arched over back, bill pointing up.

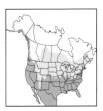

Habitat: Marshes, swamps, river and lake edges, tidal flats, mangroves, other water areas.

Voice: Harsh guttural "frahnk" or short "rok-rok" call given during aggression. Both sexes do bill clacking.

Conservation:
BBS: E ⇑ C ⇑ CBC: ⇑

33

Great Egret

Ardea alba

Identification: 39" A **large white heron** with a **yellow bill** and **black legs.** Immature is similar to adult. In breeding season adults of both sexes have long white plumes growing on their back.

Feeding: Primarily feeds by walking slowly, head erect, then striking prey. Forages in shallow water for small fish and amphibians, but also on land for insects, reptiles, and small mammals. May feed solitarily and defend feeding areas by displaying aggressively and supplanting intruders. Also feeds in large groups when food is concentrated. Has been known to steal fish from other birds.

Nesting: Nests in colonies with other herons, ibises, and cormorants or singly. Nest is flimsy platform of sticks, twigs, and reeds, placed in tree or shrub 8–40 ft. above ground or in cattails 1–4 ft. above water. Eggs: 1–6, pale bluish green; I: 23–26 days; F: 42–49 days, altricial; B: 1.

Other Behavior: Among this and other herons, greeting ceremonies between pair include calls, head stretched up and over back with bill skyward, and bill clacking, in which mandibles are snapped open and shut.

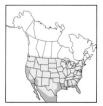

Habitat: Marshes, swamps, seashores, lake margins.

Voice: A deep, rattlelike croak.

Conservation:
BBS: E ↓ C ⇑ CBC: ↑
At turn of century, hunted for plumes used in feather trade. Since decline of hunting and ban on DDT, which had led to eggshell thinning, population has increased.

Snowy Egret
Egretta thula

Adult

Immature

Identification: 24" **White body; black bill; black legs with bright yellow feet.** During breeding, the feet and facial skin in front of the eye turn orange or red. **IMM:** Like nonbreeding adult, but legs black in front and yellow in back. Bright yellow facial skin at base of bill clearly distinguishes it from the similar imm. Little Blue Heron. Imm. plumage kept 1 year.

Feeding: Very active. Often feeds in flocks and in aggregations with other species. Has diverse foraging techniques: walking slowly or quickly, running or hopping, and using its feet to stir, rake, or probe food from bottom. Can vibrate bill in water to attract fish. Eats shrimp, fish, crabs, amphibians, snakes, and insects.

Nesting: Nests in large colonies of thousands, singly or with other herons in small colonies. Sticks and twigs compose a platform, which is placed on the ground or in tree or shrub 5–10 ft. high. Eggs: 3–5, pale bluish green; I: 20–29 days; F: 30 days, altricial; B: 1.

Other Behavior: Aggressively defends nest and feeding sites with calls, displays such as raising crest, and fights. Communal nighttime roosts outside breeding season.

Habitat: Coastal areas, marshes, river valleys, lake edges.

Voice: In breeding colonies, "wah-wah-wah"; during aggression a harsh "aah."

Conservation:
BBS: E ⇓ C ⇑ CBC: ⇑ Hunted to near extinction in late 1800s, for plumes. With protection, population now expanding.

Little Blue Heron

Egretta caerulea

Immature (l.), adult (r.)

Identification: 27" Dark overall; purplish head; blue-gray body and wings; bill two-toned — blue-gray at the base with a darker tip. **IMM:** All white with greenish-yellow legs and a two-toned bill like the adult's. Gray facial skin at the base of the bill distinguishes it from the similar imm. Snowy Egret. White becomes blotched with blue-gray as bird changes to adult plumage. Imm. plumage kept 1 year.

Feeding: Stealthily walks through shallow waters and peers down looking for prey. Eats fish, insects, amphibians. May follow other birds and catch prey stirred up by them.

Nesting: Nests colonially, often with other heron species. Nest of sticks and twigs is placed in tree or shrub 10–15 ft. above the water. Eggs: 2–5, pale bluish green; I: 20–24 days; F: 42–49 days, altricial; B: 1.

Other Behavior: Males may mate with females on neighboring territories.

Habitat: Swamps, inland marshes, and coastal areas.

Voice: During courtship a rattling chatter; low-pitched "aarh" during aggressive interactions.

Conservation:
BBS: E ⇓ C ↓ CBC: ↓ Spared during plume trade because it does not have long breeding plumes.

Tricolored Heron
Egretta tricolor

Identification: 26" **Dark blue-gray heron** with a **white belly and underwings;** white stripe down the front of the neck. Bill color varies from dark on top and yellow beneath to gray at base and darker at tip. **Imm:** Similar to adult, but brown mottling on neck and wings. Imm. plumage kept 1 year.

Feeding: Wades belly-deep in water. In addition to stalking prey by walking, it also runs or hops with wings open. Eats fish, amphibians, insects.

Nesting: Nests in large colonies, often with other herons. Platform nest of sticks and twigs lined with finer vegetation, placed in tree or shrub 6–15 ft. above the ground. Eggs: 3–7, pale bluish green; I: 21–25 days; F: 35 days, altricial; B: 1.

Other Behavior: Courtship involves circle flights, chases, and displays during which neck feathers, back feathers, and crest are raised. Bill clacking is frequent.

Habitat: Marshes, shores, mudflats, tidal creeks.

Voice: Guttural "unh" and "culh-culh" given during courtship displays. High-pitched "aah" given during aggression.

Conservation: BBS: E ⇓ C ⇑ CBC: ↑ Spared by plume trade because its plume color was not popular.

Reddish Egret

Egretta rufescens

Dark-morph adult

White-morph adult

Dark-morph immature

Identification: 30" Has 2 adult color morphs — a common dark morph and a rare white morph. Both morphs have distinctive **pink bill that looks like tip has been dipped in black ink.** The dark morph has a **blue-gray body** and **red-brown neck and head;** the white morph is all white. In both morphs the legs are dark. **IMM:** Dark morph is gray with a brownish head and all-dark bill; white morph is white with an all-dark bill and gray facial skin at the base of the bill. Imm. plumage kept 1–2 years.

Feeding: One of the most active herons. Uses wide variety of feeding techniques: runs, hops, opens one or both wings and brings them forward. Eats fish, frogs, crustaceans.

Nesting: Colonial on coastal islands. Stick nest lined with twigs, in tree or shrub. Eggs: 3–7, pale blue-green; I: 25–26 days; F: 45 days, altricial; B: 1.

Other Behavior: Courtship displays similar to those of other herons. Shakes and tosses head during greeting ceremony. See Tricolored Heron.

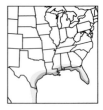

Habitat: Shorelines, tidal flats, shallow pools.

Voice: Utters guttural croaks.

Conservation: BBS: E ↑ C CBC: ↓ Also a victim of plume hunting. Its populations have recovered somewhat, but coastal development threatens it.

Cattle Egret
Bubulcus ibis

Identification: 20″ Common small heron. **White overall; short, stocky, yellow-orange bill;** legs vary from orange to yellow-green. Breeding adult has buffy-orange plumes on head, back, and breast. **Imm:** Similar to nonbreeding adult, except with dark gray legs. Imm. plumage kept until next spring.

Feeding: Typically seen away from water, feeding in fields, lawns, and along highways. Eats insects, amphibians, reptiles, mollusks. Often follows cattle or horses, watching for insects they stir up.

Nesting: In same-species colonies or with other herons. Platform nest of sticks, twigs, and reeds, placed in shrub or tree 3–30 ft. above the ground. Eggs: 2–6, bluish white; I: 21–24 days; F: 30 days, altricial; B: 1.

Other Behavior: Originally most likely from Africa, this species has widely expanded its range. It first flew across the Atlantic and spread to S. America in 1880. By 1942 it was seen in Fla. and was nesting there by the early 1950s. Deforestation and cultivation have continued to provide it with favorable habitat. It is now widespread across the country.

Habitat: Open dry areas, lawns, fields, pastures with livestock.

Voice: In colonies, a "rick-rack" call. When alarmed, gives "kok" call.

Conservation: BBS: E ↑ C ↑ CBC: ⇑ May displace some native species of herons at breeding sites.

Green Heron

Butorides virescens

Adult

Immature

Identification: 19" Small all-dark heron; compact shape; blue-green back; reddish-brown neck and chest; short bright yellow to orange legs. Looks short-necked because it holds its head close to its body. **Imm:** Similar to adult, but with brown streaking on neck and belly; wing feathers may have buff dots at tips. Distinguished from imm. night-herons by smaller size, darker back, and longer pointed bill. Imm. plumage kept 1 year.

Feeding: Crouches in branches on shore and waits for prey or wades stealthily. May also plunge or jump or stir up bottom with foot. Has been known to place an object such as a twig or insect on water to lure prey to surface. Eats fish, insects, crabs.

Nesting: Nests singly or in small colony. Nest of sticks, placed in tree or grass hummock. Eggs: 3–6, pale blue-green; I: 21–25 days; F: 34–35 days, altricial; B: 1–2.

Other Behavior: Does crest raising and tail flicking when excited. Courtship involves pursuit and circle flights. Duets of "skow"call occur between the sexes.

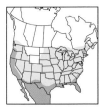

Habitat: Shores and water edges with dense vegetation, salt marshes, streams.

Voice: "Skow" call is commonly given when flushed and in flight. Aggressive call is "raah."

Conservation:
BBS: E ↓ C ↑ CBC: ↑

Black-crowned Night-Heron
Nycticorax nycticorax

Adult

Immature

Identification: 25" **Gray-and-white stocky heron; black cap; black back.** Short pale yellow legs turn reddish in breeding season. **IMM:** Brown with white streaks below; large buffy-white spots on back and wings. Told from imm. Yellow-crowned Night-Heron by its greenish-yellow lower bill (Yellow-crowned has all-dark bill); Black-crowned also has a comparatively longer, thinner bill. Imm. plumage kept 2 years.

Feeding: Although it can feed by day, this species feeds mostly at night or at dusk, either on individual feeding territories or in aggregations. Diet consists of fish, amphibians, insects, and small mammals. Eats the young of other bird species such as terns, herons, and ibises.

Nesting: In colonies or singly. Nest consists of coarse twigs, reeds, and finer material and is placed against a tussock, or in reeds, shrub, or tree up to 160 ft. high. Eggs: 3–5, pale blue-green; I: 24–26 days; F: 42–49 days, altricial; B: 1.

Other Behavior: In greeting ceremony, birds stretch necks horizontally with breeding plumes on head raised and they touch bills. Roosts in trees during the day.

Habitat: Diverse— freshwater streams, lakes, rice fields, dry grasslands, salt marshes.

Voice: Low, hoarse "quok" often heard at dusk. During nesting, "rok-rok."

Conservation: BBS: E ⇓ C ⇓ CBC: ⇑

Yellow-crowned Night-Heron

Nyctanassa violacea

Adult
Immature

Identification: 24" **Stocky gray heron; black head; buffy-white crown.** Also has a white cheek patch, a dark stocky bill, and yellow legs. **IMM:** Grayish brown overall with fine white streaks on breast and fine white dots on back and wings. Best told from imm. Black-crowned Night-Heron by its stocky all-dark bill (Black-crowned has yellowish lower bill). Imm. plumage kept 2 years.

Feeding: Feeds mostly at night, but sometimes during day. Eats a large number of crustaceans, particularly fiddler crabs and crayfish. Also eats fish, insects, mammals, and small birds.

Nesting: Solitary or in small colony with other herons. Substantial platform of coarse sticks lined with finer twigs and leaves, on ground or in tree or shrub up to 40 ft. high. Eggs: 3–5, pale bluish green; I: 21–25 days; F: 25 days, altricial; B: 1.

Other Behavior: Greeting ceremonies include crest raising, calls, bill clacking. Lots of display flights and chases occur in colonies. Roosts in tall trees or shrubs.

Habitat: Coastal as well as ponds, swamps, rivers, parkland.

Voice: Has many calls. "Quack" call is higher pitched and less harsh than Black-crowned Night-Heron's; flight call is "scaup"; a whoop is given during nest displays.

Conservation: BBS: E ⇑ C ↓ CBC: ↑

White Ibis
Eudocimus albus

Adult

Immature

Identification: 25" **Large, white, long-legged bird; long, downcurved, reddish bill.** During breeding, bill, facial skin, and legs turn bright red. **In Flight:** Wings show black tips. **Imm:** White belly and rump; brownish head and back; dark wings. Dark areas gradually change to white. Bill is pink. Imm. plumage kept 1 year.

Feeding: Feeds in groups or alone in shallow fresh or salt water. Probes the bottom with its bill. Eats crayfish, mudcrabs, frogs, and aquatic insects.

Nesting: Nests in large colonies of thousands. Loose nest of sticks and twigs, placed in tree or shrub, occasionally in low vegetation such as sawgrass and bulrushes. Eggs: 3–5, greenish white with dark marks; I: 21–23 days; F: 28–35 days, altricial; B: 1.

Other Behavior: Flies with neck outstretched. Flocks go to large nocturnal roosts at sunset in long lines or V's. This bird can also soar in circles.Other birds, such as Little Blue Herons and Great Egrets, may follow feeding White Ibises and snatch prey they have scared up.

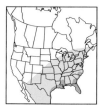

Habitat: Salt and freshwater lakes, marshes, swamps, tidal mudflats, shores.

Voice: Mostly quiet. Alarm call is nasal "hunk, hunk, hunk."

Conservation:
BBS: E ↓ C ⇑ CBC: ⇑

Glossy Ibis
Plegadis falcinellus

Summer

Winter

Identification: 23" Large, dark, long-legged bird with a long downcurved bill. SUMMER: Chestnut head and neck; pale blue line of facial skin around base of bill and up to, but not surrounding, the dark brown eye. WINTER: Streaked gray-brown head and neck; traces of pale blue facial skin still visible. IMM: Similar to winter adult, but duller. Indistinguishable from imm. White-faced Ibis. Imm. plumage kept 1½ years.

Feeding: Feeds by probing. Eats crayfish, grasshoppers, other insects, snakes, earthworms. Boat-tailed Grackles have stolen food by swarming around an ibis carrying crayfish until the ibis drops its prey.

Nesting: Colonial nester, often with other herons. Platform of sticks and aquatic vegetation, placed on the ground in cattails or in shrub or tree such as willow, mangrove, swamp maple. Eggs: 3–4, greenish blue; I: 21 days; F: 28–30 days, altricial; B: 1.

Other Behavior: Circling of flocks to great heights is a form of display not limited to breeding season.

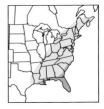

Habitat: At edges of fresh, brackish, and salt water.

Voice: Nasal grunt or repeated guttural notes.

Conservation: BBS: E ⇑ C CBC: ⇑ Probably arrived in N. America in 1800s. Since 1940, has been expanding range north along East Coast to Maine.

White-faced Ibis

Plegadis chihi

Summer

Winter

Identification: 23" Large, dark, long-legged bird with a long downcurved bill. SUMMER: Chestnut head and neck; red facial skin around base of bill; thin line of white feathers surrounding the back of the reddish eye. WINTER: Streaked gray-brown head and neck; reddish eye; dark facial skin. IMM: Similar to winter adult, but duller. Indistinguishable from imm. Glossy Ibis. Imm. plumage kept 1½ years.

Feeding: Prefers to feed in freshwater marshes. Wades and probes in shallow water. Consumes crayfish, crabs, frogs, insects, snails, fish.

Nesting: In small colonies, usually with other herons. Nest is deep cup of dead reeds and sticks lined with grass, on floating mat of dead plants or attached several ft. above water to bulrushes, shrub. Eggs: 3–4, bluish green; I: 21–22 days; F: 28 days, altricial; B: 1.

Other Behavior: Flies in lines or compact groups. Direct flight with short intervals of gliding. May circle high in air, then rapidly plunge down with feet dangling.

Habitat: Freshwater and brackish marshes.

Voice: Nasal grunting.

Conservation: BBS: E C ⇑ CBC: ⇑ Loss of wetlands and pesticide use is leading to declines in population. Populations now recovering in Ore., Calif., and Nev.

Roseate Spoonbill

Ajaia ajaja

Identification: 32" **Large, pink, long-legged wader; long spoon-shaped bill;** head is bare and light green; tail is orange. **IMM:** Mostly white or very pale pink with same distinctive bill as adult. Head is feathered for first year. Imm. plumage kept 3 years and gradually changes to full adult colors over that time.

Feeding: Feeds in shallow water by wading and moving its partially opened bill back and forth in the water and then snapping it shut when it feels live prey. Eats small fish, crustaceans, mollusks, and aquatic insects.

Nesting: Nests in rookeries with other herons, usually on islands. Deeply cupped platform nest of sticks and twigs lined with leaves and bark is placed in low tree or shrub 5–15 ft. above the water. Eggs: 1–5, white with dark marks; I: 22–24 days; F: 35–42 days, altricial; B: 1.

Other Behavior: Usually found in small flocks. During nesting season they are constantly on the move, flying from nests to feeding areas and back. During mutual pair displays, birds rub bills and present sticks to each other.

Habitat: Salt or fresh water.

Voice: Alarm call is low, repeated "huh-huh-huh."

Conservation:
BBS: E ⇑ C ⇑ CBC: ⇑ In 1800s was hunted for wings, which were sold as ladies' fans. Range has expanded since 1940, but drainage of wetlands jeopardizes feeding habitat.

Wood Stork
Mycteria americana

Adults

Adult

Identification: 40" A very **large, long-legged, white bird** with a **dark featherless head and neck;** thick, moderately downcurved bill. **IN FLIGHT:** Note black tail and broad black trailing edge of wings. **IMM:** Similar to adult, but head is feathered with gray and bill is dull yellow.

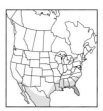

Feeding: Feeds in shallow, often muddy water by wading and groping along the bottom with its bill. Food includes small fish, frogs, snakes, small alligators, and other aquatic animals.

Nesting: In colonies. Many nests can be in same tree. Flimsy platform of sticks lined with finer material and placed in tree, preferably large cypress or mangrove, several feet above the water. Eggs: 3–4, dull white; I: 28–32 days; F: 55–60 days, altricial; B: 1.

Other Behavior: Breeding cycle may be triggered by food supply. After rains decrease and marshes dry, fish are concentrated and more available to storks, and breeding starts. If there is too much rain, and high water precludes concentration of prey, storks may skip breeding or desert eggs.

Habitat: Swamps, coastal shallows, ponds, flooded pastures.

Voice: Mostly quiet. Young have gooselike flocking note.

Conservation: BBS: E ↓ C CBC: ↓ Endangered in U.S. Declines due to loss of nesting and feeding sites. Restoration efforts are under way.

47

Black Vulture

Coragyps atratus

Adult

Immature

Identification: 25" **IN FLIGHT:** In all plumages, **large black bird; pale whitish primary feathers; short tail.** Soars with wings held in a slight dihedral; does not rock from side to side as does Turkey Vulture; periodically gives 3–4 rapid flaps. **PERCHED—ADULT:** A **large black bird; naked, wrinkled, gray head;** pale bill. **IMM:** Similar to adult, but head black, smooth, and covered with fine down; bill all dark. Imm. plumage kept 1 year.

Feeding: Feeds by scavenging on carrion in the wild or in urban areas. Finds food by sight alone, whether perched or in flight; flies higher than Turkey Vulture and may watch it and follow it to prey.

Nesting: Nest on bare ground in cave, on cliff ledge, in hollow stump, or under vegetation. Eggs: 1–3, pale greenish white with dark marks; I: 37–48 days; F: 70 days, altricial; B: 1.

Other Behavior: Roosts communally, sometimes at same spots as Turkey Vultures. When perched, may hold wings out in the sun as does Turkey Vulture.

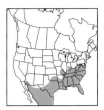

Habitat: Open country, dumps, urban areas.

Voice: Hisses, grunts, and snarls heard near the nest site and when birds are competing over food.

Conservation: BBS: E ⇑ C ↑ CBC: ↑

Turkey Vulture

Cathartes aura

Immature

Adult

Identification: 26" In Flight: In all plumages, **large all-dark bird; trailing half of wings silver. During soar, wings held in a V; bird rocks side to side and rarely flaps.** Has a smaller head and longer tail than Black Vulture. PERCHED— ADULT: **Large all-dark bird; naked red head;** pale bill. IMM: Like adult, but small head is gray; bill at first all dark, changing to pale with a dark tip. Imm. plumage kept 1 year.

Feeding: Feeds by scavenging on carrion, fresh or decayed. Finds food by sight and smell while soaring.

Nesting: Nest a scrape on bare ground, in hollow stump, cave, cliff ledge, or old building. Eggs: 1–3, dull white, occasionally with dark marks; I: 38–41 days; F: 70–80 days, altricial; B: 1.

Other Behavior: Turkey Vultures are often seen coming to and from nightly communal roosts, which may be located on tall buildings or towers and in large trees. The birds use thermals of warm air and updrafts off ridges to stay aloft; when these are no longer available and they need to flap, they usually stop flying and land.

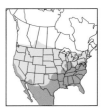

Habitat: Open country and dumps, occasionally roosts in urban areas.

Voice: Grunts and hisses heard at nest site and often during competition over food.

Conservation: BBS: E ⇑ C ↑ CBC: ⇑

Fulvous Whistling-Duck
Dendrocygna bicolor

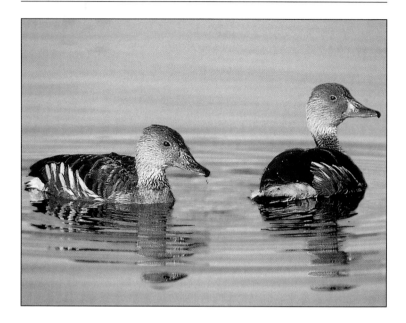

Identification: 20" **Rich buffy head and body; dark back and wings; dark bill.** White feathers create lines along the flanks. **In Flight:** Note buffy belly, black wings, and white patch on rump. Flies with head and feet lower than body, and feet extended well beyond the tail, as does Black-bellied Whistling-Duck.

Feeding: Primarily feeds at night in marshes and rice fields. Eats aquatic plants, grass and weed seeds, alfalfa, and waste grain.

Nesting: Nest of reeds lined with grasses and weeds is placed on the ground in dense vegetation or grass hummock, rarely in tree cavity. Eggs: 12–14, dull white; I: 24–26 days; F: 55–63 days, precocial; B: 1.

Other Behavior: Highly social. Usually found in groups. Female may lay eggs in other female's nest. Up to 100 eggs laid by several females were found in 1 nest. Often the duck will desert the nest. This intraspecific brood parasitism occurs in many duck species.

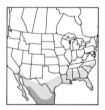

Habitat: Wet agricultural land, ponds, and marshes.

Voice: Flight call a whistling, loud "kaweee."

Conservation:
BBS: E C ⇑ CBC:→
Population declines in parts of its range due to habitat destruction and pesticide use.

Black-bellied Whistling-Duck

Dendrocygna autumnalis

Identification: 21" **Gray head; broad white eye-ring; bright red bill;** dark reddish-brown body; contrasting buff and white on wings. **IN FLIGHT:** Broad white streak down the center of upperwings; dark belly. Flies with head and feet lower than body. **IMM:** Similar to the adult, but bill is dark gray and rich brown areas of adult are gray and brown. Imm. plumage kept until following spring.

Feeding: Does much terrestrial grazing. Eats mostly sorghum grain, Bermuda grass seeds, and other plant material. Rarely mollusks and insects.

Nesting: Nest of rotted wood chips in tree cavity or nest box 8–30 ft. above the ground. May also nest on ground among vegetation. Eggs: 12–14, white; I: 25–30 days; F: 53–63 days, precocial; B: 2.

Other Behavior: Seen in large flocks. Tree nest is placed next to herbaceous plants so ducklings have soft landing spot when they jump from nest at 1 day old.

Habitat: Woodland ponds and marshes.

Voice: A series of 3–4 whistles, often given in flight.

Conservation: BBS: E C ⇑ CBC: ⇑

Tundra Swan

Cygnus columbianus

Identification: 53" **Body all white; bill black with a small yellow dash before the eye;** yellow dash not always present. The black facial skin narrows to a point before touching the eye, leaving eye more isolated on face than in the larger Trumpeter Swan. Head and neck may appear rusty due to iron staining in northern lakes. **IMM:** All-white body and neck; brownish head; pink bill with a dark tip and nostril. Imm. plumage kept until following spring.

Feeding: Eats aquatic vegetation, mollusks. In winter also eats grain.

Nesting: Platform nest of grasses and mosses, placed on an elevated hummock on small island. Eggs: 2–7, dull white; I: 35–40 days; F: 60–70 days, precocial; B: 1.

Other Behavior: Assembles in large flocks, sometimes in the thousands, to feed or rest.

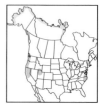

Habitat: Summers on tundra; winters on lakes, ponds, open marshes.

Voice: High-pitched whistling "kow-wow."

Conservation: CBC: ⇑

Mute Swan
Cygnus olor

Adult

Immature

Identification: 55" **Body white; bill pink to orange with black knob at base.** Swims with unique posture of neck in an S-curve and often with wings slightly raised over back. **Imm:** Light brownish with an all-dark bill. Imm. plumage kept 1 year.

Feeding: Eats leafy parts of fresh- and saltwater plants, algae, waste grain.

Nesting: Nest is a large pile of herbaceous vegetation lined with feathers, placed near water. Eggs: 4–8, pale grayish green; I: 35–38 days; F: 115–155 days, precocial; B: 1.

Other Behavior: Usually seen in city parks, but also seen in the wild. This native to Europe and Great Britain was brought to the U.S. in 1800s and stocked on estates and parks. Escapes developed into the wild population. The name "mute" was given because this swan is usually silent. It does not have the same vocal structure as our native swans and can only make hissing and snorting sounds. In flight, its wings make a repeated droning sound; our other swans have quiet wingbeats.

Habitat: Lakes, parks, coastal bays.

Voice: Usually silent.

Conservation:
BBS: E ⇑ C CBC: ⇑ In some coastal areas, Mute Swans are beginning to aggressively compete for food with native species of waterfowl.

53

Greater White-fronted Goose

Anser albifrons

Identification: 30" **A dark-headed goose with a pink or orange bill.** "White-fronted" refers to the ring of white feathers at base of bill. Variable black barring on the light brown belly; legs and feet orange. **IN FLIGHT:** Note black patches on belly and dark upperwings. **IMM:** Also dark-headed goose with a pink bill. Lacks the white on face and barring on the belly. Imm. plumage kept through following spring.

Feeding: Feeds on grasses, sedges, and grains such as wheat, rice, and barley, and on new growth in burned meadows.

Nesting: Nests in open wet tundra on hummocks or elevated ground. Nest of sticks, grasses, mosses, and down is placed in hollowed-out depression. Eggs: 4–7, creamy white; I: 22–28 days; F: 42–49 days, precocial; B: 1.

Other Behavior: Flocks may contain thousands. May also mix with Canada Geese on migration and in wintering areas, feeding in fields with them. Courtship and aggressive behavior can be seen in wintering flocks.

Habitat: Summers on tundra lakes and rivers; winters on wetlands, fields, and agricultural land.

Voice: High-pitched "leek-leek" call.

Conservation: CBC: ⇑ Declining in Pacific flyway.

Snow Goose

Chen caerulescens

Dark-morph adult (l.), light-morph immature (ctr.), light-morph adult (r.)

Adults

Identification: 29" **White goose with a pink bill.** Best distinguished from much smaller Ross' Goose by proportions; it has a **longer neck and bill** and **flatter head.** The two are often seen together on wintering grounds. IN FLIGHT: Black wing tips are prominent in flight, less so when bird is at rest. IMM: Light morph is light gray with dark legs and bill. Dark morph is all dark. Imm. plumage kept until following spring. ►Dark morph, called "Blue Goose," has a pink bill, white head and upper neck, and dark body and wings. Larger eastern form, "Greater Snow Goose," winters along Atlantic Coast and often has orange (due to iron staining) on head.

Feeding: Digs up the roots and tubers of aquatic plants. Also feeds on waste grain and tender shoots of grasses.

Nesting: Highly colonial. Nest of grasses and down is placed near the water. Eggs: 3–5, white; I: 23–25 days; F: 40–49 days, precocial; B: 1.

Other Behavior: Winters in large flocks that can number in the tens of thousands.

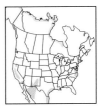

Habitat: Summers on tundra; winters on agricultural fields and wetlands.

Voice: A high-pitched honking.

Conservation: CBC: ⇓

Ross' Goose

Chen rossii

Light-morph adults

Identification: 24″ **A small white goose with a stubby pink bill.** Best distinguished from the larger Snow Goose by proportions; it is 25% smaller, with a **shorter neck and bill** and **rounder head.** The very rare "blue" morph has a pink bill, a white face and belly, and a dark body and wings. **In Flight:** Black wing tips are prominent in flight, less so when the bird is at rest. **Imm:** Light morph is similar to adult, but with a grayish wash on the head. Imm. plumage kept until following spring.

Feeding: Feeds on grasses and waste grains.

Nesting: Nests primarily on islands in lakes as a protection from mammalian predators. Concentrated nests average 15 ft. apart. Nest of grasses and mosses, concealed under vegetation. Eggs: 3–5, white; I: 21–24 days; F: 45 days, precocial; B: 1.

Other Behavior: Mostly seen in small numbers amid larger flocks of Snow Geese on wintering grounds.

Habitat: Summers on tundra; winters on agricultural fields and wetlands.

Voice: Higher-pitched honking than Snow Goose.

Conservation: CBC: ⇑

56

Brant

Branta bernicla

Western subspecies *(B. b. nigricans)*

Eastern subspecies *(B. b. hrota)*

Identification: 24" The **all-black head and bill** distinguish this **small goose** from others. Black neck, back, and wings; white rump; whitish sides with gray barring; and a belly that is white (in East) or dusky (in West). Thin white markings on either side of neck can be hard to see at a distance; they meet in front of neck in western subspecies. In FLIGHT: Note black head, neck, and chest; large white rump patch.

Feeding: Feeds on sedges, grasses, arctic plants, sea lettuce and other algae, and eelgrass.

Nesting: Semicolonial. Nests along shore of pond or stream, or on small island. Nest of seaweeds, grasses, and down is placed in low cover. Eggs: 3–5, dull white; I: 22–26 days; F: 40–50 days, precocial; B: 1.

Other Behavior: Highly social. Flocks fly low over water in long wavy lines. Courtship occurs on wintering areas. Early spring storms on breeding grounds can cause nest desertion and consequent population drop since females do not renest. Pacific populations now heavily dependent on Mexican (Baja Calif.) lagoons for wintering.

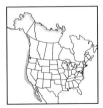

Habitat: Summers on high arctic coast; winters on coastal waters.

Voice: Soft "ruk-ruk" calls.

Conservation: CBC: ⇓

Canada Goose

Branta canadensis

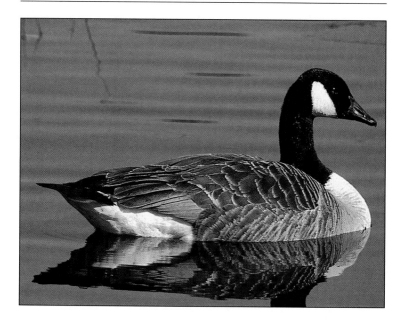

Identification: 25–45″ The most widespread and commonly seen goose. Look for its **black head and neck** and **white chinstrap.** Otherwise, brownish gray except for white rump. Varies greatly in size, with smallest forms living farthest north. IN FLIGHT: Note black neck and white chinstrap.

Feeding: Feeds on the ground and in the water. Eats submergent vegetation, grasses, winter wheat, clovers, and waste grain, especially corn.

Nesting: Nests at edges of ponds, lakes, or swamps, on rocks or grass hummocks out in the water. Nest made of sticks, mosses, and grasses lined with down. Eggs: 4–7, white; I: 28 days; F: 2–3 weeks, precocial; B: 1.

Other Behavior: Breeding range has increased due to management programs. Some birds that used to migrate now overwinter because food is provided for them by people at local ponds. Although this is a pleasant activity, it creates a major problem in many parks, golf courses, and public lands where the geese foul lawns, overgraze the grass, and may become aggressive during breeding.

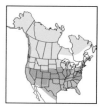

Habitat: Summers on lakes, marshes; winters on lakes, bays, fields, parks.

Voice: Male gives "ahonk." Female duets with higher "hink" call.

Conservation: BBS: E ⇑ C ⇑ CBC: ↑ Subspecies Aleutian Canada Goose is endangered in U.S. All other populations increasing.

Wood Duck

Aix sponsa

Male

Female

Identification: 18" **MALE: Distinctive colorful head; white throat, partial neck-ring, and chinstrap** all connected. Large crest is green, bill is pink, and eye is red. In eclipse plumage, male is similar to female but retains a suggestion of the white facial markings. **FEMALE: Brownish gray** with a darker crown and **broad white eye-ring** that tapers to a point in back. **IN FLIGHT:** Large head; long square tail; distinctive flight call.

Feeding: Feeds on the surface of the water, eating mostly aquatic plants like duckweed. Also eats insects, minnows, frogs, and feeds in wild rice marshes.

Nesting: Nest of wood chips and down is in natural tree cavity or human-made box 5–50 ft. above the ground or water. Eggs: 10–15, dull white; I: 27–30 days; F: 56–70 days, precocial; B: 1–2.

Other Behavior: Watch for many courtship displays, which take place through fall and winter. In inciting, female repeatedly flicks bill back over shoulder. Done near her mate and directed at intruding male. Her mate responds by raising wings and tail, turning the back of his head to her, and swimming away. She follows him.

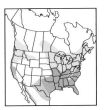

Habitat: Wooded swamps, rivers.

Voice: "Oo-eek" flight call given by female. Male gives high whistle in courtship groups.

Conservation: BBS: E ⇑ C ⇑ CBC: ↑ By 1900s was almost extinct due to hunting and habitat destruction. Now recovering due to nest-box programs.

59

Green-winged Teal

Anas crecca

Male

Female

Identification: 14" Our smallest dabbling duck. **MALE: Gray body with white vertical stripe on side** at start of wing. **Reddish-brown head; iridescent green patch extending behind eye.** In eclipse plumage, male looks like female. **FEMALE: Mottled brown; dark streak through eye; green speculum, which is usually visible; small bill.** **IN FLIGHT:** Small duck, light belly, and green speculum. ➤A similar male without the white vertical stripe may be the Eurasian subspecies, *A. c. crecca.*

Feeding: Feeds by dabbling along the edges of ponds and waterways, eating the soft parts of aquatic plants and their seeds. In the fall it visits grainfields and eats seeds, waste corn, wheat, oats, and buckwheat.

Nesting: Nest of grasses, weeds, and down is placed in depression in ground, concealed in grass or brush. Can be up to a mile from water. Eggs: 7–15, pale olive-buff; I: 21–23 days; F: 34–44 days, precocial; B: 1.

Other Behavior: One of earliest spring migrant ducks. Does courtship displays from winter through spring.

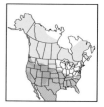

Habitat: Summers on freshwater ponds and lakes; winters also on rivers and sheltered coastal marshes.

Voice: Male gives piping "krick'et" whistle. Female gives high-pitched decrescendo quacking call of about 4 notes.

Conservation: BBS: E ⇓ C ↑ CBC: ↑

American Black Duck

Anas rubripes

Male

Females

Identification: 23" A large dark brown duck with a **paler brown head and neck;** speculum is violet. The sexes are similar. **MALE:** Olive to yellowish, unmarked bill. Eclipse plumage in the male shows practically no change. **FEMALE:** Greenish bill mottled with gray on upper surface. **IN FLIGHT:** Whitish underwings contrast strongly with the dark body.

Feeding: Feeds by tipping body tail-up. Eats aquatic vegetation, insects, small frogs, salamanders, snails, seeds, berries, and grain.

Nesting: Nest of dry leaves and grasses lined with down, placed in depression in ground close to water. Eggs: 6–12, cream or greenish buff; I: 26–29 days; F: 58–63 days, precocial; B: 1.

Other Behavior: Behavioral displays are identical to those of Mallard. Previously, the range of breeding and wintering was distinct from the Mallard's. In recent decades there has been an increased intrusion of Mallards into this area. The result is frequent hybridization with Mallards.

Habitat: Summers on fresh- and saltwater marshes; winters along coast.

Voice: Same as Mallard's.

Conservation: BBS: E ↓ C CBC: ⇓ Populations are declining due to habitat loss and hybridization with Mallards.

Mottled Duck

Anas fulvigula

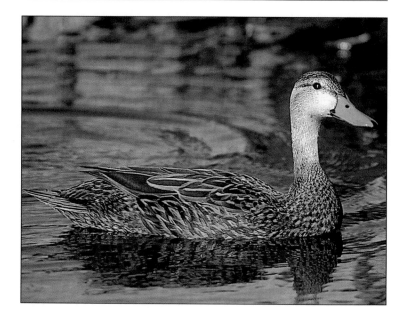

Identification: 23″ Limited to Fla. and Gulf Coast. **Large duck; mottled brown body; light buffy face and chin; bright yellow unmarked bill.** The sexes are alike. IN FLIGHT: Similar to Black Duck; greenish speculum bordered with black.

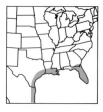

Feeding: More carnivorous than Mallard. Eats mollusks, insects, crayfish, snails, small fish, aquatic vegetation, grass, and seeds.

Nesting: Nest of reeds, aquatic vegetation, grasses, lined with feathers, placed in a depression in the ground close to water. Eggs: 8–10, pale greenish white; I: 25–27 days; F: 60–70 days, precocial; B: 1.

Other Behavior: Displays are similar to Mallard's. Mottled Ducks are relatively sedentary. Pair bonds are maintained throughout the year, and there is a prolonged breeding season.

Habitat: Freshwater or saltwater marshes; mostly coastal.

Voice: Like Mallard's.

Conservation:
BBS: E ⇓ C ⇓ CBC: ↑

Mallard
Anas platyrhynchos

Female (lower l.), males (top and r.)

Identification: 24" **MALE: Iridescent green head; yellow bill; chestnut breast.** White neck-ring can be hidden or exposed. Eclipse plumage is like female's, but with unmarked yellowish bill and reddish-brown breast. **FEMALE: Brown-streaked; orange bill broadly marked with black in the center; whitish tail feathers.** IN FLIGHT: Dark blue speculum bordered by white; underwings and body the same color.

Feeding: Male defends small feeding area in open water while female is building nest. Eats mostly aquatic vegetation, but also grain and insects.

Nesting: Nest of reeds and grasses lined with down, placed on ground near water. Eggs: 8–10, pale greenish white; I: 26–30 days; F: 50–60 days, precocial; B: 1.

Other Behavior: Mallards and other ducks in the genus *Anas* have similar complex courtship displays, and these occur fall through late winter. In inciting display, female follows her mate while repeatedly flicking her bill back over one side of her body. During head-up tail-up display, male stretches head, wing tips, and tail upward, then lowers them.

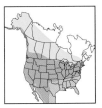

Habitat: Lakes, rivers, bays, parks.

Voice: Male does not quack; gives "rhaeb, rhaeb" call during aggression and short whistle during courtship. Female quacks in a decrescendo when uneasy or separated from male; gives "quegegege" call during inciting.

Conservation: BBS: E ⇑ C ↑ CBC: ⇓

63

Northern Pintail

Anas acuta

Male

Female

Identification: 25" **Long-necked** slender duck with **long pointed tail. MALE: Dark brown head; white breast and neck; gray flanks and wings.** Thin white line extends up sides of neck. In eclipse plumage, male looks like female, but has darker back. **FEMALE: Long neck; pointed tail; plain light brown head and neck; gray bill. IN FLIGHT:** Long neck; long thin tail; white streak on neck of male.

Feeding: Eats seeds, roots and shoots of aquatic plants, small crustaceans, corn and other grain.

Nesting: Concealed nest of leaves, grasses, and sticks lined with down is placed close to, or sometimes farther away from, water. Eggs: 6–12, greenish buff; I: 22–25 days; F: 36–57 days, precocial; B: 1.

Other Behavior: Large flocks of wintering birds often fly to cornfields to feed. Pair formation starts on wintering areas in Dec. and continues into spring migration. Head pumping by pair precedes copulation.

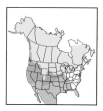

Habitat: Summers on open marshes and ponds; winters on coastal bays, lakes, and agricultural fields.

Voice: Female quacks. Male gives a fluty whistle.

Conservation: BBS: E ⇑ C ⇓ CBC: ⇓

Blue-winged Teal

Anas discors

Male

Female

Identification: 15" **MALE: Gray head; broad white crescent in front of eye.** Eclipse plumage, kept from late summer into midwinter, very similar to female's. **FEMALE: Small brown duck with a green speculum.** Differs from similar female Green-winged Teal in having **light spot at base of relatively large dark bill** and **dark eye-stripe that is darker behind eye. IN FLIGHT:** Light blue patches on forewing.

Feeding: Rarely dives. Skims the water surface with bill or reaches below the surface with head and neck. Eats seeds and vegetative parts of aquatic plants.

Nesting: Nest composed of grasses lined with down, placed in grassy cover not far from water. Eggs: 6–15, dull white; I: 23–27 days; F: 35–44 days, precocial; B: 1.

Other Behavior: Pair formation takes place midwinter through spring. Males do aggressive chin-lifting displays to one another. The female's primary display, as is the case with many surface-feeding ducks, is inciting (see Mallard for description).

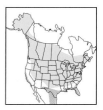

Habitat: Summers on small lakes in open grasslands; winters on marshes and protected coastal areas.

Voice: Female gives a high-pitched quacking. Male gives a peeping "tsee" note.

Conservation: BBS: E ↑ C ⇓ CBC: ⇑

Cinnamon Teal

Anas cyanoptera

Male

Female

Identification: 16" MALE: **Head, neck, and body dark cinnamon**; wings and back blackish. In eclipse plumage, male is similar to female, but has rustier plumage and a yellow or orange iris. FEMALE: Similar to female Blue-winged Teal, with **green speculum** and **light area at base of bill.** Differs by having a **darker, more uniformly colored head; little or no eye-stripe,** especially past the eye; and a **faint light area at base of bill.** IN FLIGHT: Light blue leading edge to wing, as in Blue-winged Teal.

Feeding: Prefers shallow water surrounded by grasses and herbaceous cover. Eats seeds of aquatic plants.

Nesting: Nest formed of grasses lined with down, placed in grassy or herbaceous cover, sometimes on islands. Eggs: 7–12, pinkish buff; I: 21–25 days; F: 49 days, precocial; B: 1.

Other Behavior: Hybridizes with Blue-winged Teal. Molts into breeding plumage relatively late, and courtship continues through spring migration. Nesting densities can be up to 100 pairs per square mile.

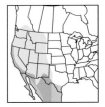

Habitat: Open shallow lakes and marshes.

Voice: Female sounds like Blue-winged Teal. Male gives series of "chuk" notes.

Conservation: BBS: E C ⇑ CBC: ↑

Northern Shoveler

Anas clypeata

Female (l.), male (r.)

Identification: 19" **Long bill widens consider-ably at the tip. MALE: Dark green head; white breast; reddish-brown flanks.** Eclipse plumage is similar to female's, but with darker back and more reddish-brown breast and flanks. **FEMALE:** A **brown-streaked duck** with a **spatula-shaped bill that is gray on top and orange along the opening. IN FLIGHT:** Large bill; pale blue forewing; green speculum.

Feeding: Feeds at water's surface by straining out small organisms with comblike edge of large bill. Eats aquatic insects and other invertebrates. Also eats duckweed and submerged aquatic plants.

Nesting: The concealed nest of grasses lined with down is placed in a depression in the ground and can be more than 100 yd. from the nearest water. Eggs: 6–14, pale greenish buff; I: 21–28 days; F: 36–60 days, precocial; B: 1.

Other Behavior: Usually found in small flocks or pairs. Much aggression is shown during displays and territorial defense.

Habitat: Summers on open shallow lakes and marshes; winters also on protected coastal areas.

Voice: Females do quacking and a decrescendo call of 5 notes, with the 1st note the loudest. Male gives low "took-a" note during courtship.

Conservation:
BBS: E C ↑ CBC: ⇑

Gadwall

Anas strepera

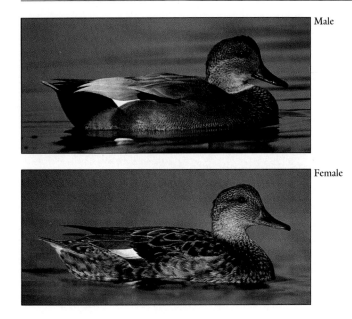

Male

Female

Identification: 21" MALE: A grayish duck with a **light brown angular head** and a **black tail.** White speculum is often visible. In eclipse plumage, looks like female. FEMALE: **Brown with a white belly** and **white speculum; bill grayish with orange along the opening.** IN FLIGHT: Note white belly and speculum.

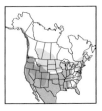

Feeding: Feeds by tipping body tail-up and by diving for food. Eats seeds and vegetative parts of aquatic plants.

Nesting: Often nests colonially on islands with good habitat. Nest of plant material and down is well hidden under dense herbaceous cover. Eggs: 7–13, white; I: 26–28 days; F: 48–60 days, precocial; B: 1.

Other Behavior: The complex courtship displays of this species are similar to those of other ducks in the genus *Anas.* Females do the inciting display. Males respond by turning the back of their head toward inciting female. Males do a number of displays. These include grunt-whistle, in which male points his bill down, raises the back of his neck, and gives a short high-pitched whistle. Gadwalls were primarily western until 1950s and 1960s, when they were introduced to the Northeast.

Habitat: Open lakes and marshes.

Voice: Female does quacking and a higher-pitched decrescendo than Mallard. Male gives whistle and "raeb-raeb" call.

Conservation: BBS: E C ⇑ CBC: ⇑

Eurasian Wigeon

Anas penelope

Male

Female

Identification: 19" A rare but regular winter visitor along both coasts, sometimes found inland. **MALE:** Look for the **reddish-brown head** with a **cream-colored crown,** and **gray sides and back.** Notice the white patch next to the dark rump. **FEMALE: Uniformly brown; small rounded head; darkish eye patch; light gray bill with black tip.** Gray morph of the female very similar to female American Wigeon.

Feeding: Feeds along the edges of ponds and waterways, eating aquatic plants such as pondweeds and eelgrass and also insects.

Nesting: Grassy nest hidden under low shrubs. Eggs: 7–10, white; I: 24–25 days; F: 40–45 days, precocial; B: 1.

Other Behavior: Breeds in Iceland and the British Isles and across northern Europe and Asia. Winters in those areas as well as around the Mediterranean and in China, Japan, and Africa. Is a regular winter visitor to the U.S. Social behavior is the same as American Wigeon's.

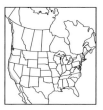

Habitat: Lakes, bays, estuaries.

Voice: Female gives abbreviated decrescendo call of 1–3 syllables. Male's calls are louder than American Wigeon's and are of 1 or 2 syllables.

Conservation: CBC: ⇑

69

American Wigeon
Anas americana

Female (l.), male (r.)

Identification: 21" MALE: **White forehead and crown; gray head; iridescent green patch through eye;** white patch before black tail. Male in eclipse plumage similar to female. FEMALE: **Brownish sides, grayish head and neck, dark eyespot,** and **light gray bill with black tip.** IN FLIGHT: White forewing; green speculum; light belly.

Feeding: Feeds on the stems, leaves, and buds of aquatic plants such as pondweeds, water milfoil, wigeon grass, wild celery, and eelgrass. May eat vegetation stirred up by diving ducks like Canvasbacks.

Nesting: Concealed in rushes or sedges, or under tree clumps, the grassy nest is generally placed rather far from water in upland meadows. Eggs: 6–12, white; I: 23–25 days; F: 36–48 days, precocial; B:1.

Other Behavior: Usually found in small flocks. As early arrivals on their southern wintering grounds, they immediately begin courtship, which lasts until March. By then, most females have paired. During courtship, competing males repeatedly give whistling calls and lift folded wings nearly vertically above back.

Habitat: Summers on lakes and marshes; winters on wet meadows, lakes, protected coastal waters.

Voice: Soft, growling "quegegege" by female during inciting. She also quacks. Male gives soft, descending 3-syllable whistle.

Conservation: BBS: E ⇑ C ⇑ CBC: ↓

Canvasback

Aythya valisineria

Male

Female

Identification: 21" A long-billed duck with a long sloping forehead. MALE: Reddish-brown head; black breast; white body; bill and tail black. In eclipse plumage is slightly browner but retains reddish-brown head and black breast. FEMALE: Grayish body; brown head and neck; long black bill; long sloping forehead. IN FLIGHT: Black bill; long sloping forehead.

Feeding: Dives to 30 ft. underwater to get roots, buds, and tubers of aquatic plants, especially pondweeds and wild celery. Also eats aquatic insects, small fish, and crustaceans.

Nesting: Bowl-shaped nest of reeds and sedges lined with down, attached to surrounding vegetation or placed on floating mass of vegetation. Eggs: 7–12, greenish olive; I: 24–29 days; F: 56–77 days, precocial; B: 1.

Other Behavior: Concentrates in large numbers on migratory and wintering grounds. Courtship continues during spring migration and includes aerial chases. Males leave females during incubation and gather in large flocks to molt. Females molt when young fledge.

Habitat: Summers on prairie lakes and marshes; winters on lakes and sheltered coastal waters.

Voice: Female gives soft "krr-krr." Male gives cooing note during courtship.

Conservation: BBS: E C ↓ CBC: ↓ Populations declining due to drainage of marshes and prairie potholes where ducks breed.

Redhead
Aythya americana

Male

Female

Identification: 20" Both sexes have **short bluish bills with black tips** and **steep rounded foreheads. MALE: Reddish head; black breast; grayish body.** In eclipse plumage has brown body but retains reddish head and dark breast. **FEMALE: Plain, warm brown body; darker brown back and wings; darker brown crown; buffy eye-ring; black-tipped bill. IN FLIGHT:** White belly; gray wings; small rounded head.

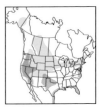

Habitat: Ponds, lakes, bays.

Feeding: Eats aquatic vegetation, including the roots, stems, and leaves of submerged plants. Also eats insect larvae, mollusks, and small crustaceans.

Voice: Male has catlike call during courtship. Female gives soft growling note.

Nesting: Basketlike nest of rushes, reeds, and cattails lined with down is attached to surrounding vegetation. Eggs: 9–13, pale buff; I: 24–28 days; F: 56–73 days, precocial; B: 1.

Conservation:
BBS: E C ⇑ CBC: ⇓

Other Behavior: A substantial portion of females do not attempt to nest; rather they "dump" their eggs in the nests of other Redheads or other species of ducks, especially Canvasbacks. The hatching success of these parasitically laid eggs is low because the host female often deserts the nest and then renests.

Ring-necked Duck
Aythya collaris

Male

Female

Identification: 16" In profile, **crown comes to a point**. MALE: All dark except for **white vertical mark in front of light gray sides; broad white band encircles grayish bill** just before black tip; a thinner band encircles base of bill. Brownish "ring" on neck is barely visible. In eclipse plumage, male like female, but with yellow iris. FEMALE: **Grayish brown with white eye-ring** and faint white line behind eye; **bill has white ring at tip;** poorly defined light area on face at base of bill. IN FLIGHT: White belly and gray speculum.

Feeding: Dives for tubers, leaves, and seeds of submerged vegetation. Also eats mollusks and insects.

Nesting: Nest of grass and mosses lined with down, placed near water's edge. Eggs: 6–14, olive-buff; I: 25–29 days; F: 49–56 days, precocial; B: 1.

Other Behavior: Found in small, often single-sex flocks during fall migration. Courtship peaks during spring migration. Copulation is preceded by bill dipping.

Habitat: Summers on open lakes, marshes; winters on large lakes and coastal areas.

Voice: Females give soft "rrrr" notes. Males give loud whistle during displays.

Conservation: BBS: E ↑ C ⇓ CBC: ↓ Populations have increased considerably in East over last 50 years.

Greater Scaup
Aythya marila

Male

Female

Identification: 18" Head shape and bill size are best characteristics for distinguishing this species from Lesser Scaup. Greater Scaup's **head is like a rounded rectangle** and never comes to a peak in the center; **slightly larger bill.** MALE: **Dark head and breast** and **dark tail** separated by gray back and **white flank.** In excellent light, note **greenish gloss on head.** FEMALE: **Dark brown; extensive white patches on either side of base of bill.** Distinguish it from female Lesser Scaup by head shape and bill size. IN FLIGHT: Long white band on inner wing extends onto wing tip.

Feeding: Dives as deep as 25 ft. underwater for up to 1 minute, eating submerged plants, crustaceans, mollusks, and snails.

Nesting: Often on islands. Nest is made of matted vegetation, grasses, and down. Eggs: 8–11, olive-buff; I: 24–28 days; F: 35–42 days, precocial; B: 1.

Other Behavior: In fall and winter often found on deeper lakes and in more saltwater habitats than Lesser Scaup.

Habitat: Summers on tundra lakes; winters on salt water and coastal ponds.

Voice: Male gives a soft "wa-hooo" note and a triple-note whistle. Female gives a growling "arrr" call.

Conservation: CBC: ⇓

Lesser Scaup

Aythya affinis

Male

Female

Identification: 17" Head and bill shapes are most useful characteristics distinguishing this species from Greater Scaup, but differences are subtle. On Lesser Scaup the **head comes to a peak at the top or near the back; bill is slightly shorter and narrower.** MALE: **Dark head and breast** and **dark tail** separated by gray back and **white flank.** In excellent light, note **purplish gloss on head.** FEMALE: **Dark brown with small white patches on either side of base of bill.** Distinguish from Greater Scaup female by shape of head and bill. IN FLIGHT: Long white band on inner wing usually does not extend to outer wing.

Feeding: Dives for submergent plant seeds, snails, insects, and crustaceans.

Nesting: Concealed nest of grasses lined with down is placed on ground, in cover within 100–200 ft. of water. Sometimes nests in tern colonies. Eggs: 8–14, olive-buff; I: 21–28 days; F: 49 days, precocial; B: 1.

Other Behavior: Highly social. Winter flocks, or "rafts," may number in the thousands.

Habitat: Summers on prairie lakes and marshes; winters on lakes, sheltered coastal areas, freshwater ponds.

Voice: Male gives faint "whee-ooo" note, a single-note whistle, and a quacking sound. Female makes a purring "kwuh" sound.

Conservation: BBS: E C ⇑ CBC: ↓

Common Eider

Somateria mollissima

Male

Female

Immature male

Identification: 25″ A large duck often seen in large flocks floating along the coast. **MALE:** Distinctive **white back and black flanks** easily seen from a distance. Long sloping "Roman nose." **FEMALE:** All **brown with profile like that of male.** **IMM:** Female much like adult; male dark with white areas of adult plumage developing first on breast and then elsewhere. Imm. plumage kept 3 years.

Feeding: Dives in sea as far as 60 ft. under water for whelks, sea urchins, crustaceans, and mollusks, especially blue mussels.

Nesting: Prefers boulder-covered islands. Nest of seaweeds, grasses, sticks, and mosses lined with down is placed on ground. Eggs: 3–5, pale greenish olive; I: 25–30 days; F: 56–70 days, precocial; B: 1.

Other Behavior: In Iceland, down from nest is collected during incubation and is used commercially; female usually does not desert nest. Cooing sounds accompany a lot of male courtship displays. Males often winter farther north than females and immatures.

Habitat: Coastal waters.

Voice: Female gives several hoarse-sounding calls. Male gives dovelike cooing sounds.

Conservation: BBS: E ⇑ C CBC: ↑ Susceptible to oil spills.

King Eider
Somateria spectabilis

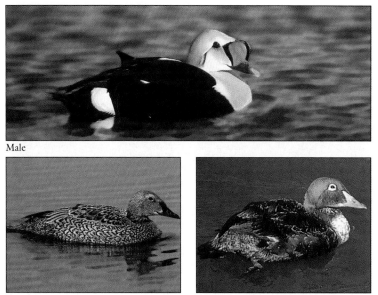

Male

Female

Immature male

Identification: 23" Stays farther north than Common Eider and so is only occasionally seen. **MALE: Orange shield over base of bill;** black back and flanks; white breast. **FEMALE: Brown duck with a Roman nose** similar to that of Common Eider but **frontal lobes of bill shorter and more rounded;** otherwise hard to distinguish. **IMM:** Female similar to adult. Male dark with no shield on bill at first; develops white of adult plumage first on breast, then on other areas. Imm. plumage kept 2–3 years.

Feeding: Dives as deep as 200 ft. underwater for mollusks, crustaceans, sea urchins, starfish. Also eats algae, eelgrass, sedges, and aquatic insects.

Nesting: Nest of feathers and down is placed on the ground near water, but can be some distance away. Eggs: 4–7, olive-buff; I: 22–24 days; F: up to 50 days, precocial; B: 1.

Other Behavior: After hatching, broods merge and "nurseries" of up to 100 ducklings are attended by several females. Stays in large flocks during winter.

Habitat: Summers on tundra; winters along subarctic coast.

Voice: Female gives hollow-sounding notes. Male makes cooing sounds.

Conservation: CBC: ↑

Harlequin Duck

Histrionicus histrionicus

Male

Female

Identification: 17″ A small compact sea duck with a short bill. MALE: A slate-blue head, breast, and back boldly patterned with white. Also has red-brown flanks. In eclipse plumage similar to female but with some white on wings. FEMALE: All dark brown; unstreaked; 3 white patches on each side of face. IN FLIGHT: Dark belly; white face patterns; long tail; small bill.

Feeding: In summer feeds on insects found in streams. In winter moves to coast and dives for mollusks.

Nesting: Concealed nest of grasses lined with down. Eggs: 4–8, light buff; I: 28–30 days; F: 40–70 days, precocial; B: 1.

Other Behavior: Has the ability to swim in torrential currents and rapidly moving streams where it forages for insects. Male's color and white spotting may provide camouflage in this environment.

Habitat: Summers on mountain rivers and streams; winters on rocky coasts.

Voice: High-pitched peeping sounds.

Conservation: CBC: ↓ A major victim of oil spills, with sharp declines in population.

Oldsquaw
Clangula hyemalis

Summer male

Winter male

Female

Identification: 19" A sea duck best recognized by its **variable light and dark plumage** and **pointed tail.** Plumage varies since adults molt 3 times each year and there is an immature plumage as well. SUMMER—MALE: **Black head and breast; large white patch surrounding eye.** FEMALE: **Dark wings; light flanks and head; large dark smudge behind cheek.** WINTER— MALE: **White head; large dark patch on side of neck.** FEMALE: **Similar to summer, but lighter.** IN FLIGHT: Note light eye patch of both sexes and long, pointed tail of male. IMM: Similar to the adult female, but variable. Imm. plumage kept 1 year.

Feeding: Can dive to 200 ft. deep. Eats crustaceans, mollusks, and larval insects.

Nesting: Concealed grassy nest. Eggs: 5–11, yellowish buff; I: 24–35 days; F: 35–40 days, precocial; B: 1.

Other Behavior: Very social. Much courtship and territorial displaying done winter to summer. Very vocal throughout year.

Habitat: Summers on tundra lakes, coastal inlets; winters along coast.

Voice: In winter males give yodeling calls. In courtship males give "ah-har-lik" call with a bill toss. Females give guttural calls during chin-lifting display.

Conservation:
CBC:→
Suffers in oil spills.

79

Black Scoter

Melanitta nigra

Males

Female

Identification: 19″ **MALE: All black** with a large **orange knob at base of bill. FEMALE: Brown; small-billed; cheek noticeably lighter than crown and nape. IN FLIGHT:** All dark with silvery wing linings; male with orange knob on bill. **IMM:** Female similar to adult female; male similar to adult female, but with yellow knob on bill showing in first winter. Imm. plumage kept 1 year.

Habitat: Summers on tundra lakes; winters along the coast.

Feeding: Usually feeds in shallow water just outside breaker zone. Sometimes frequents deeper water. Eats aquatic plants, crustaceans, and mollusks, especially mussels and limpets.

Voice: Female gives grating notes. Male gives mellow whistle during courtship.

Nesting: Concealed nest of coarse grasses lined with down, on ground close to water. Eggs: 5–8, pale pinkish buff; I: 27–31 days; F: 45–50 days, precocial; B: 1.

Conservation: CBC: ⇓

Other Behavior: Formerly called Common Scoter. The least common of the scoters. They do not breed until their second spring, when they reach sexual maturity.

Surf Scoter

Melanitta perspicillata

Male

Female

Identification: 20" MALE: Black; orange, yellow, and white bill; white patches on forehead and nape. FEMALE: Brown; large dark bill; darker crown; 2 white spots on side of face. The forward spot ends in an abrupt vertical line where it meets the bill. This can help distinguish it from the similar female White-winged Scoter. IN FLIGHT: Lighter belly on female; male with white patches on head. IMM: Females like adult female; males have colorful bill, but lack full white head markings. Imm. plumage kept 1 year.

Feeding: Dives underwater and feeds primarily on mussels and crustaceans. Eats some insects and plants.

Nesting: Concealed nest of weeds located some distance from water. Eggs: 5–8, pale buff; I: ?; F: ?, precocial; B: 1.

Other Behavior: Has the habit of diving through the breaking surf. Scoters gather into huge flocks along the coast during fall migration. Traditionally, they were hunted at this time.

Habitat: Summers on semiwooded arctic lakes and rivers; winters along the coast, very infrequently found inland.

Voice: A low guttural sound. During mating season male gives a low whistle.

Conservation: CBC: ↓

White-winged Scoter

Melanitta fusca

Male

Female

Identification: 22″ **White wing patch** on all-dark male and female is a good clue, but not always visible when wings are closed. **MALE: Black; small white mark around eye;** multicolored bill tip. **FEMALE: Brown; large dark bill; 2 whitish spots on face.** The forward spot is ovate; the shape of this spot and the white wing patch can help distinguish it from the similar female Surf Scoter. **IN FLIGHT:** All dark with bright white speculum. **IMM:** Female may have more distinct facial spots than adult; male browner and lacking eye patch of adult. Imm. plumage kept at least 1 year.

Feeding: On the coast, birds concentrate in water that is less than 20 ft. deep and feed on mussels, clams, and scallops.

Nesting: Concealed nest of sticks, leaves, and feathers, on ground near water. Eggs: 5–12, pink-buff; I: 26–29 days; F: 63–77 days, precocial; B: 1.

Other Behavior: Most widespread scoter. Migrates in flocks, often flying in long line formations.

Habitat: Summers on lakes and ponds; winters along the coast.

Voice: Females give a thin whistling note. Males give a bell-like call during courtship.

Conservation: CBC: ↓

Common Goldeneye

Bucephala clangula

Male

Female

Identification: 18" MALE: **White flanks; dark head; rounded white spot in front of and below eye.** In perfect lighting, head looks glossy green. FEMALE: **Grayish; white collar; dark brown head. Bill dark with small area of yellow at tip.** Note **thicker bill** and **more sloping forehead** than similar female Barrow's Goldeneye. IN FLIGHT: Large white speculum area; white patches on male's face. IMM: Both sexes similar to female at first. Male gradually develops adult wing and facial pattern. Imm. plumage kept 1 year.

Feeding: Dives underwater to feed on crustaceans and mollusks. Also eats aquatic insects.

Nesting: Nest in tree cavity or man-made nesting box is lined with feathers from female's breast. Eggs: 5–15, olive to light green; I: 28–30 days; F: 56–66 days, precocial; B: 1.

Other Behavior: Has spectacular and complex courtship with numerous displays. When nesting sites are scarce, female may lay eggs in another female's nest.

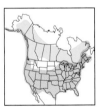

Habitat: Summers on lakes and marshes; winters on interior and coastal waters.

Voice: Relatively silent. Male gives nasal "eeent" during courtship. In flight, wings make whistling noise.

Conservation: BBS: E ⇓ C ⇑ CBC: ↓

83

Barrow's Goldeneye
Bucephala islandica

Male

Female

Identification: 19" **MALE: White flanks; dark back and head; clear white crescent in front of the eye.** In perfect lighting, head looks glossy purple. **FEMALE: A grayish duck** with a **white collar** and **dark brown head. Bill mostly yellow-orange** in western birds; dark with yellow tip in eastern birds. Note **thinner bill, darker head,** and **more vertical forehead** than similar female Common Goldeneye. **IN FLIGHT:** Large white speculum area bisected by dark bar, and note facial crescent of male. **IMM:** Both sexes similar to female at first. Male gradually develops adult wing and facial pattern. Imm. plumage kept 1 year.

Feeding: Eats mollusks, crustaceans, fish, aquatic insects.

Nesting: Uses tree cavities or nest boxes, but also can nest in rock crevice or on the ground. Eggs: 8–10, olive-green; I: 30–32 days; F: 56 days, precocial; B: 1.

Other Behavior: Male display behavior and vocalizations differ from Common Goldeneye's. Hybridization with Common Goldeneye rare.

Habitat: Summers on wooded lakes and rivers; winters on estuaries or coastal lakes.

Voice: Males give grunting and clicking notes. Females mostly silent.

Conservation: CBC: ⇑

Bufflehead
Bucephala albeola

Male

Female

Identification: 14" A small duck with a large rounded head. **MALE:** Note **conspicuous white wedge at back of dark head;** white breast and flanks. **FEMALE: Gray-brown duck; dark head; long white dash behind eye.** **IMM:** Female similar to adult; male has larger white dash than female, and this gradually develops to the full white wedge. Imm. plumage kept 1 year.

Feeding: Dives underwater and eats small mollusks, fish, snails, and crustaceans. Also eats aquatic insects.

Nesting: Nests in tree cavity 5–50 ft. high or nest box, which it lines with down. Eggs: 8–10, ivory to buff; I: 28–33 days; F: 49–56 days, precocial; B: 1.

Other Behavior: Winters in small flocks. Courtship, which begins in Jan., has high level of aggression.

Habitat: Summers on wooded lakes and rivers; winters on lakes and coastal waters.

Voice: Generally silent; female makes guttural sounds during courtship.

Conservation: CBC: ↑

Hooded Merganser
Lophodytes cucullatus

Male

Female

Identification: 18″ Note the **short thin bill** and **crested head** on this smallest of the mergansers. **MALE: Black head; white fan-shaped patch within crest** (when crest is raised); flanks brown; back is black. Black vertical line cuts diagonally down through white breast in front of flanks. **FEMALE:** Plain brown with a **darker back; red-brown crest; darker upper bill. IN FLIGHT:** Note thin bill, grayish wing linings, and rapid wingbeats **IMM:** Female like adult; male like female, but with some white in crest. Imm. plumage kept 1 year.

Feeding: Dives underwater. Eats small fish, frogs, crustaceans, mollusks, and aquatic insects.

Nesting: Nest of grasses and down, placed in tree cavity or nest box. Eggs: 6–18, white; I: 32–41 days; F: 70 days, precocial; B: 1.

Other Behavior: Courtship begins in midwinter, usually occurring in mixed groups of 3–10 birds. Females do head bobbing and pumping. Most male displays involve crest raising.

Habitat: Summers on wooded rivers and lakes; winters on similar locations as well as along the coast occasionally.

Voice: Male gives froglike note. Female makes a hoarse "gak."

Conservation:
BBS: E ⇑ C CBC: ⇑

Common Merganser

Mergus merganser

Male

Female

Identification: 25" This merganser has a **long bill that is thicker at the base,** making its **forehead appear more gently sloping** than that of the Red-Breasted Merganser. **MALE: Dark green head; creamy white breast and flank; dark back; red bill. FEMALE: Gray; red-crested head sharply delineated from white chin and breast;** red bill. **IN FLIGHT:** Thin bill, white breast on male. Flight strong and direct. **IMM:** Female resembles adult; male looks like female at first, but begins to develop adult male plumage by first spring. Imm. plumage kept 1 year.

Feeding: Dives underwater and eats mostly fish, also crustaceans and mollusks. Serrated bills of all mergansers aid in holding slippery fish prey.

Nesting: Down-lined nest of weeds and roots in tree cavity, nest box, or rock crevice, or on ground. Eggs: 8–11, buff; I: 28–35 days; F: 70–84 days, precocial; B: 1.

Other Behavior: Displays involve much chasing on water and in air, and underwater attacks.

Habitat: Summers on wooded lakes and along rivers; winters on large lakes and estuaries, usually on fresh water.

Voice: Male's courtship call is a guitarlike note. Female gives harsh sound.

Conservation: BBS: E ⇑ C ⇓ CBC: ↑

87

Red-breasted Merganser

Mergus serrator

Male

Female

Identification: 23″ This merganser has a **long bill that is thin at the base,** making its **forehead appear more abrupt and vertical** than that of Common Merganser. **MALE: Dark green crested head; white neck-ring; rusty breast;** red bill. **FEMALE: A brown duck with a red-crested head that gradually shades to the white breast;** red bill. **IN FLIGHT:** Thin bill; dark breast on male. Flight fast and direct. **IMM:** Female resembles adult; male looks like female at first, but begins to develop adult male plumage by first spring. Imm. plumage kept 1 year.

Feeding: Dives for fish, mollusks, and crustaceans.

Nesting: Nest lined with vegetation and down is sheltered under shrubs, logs. Eggs: 5–11, greenish buff; I: 29–35 days; F: 59–65 days, precocial; B: 1.

Other Behavior: Courtship begins in winter. Males do elaborate posturing and give distinct catlike call.

Habitat: Summers on rivers and lakes; winters along sheltered coastal waters, preferring salt water.

Voice: Male gives catlike "yeow-yeow." Female gives harsh double note.

Conservation: BBS: E ⇓ C CBC: ↑

Ruddy Duck
Oxyura jamaicensis

Summer male

Winter male

Female

Identification: 16" **Small stocky duck with a broad bill and a stiff tail that is often held straight up.** SUMMER—MALE: **Reddish-brown body; black head; white cheek;** light blue bill. FEMALE: **Brown; head appears 2-toned,** having a dark crown and a lighter cheek with a line through it. Keeps same plumage all year. WINTER—MALE: Similar to female, but with no line through cheek. IMM: Like adult female. Imm. plumage kept 1 year.

Feeding: Dives and feeds on aquatic plants, crustaceans, aquatic insects.

Nesting: Well-concealed nest of plant material is attached to marsh plants. Eggs: 6–10, dull white; I: 23–26 days; F: 42–52 days, precocial; B: 1–2.

Other Behavior: Birds are in large winter flocks. They start courtship on spring migration. Male's tail cocking and neck enlargement is most obvious display. Females dump eggs in nests of other females and in nests of other duck species such as Canvasbacks and Redheads.

Habitat: Summers on open lakes; winters also along coast.

Voice: Mostly silent. Males make drumming sound by beating lower mandible on breast.

Conservation:
BBS: E C ↓ CBC: ↓

The term *hawk* refers to several related bird groups, including eagles, falcons, kites, and ospreys. Vultures, not closely related, are often included because they look similar and soar with hawks.

To identify hawks, start by learning the fairly distinctive silhouette and flight behavior of each group. Then learn the most common species in each group. The Learning Pages will help you do this with adult hawks; immature hawks are more difficult to identify, but have essentially the same size, shape, and flight behavior as the adults. For each hawk shown on these pages there is the name, a brief description, and the range of wingspread (W), from the smaller male to the larger female (a sexual difference typical of hawks). For complete information on adults and immatures, see the Species Accounts.

Most hawks are not commonly seen; the ones that are, are listed below. The best way to see other hawks is during fall migration, when large numbers move south on clear days with generally north winds. Along ridges or the coast are good places to look for them.

Commonly Seen Hawks: Which Ones and Where

- **Perched along roads:**
    Most large hawks are Red-tailed Hawks, p. 111
    Most small hawks are American Kestrels, p. 116

- **Perched or soaring near water:**
    Most are Ospreys, p. 94
    Some may be Bald Eagles, p. 99

- **Soaring over land:**
    Black Vulture, p. 48, or Turkey Vulture, p. 49
    Red-tailed Hawk, p. 111

- **Perched near or attacking birds at bird feeders:**
    Sharp-shinned Hawk, p. 101

Eagles

Very large; mostly dark; very long wings; soar continuously.

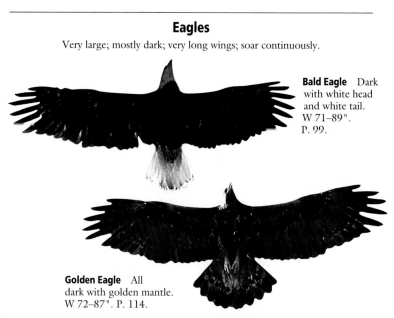

Bald Eagle   Dark with white head and white tail. W 71–89". P. 99.

Golden Eagle   All dark with golden mantle. W 72–87". P. 114.

Buteos

Large hawks; broad wings; short tails; soar a lot; seen in open areas.

Red-tailed Hawk Red tail; belly band; dark line at front edge of wing. W 43–52". P. 111.

Broad-winged Hawk Broad black and white tail bands; bold black border along tip and trailing edge of wings. W 32–36". P. 107.

Rough-legged Hawk Dark square patches on wrists of wings. W 48–56". P. 113.

Red-shouldered Hawk Whitish wing windows next to dark wing tips. W 37–42". P. 106.

Vultures

Large birds; mostly black; soar continuously, rarely beating wings.

Turkey Vulture All black with trailing half of wings light gray. W 63–71". P. 49.

Black Vulture All black with pale whitish primaries. W 55–63". P. 48.

Accipiters

Small-to-large hawks; short rounded wings; medium-to-long tail; in flight, alternate several quick flaps with glides ("flap, flap, flap, glide"); catch other birds in the air.

Sharp-shinned Hawk
Small; square-tipped tail with thin gray band at tip; looks short-necked. W 20–26". P. 101.

Cooper's Hawk
Crow-sized; long tail rounded at tip with whitish terminal band; heavyset head and long neck. W 28–34". P. 102.

Northern Goshawk
Red-tailed Hawk size; long wings; wide tail; soars more than other accipiters. W 38–45". P. 103.

Northern Harrier

Large hawk; long thin wings held in a V over back; long tail with white rump patch; tilts from side to side when soaring. W 38–48". P. 100.

Osprey

Large hawk; dark above, white below; when soaring, forms a shallow M, with wings arched forward at the wrists and bent down at the tips. W 59–67". P. 94.

Falcons

Small-to-large hawks; pointed wings; direct flight with little gliding.

American Kestrel Small falcon; thin wings with light spots on trailing edge. W 20–24". P. 116.

Merlin Medium-sized dark falcon; heavier than kestrel; angular wings; very direct flight. W 21–27". P. 117.

Peregrine Falcon Large falcon; long wings; broad tail; broad dark bar on cheek; whitish wing linings. W 37–46". P. 118.

Kites

Medium-sized hawks; long thin wings; long thin tails; graceful and buoyant fliers that often catch insects in the air.

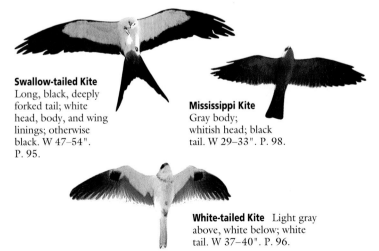

Swallow-tailed Kite Long, black, deeply forked tail; white head, body, and wing linings; otherwise black. W 47–54". P. 95.

Mississippi Kite Gray body; whitish head; black tail. W 29–33". P. 98.

White-tailed Kite Light gray above, white below; white tail. W 37–40". P. 96.

Osprey
Pandion haliaetus

Female

Male

Identification: 24" **IN FLIGHT:** In all plumages, **dark above, white below; white head; prominent black streak through eye**. When soaring and gliding, forms a **wide shallow M,** with wings bowed (wrists up and forward and wing tips pointed down). Females generally more streaked on breast than males. **PERCHED— ADULT: Dark back and tail; white head; dark streak through eye. IMM:** As adult, but pale tips to wing and back feathers; streaked crown. Imm. plumage kept 2 years.

Feeding: Eats mostly fish, usually caught by hovering over water, then diving down and catching them in its talons. Fish are carried headfirst as bird flies off.

Nesting: Large platform nest of sticks lined with moss and grass is placed on a tree, cliff, or human structure 5–200 ft. high. Eggs: 2–4, whitish with reddish-brown blotches; I: 34–40 days; F: 49–56 days, altricial; B: 1.

Other Behavior: Male brings female all of her food during breeding. Immature birds stay on wintering grounds for 2 years before returning north.

Habitat: Large lakes, rivers, coast.

Voice. A down-slurred chirp given in mild alarm; an ascending squeal given during sky-dance display

Conservation: BBS: E ⇑ C CBC: ⇑ First studies leading to 1972 ban on DDT done on declining Osprey populations, which are now recovered.

Swallow-tailed Kite
Elanoides forficatus

Identification: 22" IN FLIGHT: In all plumages, unmistakable. Long forked tail; underparts white except for tail and flight feathers, which are black. PERCHED—ADULT: Head, chest, and belly white; back and long forked tail black. IMM: Similar to adult, but shorter tail and sometimes fine streaking on breast and head. Imm. plumage kept 1 year.

Feeding: While flying, catches in its talons and eats large insects; also lizards, snakes, frogs, and small birds. Several kites may feed together.

Nesting: Platform nest of sticks, twigs, and pine needles lined with Spanish moss and lichens is placed in treetop 60–130 ft. high. Eggs: 2–4, white with dark marks; I: 28 days; F: 36–42 days, altricial; B: 1.

Other Behavior: In spring, you may see pair soaring over nesting area, with higher bird diving down on lower bird. Birds collect nest twigs by breaking them off trees with their talons as they fly by. When mates exchange places on nest, they may call "eeep" or "keeawee." In mid- to late summer, large aggregations of this species congregate around Lake Okeechobee in Fla.

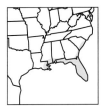

Habitat: Woodlands near marshes or swamps.

Voice: Interactions between pair are accompanied by calls like "eeep" and "kleekleeklee."

Conservation:
BBS: E ⇑ C
Declining since 1900 due to loss of woodland habitat from logging. Now only in portion of former range.

White-tailed Kite

Elanus leucurus

Immature

Adult

Identification: 15" IN FLIGHT—ADULT: **Light gray above, white below; black shoulder patches; black wrist patch on underside of pointed wings.** Distinguished from Mississippi Kite by white rather than black tail. Hunts by hovering. IMM: Similar to adult from below, but narrow dusky band near tip of tail. PERCHED— ADULT: **Gray back, white belly, black shoulders.** IMM: Black wings, brown back, rufous wash across breast, dusky band on tail. Body feathers like adult's in 2–3 months, but tail band kept 1 year.

Feeding: Eats almost exclusively small rodents, catching them by hovering above ground and dropping down.

Nesting: Platform nest of sticks and twigs lined with grass, weeds, and rootlets, placed in tree 5–60 ft. high. Eggs: 3–6, white with dark marks; I: 30 days; F: 33–37 days, altricial; B: 1–2.

Other Behavior: Gregarious with communal feeding and roosting areas from fall through spring, and communal roosts of nonbreeding birds during breeding season.

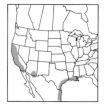

Habitat: Grasslands with scattered trees, near marshes, along highways.

Voice: A repeated short "chip chip chip"; a longer "kree-eek" given during mild alarm.

Conservation: BBS: E C ⇑ CBC: ⇑ Disappeared from original Midwest range by 1900; now increasing and expanding range.

Snail Kite

Rostrhamus sociabilis

Female

Male

Identification: 17″ Limited to central Fla. **IN FLIGHT:** In all plumages, **long, thin, hooked bill; wide white band at base of black tail; soars with wings bowed** (wrists up and wing tips down). **MALE:** Dark gray body and wings. **FEMALE AND IMM:** Mottled or streaked brown below, with distinctive light cheek and eyebrow. **PERCHED—MALE: Body dark gray; legs and facial skin red. FEMALE AND IMM: Body streaked brown; legs and facial skin orange in female and yellow in imm.** Imm. plumage kept 1–2 years.

Feeding: Eats almost exclusively *Pomacea* (large freshwater snails). Birds hover over water vegetation and grab snails with talons. Snail meat is removed from shell by the bird's long hooked bill.

Nesting: Platform nest of sticks and twigs lined with finer materials, placed in a low tree or on a hummock or bush. Eggs: 2–4, white with dark marks; I: 28–30 days; F: 23–28 days, altricial; B: 1–2.

Other Behavior: Forms communal nighttime roosts.

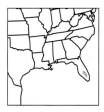

Habitat: Freshwater marshes.

Voice: Generally quiet, but may give a cackling call near nest.

Conservation: Endangered in U.S. In 1950s, drainage of Fla. wetlands caused severe declines. Managing wetlands has helped small population remain stable.

Mississippi Kite

Ictinia mississippiensis

Adult

Immature

Adult

Identification: 14" IN FLIGHT—ADULT: **Gray** with **black tail** and **whitish head.** Distinctive white patch on inner trailing edge of wings seen from above. Black tail distinguishes it from similar White-tailed Kite. IMM: Long, pointed brown wings; heavily brown-streaked belly changing to gray with small white blotches in spring; 2–3 thin white bands on black tail. PERCHED—ADULT: **Whitish head; gray underparts and back; black tail.** IMM: Body and tail as described above. Imm. plumage kept 1 year.

Feeding: Eats mostly insects caught on the wing. Catches them in its talons; and eats them while flying.

Nesting: Flat nest of twigs lined with green leaves, placed in tree 4–135 ft. high. Eggs: 1–3, bluish white; I: 29–31 days; F: 34 days, altricial; B: 1.

Other Behavior: Previous nests are often used in following years. First-year birds may become helpers at the nest of breeding birds. Migrates in flocks. Increasingly seen wandering north of its range into S. New England. Expanding range into West.

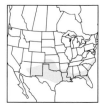

Habitat: Open woodlands, wooded streams, swamps.

Voice: Generally quiet, but gives a "kee kew, kee kew" when disturbed at the nest.

Conservation:
BBS: E ↑ C ↑

98

Bald Eagle

Haliaeetus leucocephalus

Adult

Immature

Immature

Identification: 31" IN FLIGHT—ADULT: **Very large dark bird; white head; white tail.** Massive head and bill equal to one-half or more length of tail. Soars on flat wings. IMM: **Very large dark bird; white armpits; white mottling on wing lining; undertail, if whitish, has dark edges; variable amounts of white on belly after 1st year.** PERCHED—ADULT: **White head and tail.** IMM: Told from Golden Eagle by lack of gold on head and nape, longer bill, and presence of white on belly. Imm. plumage kept 4 years.

Feeding: Eats mostly fish inland and mostly birds along coast; also carrion and some mammals, such as rabbits.

Nesting: Massive platform nest of sticks and vegetation lined with moss and grasses is placed on cliff ledge or in the fork of a tree 10–180 ft. high. Eggs: 1–3, bluish white; I: 34–36 days; F: 10–12 weeks, altricial; B: 1.

Other Behavior: Eagles congregate at feeding areas in late winter and early spring. During their soaring, look for chases and even passing of sticks between birds; these may function in courtship.

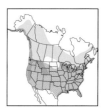

Habitat: Along coasts, lakes, and large rivers.

Voice: Has a repeated piercing scream given between pair, and a rapid series of chirps given at nest.

Conservation: BBS: E ⇑ C CBC:→ Most populations are recovering from serious declines due to use of DDT.

Northern Harrier

Circus cyaneus

Immature

Male

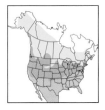

Female

Identification: 18" IN FLIGHT: In all plumages, **long slender wings held in a V; long tail; rectangular white patch on rump.** When soaring or gliding it may **tilt from side to side.** PERCHED—MALE: **Gray above; white below.** FEMALE: **Larger than male; brown above; streaked brown below.** IMM: Brown above; reddish brown to creamy brown below, with streaking only on chest. Imm. plumage kept 1 year, gradually changing to adult.

Feeding: Feeds by coursing close to the ground and quickly swooping down on its prey. Eats mice, rats, birds, snakes, frogs, and other small animals.

Nesting: Platform nest of sticks and grasses lined with fine materials is placed on the ground. Eggs: 3–9, bluish white, sometimes with dark marks; I: 31–32 days; F: 30–35 days, altricial; B: 1.

Other Behavior: Often hunts at dusk and catches prey by sound as well as sight. Their owllike facial disk of feathers may function to help them locate sounds. Males are polygamous, mating with up to 3 females. Birds may roost communally in winter.

Habitat: Open fields, grasslands, prairies, marshes.

Voice: Variety of shrill alarm calls when disturbed at nest, otherwise quiet.

Conservation: BBS: E ↑ C ⇓ CBC: ↓

Sharp-shinned Hawk
Accipiter striatus

Adult

Immature

Immature

Identification: 11" IN FLIGHT: In all plumages, **small; short rounded wings; long narrow tail.** Uses short flaps followed by glides and is often **buffeted about by wind.** Differences from Cooper's Hawk: **tail squarish at corners,** sometimes notched; **tail narrowly tipped** with off white; bird looks **short-necked.** IMM: Heavy streaking on breast *and* belly makes it look darker than imm. Cooper's Hawk. PERCHED—ADULT: **Blue-gray above,** light below with **reddish-brown barring; tail as described; crown similar to back in color.** IMM: Dark brown above, light below with thick brown streaking. Imm. plumage kept 1 year.

Feeding: Feeds by catching small birds in midair and carrying them off to eat. May hunt around bird feeders.

Nesting: Platform nest of sticks lined with bark, placed in tree 10–90 ft. high. Eggs: 3–8, whitish with dark marks; I: 30–32 days; F: 21–28 days, altricial; B: 1.

Other Behavior: Largest numbers seen on spring and fall migrations as it flies along coasts or mountain ridges.

Habitat: Summers in mixed deciduous and coniferous woods; winters in woods and near bird feeders.

Voice: A rapid series of high "kek kek kek kek" notes given during alarm.

Conservation: BBS: E ⇑ C CBC: ↑ Recent declines in Northeast noticed during migration counts.

Cooper's Hawk

Accipiter cooperii

Adult

Immature

Immature

Identification: 16" **IN FLIGHT:** In all plumages, "crow-sized"; relatively short rounded wings; very long narrow tail. Uses short flaps followed by glides and is **steady in the wind.** Differences from Sharp-shinned Hawk: **longer tail rounded at corners, often with wide white band at tip; neck wider and longer.** **IMM:** Fine streaking mostly on breast makes it look lighter bellied than imm. Sharp-shinned. **PERCHED—ADULT:** **Blue-gray above;** light below with **reddish-brown barring; crown darker than back;** tail as described. **IMM:** Dark brown above; light below with thin brown streaks. Imm. plumage kept 1 yr.

Habitat: Mixed forests and open woodlands.

Voice: Loud, repeated, high "kek kek kek kek" call given during alarm or during pair interactions.

Feeding: During breeding season has regular feeding routes where it hunts for common medium-sized birds such as Mourning Doves, jays, and starlings.

Nesting: Platform nest of sticks lined with bark, placed in tree 10–70 ft. high. Eggs: 3–6, pale blue-green with dark marks; I: 32–36 days; F: 27–34 days, altricial; B: 1.

Other Behavior: May show up at bird feeders, especially in winter, when it roams more widely for food.

Conservation: BBS: E ⇑ C ⇓ CBC: ↑ Populations may be slowly recovering after declines in the 1940s and 1950s due to use of DDT.

Northern Goshawk
Accipiter gentilis

Immature

Adult

Immature

Identification: 21" In Flight: In all plumages, large; long "muscular" wings, tapered at tip; long wide tail. Flies with **deep powerful wingbeats;** less "flap and glide" than is typical of Sharp-shinned and Cooper's Hawks. Adult: **Dark gray above; light gray beneath; dark cap; white eyebrow.** Imm: Dark brown above; lighter below with thick brown streaks on breast *and* belly, making it look darker than imm. Cooper's Hawk. Perched: See adult and imm. clues above. Imm. plumage kept 1 year.

Feeding: Feeds on birds by catching them in air, mammals by swooping down on them. Eats medium-sized birds and mammals such as grouse and squirrels.

Nesting: Platform nest of sticks lined with bark, placed in the crotch of a tree 18–75 ft. high. Eggs: 2–5, bluish white; I: 35–38 days; F: 35 days, altricial; B: 1.

Other Behavior: Birds do flight displays over territory: slow exaggerated flapping between glides; undulating flights, as bird repeatedly flies up and swoops down. Can be aggressive to humans near nest site.

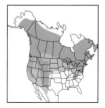

Habitat: Deep woods with mostly conifers.

Voice: Short, harsh, repeated "kek kek kek kek" used during pair interactions, and a down-slurred wail like "keeaah" given when the male brings food to the nest.

Conservation:
BBS: E ⇓ C CBC: ↑

103

Common Black-Hawk

Buteogallus anthracinus

Adult

Immature

Adult

Identification: 21" IN FLIGHT—ADULT: Black hawk; wide rounded wings; tail appears short and has wide white band through middle and fine white band at tip. Small light areas may show at base of outer primaries. IMM: Streaked brown below; short wide tail has thin wavy black and white lines and wider black terminal band.
PERCHED—ADULT: Black; tail as described; yellow legs; prominent yellow-orange facial skin and black-tipped bill. IMM: Dark back and wings; streaked below; buffy eyebrow and long dark streak off base of bill; tail as described. Imm. plumage kept 1 year.

Feeding: Hunts reptiles, amphibians, crabs, and insects by perching above wet areas or standing on bank or sandbar.

Nesting: Nest of sticks lined with grass and leaves, placed in tree 15–100 ft. high. Eggs: 1–3, white with dark marks; I: 34–37 days; F: 43–50 days, altricial; B: 1.

Other Behavior: Undulating display flights and dives may occur over the nest site. Usually seen perched.

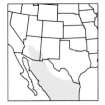

Habitat: Wooded streams, rivers, and swamps; dry canyons

Voice: A series of harsh whistles increasing and then decreasing in intensity.

Conservation:
HWI: →

Harris' Hawk

Parabuteo unicinctus

Immature

Adult

Adult

Identification: 20″ **IN FLIGHT:** In all plumages, a **dark hawk** with **reddish-brown shoulders and wing linings; long black tail has broad white band at base** and **white band at tip.** ADULT: **Dark underparts; dark flight feathers.** IMM: Light streaks on belly; whitish flight feathers. PERCHED—ADULT: **Dark brown hawk with reddish-brown shoulders;** reddish-brown leggings; long tail; white undertail coverts. IMM: Like adult but with whitish streaks on dark breast.

Habitat: Desert scrub and mesquite woodlands.

Voice: A drawn-out alarm call like "kirrrrr."

Conservation: BBS: E C ⇓ CBC: ↓

Feeding: Feeds by swooping down on prey. Eats wood rats, gophers, rabbits, squirrels, lizards, insects, and some birds.

Nesting: Platform nest of sticks and weeds lined with grass and green mesquite is placed in mesquite, cactus, or tree 10–30 ft. high. Eggs: 1–5, bluish white with marks; I: 33–36 days; F: 40–45 days, altricial; B: 1–2.

Other Behavior: A cooperative breeder with additional adults often attending a pair's nest, helping with feeding, and defending the nest. There can be up to 5 helpers at the nest. Can be polygamous, with either 1 male and several females or 1 female and several males.

Red-shouldered Hawk

Buteo lineatus

Adult

Immature

Adult

Identification: 17" IN FLIGHT: In all plumages, a long-tailed long-winged hawk with **thin crescent-shaped wing windows parallel to the dark tips of the wings.** May alternate flaps with glides like an accipiter. ADULT: Tail has **3–4 thin white bands between wide black bands.** IMM: From below, tail whitish with many narrow dark bands of equal width. PERCHED—ADULT: **Cinnamon breast; reddish shoulders; bold white spots on dark wings.** A pale race lives in S. Fla. IMM: Brown above, streaked brown and white below; tail as described. Imm. plumage kept 1 year. Imm. of Calif. race is similar to adult.

Feeding: Spots prey when perched. Eats small mammals, snakes, lizards, frogs, insects, and a few birds.

Nesting: Platform nest of sticks lined with finer materials is placed in tree 10–120 ft. high. Eggs: 2–6, bluish with dark marks; I: 28 days; F: 35–49 days, altricial; B: 1.

Other Behavior: Birds return to same nesting area repeatedly; do roller-coaster flights and dives as displays.

Habitat: Woodlands and swamps.

Voice: A down-slurred scream often given in a series during displays near nest.

Conservation:
BBS: E ↑ C ⇑ CBC: ↑

Broad-winged Hawk

Buteo platypterus

Adult

Immature

Adult

Identification: 15" IN FLIGHT—ADULT: **Broad black and white bands on tail;** wings broad, held flat during soar; wings white underneath with **conspicuous black border along tip and trailing edge.** IMM: Tail light brown with 4–5 thin dark bands, the last widest. PERCHED—ADULT: **Dark brown above; reddish-brown barring underneath.** IMM: Brown upperparts and brown streaking below; tail as described. Imm. plumage kept 1 year.

Feeding: Feeds by swooping down on prey from a perch. Eats mammals, birds, reptiles, and amphibians.

Nesting: Platform nest of sticks lined with greenery and bark, placed in tree 3–90 ft. high. Eggs: 1–4, white with dark marks; I: 30–38 days; F: 35–40 days, altricial; B: 1.

Other Behavior: Broad-wings are best known for their spectacular migrations, when they gather into flocks of thousands, rising on thermals and then gliding on to the next thermal. These migrations can be seen from various hawk-watching sites in fall. Spring migration is more dispersed except in S.E. Tex. and along the southern shores of the Great Lakes.

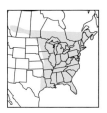

Habitat: Dry woodlands.

Voice: Most common call is a very high-pitched whistle with a short preceding syllable, like "sigeeee."

Conservation: BBS: E ⇑ C ↓ CBC: ↓ Up until the 1930s, migrating hawks were shot for sport by the thousands. Now they are all protected by law.

Short-tailed Hawk

Buteo brachyurus

Dark-morph adult   Dark-morph immature

Identification: 16" A small hawk limited to Fla.; comes in 2 color morphs. **IN FLIGHT—ADULT: Dark morph is all dark with lighter flight feathers; rare light morph has white underparts with a dark hood.** Both morphs have a short gray tail with thin dark bands, the last widest; wings held flat and curved up at tips. **IMM:** Similar to adult, but tail has thin dark and light bands of equal width. **PERCHED—ADULT: Dark morph all dark with yellow feet; light morph white underneath with dark hood and yellow feet.** **IMM:** Dark morph has mottled belly; light morph similar to adult; tail as described.

Habitat: Swamps or woodlands bordering open areas of grasses or water.

Voice: Alarm call is a high-pitched descending scream.

Conservation: CBC: ↑

Feeding: Hunts from the air; may hold still into the wind and then dive down after prey, which includes rodents, birds, amphibians, reptiles, and insects.

Nesting: Platform nest of twigs lined with fine materials, placed in tree 8–100 ft. high. Eggs: 1–3, dull white with occasional marks; I: 34 days; F: ?, altricial; B: 1.

Other Behavior: Undulating flights high in the air can be seen over the breeding territory. Seldom seen perched.

Swainson's Hawk

Buteo swainsoni

Light-morph adult

Light-morph immature

Dark-morph adult

Identification: 19″ **IN FLIGHT:** In all plumages, **long wings; long tail; pale wing linings; dark flight feathers.** Soars with wings held in a V, often tilts side to side. Dark morphs have all-dark bodies; rufous wing linings; and light undertail coverts. **PERCHED—ADULT: White chin; brown bib extending onto light chest.** Dark morph all dark. **IMM:** Dark brown above, streaked below; thick streaking on upper chest suggests biblike pattern of adult. Dark morph similar, but more heavily streaked below. Imm. plumage kept 2 yr.

Feeding: Often feeds by hopping on ground, eating insects such as grasshoppers and crickets. Also soars and catches mice, rabbits, lizards, frogs, and birds.

Nesting: Nest of sticks lined with plants, placed in tree, on cliff, or on ground. Eggs: 2–4, bluish white with dark marks; I: 28–35 days; F: 30 days, altricial; B: 1.

Other Behavior: Migrates in groups, rising on thermals, then gliding to the next thermal. Similar to Broad-winged Hawks in the East, although flocks are smaller, generally only in the hundreds.

Habitat: Prairies and open arid land.

Voice: A long high-pitched whistle.

Conservation:
BBS: E C ↑ CBC: ↓
Significant declines in S. Calif., where populations may be down 90% since 1940s.

White-tailed Hawk

Buteo albicaudatus

Adult

Immature

Adult

Adult

Identification: 20″ Limited to S. Tex. **In Flight—Adult: Long pointed wings; short white tail with a broad black band near tip.** Soars with wings in a V. **Imm:** 1st year, body all dark except for whitish breast patch and light undertail coverts. 2nd year, like adult but with dark barring on belly and dark wing linings. **Perched—Adult: Gray above, white below; conspicuous reddish-brown shoulders. Imm:** As described above. Imm. plumage kept 2 years.

Feeding: Feeds mostly on rabbits, but also small rodents, snakes, frogs, and some insects. Hunts from air. May follow tractors, like Swainson's Hawk, to get prey stirred up by plowing or harvesting.

Nesting: Platform nest of sticks lined with grass, mesquite, and its own breast feathers, placed in small tree or bush 2–40 ft. high. Eggs: 1–4, bluish white with dark marks; I: 31 days; F: 47–53 days, altricial; B: 1.

Other Behavior: Young may be fed by parents for up to 7 months after leaving the nest. Birds often hover while looking for prey and are attracted to the edges of prairie fires, where they feed on exposed prey.

Habitat: Coastal prairie.

Voice: Alarm note at the nest is a loud "kek kek kek."

Conservation: BBS: E C ⇑ CBC:↑ Threatened by loss of Tex. coastal prairie.

Red-tailed Hawk

Buteo jamaicensis

Adult

Immature

Adult

Identification: 19" Extremely variable plumage. IN FLIGHT—ADULT: **Long broad wings held in shallow V; reddish upper tail; dark mark on inner front edge of underwing; white chest; usually a belly band.** IMM: Distinctive upperwing paler on outer half; finely banded gray-brown tail; may show rectangular wing windows. PERCHED—ADULT: **Red tail; white chest; usually a belly band;** white mottling on back. IMM: Similar except for tail. Imm. plumage kept 1 year.

MORPHS: "Krider's Hawk" (in Great Plains) — Pale version of above, may lack belly band. "Harlan's Hawk" (in Northwest and Midwest) — Body, upperwings, and underwing coverts dark with white spotting; tail streaked gray with dark tip. Intergrades of all morphs.

Feeding: May perch, hover, or hold still into wind when hunting. Eats small mammals, birds, reptiles.

Nesting: Platform of sticks lined with bark and greenery, in tree 15–120 ft. high. Eggs: 1–5, bluish white with dark marks; I: 28–35 days; F: 44–46 days, altricial; B: 1.

Other Behavior: Most commonly seen hawk.

Habitat: Variety of open habitats.

Voice: A down-slurred scream like "tseeeaarr" often directed at intruders; a harsh up-slurred "klooeeek" given by fledglings and adults; and a piercing "chwirk" during courtship or territorial encounters.

Conservation: BBS: E ⇑ C ↑ CBC: ⇑

111

Ferruginous Hawk

Buteo regalis

Adult

Immature

Identification: 23″ IN FLIGHT—ADULT: Very large; white body; white underwings with chestnut on wing linings; dark-feathered legs form a V underneath. From above, note light rectangular patch on outer wings and light area at base of tail. Soars with wings in a shallow V; may also hover or hold still in wind. IMM: Similar, but lacks chestnut on wing linings and has white-feathered legs. PERCHED—ADULT: White breast; pale head, reddish shoulders; dark-feathered legs. Often perches on ground. IMM: Dark brown above; light below; white-feathered legs. Imm. plumage kept 1 year.

Feeding: Feeds by swooping down on prey from the air. Eats mostly medium-sized mammals, reptiles, insects.

Nesting: Platform nest of sticks, bones, and cow dung lined with grasses, placed on ground, cliff edge, or in tree 6–55 ft. high. Eggs: 2–6, bluish white with dark marks; I: 28–33 days; F: 44–48 days, altricial; B: 1.

Other Behavior: In breeding territory, maintains up to 5 nest sites, only 1 used. Roosts communally in Calif.

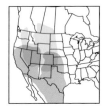

Habitat: Arid open land and grasslands.

Voice: Alarm call of a down-slurred scream used near the nest.

Conservation: BBS: E C ⇑ CBC: ⇑ Breeding range has shrunk drastically in the last few decades; by 60% in parts of Can.

Rough-legged Hawk

Buteo lagopus

Light-morph immature

Dark-morph adult

Light-morph adult

Identification: 21" IN FLIGHT—ADULT: From below, **light morphs have distinctive black rectangular patch on wrist; white tail with wide dark band at tip.** Male has darker chest than belly; female darker belly than chest. **Dark morphs have dark bodies and wing coverts; silvery barred flight feathers with dark trailing edge.** Male has black tail with 3–4 narrow white bands; female has silvery tail with dark band at tip. IMM: Similar to adult female in both morphs, but with dusky terminal band on underside of tail. Light-morph imm. has solid dark belly. PERCHED: Bodies and tails for morphs as described above.

Feeding: Often hovers while hunting, but may also hunt from perch. Eats primarily voles and lemmings.

Nesting: Platform nest of sticks and grass placed in open tundra or on cliff. Eggs: 2–7, white with dark marks; I: 28–31 days; F: 39–45 days, altricial; B: 1.

Other Behavior: Adults and immatures migrate south in winter, and both color morphs are seen.

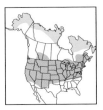

Habitat: Summers at the arctic tree line; winters in open country.

Voice: Generally silent on its wintering grounds.

Conservation: CBC: ↓

Golden Eagle

Aquila chrysaetos

Adult

Immature

Adult

Identification: 30" IN FLIGHT—ADULT: Very large; long broad wings; all dark. Soars with wings in shallow V; head projects beyond wings less than one-half length of tail. IMM: Dark, with white areas limited to base of primaries and outer secondaries on wings (imm. Bald Eagles have white on armpits) and at base of tail. PERCHED: Adult and imm. dark with golden feathers on crown and nape. Imm. plumage kept 4 years.

Feeding: Hunts by soaring and then diving down on prey such as rabbits and rodents and some birds. Feeds on road-killed deer in the West.

Nesting: Large platform nest of sticks and roots lined with finer materials is placed on cliff ledge, on ground, or in tree 10–100 ft. high. Eggs: 1–4, creamy with dark marks; I: 43–45 days; F: 72–84 days, altricial; B: 1.

Other Behavior: Starts nest building anytime during nonbreeding season when site is clear of snow. May build nest on high-power electric poles. Breeding success often tied to populations of prey such as rabbits.

Habitat: Mountains, foothills, and adjacent grasslands.

Voice: Generally quiet; repeated series of chirps when approaching the nest with food.

Conservation: BBS: E C ↓ CBC: ↓ Federal protection has curtailed some of the aerial hunting and poisoning of this species.

Crested Caracara

Caracara plancus

Adult

Immature

Identification: 23" IN FLIGHT: In all plumages, **checkered white patches at tips of bowed black wings; long white neck; long whitish tail with wide dark terminal band;** black cap; black belly. Flight usually low and direct with deep rowing wing beats. PERCHED—ADULT: **Black cap; orange-red base of bill and face; white head and neck.** IMM: Like adult, but browner with streaking underneath. Imm. plumage kept 3 years.

Feeding: Feeds on the ground, eating mostly carrion, but also turtles, small mammals, fish, crustaceans, and insects.

Nesting: Bulky platform nest of sticks and vines lined with finer materials, placed in branches of cactus, palmetto, and other trees 8–80 ft. high. Eggs: 2–4, pinkish with dark marks; I: 28 days; F: 30–60 days, altricial; B: 1.

Other Behavior: Caracaras may fly along highways in the morning looking for animals killed by cars. They often displace Turkey Vultures from food and even harass them into regurgitating what they have eaten. Increasing and expanding range in Tex.

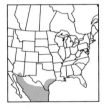

Habitat: Dry scrubland, prairie.

Voice: A cackling call can be given early in the morning. The bird's name comes from this.

Conservation: BBS: E ⇑ C ⇑ CBC: ⇑ Populations are declining, especially in Fla., due to habitat loss.

American Kestrel
Falco sparverius

Male

Male at nest

Female

Identification: 9" IN FLIGHT: Small colorful falcon; long tail; thin sickle-shaped wings. MALE: **Blue-gray wings; reddish-brown tail with broad black tip.** A line of translucent spots is visible along trailing edge of wings. FEMALE: **Wings, back, and tail reddish brown; thin dark brown bars on tail.** Spots along trailing edge of wings less conspicuous. PERCHED: **Two black sideburns on each side of face.** Male has blue-gray wings; female has lightly barred brown wings. Imm. almost identical to adults.

Feeding: Hunts by perching or hovering, then diving to catch prey. Eats voles and mice, birds, and insects.

Nesting: Natural cavity, nest box, woodpecker hole in cactus or tree, or in cliff nook, no nesting material. Eggs: 3–7, pinkish with dark marks; I: 29–31 days; F: 29–31 days, altricial; B: 1.

Other Behavior: Male does all hunting for 8–12 weeks during the breeding period; female remains at the nest. Male and female do fluttering flights when exchanging food that the male has brought to the nest.

Habitat: A wide variety of open habitats, including urban areas.

Voice: Most common call is a series of sharp staccato notes like "klee klee klee" given during disturbances at the nest.

Conservation: BBS: E ↑ C ⇑ CBC: ↑

Merlin
Falco columbarius

Female

Immature

Identification: 10" IN FLIGHT: In all plumages, **small dark falcon.** Heavier than a kestrel, with **thicker angular wings** and **powerful direct flight** that is usually low over vegetation; also has darker underwings. Sideburns indistinct. Often aggressive to other birds in flight. PERCHED— MALE: **Blue-gray above**; appears **light below** due to fine brown streaking. FEMALE: **Dark brown above** with **heavy brown streaks below** — the "chocolate falcon." IMM: Similar to adult female. Imm. plumage kept 1 year.

Feeding: Catches birds in the air, feeds secondarily on rodents, lizards, snakes, and insects.

Nesting: Uses abandoned nest of other bird, a cavity in a tree or cliff, or on the ground with no nest materials except a few sprigs of greenery. Eggs: 2–7, white with dark marks; I: 28–32 days; F: 25–35 days, altricial; B: 1.

Other Behavior: A wide variety of elaborate aerial maneuvers and calls are used in courtship displays. Food collected primarily by the male may be passed to the female in midair.

Habitat: Summers in a variety of habitats, including forest edges, farmland, urban areas; winters on coastal lowlands, prairies, marshes.

Voice: Alarm note is a high "kikikikiki."

Conservation: BBS: E ⇑ C ⇑ CBC: ↑

Peregrine Falcon

Falco peregrinus

Adult

Immature

Adult

Identification: 16" IN FLIGHT: In all plumages, **large falcon; relatively long tapered wings; long broad tail; dark crown; broad sideburn on cheek** extends below eye. Flight is direct with steady rowing beats on swept-back wings. Plumage varies from the Tundra form, which is bluish gray above with a white chest, to the Peale's form, which is darker above with a heavily spotted chest. As in most falcons, females noticeably larger than males. PERCHED—ADULT: **Bluish-gray back; barred belly; white bib; wide dark sideburn.** IMM: Brown back; streaked brown breast and belly; dark sideburn. Imm. plumage kept 1 year.

Feeding: Catches birds on the wing; eats some insects.

Nesting: A scrape in the ground on a cliff ledge 50–200 ft. high. Eggs: 3–4, creamy white with dark markings; I: 28–33 days; F: 30–42 days, altricial; B: 1.

Other Behavior: Spectacular fliers with tremendous speed when pursuing other birds. Some have been introduced into cities, where they nest on buildings.

Habitat: Open country near cliffs, urban areas, coast.

Voice: A series of harsh high-pitched sounds like "ki ki ki ki ki" given as an alarm near the nest.

Conservation:
BBS: E C ⇑ CBC:→ Extirpated in the East but now recovering slowly through protection of nests and restocking.

Gyrfalcon
Falco rusticolus

Gray-morph adult

Gray-morph immature

Gray-morph immature

Identification: 22″ IN FLIGHT—ADULT: **Large heavy-bodied falcon; long broad wings; long wide tail that tapers toward tip.** White morph all white except for lightly barred back and tail. Gray morph has gray upperparts, whitish body with gray spotting on breast and belly. Dark morph is dark with pale streaking on breast. From below, gray and dark morphs show darker wing linings than flight feathers. IMM: Similar to adults but browner; more streaked below. PERCHED—ADULT: **White morph mostly white; darker morphs have gray or brown back and streaked breast.** IMM: Similar to adults, but darker and with a bluish, rather than yellowish, base to bill.

Feeding: Hunts by catching other birds in midair, such as ptarmigans and grouse; eats some small mammals.

Nesting: Scraped depression on cliff ledge or uses abandoned nest in tree. Eggs: 3–8, pale yellowish with dark marks; I: 28–36 days; F: 49–56 days, altricial; B: 1.

Other Behavior: Gyrfalcons that range into southern Can. and northern U.S. in winter are usually immatures.

Habitat: Arctic tundra to tree line.

Voice: Alarm note is a harsh "kikikikiki."

Conservation: CBC: ↑ There is pressure worldwide on these birds, for they are collected from the wild and sold to falconers in other countries for large sums of money.

Prairie Falcon

Falco mexicanus

Identification: 16" IN FLIGHT: Large falcon; long pointed wings; long tail. From below, note **prominent dark wing linings and armpits that contrast with its light-colored body and light translucent flight feathers.** These traits distinguish it from the similar Peregrine Falcon. From above, has dark back and wings and lighter tail. PERCHED: **Brown back and brown-streaked front. Dark cheek bar is thinner than in most Peregrine Falcons.** IMM: Similar to adult, but more streaking on breast and a blue-to-yellow cere (rather than orange as in adult).

Feeding: Catches birds in midair or on ground, and mammals after swift swoop.

Nesting: Scrape in a cliff ledge 20–400 ft. high. Eggs: 2–7, pinkish white with dark marks; I: 28–32 days; F: 35–42 days, altricial; B: 1.

Other Behavior: Strongly territorial during the early stages of breeding; less so later.

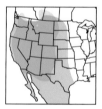

Habitat: Plains, grasslands, and other open country

Voice: Alarm notes include a harsh series of short notes like "kikikikiki."

Conservation: CBC: ↑ This species, owing to prey differences, was not as adversely affected as Peregrines by pesticide residues.

Plain Chachalaca

Ortalis vetula

Identification: 22" Limited to S. Tex. **Large, brown, chickenlike bird** with a **very long white-tipped tail.** Male has patch of skin on throat which is bright red during breeding and gray at other times of year.

Feeding: Forages in trees and bushes for berries, plant shoots, and leafy material. Eats insects. Sometimes comes to bird feeders where seed is sprinkled on ground.

Nesting: Frail nest of sticks and leaves is placed in tree fork, bush, or vine. May refurbish nest of other species. Eggs: 2–4, cream; I: 22–25 days; F: up to 21 days, precocial; B: 1.

Other Behavior: Listen for loud, cacophonous calling of the flock in early morning and evening. Both sexes join in, and females have higher voices than males. Each bird has 3-syllable call of "cha-cha-lac," but when the group sings together it sounds like continuous "chachalaca, chachalaca."

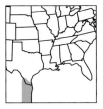

Habitat: Open tropical forests and thickets.

Voice: Loud "cha-cha-lac" call.

Conservation:
TREND UNKNOWN.

Gray Partridge

Perdix perdix

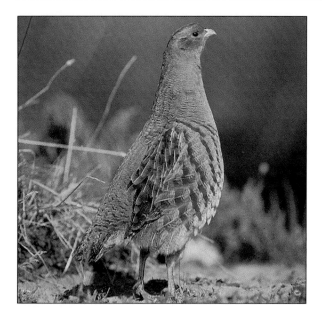

Identification: 13" **Rusty face and throat; gray breast; brown barring on flanks.** Male has large brown patch on whitish belly; female lacks patch. **IN FLIGHT:** Note chestnut tail feathers.

Feeding: Eats grain, weed, and grass seeds; also leaves and insects.

Nesting: Nest is a scraped depression lined with grasses, weeds, and feathers, near rocks or taller vegetation. Eggs: 15–17, olive; I: 23–25 days; F: 13–15 days, precocial; B: 1.

Other Behavior: Native to Europe and Asia, but introduced into N. America and now widespread. In fall, forms covey of about 10–30 birds, which remain together throughout winter.

Habitat: Open farmlands and hedgerows.

Voice: Unmated male gives rusty-gate "kee-uck" sound to advertise for female.

Conservation: BBS: E ⇓ C ⇑ CBC: ↓

Ring-necked Pheasant

Phasianus colchicus

Male

Female

Identification: 33″ A large chickenlike bird with a **long pointed tail. MALE: White neck-ring; green head; red wattles.** Body is a mixture of iridescent greens, browns, and golds. Two other forms can be seen: one with white on the wings and another lacking the white neck-ring. **FEMALE: Rich brown with dark markings on wings and back.**

Feeding: At bird feeders, eats cracked corn and mixed seed from the ground. In the wild, eats waste grain, weed seeds, acorns, berries, and insects.

Nesting: Nest of grasses and leaves placed on the ground is concealed among grasses or shrubs. Eggs: 10–12, brownish olive; I: 24 days; F: 10–11 weeks, precocial; B: 1.

Other Behavior: One of the most conspicuous aspects of pheasant behavior is the crowing of the male. It sounds like "skwagock," and is accompanied by an audible wing whir. This is territorial advertisement, and it is most frequent in the spring, in the early morning and late afternoon. Some males have just 1 mate, but 45% of males have a harem of females with whom they mate.

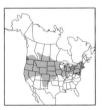

Habitat: Farmlands with woods edges and hedgerows.

Voice: Male gives "skwagock" call. Female responds to him with "kia-kia" call.

Conservation: BBS: E ⇓ C ↓ CBC: ⇓ First introduced into N. America in 1850s. Now widespread.

123

Spruce Grouse

Dendragapus canadensis

Male

Female

Identification: 15" **MALE: Black chin and breast; red eye combs. Tail is black with a reddish-brown tip** except in the Northwest, where the so-called Franklin's Grouse form has an all-black tail. **FEMALE: Brownish overall with black barring on breast and belly;** tail as in male. Females come in reddish and grayish color phases.

Feeding: Feeds on the ground and in trees, eating needles and buds of conifers; also wild berries, grass seeds, and insects. In winter exclusively eats conifers.

Nesting: Grassy nest is placed in well-concealed location in brush or thicket. Eggs: 6–7, buff with dark marks; I: 23 days; F: 10 days, precocial; B: 1.

Other Behavior: In territorial display males do nearly vertical flutter flights, producing a drumming sound by rapidly beating wings. In western race called Franklin's Grouse, the males twice clap their wings above their back during this display. Often very tame.

Habitat: Dense coniferous forests with occasional clearings.

Voice: Male may make hissing sound when female is near. Female makes low warning calls to chicks.

Conservation:
BBS: E ⇓ C CBC: ⇑
As with many grouse, populations fluctuate cyclically.

Willow Ptarmigan

Lagopus lagopus

Summer male

Summer female

Identification: 15" SUMMER—MALE: Reddish-brown head and neck; brown body; white on wings and belly. FEMALE: Mottled brown with black tail; heavier bill than similar female Rock Ptarmigan. WINTER: All white except for black tail. •Willow and Rock Ptarmigans are very similar. The females are hard to distinguish in the field; both are mottled brown with black tails in summer and all white with black tails in winter. Their black tail in all seasons distinguishes them from the otherwise similar White-tailed Ptarmigan.

Feeding: Buds from woody plants, seeds, insects.

Nesting: Nest a shallow depression in ground lined with grass, moss, and feathers, placed by grass clump or base of log. Eggs: 6–7, yellowish with darker marks; I: 21–22 days; F: 9–10 days, precocial; B: 1.

Other Behavior: Red eye combs of males are swollen during displays. Songs are given by males at end of courtship display flights. Females cover the nest with vegetation when they briefly leave it during incubation.

Habitat: Summers on shrubby alpine areas; winters at lower elevations.

Voice: Call a loud "tobacco tobacco."

Conservation: TREND UNKNOWN.

125

Rock Ptarmigan
Lagopus mutus

Summer female

Winter male

Summer male

Identification: 13" SUMMER—MALE: Grayish-brown head and neck; brown body. FEMALE: Mottled brown with black tail; smaller bill than similar female Willow Ptarmigan. WINTER— MALE: All white except for black tail and black streak through eye. FEMALE: All white with black tail. •Rock and Willow Ptarmigans are very similar. The **females are hard to distinguish in the field;** both are mottled brown with black tails in summer and all white with black tails in winter. Their **black tail in all seasons** distinguishes them from otherwise similar White-tailed Ptarmigan.

Feeding: Leaf and flower buds and catkins from woody plants, seeds, insects.

Nesting: Nest a shallow depression in ground lined with grass, moss, and feathers, placed in rocky area. Eggs: 6–9, buff with dark brown splotches; I: 21–24 days; F: 12–14 days, precocial; B: 1.

Other Behavior: Nests in barren areas. In spring males develop red eye combs, which are used in courtship displays. Migrates from north when snow covers food.

Habitat: Tundra and barren rocky slopes.

Voice: Gives a long snoring call.

Conservation: TREND UNKNOWN.

126

Ruffed Grouse
Bonasa umbellus

Male

Identification: 17" MALE: **Note brown or gray tail with dark subterminal band;** sides of neck (the ruff) black; belly and chin light. Crest on head erected when bird is alarmed. FEMALE: **Browner and more barred below; central brown gap in the dark tail band;** black ruff is smaller.

Feeding: Feeds on berries, leaves, buds, seeds, and insects.

Nesting: Nest lined with leaves, twigs, and feathers, placed in scraped depression and concealed under brush or shrub. Eggs: 6–15, buff with light marks; I: 21–28 days; F: 10–12 days, precocial; B: 1.

Other Behavior: Male advertises his territory to prospective mate by drumming from a favorite spot, usually a fallen log. Drumming sound is made by bracing tail against log and giving a series of strong wingstrokes. He also struts before female with tail fanned and neck ruff raised. Female raises brood. She will feign injury if disturbed during incubation. Ruffed Grouse can at times be very tame. They occasionally approach humans and may even act aggressively.

Habitat: Forests with mostly deciduous trees.

Voice: A sharp "quit-quit" alarm note. Female gives cooing and clucking notes.

Conservation: BBS: E ↑ C ⇓ CBC: ↑

Greater Prairie-Chicken
Lesser Prairie-Chicken

Tympanuchus cupido   *Tympanuchus pallidicinctus*

Greater Prairie-Chicken male

Lesser Prairie-Chicken male

Identification: Greater 17", Lesser 16" Both species have **dark barring on brown back and on whitish chest and belly;** tail is dark and rounded. Lesser Prairie-Chicken is slightly smaller and paler. Ranges do not overlap. **MALES: Fleshy yellow eye combs.** In display, Lesser shows orange-red air sacs on sides of neck; Greater shows yellow-orange air sacs. **FEMALES:** Thin yellow eye combs and no air sacs.

Feeding: Both eat grasshoppers, seeds, and grain.

Nesting: GREATER: Grassy nest in depression. Eggs: 7–17, olive with dark marks; I: 23–24 days; F: 7–10 days, precocial; B: 1. **LESSER:** Grassy nest in depression. Eggs: 11–13, yellowish with brown marks; I: 22–24 days; F: 7–10 days, precocial; B: 1.

Other Behavior: Males display in groups with tails erect, wings drooped, then deflate air-filled sacs, making booming noise in Greater, and gobbling noise in Lesser Prairie-Chicken. Males then jump and run at each other with sacs inflated. Females mate with dominant male, raise broods alone.

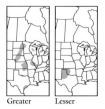

Greater   Lesser

Habitat: Greater lives on tallgrass prairie; Lesser on short-grass prairie.

Voice: Booming and gobbling.

Conservation: Greater:
BBS: E ⇑ C ↑ CBC: ↓
Lesser:
POP. DECLINING. Subspecies of Greater, Attwater's Prairie-Chicken, endangered in U.S.

Sharp-tailed Grouse

Tympanuchus phasianellus

Male

Identification: 18" **Dark spots on light brown back and on whitish chest and belly; tail is pointed,** with squared-off central feathers projecting well beyond the others. In display, male exposes purple air sacs on either side of neck. IN FLIGHT: Note white on sides of tail.

Feeding: Feeds on the ground, eating plant parts, berries, grains, insects.

Nesting: Nest a scraped depression lined with grasses, ferns, and leaves, in grass or under shrub. Eggs: 5–17, light brown with darker marks; I: 21–24 days; F: 7–10 days, precocial; B: 1.

Other Behavior: As with some other species of grouse, males display communally in groups at a traditional site called a lek. With tails fanned and wings drooped, they make cooing sound by deflating neck air sacs. They also jump and run at one another. Females come and mate with the dominant male, who usually is the one occupying the center spot in the group. Females then go off to nest and raise the young by themselves.

Habitat: Grasslands, shrublands, and partially cleared boreal forest.

Voice: Males make cooing sound.

Conservation: BBS: E ⇑ C ⇑ CBC: ⇑ Declining in much of its range due to habitat loss by conversion of grasslands to agricultural areas.

Wild Turkey
Meleagris gallopavo

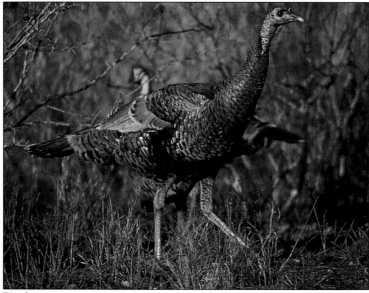

Female

Identification: 36–49" Its **large size** and **familiar turkey shape** make it unmistakable. Body is dark and iridescent; **head is naked.** MALE: Larger and more iridescent than female and with tuft of hairlike feathers on breast. FEMALE: Smaller than male, has less iridescence, and usually lacks tuft on breast.

Feeding: Feeds on the ground, eating nuts, acorns, and seeds. Also eats grains, vegetation, insects, frogs, lizards.

Nesting: Nest is placed in a natural or scraped depression and lined with leaves and grasses. Eggs: 6–20, whitish buff with marks; I: 27–28 days; F: 6–10 days, precocial; B: 1.

Other Behavior: Spends the winter in same- or mixed-sex flocks. In courtship, male struts and gobbles with tail fanned. Female responds with yelping call. Male may mate with many females. Female raises young. Domestic turkey is a subspecies that had been tamed and taken from Mexico to Europe by Spanish in 16th century. English settlers brought domestic turkey back to N. America.

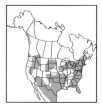

Habitat: Open forests, forest edges, wooded swamps.

Voice: Gobbling, yelping, and clucking notes.

Conservation: BBS: E ⇑ C ⇑ CBC: ⇑ Habitat loss and hunting had previously reduced populations. Has now been reintroduced into much of former range.

Northern Bobwhite

Colinus virginianus

Female (l.), male (r.)

Identification: 10" Both sexes have a **light eyebrow and chin** and a wide **dark streak through the eye.** Sides are streaked with reddish brown and tail is gray. **MALE: White eyebrow and chin. FEMALE: Buffy eyebrow** and chin.

Feeding: Feeds on grass seeds, grains, leaves, fruits, tender plant parts, and insects. Also comes to bird feeders for seed placed on the ground.

Nesting: Nest a scrape in the ground lined with grasses, moss, pine needles, placed usually within 50 ft. of a clearing. Eggs: 12–14, white; I: 23 days; F: 14 days, precocial; B: 1.

Other Behavior: The famous "bob-white" call is best clue to presence of this wary bird. Call is given most loudly and frequently by unmated males in spring and early summer, around the areas where mated pairs are breeding. After chicks hatch, family feeds and stays as tight flock. Parents will give alarm call, and may do distraction display when threatened by possible predator. In winter, multiple family groups form a covey of about 12–16 birds that feed and roost together in a fixed range. Each night the covey sleeps on the ground in a tight circle with tails pointed inward.

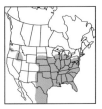

Habitat: Farmland, brushy fields, open woodland.

Voice: Wide variety of calls include "toilick" for alarm; "koilee" by covey at dawn and dusk; and "bob-white" by males.

Conservation: BBS: E ⇓ C ↓ CBC: ⇓ Does not survive harsh winters in North.

Scaled Quail

Callipepla squamata

Identification: 11" **White-tipped crest** is distinctive. Gray feathers on breast and back tipped with black, making them look like scales. Sexes similar.

Feeding: Feeds on ground, eating grass and weed seeds.

Nesting: Concealed nest lined with grasses and feathers is placed in a scraped depression in grass or shrubbery. Eggs: 9–16, creamy white, plain or with light marks; I: 21–23 days; F: ?, precocial; B: 1.

Other Behavior: During breeding, unmated males call from exposed perches to attract potential mates. Females may defer egg laying until summer rainy season starts. In fall, families form into a large covey of 50 or more birds that feed and roost together. May hybridize with Gambel's Quail.

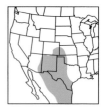

Habitat: Arid grassland and scrub.

Voice: "Pey-cos" location call given by both sexes when separated. Unmated male gives "whock" call.

Conservation: BBS: E C ⇓ CBC: ⇓ Species was introduced into Wash. and Nev.

Yellow Rail

Coturnicops noveboracensis

Identification: 7" Very secretive; **heard more than seen.** Calls mostly at night during breeding season. **Tiny, brownish, chickenlike bird; wide dark streaks on back crossed by fine white lines;** buffy breast. Short bill varies from yellowish to dark. **IN FLIGHT:** Note white patch on trailing edge of wings.

Feeding: Feeds in shallow water, eating snails, insects, and some seeds and grasses.

Nesting: Canopied saucerlike nest of fine grass lined with finer material, placed on ground or in surrounding stems a few inches above water. Eggs: 7–10, yellow-buff with dark marks; I: 16–18 days; F: 35 days, precocial; B: ?

Other Behavior: This bird is so secretive its behavior is hard to observe. Its call, which is given occasionally in the middle of the day, is most often heard at the end of the day and at night. It seems to occur primarily at the beginning and middle stages of the breeding cycle.

Habitat: Summers on wet meadows, marshes; winters on grasslands, fields, coastal marshes.

Voice: Call sounds like 2 small stones clicking together in a regular rhythm, like "tik tik, tik tik tik" repeated.

Conservation: BBS: E C ⇑ CBC: ↑ Populations declining due to habitat loss and pesticides.

133

Black Rail

Laterallus jamaicensis

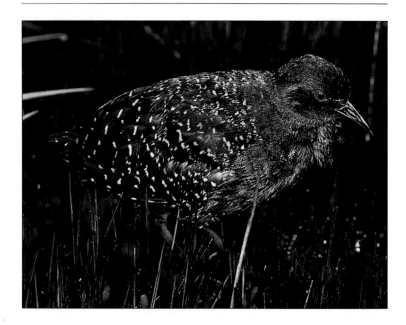

Identification: 5½" Our smallest rail and almost as secretive as the Yellow Rail. Listen for its nocturnal call. **Black; fine white spotting on wings;** brown on back of neck. More likely to scurry away through the marsh grasses than take flight.

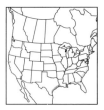

Feeding: Feeds in shallow water and on the ground, eating insects and aquatic plant seeds.

Nesting: Cuplike nest of soft grasses with a grass canopy, placed on the ground. Eggs: 6–13, white with buffy marks; I: 16–20 days; F: ?, precocial; B: ?

Other Behavior: Rarely seen but can be heard, especially at night. Very little is known about other aspects of this species' behavior.

Habitat: Salt and freshwater marshes, wet meadows.

Voice: A repeated "kikidoo, kikidoo, kikidoo."

Conservation: CBC: ↑

Clapper Rail
King Rail

Rallus longirostris   *Rallus elegans*

Clapper

King

Identification: Clapper 14", King 15" Similar-looking **large rails** with **long slightly downcurved bills.** Note habitat and range differences. **CLAPPER: Back feathers dark-centered with broad gray edges,** giving back a grayish look. Breast color varies regionally from gray to reddish brown. **KING: Back feathers dark-centered with broad reddish-brown edges,** giving back a reddish-brown look. Head, neck, and breast are always reddish brown and flank stripes more distinct.

Feeding: Feed in shallow water and on mudflats, eating crabs, crayfish, small fish, insects, and some plants.

Nesting: Clapper nest a cupped platform of grasses and aquatic plants, placed on the ground. Eggs: 5–12, buff with dark marks; I: 20–23 days; F: 63–70 days, precocial; B: 2. King nest a canopied platform of dried aquatic plants, placed on a mound 6–8 in. above water. Eggs: 6–15, buff with dark marks; I: 21–24 days; F: 63 days, precocial; B: 2.

Other Behavior: These species occasionally hybridize.

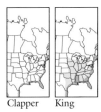

Clapper   King

Habitat: Clapper on salt marshes; King on fresh and brackish marshes.

Voice: Clapper: harsh notes varying in speed, like "chit chit chit, chit, chit — chit — chit." King: similar but evenly spaced.

Conservation:
Clapper:
BBS: E ⇑ C ↑ CBC: ↓
King:
BBS: E ⇓ C ↓ CBC: ↑

135

Virginia Rail

Rallus limicola

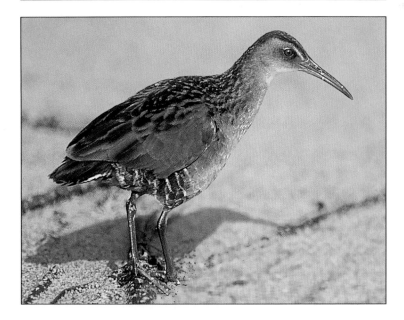

Identification: 9 " **Small rail; long bill;** similar in coloration to much larger King Rail. **Back feathers dark-centered with reddish-brown edges; face gray** (rather than buff as in King Rail); bill can be reddish, especially at base.

Feeding: Feeds in mudflats by probing in the mud with bill searching for worms, snails, and aquatic insects.

Nesting: Loose, canopied, cuplike nest of coarse grasses, reeds, and sedges, placed on ground a few inches above mud or water. Eggs: 5–12, buff with dark marks; I: 18–20 days; F: 25 days, precocial; B: 1–2.

Other Behavior: Heard more than seen. Calls are given most at dawn and dusk, but may occur sporadically at other times of day or night. Pair does courtship feeding and mutual preening.

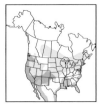

Habitat: Summers on freshwater and brackish marshes; winters also on salt marshes.

Voice: Call of territorial male is a metallic "kit kidit kidit kidit kidit." Also gives a "kikikikeeer" and a series of descending grunts.

Conservation:
BBS: E ⇩ C ⇩ CBC: ⇑

Sora

Porzana carolina

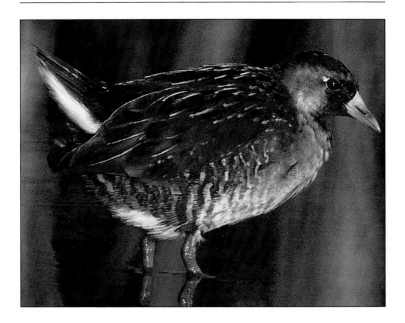

Identification: 9" Small, brownish, chickenlike bird; **black face** and upper throat; **bright yellow bill**. Back is dark brown with fine white streaks; belly is gray with dark barring. In winter, gray edges to face and throat feathers hide the black markings in these spots.

Feeding: Feeds in the water and on the ground, eating aquatic insects and weed seeds.

Nesting: Saucerlike nest of dead cattail leaves, reeds, and sedges, attached to surrounding plant stems a few in. above water. Eggs: 6–18, buff with dark marks; I: 18–20 days; F: 21–25 days, precocial; B: 1–2.

Other Behavior: As with other rails, Sora's body is compressed laterally, which may help it move more easily throughout its reedy environment. Any sudden sound near breeding ground may start the birds calling. They tend to leave breeding ground on night of first frost. Soras migrate at night, like most rails.

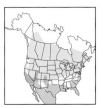

Habitat: Salt and freshwater marshes, wet meadows.

Voice: A common call is a plaintive ascending "puweee, puweee." Also gives call like a descending whinny that slows down near the end.

Conservation: BBS: E ↓ C ⇓ CBC: ↑

Purple Gallinule

Porphyrula martinica

Adult

Immature

Identification: 13" **Ducklike; blue head and underparts; yellow-tipped red bill.** Back is green; legs are yellow; light blue patch on forehead. Usually seen walking about over lily pads or other marsh vegetation. **Imm:** Brownish overall, lightest underneath; bill dark with yellowish tip. Distinguished from similar imm. Common Moorhen by lack of white line along flank. Imm. plumage kept through fall and sometimes into late winter.

Feeding: Feeds in shallow water, eating grains, (especially wild rice), weed seeds, frogs, and aquatic insects. Often walks on top of lily pads when feeding.

Nesting: Platform nest of sedges, suspended in plant stems 1–5 ft. high or directly on island of floating vegetation. Eggs: 5–10, pinkish buff with dark marks; I: 22–25 days; F: 63 days, precocial; B: 1–2.

Other Behavior: Young may help raise and defend young of subsequent broods. Often disperses widely after nesting.

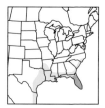

Habitat: Freshwater marshes.

Voice: A wide variety of sounds, many like the clucks of a chicken; others are short grating noises.

Conservation: BBS: E ⇓ C ⇓ CBC: ⇑

Common Moorhen

Gallinula chloropus

Summer adult

Winter adult

Immature

Identification: 14" **SUMMER: Dark; ducklike; black head; yellow-tipped red bill;** also has red forehead and white line of feathers along flanks. Often seen swimming. **WINTER:** Like summer, but with brownish yellow-tipped bill and brownish forehead. **IMM:** Brownish gray overall; whitish throat; dark bill. White line along flanks distinguishes it from similar imm. Purple Gallinule. Imm. plumage kept until midwinter. Red forehead does not fully develop until late next summer.

Feeding: Feeds by walking over aquatic vegetation or by swimming and diving. Eats seeds, grasses, small snails, and aquatic and land insects.

Nesting: Platform nest of cattail stems lined with grasses, placed on ground or suspended in vegetation 4–6 in. high. Eggs: 4–17, olive-buff with dark marks; I: 19–22 days; F: 40–50 days, precocial; B: 2–3.

Other Behavior: Courtship display may include head held low, wings raised, and white undertail exposed. Young of 1st broods may help in feeding later broods.

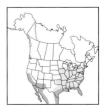

Habitat: Freshwater marshes, ponds, lakes.

Voice: A wide variety of sounds, many like the clucks of a chicken; others are short grating noises.

Conservation: BBS: E ↓ C ⇓ CBC: ⇑

American Coot

Fulica americana

Adult

Immature

Identification: 15″ **Slate-colored; ducklike; white bill;** partial ring around tip of bill. IMM: Grayish overall; whitish chin and throat; bill light-colored with no partial ring at tip. Imm. plumage gradually changes to adult through winter.

Feeding: Feeds on water by diving or tipping its body like a duck, eating seeds, leaves, roots, and small aquatic animals. Also feeds on land.

Nesting: Platform nest of stems lined with finer material, placed on a floating mass of vegetation attached to surrounding stems. Eggs: 8–12, pink-buff with dark marks; I: 21–25 days; F: 49–56 days, precocial; B: 1–2.

Other Behavior: Many conspicuous visual displays easily seen. Coots defend breeding and feeding territories by charging at other birds and running across water. In courtship, male may chase female with flapping wings or swim with head and neck held close to the water, wing tips raised, and tail lifted, displaying white patches. Birds may build up to 9 nests and then chose 1 for eggs. Occasionally, female coots will lay eggs in another coot's nest.

Habitat: Summers on marshy lakes; winters also along the coast.

Voice: A wide variety of calls, most of which sound like the toots of a tiny toy trumpet.

Conservation: BBS: E ⇊ C ↓ CBC: ↓

Limpkin

Aramus guarauna

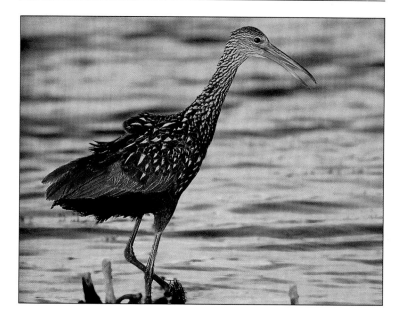

Identification: 26″ Large, brown, heronlike bird speckled with white; bill is long and slightly downcurved.

Feeding: Feeds in shallow water, eating snails, mussels, and other small aquatic animals.

Nesting: Platform nest of reeds and grasses lined with finer materials, placed on ground or in tree or shrub up to 45 ft. high. Eggs: 4–8, buff with dark marks; I: ?; F: ?, precocial; B: 2–3.

Other Behavior: Its bill is especially adapted to breaking open hard shells and extracting meat from snails.

Habitat: Freshwater swamps, marshes.

Voice: A series of drawn-out screams like "kareeow, kareeow, kareeow," often given at night.

Conservation: BBS: E ⇓ C CBC: ↑

Sandhill Crane

Grus canadensis

Identification: 45″ **Tall, gray, heronlike bird; dark red patch on forehead;** black bill. Some feathers on back and wings are rusty-colored, possibly due to staining as bird preens with iron-laden mud on its bill. **Imm:** Grayish with more extensive rust coloring; forehead lacks dark red patch; bill orangish. Imm. plumage kept about 2 years.

Feeding: Feeds by picking or probing with bill, eating seeds, agricultural grains, and small animals.

Nesting: Moundlike nest of marsh plants, grasses, and weeds, placed on ground or in shallow water. Eggs: 1–3, olive with dark marks; I: 28–32 days; F: 90 days, precocial; B: 1.

Other Behavior: These birds form huge flocks in winter and during migration, when they feed primarily in agricultural fields and then roost at night in the center of shallow lakes or large shallow rivers. Courtship displays are easily seen during migration and involve graceful jumps off the ground in a dancing manner. Subspecies *G. c. pulla*, in Miss., is endangered.

Habitat: Summers on prairies and tundra; during winter, roosts on shallow water and feeds in agricultural fields.

Voice: A low-pitched "karooo karooo karooo."

Conservation: BBS: E ⇑ C ↑ CBC: ↑ Dependent on unprotected migration stopovers in Midwest.

Whooping Crane

Grus americana

Identification: 55" Tall, white, heronlike bird; black facial mask; dark red crown. IN FLIGHT: Note the black wing tips. IMM: White except for rust-colored head and wing tips; lacks adult facial markings. Imm. plumage kept 1 year.

Feeding: Feeds in shallow water or mudflats eating crabs, shrimp, clams, and snails, as well as amphibians, reptiles, and plant parts.

Nesting: A mound of wetland plants and grasses placed in shallow water. Eggs: 1–3, creamy buff with dark marks; I: 34–35 days; F: 100–115 days, precocial; B: 1.

Other Behavior: Family groups of several birds defend winter feeding territories. Courtship displays are typical of many cranes and include high leaps between the pair and bills pointing up and down. In order to help keep the bird from extinction, eggs laid by captive birds have been placed in Sandhill Crane nests and these parents raise the Whooping Crane young.

Habitat: Summers on freshwater marshes; winters on saltwater marshes.

Voice: A loud, repeated "kalooo kaleeooo."

Conservation: Endangered in U.S. and Can. Only about 200 birds alive. Being reintroduced into Fla.

Most people see their first shore-birds in mid-to-late summer, when they are on vacation and near the coast. At this time, as well as in spring, large numbers of shore-birds stop over to feed along sandy beaches and mudflats as they migrate south from their breeding grounds in the Arctic. A few very common species make up about 80–90% of what you see. If you start by learning to identify these species, it will then be much easier to learn the others.

Most of these common species migrate inland as well as along the coasts. So if you live inland, look for shorebirds along mudflats and shallow edges of streams, rivers, ponds, and lakes.

In fall, you will see young and adult shorebirds. Adults are often in transition between their summer and winter plumages; young are in their juvenal plumage and by late fall may be molting into their win-ter plumage. Because of this, you may see a lot of variation within the same species. For complete descriptions of these birds, refer to their main accounts on the pages mentioned.

MOST COMMON SHOREBIRDS ON MUDFLATS AND BEACHES

Semipalmated

Least

Smallest Sandpipers Sometimes called "peeps." Smallest shorebirds; brown-ish; feed along mudflats. In fall, Semipalmated Sandpiper (p. 170) is most common peep in Northeast; Western Sandpiper (p. 171) is common in mid-Atlantic and Southeast; Least Sandpiper (p. 172) is common throughout.

Sanderling Small; grayish; black legs; chases the edges of waves as it feeds. P. 169.

Semipalmated Plover Small; stubby bill; dark brown above; single dark neck-ring. P. 150.

Dunlin Medium-sized; long bill that droops slightly at the tip; may have some black on belly from summer plumage. P. 177.

Ruddy Turnstone Medium-sized; black bib; orange legs set far back on body. P. 167.

Long-billed

Black-bellied Plover Medium-sized; short thick bill; often some black on belly from summer plumage; in flight, look for black armpits. P. 146.

Short-billed and Long-billed Dowitchers Medium-sized; very long straight bills; feed by probing sand with rapid sewing-machine action. Pp. 181, 182.

Greater and Lesser Yellowlegs Large and medium-sized; long yellow-to-orange legs; long thin bills; slender graceful birds; whitish marks on dark upper-parts. Pp. 157, 158.

Lesser

Black-necked Stilt Large; black above and white below; long pink legs. P. 155.

Willet Large; long heavy bill; long grayish legs; in flight, shows black wings with bold white stripe down center. P. 160.

Whimbrel Large; long downcurved bill; 2 dark stripes on crown; dark eyeline. P. 163.

Black-bellied Plover
Pluvialis squatarola

Summer

Winter

Transition to winter

Fall juvenile

Identification: 12″ SUMMER: **Whitish crown; black from face to belly; white undertail coverts.** Female has white flecks in black areas. WINTER: **Grayish overall; darker above than below; faint eyebrow. Relatively larger head and longer bill** than similar golden-plovers. IN FLIGHT: All plumages show distinctive **black armpits; wide white wing-stripe; white rump.** FALL JUV: Like winter adult, but wings and back darker and with pale whitish-yellow spots; underparts finely streaked. Can be very similar to winter golden-plovers; note bill proportions and flight marks.

Feeding: Feeds on marine worms, insects, crustaceans, and mollusks in salt marshes and broad tidal flats. Also eats grasshoppers, earthworms, and seeds.

Nesting: Nest is a scraped depression of grasses and mosses. Eggs: 4, pale greenish with marks; I: 26–27 days; F: 30–35 days, precocial; B: 1.

Other Behavior: Birds often fly and roost in flocks, but scatter when feeding.

Habitat: Summers on arctic tundra; winters on sandy beaches, mudflats, and plowed fields near coast.

Voice: Distinctive melancholy 3-note whistle, with the 2nd syllable lower in pitch, like "tleeooee."

Conservation:
CWS: E ↓ C→ CBC: ↑

American Golden-Plover

Pluvialis dominicus

Summer

Fall juvenile

Identification: 10" **SUMMER: Dark crown; black face and underparts, including undertail coverts.** Wide white neck-stripe that stops at shoulder. **WINTER: Grayish brown above, usually with golden dots on back; grayish below; tends to have white eyebrow.** Smaller head and bill than similar Black-bellied Plover. Tips of folded wings project noticeably beyond tail. **IN FLIGHT:** All plumages show **dark wings** (no wing-stripe); **dark rump; gray armpits.** **FALL JUV:** Similar to winter adult, but more golden on crown, back, and wings.

Feeding: Feeds on insects, worms, seeds.

Nesting: Nest a scrape in the ground. Eggs: 4, tinged green with dark blotches; I: 26–27 days; F: 22 days, precocial; B: 1.

Other Behavior: One of our longest-distance migrants.

Habitat: Summers on arctic tundra; winters on plowed fields, short-grass fields, mudflats.

Voice: A short "queedle."

Conservation: CWS: E→ C→ CBC: ↓

Snowy Plover

Charadrius alexandrinus

Summer male

Identification: 6" In all plumages, **pale sandy above; partial neck-ring; thin, pointed, black bill; gray legs.** SUMMER: Male has dark bar across forehead, dark eye patch, and dark partial neck-ring. Female is light brown in these areas. WINTER: Both sexes like summer female. FALL JUV: Like summer female, but legs can be pale gray.

Feeding: Feeds by quickly running then picking up food, or probing on beaches and at surf line. Eats marine worms, small crustaceans, and, inland, insects.

Nesting: Nest a shallow depression on salt flat or open beach. Eggs: 2–3, buff with dark marks; I: 25–30 days; F: 31 days, precocial; B: 1–2.

Other Behavior: Breeding may be loosely colonial. In the East, there is 1 brood per year. In the West, there can be 2 broods per year. Female leaves young within 6 days to male's care, and she renests with new male. Male may also choose to renest with new female. In 1980s, population declines of 70–80% were recorded in Calif.

Habitat: Sandy beaches; alkaline lakes in West.

Voice: Low, whistled flight call like "ku-wheet."

Conservation: CBC: ⇓ Population is declining due to loss of nesting habitat and nest destruction on beaches.

Wilson's Plover

Charadrius wilsonia

Male

Female

Identification: 8″ Brown above, white below; **single wide neck-ring; heavy black bill** comparatively long for a plover. MALE: Neck-ring black. FEMALE: Neck-ring brown and can narrow in center to a thin line or, in winter, be incomplete. JUV: Like adult female.

Feeding: Feeds on higher, drier parts of beach. Eats mollusks, marine worms, insects, and especially fiddler and other land crabs.

Nesting: Nest a scraped depression sometimes lined with bits of stones, shells, and plants, on sand or gravel above tide line. Eggs: 4, creamy buff with dark marks; I: 23–25 days; F: 21 days, precocial; B: 1.

Other Behavior: Found in small flocks or with other species of plovers or shorebirds. To protect nest or brood, female (or male) does distraction display. She moves away from nest while fluttering wings and tilting to the side. Potential predator follows her, interpreting that she is injured.

Habitat: Coastal dunes and flats.

Voice: A single unmusical "wheet," or a deeper double whistle.

Conservation: BBS: E ⇓ C ⇑ CBC: ⇓ Declines may be due to increased populations of predators, such as gulls, crows, and raccoons, which have increased along with humans.

Semipalmated Plover

Charadrius semipalmatus

Summer

Winter

Identification: 7″ In all plumages, **dark brown above; dark neck-ring is complete.** SUMMER: **Black bar across forehead and from eye to bill;** black neck-ring. **Bill orange with dark tip; legs orange.** WINTER: **Black areas of summer plumage are brown; bill mostly dark;** legs dull orange. FALL JUV: Like dull winter adult; back and wing feathers lightly scalloped.

Feeding: Feeds by running then stopping and picking up prey item, then running again. Also may stir up prey by vibrating 1 foot on the ground. On migration and in winter, eats mainly marine worms.

Nesting: Nest a slight depression that may contain bits of shells or grass, on sandy or gravelly area. Eggs: 4, buffy brown with dark marks; I: 23–25 days; F: 21–31 days, precocial; B: 1.

Other Behavior: These little plovers space themselves out while feeding and aggressively defend their own feeding spots. May be seen running around with Sanderlings on exposed sandy beaches. Tend to roost by themselves in small groups.

Habitat: Summers on tundra; winters on muddy shores, tidal flats, sandy beaches.

Voice: A clear rising whistle like "chee-wee"; also an accelerating chortling note when defending feeding territory.

Conservation: CWS: E→ C→ CBC: ↑

Piping Plover
Charadrius melodus

Summer

Winter

Identification: 7" In all plumages, **pale sandy above; neck-ring complete or incomplete; short thick bill.** SUMMER: **Bill orange with black tip; legs bright orange;** black neck-ring and bar across forehead. Female less distinctly patterned than male. WINTER: **Bill all black;** legs pale orange; neck-ring and forehead pale sandy. IN FLIGHT: Note white base of tail. FALL JUV: Similar to winter adults.

Feeding: Feeds on crustaceans, mollusks, fly larvae, and marine worms and other small marine animals and their eggs.

Nesting: Nest a hollow in sand, sometimes lined with shells and pebbles; occurs on sandy or pebble beach above high-water mark, or on lakeshore. Eggs: 3–4, gray to buff with dark dots; I: 26–28 days; F: 21–28 days, precocial; B: 1.

Other Behavior: Territorial when nesting, with nests spaced at least 200 ft. apart. Seen in small flocks or singly during migration and in winter.

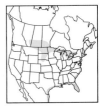

Habitat: Sandy beaches, lakeshores.

Voice: A whistled "peep" or a 2-note "peep-lo."

Conservation:
CWS: E ↓ C ↓ CBC: ↓ Interior population endangered in U.S. and Can. Habitat destroyed by development, vehicles, and human activity on beaches.

Killdeer

Charadrius vociferus

Identification: 10″ Only North American plover with **2 neck-rings**. Light **reddish-brown rump** is easily seen when bird flies or displays. Dark brown above, white below. FALL JUV: Like adult, but with buffy edges on feathers of back and wings; these edges wear off in fall.

Feeding: Eats mostly insects.

Nesting: Nest is a scraped depression in bare ground with pebbles added. Eggs: 3–4, pale brown with darker marks; I: 24–28 days; F: 25 days, precocial; B: 1–2.

Other Behavior: Most frequently encountered by humans not at the shore, but in suburban settings. Nests on athletic fields, agricultural fields, lawns, gravel rooftops, or any area that has short sparse vegetation. Can be very noisy and give a variety of calls, such as when flying overhead, or on the ground during territorial interactions. Killdeers are famous for their predator-distracting "broken-wing display," in which they appear to be injured and run along the ground dragging their wing, leading a potential predator away from nest or chicks.

Habitat: Open ground with gravel or short grass; suburban or rural.

Voice: Many varied calls. The most common is a repeated 2-part "kill-deah."

Conservation: BBS: E ↑ C ↓ CBC:→

Mountain Plover

Charadrius montanus

Summer

Identification: 8″ SUMMER: **White forehead with black bar above it; large dark eye; unmarked white beneath;** dark line between eye and black bill. WINTER: Like summer but lacks dark marks on forehead and before eye and has buffy breast.

Feeding: Eats insects, especially grasshoppers, beetles.

Nesting: Nest a scraped depression on bare ground, lined with grasses, rootlets, and cow manure chips. Eggs: 3–4, olive with spotted marks; I: 28–31 days; F: 33–34 days, precocial; B: 2.

Other Behavior: Found on short-grass plains and fields, not mountains. Runs away on foot when approached. Female can sometimes mate with more than 1 male. She will leave 1st clutch of eggs for male to incubate. She then mates with another male and incubates the 2nd clutch herself. In winter flocks may number in the hundreds.

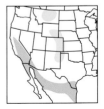

Habitat: Summers on dry prairies and short-grass plains; winters on plowed agricultural fields.

Voice: Low drawn-out whistle.

Conservation: BBS: E C ⇓ CBC:→ Endangered in Can. Prairie habitat is lost to development. New surveys show 50–90% decline in range and population.

American Oystercatcher

Haematopus palliatus

Identification: 19″ Long bright red bill; black head; dark brown back; white belly. **In Flight:** In all plumages, white at base of tail; white wing-stripe on inner flight feathers. **Imm:** Brown head and back feathers; brownish bill with some red at base. Imm. plumage kept 1 year.

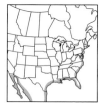

Feeding: Eats mostly oysters, also clams and other bivalves. Feeds by either stabbing or hammering technique. In stabbing, the bird stabs through the adductor muscles of open oyster, then inserts closed bill and forces shell apart. In hammering, the bird strikes the closed oyster with repeated blows, making a hole, then cuts the adductor muscle and pries apart the shell. These techniques are learned, and the young emulate their parents.

Nesting: Unlined nest placed in shallow depression on little mound of sand on open beach above high-tide mark. Eggs: 2–4, buffy with brown blotches; I: 24–29 days; F: 35 days, precocial; B: 1.

Other Behavior: Conspicuous and noisy. Feeds in small flocks in winter. The young, after hatching, are fed for 60 days by the adults, for their bills are not yet strong enough to open oysters.

Habitat: Coastal islands, beaches, and mudflats.

Voice: A loud "wheep, wheep." Also a shorter sound like "crik."

Conservation: BBS: E ⇑ C CBC: ↑ Range is expanding into N.Y. and Mass., where it used to breed in the 1800s.

Black-necked Stilt

Himantopus mexicanus

Female

Identification: 14" Black above; white below; long pink legs. MALE: Dark areas all black. FEMALE: Dark areas dark brown and faded by end of summer.

Feeding: Strides about and uses its long needlelike bill to pick up food on or just below the water surface, or on muddy shore. Wades to belly-deep on long legs. Eats larvae, nymphs, and adults of many aquatic insects, especially brine flies. Also eats crayfish, small fish, seeds.

Nesting: In small colonies, usually in marshy areas. Nest a depression on ground, lined with sticks, shells, and mud, on hummock or small island. Eggs: 3–4, buff with dark marks; I: 25 days; F: 28 days, precocial; B: 1.

Other Behavior: May move to new breeding areas from year to year if nesting localities dry up or become too flooded.

Habitat: Shallow water in marshes, ditches, ponds, salt ponds, or fields.

Voice: A loud "kek-kek-kek."

Conservation: BBS: E ⇑ C ⇓ CBC: ⇑

American Avocet

Recurvirostra americana

Summer male (l.), female (r.)

Winter

Identification: 18" **Long, thin, upturned bill; black on wings and back; white body.** Female has shorter, more strongly upcurved bill.
SUMMER: **Head and neck rich cinnamon.**
WINTER: **Head and neck whitish. IN FLIGHT:** Striking pattern of black and white on wings and back.

Feeding: Feeds in flocks. Thrusts bill underwater and swings it from side to side, feeling for prey. Can swim in deep water. Eats crustaceans, fish, aquatic insects, seeds.

Nesting: Usually in colonies. Nest a shallow depression with minimal lining, out in open on mudflat, marsh, beach. If waters rise, may build up nest with sticks and weeds. Eggs: 4, olive with dark spots; I: 23–25 days; F: 27–35 days, precocial; B: 1.

Other Behavior: Noisy and aggressive in breeding colonies and will dive-bomb intruders. Mostly silent on migration. A bird of saline lakes. One of their main concentrations is at Great Salt Lake, where there are hundreds of thousands in summer.

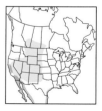

Habitat: Summers on shallow inland lakes; winters on coastal flats.

Voice: A loud penetrating "kleet."

Conservation:
BBS: E C ↑ CBC: ↓

Greater Yellowlegs

Tringa melanoleuca

Summer

Fall juvenile

Identification: 14" Long yellow-to-orange legs; whitish marks on dark upperparts. **Distinguish from similar Lesser Yellowlegs by size** when they are together — Lesser noticeably smaller — and **by proportion of bill to head size** when they are alone. Greater's bill is about 1½ times the length of its head; Lesser's bill is about equal to length of its head. Also see Voice. **SUMMER:** Head and neck heavily streaked with black; sides heavily barred with black. **WINTER:** Grayish overall with faint streaking on head and neck; dark bill is gray at base. **FALL JUV:** Similar to winter adult, except breast has fine distinct black streaks; back is finely spotted.

Feeding: Feeds in water, often dashing about. Picks at or skims surface, or swings bill back and forth through water. Eats fish, insects, worms, snails, berries.

Nesting: Nest a depression in the ground. Eggs: 4, buff with marks; I: 23 days; F: 18–20 days, precocial; B: 1.

Other Behavior: Both yellowlegs regularly seen together. Usually occurs singly or in small flocks.

Habitat: Summers on subarctic forest bogs; winters on coastal marshes.

Voice: Descending series of 3–4 notes, like "whew-whew-whew."

Conservation:
CWS: E→ C→ CBC: ↑

Lesser Yellowlegs
Tringa flavipes

Summer

Fall juvenile

Identification: 10″ Long yellow-to-orange legs; whitish marks on dark upperparts. **Distinguish from similar Greater Yellowlegs by size** when they are together — the Greater is noticeably larger — and **by proportion of bill to head size** when they are alone. Lesser's bill is about equal to the length of its head; Greater's bill is about 1½ times the length of its head. Also see Voice. SUMMER: **Head and neck finely streaked with black; sides lightly barred with black.** WINTER: **Upperparts grayish with faint streaking on head and neck; bill all black.** FALL JUV: Similar to winter adult, except breast has indistinct brownish streaks; back finely spotted.

Feeding: Feeds in shallow water, methodically walking and probing; rarely as animated as the Greater Yellowlegs. Eats fish, insects, worms, snails, berries.

Nesting: Nest is a grass-lined depression in the ground. Eggs: 4, yellow-buff, marked; I: 22–23 days; F: 18–20 days, precocial; B: 1.

Other Behavior: May defend winter feeding territories.

Habitat: Summers on subarctic forest bogs; winters on coastal marshes.

Voice: Usually a 2-note "tu tu"; less musical than Greater Yellowlegs' call.

Conservation:
CWS: E→ C→ CBC: ↑

Solitary Sandpiper

Tringa solitaria

Summer

Identification: 8 " Often found alone or in small groups at freshwater ponds and puddles. SUMMER: **Streaked brown head and neck; dark wings with whitish dots; greenish legs; bold white eye-ring;** repeatedly bobs head. The similar Lesser Yellowlegs has yellow legs and a finer eye-ring. WINTER: **Similar to summer, but head and neck appear unstreaked gray-brown.** IN FLIGHT: Wings all dark above and below; tail barred on sides.

Feeding: Feeds in shallow water, picking at surface or probing in the water or mud. May also walk through water shaking forward foot to stir up insects from bottom. Eats aquatic insects, grasshoppers, small crustaceans, frogs.

Nesting: Adds a little material to deserted nests of other birds such as Common Grackle, American Robin, or Rusty Blackbird. Nest located in coniferous tree up to 36 ft. high. Eggs: 4, greenish buff with dark marks; I: 23–24 days; F: ?, precocial; B: 1.

Other Behavior: Often found in small muddy puddles, partially dried up in late summer.

Habitat: Summers on boreal bogs; winters on small ponds.

Voice: A high-pitched 3-note "wheet, wheet, wheet."

Conservation: CWS: E ↓ C→ CBC: ↓

159

Willet

Catoptrophorus semipalmatus

Winter

Summer

Winter

Identification: 15" SUMMER: Long, straight, rather heavy bill; long grayish legs; brown streaking on head and neck; brown barring on breast. WINTER: Body plain gray-brown above; whitish below. IN FLIGHT: Distinctive **bold white wing-stripe on black wing.**

Feeding: Feeds on mud- and sandflats by probing with its bill. Eats insects, crustaceans, mollusks, grasses, seeds.

Nesting: Nest a hollow lined with dry grasses and sedges, on open area up to several hundred yards from water. Often concealed by grasses. Eggs: 4, olive with dark marks; I: 22–29 days; F: ?, precocial; B: 1.

Other Behavior: On breeding grounds, Willets are quite noisy. They flash white wing marks during aerial displays. On the ground and in flight, give the "pill-will-willet" song. Will perch on trees and fence posts to watch intruder and give alarm calls. Range in East is expanding.

Habitat: Summers on coastal marshes in East and prairie marshes in West; winters on coastal marshes, beaches, and mudflats.

Voice: Named after song given on breeding ground, "pill-will-willet." Alarm notes sound like "kip-kip-kip."

Conservation:
CWS: E→ C→ CBC: ↓

Spotted Sandpiper

Actitis macularia

Summer

Winter

Identification: 8" Distinctive flight and tail bobbing help identify this bird. **SUMMER: Large dark spots on white underparts; repeatedly bobs tail while walking;** bill pinkish orange with darker tip. Female more boldly patterned than male. **WINTER: Grayish above; pure white below; bill is dark. IN FLIGHT: Flies with stiff wings beating in a shallow arc.**

Feeding: Feeds along water edges, eating flies, worms, small crustaceans, fish, beetles.

Nesting: Nest a shallow depression lined with a few grasses. Eggs: 4, buff with brown spots; I: 21 days; F: 21 days, precocial; B: 1–5.

Other Behavior: Most common on inland lakes and streams, where it breeds in summer; less common on seashore. In a majority of cases Spotted Sandpipers are polyandrous, the female having 2 or more males as mates. She courts the male, lays a clutch of eggs for him to incubate and raise, and immediately leaves him to court another male. Up to 4 or 5 males have been reported for 1 female.

Habitat: Summers along rivers, lakes, and seashore; winters along edges of fresh or salt water.

Voice: In alarm or aggression gives series of short whistles like "weet weet weet." During courtship gives "peetaweet peetaweet."

Conservation:
CWS: E→ C→ CBC: ↑

161

Upland Sandpiper

Bartramia longicauda

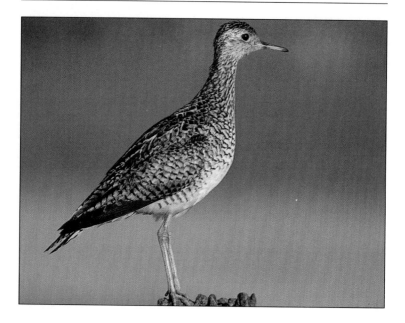

Identification: 12″ Proportionally **small head** and **large dark eye; short yellow bill and yellow legs; long neck; long tail** projects well beyond wing tips when bird is standing. IN FLIGHT: Underwings heavily barred with brown and white; wings often held above back for short period after landing.

Feeding: Feeds in grasslands. Eats worms, grasshoppers, beetles, and other insects.

Nesting: Sometimes in loose colonies. Nest a depression lined with grasses, on prairie, meadow, or field. Eggs: 4, creamy buff; I: 21–27 days; F: ?, precocial; B: ?

Other Behavior: On breeding grounds does aerial and ground displays. Upon landing, often holds wings raised. Perches on fence posts. May act tame.

Habitat: Prairies and meadows.

Voice: In flight, calls "pulip, pulip." On breeding ground gives a reedy wolf whistle.

Conservation: CWS: E ↓ C ↓

Whimbrel

Numenius phaeopus

Identification: 17" Large brown shorebird; **long downcurved bill; 2 dark stripes on crown;** dark streak through eye. **IN FLIGHT:** Underwings brown and belly pale.

Feeding: Feeds on wetlands, grasslands, shores. Probes or picks at insects, marine worms, crustaceans, mollusks. Also eats fiddler crabs and, in Arctic, berries.

Nesting: Nest a depression in tundra, heath, or bog. Eggs: 4, greenish olive with marks; I: 22–24 days; F: 35–42 days, precocial; B: 1.

Other Behavior: In large flocks on migration and at evening roosts. Birds defend individual feeding territories at low tide and then roost together in flocks at high tide. May fly long distances from feeding to roosting areas.

Habitat: Summers on tundra; winters along fresh or salt water and on agricultural fields.

Voice: Loud, repeated, whistlelike "whi whi whi whi whi" and many other calls.

Conservation: CWS: E→ C→ CBC: ↓

Long-billed Curlew
Numenius americanus

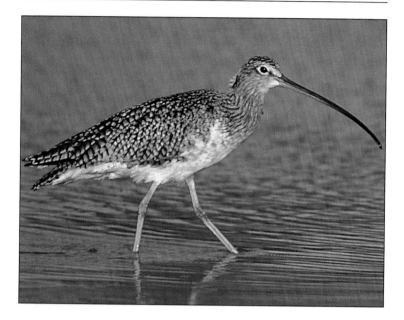

Identification: 23″ **Extremely long downcurved bill,** equal in length to more than half the length of the body; **crown finely streaked with brown;** neck and underparts washed with cinnamon. Female has much longer bill than male. **IN FLIGHT:** Cinnamon underwings. **FALL JUV:** Similar to adults, but with shorter bill for first few months; at this time its bill is not much longer than that of a Whimbrel.

Feeding: Probes into mud for crabs and other invertebrates. Also eats grasshoppers, beetles, insects, and eggs of other birds.

Nesting: Nest a slight hollow lined with weeds, grasses, and cow manure chips, on prairie, meadowland, or short-grass area. Eggs: 4, white to buff or olive with brown marks; I: 27–30 days; F: 32–45 days, precocial; B: 1.

Other Behavior: On breeding territories does roller-coaster display flights. Feeds in flocks and flies in line formations.

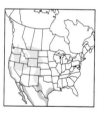

Habitat: Summers on grasslands; winters on coastal grasslands, fields, mudflats.

Voice: A loud rising "cur-lew."

Conservation: CWS: E C ↓ CBC: →

Hudsonian Godwit

Limosa haemastica

Transition to winter plumage

Summer

Fall juvenile

Identification: 15" **SUMMER: Large** shorebird; **long slightly upturned bill pink at base;** body brown above, reddish brown below with variable amounts of dark barring. Female larger, longer-billed, and paler underneath than male. **WINTER: Bill as in summer;** body gray above, white below. **IN FLIGHT:** In all plumages, **black tail; white rump; black wing linings; white wing-stripe. FALL JUV:** Dark brown back and wings; lighter edges to feathers; light grayish brown on chest.

Feeding: Feeds by probing shallow waters, beaches, and mudflats. Eats crustaceans, mollusks, marine worms, and insects.

Nesting: Nest a saucerlike depression lined with dead leaves, on moist bog, marsh, or dry hummock, often near birches. Eggs: 4, brownish olive with marks; I: 22–23 days; F: 25–30 days, precocial; B: 1.

Other Behavior: In spectacular fall migration, most fly from Hudson Bay to Patagonia and Tierra del Fuego. Flights are over 3,000 miles, often nonstop. Winters at southern tip of S. America. In spring, migrates through center of N. America.

Habitat: Summers on tundra near tree line; winters on mudflats and flooded fields.

Voice: On breeding ground, call is loud "quee-quip."

Conservation: CWS: E → C→ During spring migration, key staging areas exist in Tex. and La. and in Can.

Marbled Godwit

Limosa fedoa

Summer

Winter

Identification: 18" Large shorebird; **long slightly upturned bill is pink at base; back and wings are cinnamon marked with black.** SUMMER: Underparts heavily barred. WINTER: Underparts buffy with no barring. IN FLIGHT: **Underwings cinnamon. FALL JUV: Similar to adult.**

Feeding: Probes with its bill on tidal flats, eating worms, mollusks, and crustaceans. Also eats grasshoppers and seeds and tubers of pondweeds and sedges.

Nesting: Semicolonial. Nest a hollow, with minimal lining, on prairie wetland. Eggs: 4, green-brown with dark marks; I: 21–23 days; F: 21 days, precocial; B: 1.

Other Behavior: During breeding, males do circling flight displays. Usually found in small groups.

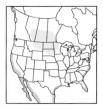

Habitat: Summers on moist grass-lands; winters along coast.

Voice: During breeding, calls "god-wit."

Conservation: CWS: E ↓ C ↓ CBC: ↓

Ruddy Turnstone

Arenaria interpres

Summer

Winter

Identification: 8 " **Black bib** and **orange legs** in all adult plumages. SUMMER: **White head; bright chestnut on back and wings.** Female tends to have more brown wash on head and nape and more streaking on crown. WINTER: **Back, wings, and head brown;** 2 white patches enclosed by bib. IN FLIGHT: Conspicuous white stripes on wings and back.

Feeding: Feeds by turning over stones, shells, earth, seaweeds, and other objects with its strong bill. Also digs with bill in sand. Eats sand fleas, mollusks, crustaceans, insects, worms.

Nesting: Nest a shallow depression lined with mosses, grasses, leaves, seaweed, next to rock or vegetation. Eggs: 3–4, greenish olive with dark marks; I: 22–24 days; F: 19–21 days, precocial; B: 1.

Other Behavior: Feeds singly, in small groups, or with flocks of other shorebirds. May feed on eggs of colonial seabirds in West and frequents garbage dumps in the North. Eastern population depends heavily on Delaware Bay for food during spring migration.

Habitat: Summers on high arctic tundra; winters on sandy and rocky beaches.

Voice: A common call is a grating "tuk-e-tuk." Also gives low staccato sound, or a low "tuk" note.

Conservation:
CWS: E→ C→ CBC: ↑

Red Knot
Calidris canutus

Summer

Winter

Identification: 11" SUMMER: **Reddish-brown face and underparts; gray, black, and rufous back; short straight bill** (about same length as head); legs dark gray. WINTER: Plain **gray back; gray breast; white belly;** legs greenish.

Feeding: Feeds on beaches and in muddy areas, eating mollusks, worms, fish, the eggs of king crabs, and seeds.

Nesting: Nest a hollow lined with leaves and lichens, on high rocky tundra. Eggs: 4, buff-olive, spotted with brown; I: 21–22 days; F: 18 days, precocial; B: 1.

Other Behavior: Feeds and roosts in tight flocks of hundreds of birds. May associate with other shorebirds like Ruddy Turnstones, Dunlins, and Black-bellied Plovers. Like Hudsonian Godwits and several other shorebirds, this species makes tremendous overwater flights of more than 2,000 miles from Hudson Bay to S. America during fall migration. Spring migration is primarily along the East Coast, where a key stopover point for feeding is the Delaware Bay.

Habitat: Summers on tundra; winters on coastal beaches and mudflats.

Voice: A low harsh "knut" while feeding; a soft "kuret" while flying.

Conservation: CWS: E ↓ C→ CBC: ⇑

Sanderling
Calidris alba

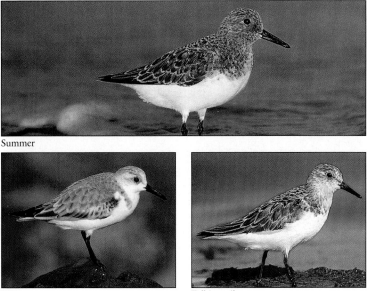

Summer

Winter   Fall juvenile

Identification: 8" Most often seen in winter plumage **chasing the edges of waves** on sandy beaches. **Summer: Upperparts reddish to orange-brown with darker brown streaking; belly white; legs black. Winter: Pale gray above; white below; black legs;** black shoulder may be visible. Straight comparatively short bill. **In Flight:** All plumages have bold white wing-stripe. **Fall Juv:** Like winter adult but darker above, with brown and black mixed with the gray.

Feeding: On beaches and mudflats. Probes with its bill. Eats minute crustaceans, mollusks, marine worms, and insects.

Nesting: Nest a scraped depression on dry tundra. Eggs: 4, olive-green with dark marks; I: 24–31 days; F: 17 days, precocial; B: 1–2.

Other Behavior: These little sandpipers are always scurrying along at the surf line, like windup toys. They run back and forth, following advancing and receding waves. On breeding grounds, female may be polyandrous, laying several clutches of eggs that are each attended by a different male.

Habitat: Summers on arctic tundra; winters along sandy coasts.

Voice: A quiet "kip" in flight.

Conservation: CWS: E ↓ C→ CBC: ↓ Drastic population declines; up to 80% declines in last 10 years in East.

Semipalmated Sandpiper

Calidris pusilla

Summer

Winter

Fall juvenile

Identification: 6¼" All plumages have **dark legs; short, relatively straight, blunt-tipped bill; grayish-brown appearance.** SUMMER: **Grayish brown on back,** with some black but little or no reddish brown; **whitish breast;** little or no streaking on flanks. WINTER: **Uniform grayish brown above; light streaking on breast.** FALL JUV: Grayish brown above, with black tips and pale edgings to back feathers. Finely streaked darker crown makes eyebrow look light. Variable, with some birds quite reddish brown on back.

Feeding: Feeds on sandy or muddy flats with its head down and snatching up food. Eats crustaceans, mollusks, marine worms, and aquatic insects.

Nesting: Nest a depression on flat ground, often near a birch tree. Eggs: 4, buff to yellow with dark marks; I: 18–22 days; F: 19 days, precocial; B: 1.

Other Behavior: Gregarious. Can be found in huge numbers in favored feeding places along migration routes in East. Rare during migration in West.

Habitat: Summers on tundra; winters on tidal flats.

Voice: Typical flight call a short low-pitched "cherk."

Conservation: CWS: E ↓ C→ CBC: ⇓ Populations recently declining. Two key spots for their survival during migration are Delaware Bay in spring and Bay of Fundy in fall.

Western Sandpiper

Calidris mauri

Summer

Winter

Fall juvenile

Identification: 6½" All plumages have **dark legs; relatively long sharp-pointed bill, usually drooping slightly at the tip.** SUMMER: **Contrasting reddish-brown markings on shoulder; reddish brown also on crown and ear patch.** Black chevron marks from breast continue down along flanks. WINTER: Uniform grayish brown above; light streaking on breast. Best distinguished from very similar Semipalmated Sandpiper by bill and voice. FALL JUV: Typically shows contrasting rusty-edged feathers on sides of grayish back.

Feeding: Often feeds in deeper water or farther out on mudflats than Semipalmated or Least Sandpipers. Eats crustaceans, mollusks, worms, and aquatic insects.

Nesting: Nest a depression on moist tundra or mossy slopes. Nest may be concealed under shrubs. Eggs: 4, buff, marked with brown; I: 20–22 days; F: 19 days, precocial; B: 1.

Other Behavior: Gregarious and can occur in flocks of thousands, especially in West. Sometimes aggressively defends feeding territory; other times feeds peaceably.

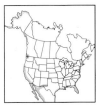

Habitat: Summers on tundra; winters on coastal beaches and mudflats.

Voice: A high-pitched "dzheet."

Conservation: CBC: ↓

Least Sandpiper

Calidris minutilla

Summer

Winter

Fall juvenile

Identification: 6″ In all plumages, **yellowish or greenish legs; short, thin, pointed bill; smallest of "peeps."** Crouched appearance when feeding. SUMMER: **Dark brown above; brown wash on breast, with dark streaks ending abruptly on upper breast;** feathers along sides of back have black centers. WINTER: **More evenly grayish on upperparts, but still darker than other winter peeps, especially on breast.** FALL JUV: Similar to summer adult, but breast only faintly streaked and washed with buff; richly colored above; distinct white stripes on back.

Feeding: Often found feeding in muddy, grassy areas closer to shore than other peeps. Eats insects, mollusks, crustaceans, and marine worms.

Nesting: Nest a shallow depression on bog or upland. Eggs: 4, pinkish buff with dark marks; I: 19–23 days; F: ?, precocial; B: 1.

Other Behavior: Roosts near feeding areas, alone or in small groups, among marsh vegetation or on upper beach in wrack line.

Habitat: Summers on tundra and bogs near tree line; winters along coastal and inland marshes.

Voice: Flight note a high-pitched "kreeet."

Conservation:
CWS: E ↓ C→ CBC: ↓

White-rumped Sandpiper

Calidris fuscicollis

Summer

Winter

Fall juvenile

Identification: 7½" In all plumages, **wings extend beyond tail** when bird is standing (also true of Baird's Sandpiper); **white rump seen in flight** or when bird preens; noticeably larger than other "peeps" except Baird's. **SUMMER: Reddish brown on crown and sides of back** (similar to summer Western Sandpiper); **streaks on breast extend down along flanks as small chevrons.** **WINTER:** Evenly grayish brown above and on breast; white eyebrow. **FALL JUV:** Breast buffy with fine streaks; usually no streaks along sides; upperparts similar to summer adult's, but more richly colored.

Feeding: Feeds by probing in mud or shallow water. Eats marine worms, insects, snails.

Nesting: Nest of grass, moss, and leaves on hummock. Eggs: 4, light green with dark marks; I: 22 days; F: 16–17 days, precocial; B: 1.

Other Behavior: Found in single-species flocks, or mixed in with other shorebirds. On breeding grounds males do display flights. The male is polygynous.

Habitat: Summers on tundra near coast; winters on muddy areas near coast.

Voice: A high thin "jeeet."

Conservation:
CWS: E→ C→ CBC: ⇓

173

Baird's Sandpiper

Calidris bairdii

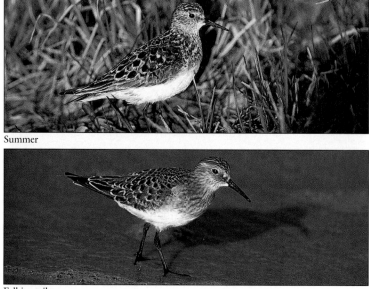

Summer

Fall juvenile

Identification: 7″ In all plumages, **wings extend well beyond tail** when bird is standing (also true of White-rumped Sandpiper); **dark rump.** SUMMER: **Buffy wash on face and breast; fine streaking on breast that does not extend along sides;** back looks splotchy with dark-centered feathers. WINTER: This plumage is acquired on wintering ground in S. Am. and only briefly seen in spring as birds start to enter N. Am. Similar to summer plumage, but duller, paler, and not so buffy. FALL JUV: More evenly brown plumage; light-edged feathers on back give it a scalloped effect.

Feeding: Rapidly moves along and picks up food on inland wetlands or grasslands. Eats insects.

Nesting: Nest a shallow depression on tundra. Eggs: 2–4, pink to olive-buff with markings; I: 19–21 days; F: 16–20 days, precocial; B: 1.

Other Behavior: Seen in small groups or singly. Adults migrate inland through the interior; juveniles migrate through interior and along both coasts.

Habitat: Summers on dry tundra; winters on inland and coastal lakes and marshes, mudflats, and grasslands.

Voice: A low trilling "preet," or a grating "krrt."

Conservation: CWS: E C→ CBC: ↓

Pectoral Sandpiper

Calidris melanotos

Adults

Fall juvenile

Identification: 9" Most often seen at grassy edges of salt or freshwater marshes, rather than with other shorebirds on mudflats. In all plumages, **dense brown streaking on breast stops abruptly at white belly;** legs yellowish; bill droops slightly at tip. Male is distinctly larger and darker-breasted than female. Summer and winter plumages similar. FALL JUV: Similar to adults, but finer streaking on buffy breast; broader white edges on back feathers form 2 white V's.

Feeding: Eats insects, grass seeds, worms, fiddler crabs.

Nesting: Concealed, well-built cup of grasses and leaves lined with finer material, on upland tundra or grassland. Eggs: 4, pale buff-olive with brown splotches; I: 21–23 days; F: 18–21 days, precocial; B: 1.

Other Behavior: Promiscuous breeding system. Males mate several times. Females visit other males. Male has an air sac beneath the breast, which emphasizes the demarcation line of streaking. Male pumps the sac in and out in flight display.

Habitat: Summers on wet tundra; winters along grassy marshes.

Voice: Flight call is a low "churk." In courtship flight male gives "oo-ah" hooting sound 2–3 times per second.

Conservation: CWS: E→ C→ CBC: ↓

Purple Sandpiper

Calidris maritima

Winter

Identification: 9" A dark shorebird, seen mostly in winter along rocky shores. SUMMER: Long, thin, slightly drooped bill, yellowish at base; short yellow legs; brown spots on breast and flanks; neck and head finely streaked; crown buffy with dark streaks. WINTER: Like summer, but clear gray head and neck; gray back; gray spots on white belly. IN FLIGHT: Dark above with white wing-stripe and white on sides of rump. FALL JUV: Similar to breeding adult, but browner overall and more finely streaked on breast.

Feeding: Forages on rocky shores, jetties, breakwaters, and reefs, probing among seaweed and crevices. Eats crustaceans, mollusks, insects, algae, grasses, seeds.

Nesting: Nest a hollow lined with grasses, among low heath plants on tundra. Eggs: 4, greenish with dark brown spots; I: 21 days; F: 21 days, precocial; B: 1.

Other Behavior: Found in small flocks in winter, often mixed with Ruddy Turnstones. Acts tame, but habitat of rocky coasts makes them hard to approach.

Habitat: Summers on tundra; winters along rocky coasts.

Voice: Flight call is a "weet," or sometimes 2 syllables, "wheet wit."

Conservation: CWS: E→ C CBC: ⇑

Dunlin

Calidris alpina

Summer

Winter

Transition to winter

Fall juvenile

Identification: 8" **Long bill, drooping at the tip; black legs.** SUMMER: Whitish face and underparts, with **large black patch on belly;** back reddish brown; crown variably streaked reddish brown. WINTER: **Plain, with head, neck, and breast gray-brown; wings and back gray; belly white.** FALL JUV: Buffy breast and head; reddish-brown back; lines of dark spots extend from lower breast onto belly and flanks. This plumage rarely seen since juveniles molt into winter plumage on breeding ground before migrating south.

Feeding: Feeds mostly on mudflats or, at times, on beaches. Probes with its bill for crustaceans, mollusks, marine worms, and insects.

Nesting: Nest placed on a hummock. Eggs: 4, green to olive-buff with spots; I: 19–22 days; F: 18–25 days, precocial; B: 1.

Other Behavior: Roosts on beaches or upland fields. Can be found in huge flocks that put on impressive aerial maneuvers when flushed, or when pursued by a predator.

Habitat: Summers on tundra; winters on beaches, coastal mudflats.

Voice: Flight call a harsh "kreee."

Conservation:
CWS: E→ C CBC: ↓

177

Stilt Sandpiper

Calidris himantopus

Summer

Winter

Identification: 8½" Legs long and greenish; bill long, thin, and slightly drooped at tip. SUMMER: Dark with heavy barring on breast and belly; whitish eyebrow; reddish-brown ear patch. WINTER: Grayish overall with white belly and white eyebrow. IN FLIGHT: All plumages have white rump; no wing-stripe. FALL JUV: Upperparts black and brown; belly white; buffy edges on feathers create a strongly scalloped effect; whitish eyebrow.

Feeding: Feeds in compact flocks. Probes with its bill and may plunge head underwater. Eats small mollusks, mosquito larvae, worms, and parts of aquatic plants.

Nesting: Nest a scrape on relatively dry sedge meadows. Eggs: 4, pale green to olive with dots; I: 19–21 days; F: 17–18 days, precocial; B: 1.

Other Behavior: Rapid feeding motion is like that of dowitchers, with which it often occurs, but it brings its bill completely out of water more often than those species. Also found feeding in single-species groups. Migrates through the Great Plains; rare sightings in fall on West Coast are mostly juveniles.

Habitat: Summers on tundra; winters on ponds and marshes near coast.

Voice: Flight call is a rattling trilled "kirr."

Conservation:
CWS: E→ C→ CBC: ⇑

Buff-breasted Sandpiper

Tryngites subruficollis

Adult

Fall juvenile

Identification: 8" **Buffy face, breast, and belly,** with some dark spotting along sides of breast; bill short; legs yellow. Summer and winter plumages alike. Male considerably larger than female. **IN FLIGHT:** Bright white underwings. **FALL JUV:** Similar to adult, but back feathers edged with white instead of buff.

Feeding: Feeds on insects, spiders, seeds of aquatic plants.

Nesting: Nest a shallow cavity on dry tundra. Eggs: 4, white to buff or olive with spots; I: ?; F: ?, precocial; B: 1.

Other Behavior: Promiscuous mating system in which males display in groups. Females arrive and mate with them, then nest elsewhere and raise the broods alone. Migrates mostly through central N. America; rare occurrences on the coasts are mostly juveniles during fall migration.

Habitat: Summers on dry arctic tundra; winters on short-grass areas and dry lake margins.

Voice: Flight call is a low "pr-r-reet."

Conservation: CWS: E C ↓ Nearly hunted to extinction in late 1800s.

Ruff

Philomachus pugnax

Summer male

Fall juvenile

Identification: 9–11″ This Eurasian species is a rare migrant along the coasts and casual in the rest of N. Am. Extremely variable in plumage, but can be recognized by its distinctive shape. **Small head; long neck; large plump body; bill relatively short and slightly downcurved.** SUMMER: Males vary from white to rufous to black; always have distinctive erectile ear tufts and neck feathers. Female (reeve) dark with light belly; black blotches on breast and flanks WINTER: Gray-brown above; whitish below; some grayish-brown mottling on breast. Female like male but smaller. FALL JUV: Dark back feathers fringed with buff; head and breast unstreaked and buffy.

Feeding: Eats aquatic insects, mollusks, and crustaceans.

Nesting: Grass-lined hollow on tundra marsh. Eggs: 4, greenish; I: 20–23 days; F: 25–27 days, precocial; B: 1.

Other Behavior: Males do courtship on communal display grounds called leks. Darker males hold territories in center of lek; paler males move around the edges. Females visit and mate with 1 or several males.

Habitat: Summers in Eurasia; during migration seen on grasslands, fresh or saltwater pools, mudflats.

Voice: Usually quiet.

Conservation: CBC: ↓

Short-billed Dowitcher

Limnodromus griseus

Summer *griseus*

Winter

Summer *hendersoni*

Fall juvenile

Identification: 11–11½" **Medium-sized; long straight bill; greenish legs.** Three subspecies. SUMMER: *L. g. griseus* (seen in Northeast, S. to N.J.) has an orange-blotched chest with dense black spotting and a white belly; *L. g. hendersoni* (seen in Midwest and Southeast S. of N.J.) has a reddish-brown chest and belly and minimal dark spotting; *L. g. caurinus* (seen west of the Rockies) is usually heavily spotted underneath, with white limited to the lower belly. WINTER: Gray-brown above; whitish below. Short-billed and Long-billed Dowitchers **best distinguished by voice.** FALL JUV: Back feathers broadly edged and internally marked with reddish buff; breast buffy and speckled with darker marks.

Feeding: Feeds by rapidly probing in sewing-machine-like motion. Eats marine worms, mollusks, some insects.

Nesting: Hollow in moss or wet meadow. Eggs: 4, buff-green with marks; I: 21 days; F: ?, precocial; B: 1.

Other Behavior: Roosts in large groups.

Habitat: Summers on bogs at northern limit of coniferous forests; winters on coastal mudflats.

Voice: Flight call is a medium-pitched repeated "tututu."

Conservation:
CWS: E ↓ C→ CBC: ⇑

Long-billed Dowitcher

Limnodromus scolopaceus

Summer

Winter

Fall juvenile

Identification: 11–11½" Medium-sized shorebird; long straight bill; greenish legs. **SUMMER:** Underparts entirely reddish brown with heavy barring on breast and flanks; no white belly. **WINTER:** Gray-brown above; whitish below. Long-billed and Short-billed Dowitchers **best distinguished by voice. IN FLIGHT:** In all plumages, **both Long-billed and Short-billed show a distinctive white wedge on lower back and a barred tail.** **FALL JUV:** Back feathers, narrowly edged with dark reddish brown, lack internal markings of Short-billed Dowitcher; breast mostly gray with little speckling.

Feeding: Feeds using up-and-down probing motion with bill, like a sewing machine. Eats insects, mollusks, crustaceans, marine worms.

Nesting: Nest a scraped depression in a wet meadow. Eggs: 4, brown to olive with marks; I: 20 days; F: ?, precocial; B: ?1.

Other Behavior: Most common in standing freshwater situations, rather than on extensive tidal flats.

Habitat: Summers just north of tree line; winters on freshwater ponds and marshes.

Voice: Flight call is a high-pitched thin "keeek," sometimes given in a series.

Conservation: CWS: E C→ CBC: ⇑

Common Snipe

Gallinago gallinago

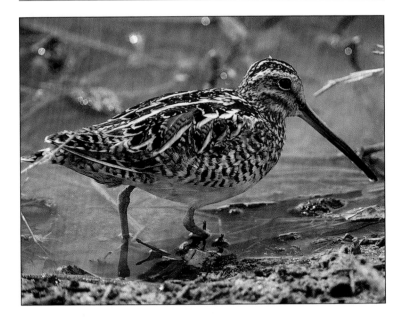

Identification: 11″ A bird of wet meadows and boggy areas. **Extremely long straight bill; plump body; short legs.** Black and white stripes on head; **conspicuous white stripes on dark back.** IN FLIGHT: Flies in a zigzag manner; wings are pointed.

Feeding: Feeds in wet areas by plunging its bill into soft ground. Eats larvae of craneflies and other insects, earthworms, crayfish, mollusks, frogs, seeds.

Nesting: Nest of grasses, leaves, and moss, placed in a scraped depression in a bog. Eggs: 4, olive-buff with spots; I: 18–20 days; F: 14–20 days, precocial; B: 1.

Other Behavior: Both sexes do unusual aerial display during breeding (female does it mostly at beginning of breeding season). Bird rises 300–360 ft. in air, then dives down. Air vibrating through the 2 outer tail feathers makes bleating or whinnying sound. This is done most over nesting area in early morning or early evening.

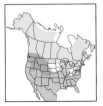

Habitat: Wet meadows, marshes, bogs.

Voice: When flushed, gives nasal "scaip" note. Sings "wheet-wheet" notes from perches on breeding ground.

Conservation:
CWS: E ↓ C ↓ CBC: ↓

American Woodcock

Scolopax minor

Identification: 11" **Extremely long straight bill; large dark eye; large head; short neck;** dark back; buffy breast. **IN FLIGHT:** Short rounded wings clatter when bird is flushed.

Feeding: Probes deep in soil with long bill, which it can open below surface to grab prey. Can eat its weight in earthworms within 24 hours; also eats insects, seeds.

Nesting: Nest is a scraped depression in ground lined with a few twigs or grasses, placed within 100–200 yd. of male's display ground. Eggs: 4, buff with brown splotches; I: 20–21 days; F: 28 days, precocial; B: 1.

Other Behavior: Listen for the "peeent" call and watch for displaying woodcocks in open fields in spring. Displays are given at dawn, dusk, and all night when the moon is full. Male rises in the air in wide circles. After he reaches about 50 ft., his wings start to make a twittering sound as he flies higher. At 200–300 ft. the twittering stops and he gives a canarylike flight song while starting a zigzag descent. Several males may display in the same field. Females are attracted to the area and mate with the males. Males continue to display after mating and may mate with other females. After mating, a female will raise her brood on her own.

Habitat: Woods and thickets bordered by open areas.

Voice: A nasal "peeent" given by both sexes. Flight display call a high-pitched twittering.

Conservation: BBS: E ⇓ C CBC: ↓ Continentwide declines of 14% in each of last few years due to loss of early-successional forest habitat.

Wilson's Phalarope

Phalaropus tricolor

Summer female

Summer male

Adult, 1st winter

Identification: 9" The phalarope most often seen inland. **Bill is very long and very thin. SUMMER: Broad dark streak goes through eye and continues down neck;** light reddish-brown wash on breast. The more colorful female has a gray crown; male has a blackish crown. **WINTER:** Gray and unstreaked above; white below; **thin grayish line through eye;** legs greenish black. **IN FLIGHT:** No wing-stripes; whitish rump. **JUV:** Back feathers strongly edged with buff; pale thin eye-stripe; legs yellow. Juv. plumage kept for only brief period.

Feeding: Wades along muddy shores and shallow water, whirling around while stabbing the water's surface. Eats brine shrimp, mosquito larvae, insects.

Nesting: Semicolonial. Nest a grass-lined hollow, concealed in grass or marsh. Eggs: 4, buff with blotches; I: 20 days; F: 20 days, precocial; B: 1–2.

Other Behavior: Females are larger than males and occasionally mate with more than 1 male. Male builds the nest, incubates the eggs, and raises the young.

Habitat: Summers on marshy areas of meadows or lakes; winters along shallow edges of saline lakes.

Voice: A soft grunting "aangh" note.

Conservation: CWS: E→ C→ CBC: ↓ Being affected by loss of breeding and feeding areas. Range expanding in West.

185

Red-necked Phalarope

Phalaropus lobatus

Summer female

Summer male

Winter

Identification: 7″ Migrates primarily at sea but occasionally shows up inland, especially in fall. **Small phalarope with a short very thin bill. Summer: Bright reddish-brown patch on side of dark gray neck;** on female this patch continues across breast. **Winter: Dark patch through eye; back is gray and black with a suggestion of white streaks; white forehead and crown. In Flight:** White wing-stripe. **Fall Juv:** Wide dark patch behind eye; dark back with 2 buffy streaks on either side.

Feeding: Feeds by picking prey from the water's surface, often while rapidly twirling about. Eats insects, mollusks, crustaceans.

Nesting: Grass-lined scrape in moist tundra. Eggs: 4, olive with brown dots; I: 19 days; F: 20 days, precocial; B: 1–2.

Other Behavior: Females can be polyandrous. Massive fall staging areas in West, especially at Great Salt Lake, Utah (600,000 birds) and Mono Lake, Calif. (80,000 birds).

Habitat: Summers on marshy tundra ponds; winters primarily at sea

Voice: A low-pitched "twick."

Conservation: CWS: E ↓ C→ CBC: ⇓ Eastern Canadian staging populations have shown significant recent shifts or possible declines.

Red Phalarope

Phalaropus fulicaria

Summer female

Summer male

Winter

Identification: 8" Migrates almost exclusively at sea. **Chunky phalarope with a short, thick, blunt-tipped bill.** SUMMER: **Bill is yellow with dark tip;** deep reddish-brown underparts; white patch over eye. In more colorful female, white patch is well defined and encompasses eye; in male, it is less defined and is mostly behind the eye. WINTER: **Wide dark patch through eye; gray unstreaked back; white forehead and crown.** IN FLIGHT: White wing-stripe. FALL JUV: Similar to summer male, but pinkish buff on breast and dark bill.

Feeding: Spins around on water and eats aquatic insects, larval fish, crustaceans.

Nesting: Nest a grassy scrape, often domed over with grasses. Eggs: 4, gray to olive with dark spots; I: 19 days; F: 16–21 days, precocial; B: 1–2.

Other Behavior: Males incubate and raise young. Females can be polyandrous. Like Red-necked Phalarope, this species may be blown toward shore by storms during its offshore migrations.

Habitat: Summers on tundra ponds near arctic coast; winters at sea.

Voice: A high-pitched shrill "wit."

Conservation: CWS: E ↓ C→ CBC: ⇑

Pomarine Jaeger
Stercorarius pomarinus

Light-morph immature

Light-morph adult

Identification: 22″ Light and dark morphs, and intermediate forms, occur. Light morphs greatly outnumber dark morphs. **IN FLIGHT: Large-bodied; thick-necked; wings wide at base; wingbeats deep, slow, and steady. Central tail feathers long, twisted, and spoon-shaped** (can be missing or broken); **flash of white at base of primaries on underwing.** Light morph has variable **mottled barring on flanks under wings; chestband, when present, mottled.** Dark morph all dark except for white on primaries. **JUV/IMM:** Central tail feathers, no matter how short, are rounded at tip. Imm. plumage kept 3–4 years.

Feeding: During breeding eats lemmings and voles, also other birds and their eggs; during winter, captures fish off ocean surface, also robs other birds of food.

Nesting: Nest is unlined depression in ground. Eggs: 1–2, brown with darker markings; I: 26 days; F: 31–37 days, precocial; B: 1.

Other Behavior: During migration, seen singly or in small flocks.

Habitat: Summers on tundra; winters at sea.

Voice: Generally quiet off breeding ground, but may be heard calling during migration.

Conservation:
CBC: ⇑

Parasitic Jaeger

Stercorarius parasiticus

Light-morph adult

Dark-morph adult

Identification: 18" Light and dark morphs, and intermediate forms, occur. Either morph can be common. IN FLIGHT: Compared to Pomarine Jaeger, **neck and body slightly thinner, wings narrower at base; central tail feathers long and pointed** (can be missing or broken); **white at base of primaries on underwing.** Alternates **quick wingbeats with short glides. In light morph, flanks under wings clear white; chestband** (when present) **smooth gray. Dark morph all dark except for white on primaries.** JUV/IMM: Tail feathers, no matter how short, are pointed. Imm. plumage kept 3–4 years.

Feeding: Breeding birds eat small mammals, birds, insects, berries; winter birds steal fish from other birds, scavenge, and prey on other birds, such as terns.

Nesting: Nest a shallow scrape lined with sparse vegetation. Eggs: 1–3, brown or greenish with darker marks; I: 25–28 days; F: 25–30 days, precocial; B: 1.

Other Behavior: May nest in loose colonies or alone. Most frequently seen jaeger from shore in West.

Habitat: Summers on tundra; winters at sea.

Voice: Generally quiet off breeding ground, but may make sounds at sea.

Conservation:
CBC: ↑

Long-tailed Jaeger

Stercorarius longicaudus

Light-morph adult

Identification: 22" Light morph most common; dark morph extremely rare. Smallest of the N. American jaegers (although tail feathers make it long overall). **IN FLIGHT: Slim-bodied; wings narrow at base; wingbeats graceful, buoyant, ternlike. Very long central tail feathers pointed** (can be missing or broken); no white at base of primaries on underwing. **Light morph white on chest with no chestband; gray back and wings, with primaries and trailing edge darker** **JUV/IMM:** Central tail feathers, no matter how short, rounded at tip. Imm. plumage kept 3–4 years.

Feeding: Eats mice and lemmings, also insects, fish, and eggs and chicks of other birds.

Nesting: Nests singly or in loose colonies. Nest a shallow depression in ground lined with some vegetation. Eggs: 1–2, brown or greenish with darker marks; I: 23 days; F: 21 days, precocial; B: 1.

Other Behavior: During migration, seen farther offshore than other jaegers; may pursue Arctic Terns.

Habitat: Summers on tundra; winters at sea.

Voice: Generally quiet off breeding ground.

Conservation: TREND UNKNOWN.

Gulls are generally seen along the coasts and near other water, such as large rivers and lakes. There are two aspects to learning gulls: identifying adults and identifying immatures.

Identifying Adult Gulls

You can recognize a gull as an adult by its lack of brown plumage and its whitish tail with no dark bars; immature gulls usually have some dark areas on their tail and usually some brown in their body and/or wing plumage (especially in earlier years). Adult gulls have both a summer and a winter plumage. Gulls whose heads are white in summer usually have just a little brown streaking on their heads in winter; gulls whose heads are black in summer change to having a partial grayish hood or a dark spot behind the eye in winter.

Start learning to identify adult gulls by looking for the most common species. The Learning Pages show these species in both summer and winter plumage. For complete information, see their individual accounts. To identify gulls, look at overall size; whether the head is white or patterned; color and shape of the bill, and the marks on it, if any; the color of the back and wings; and the patterns on the outer wings when in flight.

Identifying Immature Gulls

Immature gulls can be more difficult to identify, for several reasons. One is that gulls take from 2 to 4 years to reach adult plumage and, in each of those years, they generally have a winter and a summer plumage. Thus, after its initial juvenal plumage, a 2-year gull can have up to 4 additional plumages (1st winter, 1st summer, adult winter, adult summer); a 4-year gull has up to 8 different plumages in addition to its juvenal plumage. (If 1st summer and 1st winter plumages are essentially the same, they are jointly called 1st-year plumage.) There is not room to cover all of these immature plumages in a field guide.

In this guide, we describe adult and 1st-year plumages in detail. There are two reasons for this: there are more 1st-year gulls than any other age class of immatures, due to mortality of immatures in later years; and 1st-year plumages are better defined than those of later years, when individual variations in coloration and timing of molt begin to occur.

Some Tips on Adult Eastern Gull Identification

- **One species has a black back and black wings:**
  Great Black-backed Gull, p. 203
- **Two species have pale backs and wings and no black on wing tips (referred to as white-winged gulls):**
  Glaucous Gull, p. 202
  Iceland Gull, p. 200
- **Most other gulls have gray backs and gray wings with black wing tips.**
- **The largest gulls are 4-year gulls; medium-sized gulls are 3-year gulls; and small gulls are 2-year gulls.**
- **One gull has a black ring on its bill:**
  Ring-billed Gull, p. 198
- **Only one gull has a red bill in winter:**
  Black-headed Gull, p. 196
- **One gull lives mostly at sea and is only occasionally seen from land:**
  Black-legged Kittiwake, p. 204

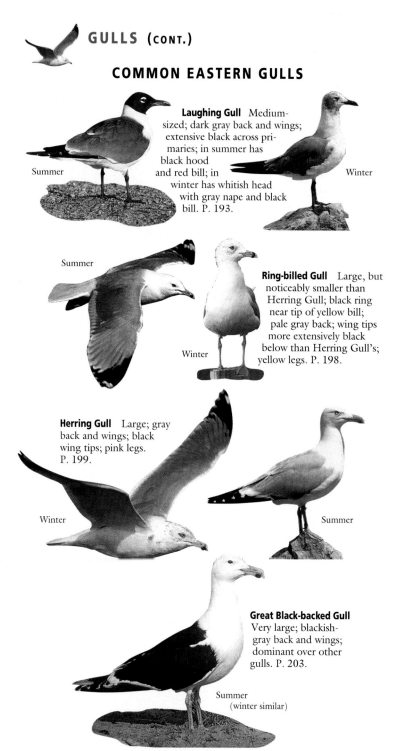

COMMON EASTERN GULLS

Laughing Gull Medium-sized; dark gray back and wings; extensive black across primaries; in summer has black hood and red bill; in winter has whitish head with gray nape and black bill. P. 193.

Summer

Winter

Summer

Ring-billed Gull Large, but noticeably smaller than Herring Gull; black ring near tip of yellow bill; pale gray back; wing tips more extensively black below than Herring Gull's; yellow legs. P. 198.

Winter

Herring Gull Large; gray back and wings; black wing tips; pink legs. P. 199.

Winter

Summer

Great Black-backed Gull Very large; blackish-gray back and wings; dominant over other gulls. P. 203.

Summer
(winter similar)

192

Laughing Gull
Larus atricilla

Summer

Immature, 1st winter

Winter

Immature, 1st winter

Identification: 17" SUMMER: Black hood; dark red, large, slightly downcurved bill; all-white tail. White crescents above and below eye thin and usually do not meet behind eye (true for all ages). WINTER: Like summer, but **head whitish with gray wash on nape; bill black; wings tipped with white.** IN FLIGHT: **Wings narrow, pointed, and dark gray; extensive black across primaries** (seen from above and below). IMM—1ST YEAR: Black bill; faint gray-brown half-hood; gray back; breast gray (rather than white as on imm. Franklin's Gull). IN FLIGHT: Brown wings with extensive black on tips and just inside trailing edge; wide black band completely crosses tip of white tail. Three-year gull.

Feeding: Eats fish, crabs, shrimp, aerial insects, garbage.

Nesting: Nests colonially. Nest of grasses and sedges, placed on ground. Eggs: 3–4, brownish with dark marks; I: 19–22 days; F: 35–40 days, precocial; B: 1.

Other Behavior: Only breeding gull in the Southeast.

Habitat: Coastal; may wander slightly inland.

Voice: Typical call sounds like high-pitched laugh — "ha ha ha ha."

Conservation: BBS: E ⇑ C ⇑ CBC: ⇑ Declines in 1940s from larger gulls displacing them on breeding grounds. Populations increasing in last 25 years.

Franklin's Gull

Larus pipixcan

Summer

Immature, 1st winter

Winter

Immature, 1st summer

Identification: 14" **SUMMER: Black hood; dark red, short, straight bill. White crescents above and below eye are thick** and usually meet behind eye (true for all ages). **WINTER: Like summer, but head whitish with dark half-hood; bill black. IN FLIGHT: Dark gray upperwings separated from rounded black wing tip by white band; underwings white except at tip; tail with grayish center. IMM—1ST WINTER:** Black bill; dark half-hood; gray back; white breast. Eye crescents as in adult. **IN FLIGHT:** Brown wings with black tips; narrow black tail band does not cross outer feathers. **1ST SUMMER:** Wings now gray with black tips; tail with faint band or none. Three-year gull.

Feeding: Eats aerial insects, worms in agricultural fields.

Nesting: Colonial. Nest of grasses on ground or floated in shallow water. Eggs: 2–3, greenish brown with marks; I: 18–20 days; F: 35–40 days, precocial; B: 1.

Other Behavior: A gull of the prairies during breeding.

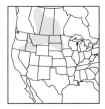

Habitat: Summers on northern prairie lakes; mostly coastal in winter.

Voice: Common call a "weea weea weea."

Conservation: CBC: ↑

Little Gull

Larus minutus

Summer

Immature, 1st winter

Summer

Immature, 1st winter

Identification: 11" SUMMER: **Smallest of all gulls. Black hood;** thin black bill. WINTER: Like summer, but black hood is replaced by **gray cap** and **black ear patch.** IN FLIGHT: **Upperwing light gray; underwing entirely dark gray to black, with conspicuous white trailing edge; rounded white-fringed wing tip.** IMM—1ST WINTER: Gray cap; black ear patch; thin black bill. 1ST SUMMER: Tail and upperwing patterns faded; incomplete black hood. IN FLIGHT: Upperwing shows **dark M pattern;** thin black band across tip of tail. Two- to three-year gull.

Feeding: Feeds like terns, flying down to the water surface to pick up small fish. Also eats aerial insects.

Nesting: Colonial. Nest of grasses and reeds, placed on the ground, often at water's edge. Eggs: 2–3, brownish with darker marks; I: 23–25 days; F: 21–24 days, precocial; B: 1.

Other Behavior: Often found in flocks with Bonaparte's Gulls. When with other gulls, they are easy to recognize because of their small size and rounded wings.

Habitat: Coastal, the Great Lakes, inland lakes and reservoirs.

Voice: Call a "ca ca ca."

Conservation: CBC: ↑ Formerly limited to Europe and Asia, now has bred in N. Am. since 1962. Seen regularly in Great Lakes and along Northeast Coast.

Black-headed Gull

Larus ridibundus

Summer

Winter

Immature, 1st winter

Identification: 15" **Summer: Dark brown hood** (can appear black in spring); **red legs and bill;** thin white eye crescents. **Winter:** Same **red legs and bill** of summer, but **head white with black ear patch. In Flight:** In all plumages, **outer wing dusky below, with bright white leading edge above and below. Imm—1st Winter:** Black ear patch; pale bill with black tip; dark shoulder bar. **1st Summer:** Incomplete brown hood. Two-year gull

Feeding: Feeds in many ways: walking on ground to get insects, earthworms, trash; flying over water or land and dipping down to get insects and fish; feeding on the surface of the water while swimming.

Nesting: Colonial or solitary nester. Nest a scrape in ground lined with grasses, or a mound of vegetation on the ground. Eggs: 2–3, grayish green with darker marks; I: 23–26 days; F: 35 days, precocial; B: 1.

Other Behavior: First seen in N. America at Newburyport, Mass., in 1930. Individuals often return to the same wintering spot each year. Often found among flocks of Bonaparte's Gulls.

Habitat: Coastal.

Voice: High-pitched "craah."

Conservation: ICN: ↑ CBC: ↓ Range expanding westward since 1900. Now breeds on islands off Nova Scotia and on Newfoundland; increasingly seen along N.E. Coast; has been recorded in almost every state.

Bonaparte's Gull
Larus philadelphia

Summer

Immature, 1st winter

Winter

Immature, 1st winter

Identification: 13" SUMMER: **Black hood; orange-red legs; thin white eye crescents; black bill.** WINTER: Like summer, but with **black ear patch and pinkish-red legs.** IN FLIGHT: **Outer wing has white wedge on leading edge and narrow black trailing edge. Buoyant, ternlike flight.** IMM—1ST WINTER: Black ear patch; bill black, sometimes reddish at base. 1ST SUMMER: Similar to 1st winter, but with incomplete black hood. IN FLIGHT: From below, as in adult. From above, dark shoulder bar and dark trailing edge on inner wing. Two-year gull.

Feeding: Feeds on fish, dipping to water's surface in flight; eats worms and aerial and ground insects when inland.

Nesting: Nest of sticks and twigs lined with grass and moss, placed on horizontal branch of spruce or fir tree 5–20 ft. high. Eggs: 3, olive-brown with darker marks; I: 24 days; F: about 30 days, precocial; B: 1.

Other Behavior: After breeding, large flocks gather on large lakes and saltwater bays. Often feeds with terns.

Habitat: Summers in northern coniferous forests; winters on coasts and inland waterways.

Voice: Common call is a repeated nasal "cherr."

Conservation: BBS: E ⇑ C CBC: ⇑

Ring-billed Gull
Larus delawarensis

Summer

Immature, 1st year

Winter

Immature, 1st year

Identification: 19" SUMMER: **Pale gray mantle; dark ring just before tip of thin yellow bill; yellow legs;** yellow eye. WINTER: Like summer, but **light brown spotting on crown and nape.** IN FLIGHT: **Light gray back and wings; black wing tips have small white dots and are more extensively black below than Herring Gull's.** IMM—1ST YEAR: Pale dark-tipped bill; gray back; brown wings; light brown mottling on breast and belly; pink legs. IN FLIGHT: Clearly defined tail band contrasts with white tail base. Three-year gull.

Feeding: Gulls outside a fast-food restaurant are almost always Ring-billed Gulls; they seem to have found a niche. They also eat worms from plowed fields, eggs from nesting seabirds, and flying dispersing ants.

Nesting: Usually colonial nester. Nest of grasses, pebbles, sticks, placed on ground. Eggs: 3, light brown with dark marks; I: 21 days; F: ?, precocial; B: 1.

Other Behavior: Coming into conflict with humans, especially near airports, where they can get in the way of planes.

Habitat: Coasts, lakes, dumps, fields, fast-food locations.

Voice: "Hyah hyah" and other calls.

Conservation: BBS: E ⇑ C ⇑ CBC: ⇑ Since 1970, populations have increased around Great Lakes and in urban areas.

Herring Gull

Larus argentatus

Summer

Immature, 1st year

Winter

Immature, 1st year

Identification: 25" SUMMER: **Pale gray back; pinkish legs; yellow bill with red spot near tip of lower mandible; yellow eye.** WINTER: Like summer, but with **brown-streaked head and neck.** IN FLIGHT: Wing tips less extensively black than in Ring-billed and California Gulls and with small white dots. IMM—1ST YEAR: Uniformly mottled brown head and body; bill black with pale base (at first just lower mandible). IN FLIGHT: Wide all-dark tail; brown rump; black wing tips and prominent pale windows on inner primaries. Four-year gull.

Feeding: Eats mussels, clams, fish, garbage, rodents, insects, young of other gulls; steals from other birds.

Nesting: Nests colonially. Nest a scrape in ground lined with grasses and seaweed. Eggs: 3, brownish with dark marks; I: 26 days; F: about 35 days, precocial; B: 1.

Other Behavior: During long-call, head is dipped down and then raised up; an aggressive display. During choking-call, body is tipped forward and bird may scrape feet backward; a courtship or territorial display.

Habitat: Coasts, dumps, lakes, rivers, fields.

Voice: Long-call is like "ow ow ow keekeekee kyow kyow kyow"; choking-call is like "huoh huoh huoh"; alarm call is "ga ga ga ga."

Conservation: BBS: E ⇓ C ⇑ CBC: ↑

Iceland Gull

Larus glaucoides kumlieni

Winter

Immature, 1st year

Immature, 1st year

Identification: 25" SUMMER: **Pale overall; dark pink legs; red spot near tip of lower mandible; bill smaller, shorter, and more pigeonlike than in Glaucous Gull; yellow eye.** WINTER: Like summer, but with **light brown spotting on head and shoulders.** IN FLIGHT: From below, **wing all light except for gray dots on trailing edge of white tip;** from above, **wings pale gray with 2 thin frosty gray to gray-brown (never black) stripes along tip.** IMM 1ST YEAR: Uniformly pale brown body (can appear almost white); bill usually all black. IN FLIGHT: Tail grayish or buff, sometimes with diffuse band at tip; wing tips lighter than rest of wings. Four-year gull.

Feeding: Eats mostly fish caught by fluttering over the surface of the water or by making shallow dives. Also feeds on land, eating carrion and eggs of other birds.

Nesting: Colonial. Nest of grass, seaweed, and moss, placed on the ground. Eggs: 2–3, reddish brown with darker marks; I: ?; F: ?, precocial; B: 1.

Other Behavior: Sometimes feeds near seals.

Habitat: Coastal, sometimes wintering on Great Lakes.

Voice: Generally quiet in winter, when it is most often seen.

Conservation:
CBC: ⇑

Lesser Black-backed Gull

Larus fuscus

Summer

Immature, 1st year

Winter

Immature, 1st year

Identification: 22" SUMMER: **Dark gray back with black wing tips; yellowish legs; yellow eye.** WINTER: Like summer, but with **substantial gray streaking on head.** IN FLIGHT: **Upperwings dark gray with darker black wing tips; 1–2 white dots in wing tip.** IMM—1ST YEAR: Body gray-brown (darker than Herring Gull's); blackish blotches on sides of breast and flanks; paler belly and head; bill black. IN FLIGHT: From above, 2 dark bands on trailing edge of inner wing; clearly defined black band on tail. From below, no wing windows as in Herring Gull. Four-year gull.

Feeding: Eats fish, insects, small mammals, refuse, and food stolen from other birds, especially Herring Gulls.

Nesting: Colonial nester. Nest a substantial mound of seaweed, grasses, and other debris, placed on the ground. Eggs: 3, olive with little or no marking; I: 24–27 days; F: 30–40 days, precocial; B: 1.

Other Behavior: Most sightings are during winter, but increasingly, they can be seen in any season.

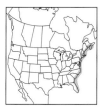

Habitat: Coastal.

Voice: Lower-pitched versions of Herring Gull calls.

Conservation: CBC: ↑ Populations increasing in Europe, where it breeds, which may be why we see more of this species along East Coast in winter. May now be breeding in N. America.

201

Glaucous Gull

Larus hyperboreus

Summer

Immature, 1st year

Winter

Immature, 1st year

Identification: 28" **SUMMER: Large; pale gray back and wings with white wing tips;** heavy relatively long bill; pink legs; yellow eye. **WINTER:** Like summer, but with **pale brown streaking on head and upper breast. IN FLIGHT: Broad pale gray wings with extensive white on wing tips** (no darker gray or black on wings). **IMM—1ST WINTER:** Pale buff to almost all white; bill pinkish with sharply defined dark tip. **1ST SUMMER:** Even paler. Four-year gull.

Feeding: During breeding season, eats lemmings and voles, as well as young and eggs of other seabirds and ducks. Also eats small fish, mollusks, crustaceans, and carrion, and feeds at dumps.

Nesting: Often colonial nester. Nest a mound of seaweed and other vegetation, placed on ground or cliff ledge. Eggs: 2–3, olive with darker marks; I: 27–28 days; F: 45–50 days, precocial; B: 1.

Other Behavior: Glaucous Gulls often rob other birds of food, attacking ducks or other diving birds just as they surface after catching prey. They also eat other adult seabirds.

Habitat: Coasts, large inland lakes, landfills.

Voice: Generally quiet, but has a variety of low hoarse calls.

Conservation: CBC: ⇑

Great Black-backed Gull

Larus marinus

Summer

Immature, 1st year

Summer

Immature, 1st year

Identification: 30" SUMMER: The **largest gull; black back; pink legs.** WINTER: Like summer, and **head remains almost all white. IN FLIGHT: Upperwings blackish gray with black tips; 2 large mirrors in wing tips.** IMM—1ST YEAR: Gray-brown checkered back with a contrasting whitish head and paler underparts; massive bill black with outermost tip light. **IN FLIGHT:** Single dark band of feathers on inner trailing edge of upperwings; tail whitish with blackish terminal band that tapers to each side. Four-year gull.

Feeding: Feeds on a variety of items, but is especially efficient predator on other birds, including shearwaters, puffins, and terns, often grabbing them with its bill in flight and shaking them to break their necks. Also eats small mammals and fish.

Nesting: Often colonial nester. Nest a mound of seaweed and other vegetation, placed on ground or ledge. Eggs: 2–3, olive with darker marks; I: 27–28 days; F: 49–56 days, precocial; B: 1.

Other Behavior: Being large, it dominates other gulls.

Habitat: Coastal and Great Lakes.

Voice: Low-pitched "cowp cowp cowp" and other calls.

Conservation: BBS: E ↓ C CBC: ⇑ Breeding range and populations have expanded down East Coast and into Great Lakes in last 50 years. May be a threat to breeding puffins and terns in Northeast.

Black-legged Kittiwake
Rissa tridactyla

Summer

Immature, 1st year

Winter

Immature, 1st year

Identification: 16" SUMMER: Small, unmarked, **yellow bill; black legs.** WINTER: Like summer, but with **dark gray smudge behind eye; gray nape.** IN FLIGHT: Gray wings with **triangular all-black wing tip.** IMM—1ST WINTER: Black bill; white body with wide black collar and small ear patch; white tail has thin black terminal band. 1ST SUMMER: Bill paler; lighter collar; tail band and M pattern on upperwings faint. IN FLIGHT: Dark lines on upperwings form large M. Two-year gull.

Feeding: Eats primarily fish picked from the surface of the ocean.

Nesting: Colonial nester. Nest of mud, seaweed, and grass, placed on small ledge of cliff or on building. Eggs: 1–3, yellowish with dark marks; I: 25–32 days; F: 33–55 days, precocial; B: 1.

Other Behavior: Gathers into large flocks during migration in spring and fall. Usually feeds in smaller flocks during winter. Flocks follow fishing ships at sea to feed on refuse.

Habitat: Summers on coastal cliffs; winters at sea.

Voice: "Kekekek" and "kittewake."

Conservation: BBS: E ⇑ C CBC: ⇓

Gull-billed Tern
Sterna nilotica

Summer

Summer

Identification: 15" **SUMMER:** Short, stocky, black bill; black legs; black cap and nape. **WINTER:** Like summer, but **head whitish with dark ear patch. IN FLIGHT: Pale gray back and wings; short only slightly forked tail.** Only tips of primaries are dark. **JUV:** Like winter adult, but outer wing darker and bill paler at base.

Feeding: Most often feeds on insects caught in the air or flutters down to pick from surface of water or land. Only rarely dives after fish as other terns do.

Nesting: Nest a shallow depression in sand lined with bits of shells or grass. Eggs: 3, yellowish; I: 22–23 days; F: 28–35 days, precocial; B: 1.

Other Behavior: Often nests singly or in small groups at the edge of colonies of other terns, such as Common Tern, Least Tern, and Black Skimmer.

Habitat: Coastal areas, fields, lakes, marshes.

Voice: "Katydid" or "kaydid."

Conservation:
BBS: E ↑ C ⇑ CBC: ↓ Historically, hurt by egg collectors and plume hunters. Populations seem to be declining in East, stable in Southeast, and may be increasing along Gulf Coast.

205

Caspian Tern

Sterna caspia

Summer

Winter

Winter

Identification: 21" Only large tern regularly seen inland. **SUMMER: Large; crested; black cap; massive blood-red bill** (sometimes slightly darker at tip). **WINTER:** Like summer, but **cap splotchy, gray, and extends over forehead to bill. IN FLIGHT: Broad wings; slow powerful flight;** from below, **extensive dark on wing tip. JUV:** Like winter adult, but bill orange; upperparts lightly marked with dark bars and V's.

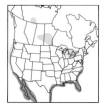

Habitat: Coasts and inland along rivers and lakes.

Feeding: Catches fish by diving completely underwater from air; also may pick fish off the surface of the water.

Voice: A harsh "cahar" and "kwok."

Nesting: Nests singly or in colonies. Nest a depression in ground lined with grasses and seaweed, located on sandy beaches. Eggs: 2–3, pinkish with darker markings; I: 20–22 days; F: 28–35 days, precocial; B: 1.

Conservation: BBS: E ⇑ C ⇑ CBC: ↑

Other Behavior: May steal fish from other seabirds. When fishing, generally flies low over water, but when traveling back to nest, will fly high and even soar in circles to gain altitude.

Royal Tern

Sterna maxima

Summer

Summer

Winter

Identification: 20" Seen only on coast. SUMMER: **Large; all-orange bill; crested black cap.** WINTER: Like summer, but **forehead white; crown pale gray to white; nape black.** IN FLIGHT: From below, note **dark on outermost primary and trailing edge of wing tip.** JUV: Bill yellowish. IN FLIGHT: From above, dark primaries and bold dark bars on inner portion of wings.

Feeding: Dives into water from 40–50 ft. high to catch fish.

Nesting: Colonial nester. Nest a shallow scrape in sand, lined with bits of grass. Eggs: 1–2, buffy with darker dots; I: 20–22 days; F: 28–35 days, precocial; B: 1.

Other Behavior: Often migrates in large flocks with other tern species. Nesting colonies can reach 10,000 birds along Gulf Coast.

Habitat: Coast.

Voice: Calls include a whistled "tooree" and a harsh "keeer."

Conservation: BBS: E ↓ C ⇓ CBC: ↓

Sandwich Tern

Sterna sandvicensis

Summer

Winter

Winter

Identification: 17" **SUMMER:** Black cap; long, thin, black bill with yellow tip; black crest. **WINTER:** Like summer, but **white crown; black patch on nape extends to eye** (winter plumage may appear as early as midsummer). **IN FLIGHT:** Silvery upperwings; outer 4–5 primaries darker than inner ones. **JUV:** Bill is shorter than adult's and all black; head like winter adult's; broad dark tip on tail; outer primaries all dark.

Feeding: Catches small fish by diving from high in air. Often feeds farther out to sea than other terns.

Nesting: Colonial nester. Nest a shallow scrape in the sand. Eggs: 1–2, pinkish; I: 21 days; F: 35 days, precocial; B: 1.

Other Behavior: Associates very closely with Royal Tern on wintering and breeding grounds. Chicks from both species may be found together on breeding grounds. Like Royal Tern, it is frequently transported north by hurricanes.

Habitat: Coastal.

Voice: "Kirrik."

Conservation:
BBS: E ⇑ C CBC: ⇑

Roseate Tern

Sterna dougallii

Summer

Summer

Juvenile/immature

Identification: 15″ SUMMER: **Medium-sized; pale; long, thin, black bill** (has red base only during breeding); **whitish tail extends far beyond tips of folded wings.** Black cap and nape kept well into fall. WINTER: Adult winter plumage generally not seen in U.S. and Can. IN FLIGHT: Note **mostly white trailing edge on underside of wing tip; long forked tail; stiff fluttery wingbeat.** JUV/IMM: Dark head with dusky streaks on white forehead; brownish back; dark shoulder bar; distinctive underwings as in adult; black bill and legs.

Feeding: Catches small fish by diving to water from air.

Nesting: Colonial nester. Nest a scrape in ground, protected by a clump of grass or other vegetation. Eggs: 1–2, olive with darker spots; I: 21–25 days; F: 28 days, precocial; B: 1.

Other Behavior: About 85% of all northeastern Roseate Terns breed on just 2 coastal islands. This makes the population very vulnerable. They often nest with Common Terns and are readily displaced by larger gulls.

Habitat: Coast and coastal islands.

Voice: One distinctive call is a soft "chevik."

Conservation: ICN:→ Endangered in Can. and U.S., except Fla. Larger gulls prey on eggs and chicks. In past, hurt by plume trade and nesting habitat loss.

Common Tern
Sterna hirundo

Summer

Juvenile

Summer

Immature

Identification: 15" SUMMER: Medium-sized; pale gray underparts contrast with white undertail coverts; orange-red bill, usually black-tipped; white black-edged tail; tips of folded wings project just past tail. Black cap kept well into fall; molt occurs mostly after migration. WINTER: Like summer but **forecrown white; nape and bill black; underparts white; dark shoulder bar.** IN FLIGHT: Below, **gray body; fairly wide black trailing edge on wing tip.** Above, **outer primaries darker than rest of wing.** Dark shoulder bar in winter. JUV/IMM: Forehead light brown wearing to white; dark nape; dark shoulder bar; back brownish wearing to gray; underwings as in adult; bill red-based at first, then mostly black; legs red.

Feeding: Feeds on small fish by diving into water.

Nesting: Colonial. Nest scrape in ground. Eggs: 3, buffy with spots; I: 21–27 days; F: 28 days, precocial; B: 1.

Other Behavior: Courting male flies with fish in beak.

Habitat: Lakes, coast.

Voice: Short "kip" and harsh "keear."

Conservation: BBS: E ⇓ C ⇑ CBC: ↓ Populations have decreased almost 75% since 1920s due to breeding habitat loss, competition with gulls for nesting sites, and predation by gulls and Great Horned Owls.

Arctic Tern

Sterna paradisaea

Summer

Summer

Summer

Juvenile/immature

Identification: 16″ **SUMMER:** Medium-sized; short all-red bill; white black-edged tail extends well beyond tip of folded wing; black cap and nape; **very short legs. WINTER:** Adult winter plumage not seen in U.S. and Canada. **IN FLIGHT:** From below, note **distinctive very narrow black trailing edge on wing tip; long forked tail; pale gray underparts. JUV/IMM:** Light forehead; dark nape; faint shoulder bar; distinctive underwings as in adult; black bill; reddish legs; white trailing edge of inner wing.

Feeding: Often hovers over water, then dives to pick fish off the surface; seldom plunge-dives as many other terns do.

Nesting: Colonial. Nest a scrape in ground, sometimes lined with grass bits, located on a beach or ledge. Eggs: 2–3, olive with darker marks; I: 23–27 days; F: 28 days, precocial; B: 1.

Other Behavior: A long-distance migrant, spending the breeding season in the Arctic and wintering as far south as Antarctica — a round trip of about 22,000 miles.

Habitat: Summers on lakes, rivers, coast; winters at sea.

Voice: A harsh "kee-yeer."

Conservation: ICN: ↑ Population drastically reduced by plume trade in late 1800s. With protection, it is slowly recovering.

Forster's Tern
Sterna forsteri

Summer

Winter

Summer

Juvenile/immature

Identification: 15″ SUMMER: Medium-sized; orange-red bill with black tip; underparts white; gray white-edged tail extends well beyond tips of folded wings; black cap and nape. Molts in August into winter plumage. WINTER: Like summer, but with **black patch from eye to ear; white forehead; pale to dark gray nape; no dark shoulder bar; black bill. IN FLIGHT: Below, white belly; fairly wide dark gray trailing edge on wing tip. Above, primaries and secondaries silvery white; in early summer, tips of primaries darken. In winter, wings all pale with no shoulder bar.** JUV/IMM: Black patch from eye to ear. Crown and back light brown wearing to white and gray; above, wings dusky with no obvious shoulder bar.

Feeding: Eats aerial insects; plunge-dives for fish.

Nesting: Colonial. Nest a scrape in ground. Eggs: 3–4, olive with marks; I: 22–23 days; F: ?, precocial; B: 1.

Other Behavior: Winters in U.S.

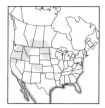

Habitat: Lakes, marshes, coast.

Voice: A short "keer" and "zreep" and "kip."

Conservation: BBS: E ⇑ C ⇑ CBC: ⇑ Breeding grounds very susceptible to human disturbance. Has recently expanded range north along Atlantic Coast.

Least Tern

Sterna antillarum

Summer

Summer

Summer

Identification: 9" SUMMER: **Very small; black cap; white forehead; yellow bill** with tiny black tip. WINTER: Like summer, but more **extended white on forehead; bill black. IN FLIGHT: Narrow wings; rapid wingbeats;** distinctive **black leading edge of outer wing;** short shallow-forked tail. FALL JUV: Whitish crown and forehead; black line through eye and often around nape; black bill; dark V's on feathers of upperparts. IN FLIGHT: Wings show dark leading edge and dark tips.

Feeding: Catches small fish by plunge diving into water or skimming over the surface.

Nesting: Colonial or solitary. Nest a shallow scrape in the sand. Eggs: 2, olive with darker marks; I: 20–22 days; F: 28 days, precocial; B: 1.

Other Behavior: As with all tern nesting colonies, it is best not to disturb them. When the adults fly up in alarm, it is a chance for gulls and other birds to fly in and eat eggs and young. May nest on gravel roofs of large buildings in Fla. in response to beach disturbance.

Habitat: Coast and along major rivers.

Voice: A repeated "kip kip kip" and a harsh "zreeet."

Conservation: BBS: E ⇓ C ⇓ CBC: ↓ In late 1800s, plume trade killed up to 100,000 birds each year. West Coast subspecies *C. a. "browni"* and interior pop. endangered in U.S.

213

Black Tern

Chlidonias niger

Summer

Summer

Winter

Identification: 10″ SUMMER: Small; head and body are black. IN FLIGHT: Wings and tail uniformly dark gray. WINTER: White underparts; dark gray upperparts; partial blackish cap; black patches (or "half collar") on either side of breast. IN FLIGHT: Dark gray above, white below. FALL JUV: Similar to winter adult, but with a grayish cap and a brownish back.

Feeding: Eats insects from air and by fluttering down to pick them off vegetation. Often feeds over meadows and agricultural lands. Feeds on fish when along coast and out at sea.

Nesting: Colonial. Nest a loose construction of reeds, placed at water's edge or floating on surface. Eggs: 3, olive with dark marks; I: 21–22 days; F: 21–28 days, precocial; B: 1.

Other Behavior: Birds nest in vegetation of marshes and become very excited if you approach the nest. Seeing their fluttering over the area and hearing their "kreeek" calls should warn you to back up and cause no further disturbance to the nest. See Conservation.

Habitat: Summers on wet meadows, marshes, ponds; winters on coast and at sea.

Voice: Short "krik" or longer "kreeek."

Conservation: BBS: E ⇓ C ⇓ CBC: ↓ Population declining, possibly due to loss of freshwater marsh nesting sites, pesticide use, and disturbance by humans.

Black Skimmer

Rynchops niger

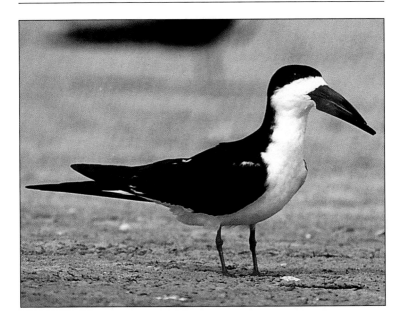

Identification: 18" Strikingly **black above and white below; large, red, black-tipped bill** with lower portion longer. In winter, plumage duller with faint white collar. IMM: Similar to adult, but upperparts mottled brown.

Feeding: Unique and entertaining feeding method of rapidly flying over water and skimming the surface with its longer lower mandible until it hits a fish, and then snapping it up.

Nesting: Colonial. Nest a hollow in the sand. Eggs: 4–5, whitish with dark marks; I: 21–23; F: 23–25, precocial; B: 1.

Other Behavior: When the bird is skimming over water, note that it must fly with its wings held high in order to stay clear of the water; at other times, flies with deeper wingbeats. Often nests in colonies with terns. Occasionally roosts on gravel roofs in Fla.

Habitat: Coast.

Voice: Variety of short low-pitched calls.

Conservation: BBS: E ⇓ C ⇓ CBC: ⇓

Dovekie
Alle alle

Winter

Summer

Identification: 8″ **SUMMER: Very small; black head and back; white belly;** short stocky bill. When flying, wings move so fast, they are a blur. **WINTER:** Similar to summer, but **chin and throat white.**

Feeding: Dives underwater from surface and uses its wings to swim; feeds on crustaceans and plankton.

Nesting: Colonial. Nest a rock crevice lined with small pebbles. Eggs: 1, bluish white; I: 24 days; F: 28 days, precocial; B: 1.

Other Behavior: Seen mostly off the coast in winter, after leaving its breeding grounds in the far north. During dives, can stay underwater up to 1 minute; usually underwater for only 30 seconds. Occasionally blown onto shore or inland by gales in late fall. May be the most abundant of all Alcids (murres, murrelets, auklets, puffins). Some are mistakenly caught in fishing nets.

Habitat: Summers along coastal cliffs; winters at sea.

Voice. Most vocal on breeding grounds; gives a variety of chattering calls.

Conservation: CBC: ⇑

Common Murre
Thick-billed Murre
Uria aalge   Uria lomvia

Summer Common

Winter Common

Summer Thick-billed

Winter Thick-billed

Identification: Common 17", Thick-billed 18" SUMMER: Both species have **dark head, neck, and upperparts; white underparts; long black bill.** COMMON: Slender, pointed, all-black bill; line between white and black on throat smoothly rounded; brownish cast to head and back. THICK-BILLED: White line along gape of thick relatively short bill; line between white and black on throat comes to a point; head and back black. WINTER—COMMON: Cheek and throat white; dark streak through cheek. THICK-BILLED: Cheek and throat white.

Feeding: Feed on fish by diving underwater from the surface. Usually dive 10–25 ft. down, but have been caught in crab traps at 300 ft.

Nesting: Colonial nesters. For both species, no nest built except for a few pebbles brought to the nest site; eggs laid directly on ledge of cliff. Eggs: 1, blue-green with darker marks; I: 32–33 days; F: 21 days, precocial; B: 1.

Other Behavior: Young leave nest before they can fully fly, gliding down from nesting cliffs to the sea.

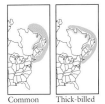
Common   Thick-billed

Habitat: Summer on coastal cliffs; winter at sea.

Voice: Make sounds like their name, like "murrr"; also low growling sounds.

Conservation:
Common:
CBC: ⇓
Thick-billed:
CBC: ⇑
Both species susceptible to gill nets and oil spills.

217

Razorbill

Alca torda

Winter

Summer

Identification: 17″ **SUMMER:** Thick-necked; large vertically compressed bill; white bar across tip of bill, and white line from top of bill to eye; pointed tail often cocked. **WINTER:** Similar, but with **white throat; no white line from bill to eye.** **IMM:** Similar to winter adult, but lacks white lines on smaller bill. Imm. plumage kept 1 year.

Feeding: Catches mostly fish by diving underwater from the surface and pursuing them. Can carry up to 9 fish at a time in its bill. Generally dives only a few ft. in shallow water to feed on bottom, but can dive to over 300 ft. and stay underwater for almost a minute.

Nesting: Colonial nester. Nest a few stems and twigs or none, placed on a ledge, between boulders, or in a burrow. Eggs: 1, bluish green; I: 34–39 days; F: 12–24 days, precocial; B: 1.

Other Behavior: Chicks leave nest at night and glide or climb down to water. Adults and chicks get together on water by recognizing each other's calls. Sometimes blown toward shore by autumn gales.

Habitat: Summers along coastal cliffs; winters at sea.

Voice: Variety of low croaking sounds.

Conservation: CBC: ⇓

Black Guillemot

Cepphus grylle

Summer

Winter

Identification: 13" SUMMER: **All black with
conspicuous white patches on wings. WINTER:
White below; barred black and white above;
white patch on black wing still conspicuous. IN
FLIGHT:** White patches on upperwing and white
lining to underwing. **IMM:** Similar to winter adult,
but white wing patch flecked with brown.

Feeding: Eats mostly fish and some crustaceans. Feeds in
shallow water during breeding, and deeper water during
winter. Can dive as much as 150 ft. deep and stay
underwater almost 2 minutes.

Nesting: Nest a shallow scrape in ground, placed in
protected place, such as under boulder, among
driftwood, or in natural sand burrow. Eggs: 1–2,
whitish with dark marks; I: 28–31 days; F: about 40
days, precocial; B: 1.

Other Behavior: Since these birds do not migrate long
distances, they are regularly seen near breeding areas in
winter. They prefer to stay near the coast, rather than at
sea, throughout the year.

Habitat: Coastal.

Voice: High-
pitched squeals.

Conservation:
BBS: E ⇑ C CBC: ↑

Atlantic Puffin

Fratercula arctica

Summer

Identification: 13" **SUMMER: Only puffin in East; distinctive, large, colorful bill;** white face; black collar; white belly. **WINTER:** Like summer, but **face grayish; bill duller. IMM:** Similar to winter adult, but bill smaller, more pointed, and gray with dark reddish tip. Imm. plumage kept up to 5 years.

Feeding: Eats mostly small fish, also crustaceans and squid.

Nesting: Nest a burrow dug by the birds, usually under boulders. Eggs: 1, whitish with faint marks; I: 35–45 days; F: 43–55 days, precocial; B: 1.

Other Behavior: Parents feed young small fish, which they carry crosswise in their bill. They are able to catch new fish while not letting the previously caught fish escape. Usually carry 5–12 prey items per trip, but have been seen to carry 60 prey items in a single load. This species has been successfully reintroduced on some islands off Maine coast.

Habitat: Coastal islands and out at sea.

Voice: Short harsh call like "urrr"; also longer calls.

Conservation: CBC: ⇓

Rock Dove (Pigeon)
Columba livia

Typical version

Variations

Identification: 13″ The familiar Pigeon. Due to breeding by humans, colors can range from all white to all black, with just about anything in between. Most often **dark gray head; iridescent neck; light gray back; 2 dark wing bars. IN FLIGHT: Note squared tail with dark band at tip; white rump.**

Feeding: Feeds on the ground, eating grain, seeds, crumbs, and other garbage in cities. At bird feeders, eats scattered seed and cracked corn.

Nesting: Saucerlike nest of roots, stems, and leaves, placed on building ledge, rafters, beams under bridge, or inside barn. Eggs: 1–2, white; I: 18 days; F: 25–29 days, altricial; B: 2–5.

Other Behavior: Pigeons have many courtship displays. Breeding birds do wing-clapping flight, in which they clap wings as they take flight, then glide with wings held in a V. In bowing display, male spreads tail and fluffs neck feathers while bowing and circling in front of female; between bows, male runs for short distance, dragging tail on ground. First introduced into N. America in 1606. Now widespread.

Habitat: Cities, parks, bridges, steep cliffs.

Voice: At nest site, call by male or female is "k't'coo"; during courtship display male gives "oorook'tookoo." Wing-clapping sound made during display flights.

Conservation: BBS: E ↑ C ↓

221

Eurasian Collared-Dove

Streptopelia decaocto

Identification: 12" Large; pale; black collar on nape. IN FLIGHT: Pale above and below; squared-off tail has white on corners.

Feeding: Feeds on seeds, grain, or crumbs picked up from the ground; also eats berries.

Nesting: Flat nest of twigs and stems, placed in tree or bush or on building ledge. Eggs: 2, white; I: 14–16 days; F: 15–18 days, altricial; B: 2–5.

Other Behavior: Originally from Eurasia. Was introduced into the Bahamas and has spread to Florida with recent reports from Georgia, Louisiana, and Arkansas. Further range expansion expected. In display flight, bird flies up with clapping wings, then glides.

Habitat: Open country with trees and scrub, usually near cultivated areas; also towns.

Voice: Soft "coo, coo, coo-oo."

Conservation: Population increasing.

White-winged Dove

Zenaida asiatica

Identification: 11" Light gray-brown; heavyset; **conspicuous white line along edge of closed wing;** small black dash below cheek; red eye surrounded by blue skin. **IN FLIGHT: Conspicuous white patches across center of wings;** tail rounded with white on either side.

Feeding: Feeds on ground or by clinging to plants from which it is eating. Eats weed, flower, and other plant seeds, acorns, cactus fruit, and waste grain such as sorghum. May come to seed on ground under feeders.

Nesting: Sometimes colonial. Saucerlike nest of sticks, twigs, grass, weed stems, placed at fork of horizontal branch or on top of deserted nest in tree 4–25 ft. high. Eggs: 1–4, creamy white; I: 13–14 days; F: 13–16 days, altricial; B: 2–3.

Other Behavior: Often roosts and nests colonially, especially in mesquite thickets. Flies singly, in pairs, or in small groups, and congregates in large numbers at good feeding areas. When nest-calling near female, male spreads tail and wings. Nesting habitat destroyed in S. Tex. in early 1900s. Now expanding northward in suburban areas.

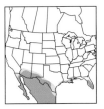

Habitat: Throughout dry areas of Southwest, including suburbs.

Voice: A distinctive "who cooks for you?" Much like a softer version of the Barred Owl's.

Conservation: BBS: E ⇑ C ↑ CBC: ⇑

223

Mourning Dove

Zenaida macroura

Male

Identification: 12" Sleek; gray-brown; **long pointed tail; black dots on wings.** Male has light gray crown and iridescent sides of neck; female is evenly brown on head and neck. **IN FLIGHT: Long pointed tail; shorter outer tail feathers broadly tipped with white.**

Feeding: Common at bird feeders, where it feeds on scattered seed, or takes seed from trays or hoppers. Eats weed, grass, and grain seeds, and some insects.

Nesting: Loose, flat nest of twigs, grass, weeds, and pine needles, placed in a vertical fork or horizontal branch of a tree 3–30 ft. high or, rarely, on the ground. Eggs: 2, white; I: 14–15 days; F: 12–14 days, altricial; B: 2–3.

Other Behavior: Unmated males do aerial display in which they clap wings as they rise up, then descend in long spiral glide with wings held slightly lower than body. From perches, courting male does conspicuous cooing in which he puffs out his throat and bobs tail. When cooing on ground in front of female, male repeatedly bows head and gives long coo.

Habitat: Can be found in almost any open habitat, including suburban areas.

Voice: Unmated males give a commonly heard "ooahoo oo oo oo." Breeding males and females can give a short "ooahoo" near the nest.

Conservation: BBS: E ↑ C ↓ CBC: ⇑

Inca Dove

Columbina inca

Identification: 8" Small; dark-tipped feathers create **scalloped effect all over body; tail almost as long as rest of body. IN FLIGHT:** Reddish-brown wing tips; long tail with white along sides and corners.

Feeding: Feeds on the ground, eating weed seeds and grain. Sometimes feeds alongside poultry. May come to bird feeders and eat seed scattered on ground.

Nesting: Saucerlike nest of twigs, sticks, grass, leaves, and rootlets lined with grass, placed on horizontal limb of bush or tree, or sometimes in hanging planter. May reuse nest of other bird such as Mourning Dove. Eggs: 2, white; I: 14 days; F: 14–16 days, altricial; B: 2–5.

Other Behavior: Does bowing display with tail held vertical and fanned, showing markings. In summer, nonbreeding adults and immatures form loose flocks, which may congregate in large numbers in good feeding areas. Roost communally in flocks with birds perched close together, sometimes even roosting on top of other flock members.

Habitat: Cactus and mesquite country; suburbs, parks, and gardens.

Voice: A continually repeated "werl-pool."

Conservation: BBS: E C ↑ CBC: ↑ Range expanding eastward along Gulf of Mexico.

225

Common Ground-Dove
Columbina passerina

Male

Identification: 7″ Very small; gray; scalloped effect on head and breast only; black-tipped reddish bill; short tail often raised. MALE: Pinkish gray. FEMALE: Gray. IN FLIGHT: Reddish-brown wing tips; short dark tail with white spots at the corners.

Feeding: Feeds on the ground, eating weed, grass, and waste grain seeds, crumbs, insects, and small berries. May come to seed on ground under feeders.

Nesting: Saucerlike nest of sticks, rootlets, and grass, placed on the ground, on the beach, in woods, in cultivated field, or occasionally in low bush. Eggs: 2–3, white; I: 12–14 days; F: 11 days, altricial; B: 2–4.

Other Behavior: Male bows with lowered head when cooing at female. Spends most of the time on the ground, usually in pairs or small groups. Unafraid of humans.

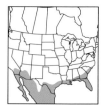

Habitat: Open areas at the edge of vegetation, including suburbs.

Voice: An ascending "coo ah, coo ah."

Conservation:
BBS: E ⇓ C ⇓ CBC: ⇓

White-tipped Dove

Leptotila verreauxi

Identification: 12″ Limited to S. Tex. **Large; stocky; pale forehead; whitish chin;** dark unmarked wings; pale belly. **IN FLIGHT: From above, wings dark; from below, wings have reddish-brown lining; tail squarish and white-tipped at corners.**

Feeding: Feeds on ground or in low branches, eating seeds of grasses, grains, mesquite, prickly pear cactus, and other plants. Also eats crickets.

Nesting: Saucerlike nest of sticks, twigs, grass, and weed stems, placed on the ground or on the fork of a horizontal branch up to 40 ft. high. Eggs: 2–3, creamy white; I: 14 days; F: 15 days, altricial; B: 1 or more.

Other Behavior: Shy and solitary. Forages under dense shrubbery. When flushed, flies off with a clatter of wings.

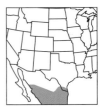

Habitat: On the ground in woodlands with dense underbrush.

Voice: Distinctive, long, low-pitched call is like sound made by blowing across the top of an empty bottle.

Conservation:
BBS: E C ⇧

Black-billed Cuckoo

Coccyzus erythropthalmus

Adult

Immature

Identification: 12" **Black downcurved bill; red eye-ring; long tail** with pairs of narrowly white-tipped feathers progressing down the dark underside of the tail. **IN FLIGHT: Wings and upperparts dark brown; tail feathers narrowly tipped with white.** IMM: Similar to adult, but with buffy eye-ring and less prominent white tips on tail feathers. Imm. plumage kept into winter.

Feeding: Eats insects, especially caterpillars; also spiders, frogs, lizards, small mollusks, fishes, and berries.

Nesting: Platform nest of twigs and grasses, lined with ferns, rootlets, catkins, placed near the trunk of a tree 2–20 ft. high. Eggs: 2–5, bluish green; I: 10–14 days; F: 9–14 days, altricial; B: 1.

Other Behavior: On rare occasions, lays eggs in nests of other birds, such as Yellow-billed Cuckoo, Gray Catbird, Wood Thrush, Yellow Warbler, and Chipping Sparrow. This activity occurs during times of food abundance, such as when there is an outbreak of caterpillars.

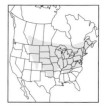

Habitat: Woods edges, thickets, hedgerows.

Voice: A soft repeated "cucucu, cucucucu."

Conservation:
BBS: E ↓ C ↓

Yellow-billed Cuckoo

Coccyzus americanus

Adult

Adult

Identification: 12″ **Downcurved bill black above, yellow below; long tail** with 3 pairs of large white ovals on its dark underside. **In Flight: Wings reddish brown on outer half; tail feathers broadly tipped with white. Imm:** Similar to adult, but with less prominent white ovals on underside of tail; bill may be all dark or partly yellow; similar to imm. Black-billed Cuckoo. Imm. plumage kept into winter.

Feeding: Eats mostly hairy caterpillars, such as tent caterpillars; also eats cicadas, beetles, grasshoppers, crickets, and other insects, berries, frogs, and lizards.

Nesting: Platform nest of twigs, lined with leaves, grasses, mosses, rootlets, placed on the horizontal limb of a tree or bush 3–20 ft. high. Eggs: 1–5, pale bluish green; I: 9–14 days; F: 7–9 days, altricial; B: 1–2.

Other Behavior: Heard more than seen. Quite shy. Stays in dense canopy of trees or tangles of undergrowth. On rare occasions, lays eggs in nest of Black-billed Cuckoo.

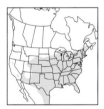

Habitat: Open woods, thickets, riparian habitats.

Voice: Sounds like "kukukukakaka kalp kalp kalp," slowing near the end.

Conservation:
BBS: E ↓ C ↓ CBC: →

Mangrove Cuckoo

Coccyzus minor

Identification: 12″ **Gray head; black ear patch; long downcurved bill black above, yellow below; buffy belly; long tail** with 3 pairs of large white ovals on its dark underside. **In Flight: Buffy belly; no reddish brown on wings. Imm:** Similar to adult, but with less prominent white ovals on tail; dark gray ear patch. Imm. plumage kept into winter.

Feeding: Eats grasshoppers, caterpillars, and other insects; also spiders, fruits, and berries.

Nesting: Platform nest of twigs, placed in tree or dense thicket. Eggs: 2, greenish blue. I: about 12 days; F: about 14 days, altricial; B:1–2.

Other Behavior: Shy and elusive. Stays in hardwood hammocks and mangrove thickets.

Habitat: Mangrove swamps.

Voice: A guttural slowly repeated "gaw gaw gaw."

Conservation: TREND UNKNOWN.

Greater Roadrunner
Geococcyx californianus

Identification: 22″ Long legs; long tail; **streaked brown;** blue-and-red streak behind eye; **usually on the ground;** when stopped, often raises crest and tail. IMM: Lacks colorful streak behind the eye.

Feeding: Feeds on the ground, eating insects, small rodents, the eggs and young of other birds, small snakes including rattlesnakes, spiders, lizards, and fruit.

Nesting: Platform nest of sticks lined with roots, feathers, grasses, snakeskins, mesquite pods, and dried horse or cattle manure, placed in low cactus, tree, or bush 3–15 ft. high. Eggs: 4–6, yellowish white; I: 20 days; F: 17–19 days, altricial; B: 1–2.

Other Behavior: Can run up to 15 miles per hour in pursuit of lizards or insects. Pair lives on its territory year round.

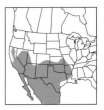

Habitat: On ground in woodlands, brushlands, grasslands; often arid areas.

Voice: A series of low dovelike coos, descending in pitch.

Conservation: BBS: E C ↓ CBC: ↑

Smooth-billed Ani
Groove-billed Ani
Crotophaga ani   Crotophaga sulcirostris

Smooth-billed

Groove-billed

Identification: Smooth-billed 14", Groove-billed 13" SMOOTH-BILLED: Limited to S. Fla. **Black; long tail;** distinctive **bill thick with a thin keel on upper part;** long tail often bent down beneath body. GROOVE-BILLED: Limited to S. Tex. **Black; long tail;** distinctive **bill very thick and often has fine grooves;** tail may be bent forward or to one side.

Feeding: Both feed in shrubs or on the ground, often in pastures near grazing cattle. Eat insects, fruits, and berries. May actually pick insects off the backs of cattle.

Nesting: Nest of both a mass of twigs lined with fresh green leaves, placed in thorny shrub or tree, to 25 ft. high. Eggs: Group of females each lay 2–4 blue eggs in 1 nest; I: 14 days; F: 7–10 days, altricial; B: 1–2.

Other Behavior: Communally live in groups of 1–4 monogamous pairs in which all members of the group take part in raising the young. May roost in groups of 30–40. Flight of both species consists of awkward hard flapping followed by a glide.

Smooth   Groove

Habitat: Farmlands, hedgerows, woods, orchards, lawns.

Voice: Smooth-billed: an ascending metallic "coo-leeek." Groove-billed: call rises, then drops, like "kwee-oh." May be rapidly repeated.

Conservation: Smooth-billed: BBS: E ⇓ C CBC: ⇓ Groove-billed: BBS: E C ⇑ CBC: ↓

232

Barn Owl
Tyto alba

Identification: 18" Pale; slim **long-legged** owl; **large, white, heart-shaped facial disk;** dark eyes; breast white to buffy and sparsely spotted.

Feeding: Locates prey almost entirely by sound. Typically flies 10 ft. over marshes, meadows, and woodlands hunting mice and rats, which it grabs in its talons. Also eats insects, bats, and reptiles.

Nesting: Nests in barns and other old buildings, tree hollows, church steeples, old burrows of woodchucks or badgers, and in holes in banks and cliffs, which it may enlarge. Will use human-made nest boxes. No nest material is added. Eggs: 4–7, white; I: 32–34 days; F: 45–58 days, altricial; B: 1–2.

Other Behavior: Barn Owl has the most acutely developed sense of hearing of all the owls. It can pinpoint prey with 100% accuracy in total darkness. It can hear a mouse's footsteps on packed earth 30 yd. away. Because of this, it can be extremely beneficial to farmers who want to get rid of mice around barns. In winter it roosts in conifers, abandoned buildings, and other dark places.

Habitat: Open farmlands, grasslands, deserts, and suburbs.

Voice: Mostly harsh hissing or screeching sounds; some metallic clicks.

Conservation: CBC: ↑

Eastern Screech-Owl

Otus asio

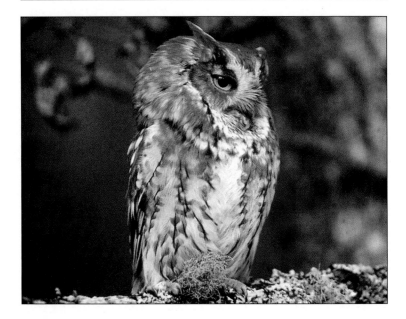

Identification: 9" **Small owl** with **yellow eyes** and **ear tufts** (which can be lowered and hidden). Only small owl in the East with ear tufts. Occurs in red or gray morphs.

Feeding: Eats mice, insects, amphibians, birds. May feed in cities on insects attracted to streetlamps.

Nesting: Nests in tree cavity, old woodpecker hole, or birdhouse. No nest material added. Eggs: 3–5, white; I: 21–28 days; F: 30–32 days, altricial; B: 1.

Other Behavior: Territory is only the area right around nest site. Defense starts in late winter as male claims several nest holes; involves whinny call, long trill, and chases. As with all owls, male has lower voice than female, and he is smaller in size. Male feeds female while she is incubating eggs. Young cannot fly well when leaving nest hole, and may use beak and talons to crawl out and up onto a branch. Roosts, as well as nests, in natural cavity or nest box; the same pair may occupy a site for 7 or more years.

Habitat: Woods, swamps, parks, suburbs.

Voice: Eerie whinny, rising and falling in pitch; long trill on 1 note.

Conservation: BBS: E ↑ C ⇓ CBC: ⇑

234

Great Horned Owl

Bubo virginianus

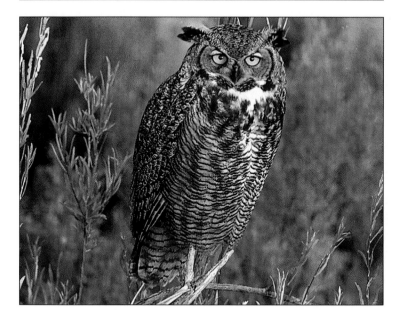

Identification: 22″ **Very large; widely spaced ear tufts;** yellow eyes; **white throat** that sometimes continues in a thin V down the chest.

Feeding: This large fearsome hunter will capture a wide variety of prey, ranging from insects to prey the size of a Great Blue Heron. Eats squirrels, mice, rabbits, snakes, skunks, weasels, porcupines, domestic cats, crows, Ospreys, as well as other owls and hawks, including Barred Owl and Red-tailed Hawk.

Nesting: Uses old nest of hawk, heron, squirrel, or tree hollow or cliff ledge; adds feathers from its breast to nest. Frequently uses Red-tailed Hawk nest since both live in same habitat. Eggs: 1–4, white; I: 28–30 days; F: 35 days, altricial; B: 1.

Other Behavior: Crows frequently mob this owl, and their drawn-out caws are often a clue to the owl's presence. The owl is more inconvenienced than disturbed by this and often just temporarily shifts its location. Great Horned, and all other owls, cough up pellets of undigested bones, fur, and feathers. Great Horned Owl's pellets are 3–4 in. long, and accumulate on the ground under its roosting spot. Has most widespread range of all N. American owls.

Habitat: Extremely varied; woods, deserts, suburbs.

Voice: Four to six deep resonant hoots, given in various rhythms by different individuals; often like "hoohoohoo hoohoo hoo." Female hoots higher-pitched.

Conservation: BBS: E ⇑ C ↑ CBC: ↑

Snowy Owl
Nyctea scandiaca

Adult

Immature

Identification: 24″ **Large white owl;** yellow eyes; **variable amounts of black spots and barring.** Immatures darker than adults; females darker than males. Thus, immature females are the darkest, with almost equal amounts of white and black on body and wings; adult males are almost pure white.

Feeding: Frequently hunts during the day. Eats mainly rodents, Arctic and Snowshoe Hares, fish, birds (including waterfowl), and carrion. When breeding, eats mostly lemmings.

Nesting: Nest on tundra, in shallow depression on top of mound, or on gravel bank, is lined with scattered feathers and bits of moss. Eggs: 3–10, white, clutch size is larger when prey are abundant; I: 32–39 days; F: 14–28 days, altricial; B: 1.

Other Behavior: Southward migration in winter is irruptive. Some years many more owls are seen than in others. This may or may not be correlated with lemming population cycle. Most of the birds that move south into U.S. in winter are immatures.

Habitat: Open tundra, or similar habitats south of the tundra, such as airports, beaches, marshes.

Voice: Barking noises on breeding grounds; quiet during winter.

Conservation: CBC: ↓

Northern Hawk Owl

Surnia ulula

Identification: 16" Medium-sized owl; long tail; grayish facial disks with wide black borders. Has no ear tufts; eyes are yellow; grayish underparts are heavily barred with brown. Birds that come south in winter are often seen perched along roadsides or fields when hunting.

Feeding: Hunts by swooping down on prey, then returning to perch. Will use favorite perch regularly, often for a period of years. Can also rapidly maneuver through woods, like Cooper's Hawk. Eats voles, mice, and lemmings in summer; in winter, eats more birds, including grouse and ptarmigan, also rabbits.

Nesting: Nests in hollowed end of broken-off dead tree; also uses old woodpecker hole or tree cavity. Eggs: 3–9, white; I: 25–30 days; F: 25–35 days, altricial; B: 1.

Other Behavior: Unafraid of humans. Much more of a daytime hunter than other owls. Has excellent daytime sight, and vision plays a more important role in its hunting than hearing, which is not as acute as that of other owls.

Habitat: Northern conifer woods and bogs, swamps, and woods; roadsides and fields.

Voice: Variety of calls, including whistled trills, rattles, screams, and a "kikikiki."

Conservation: CBC: ↓

Elf Owl

Micrathene whitneyi

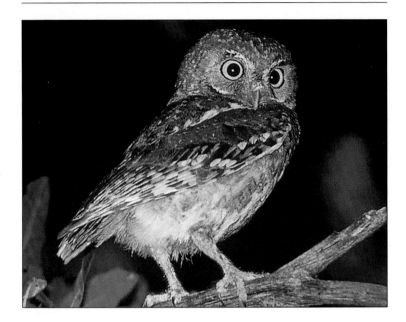

Identification: 6" **Our smallest owl; yellow eyes; short tail; no ear tufts.** Distinguished from Northern Saw-whet Owl by smaller size and lack of streaks on underparts.

Feeding: Eats insects, scorpions, spiders, centipedes, mice, and shrews. Hunts nocturnally.

Nesting: Nests in old woodpecker hole in hardwood tree or saguaro cactus; no nest material added. Eggs: 2–5, white; I: 24 days; F: 28–33 days, altricial; B: 1.

Other Behavior. Uses separate cavity for roosting and breeding. Roosts during day in tree cavity or in dense thickets, where its coloration makes it very difficult to detect. When female is incubating, male may roost with other males.

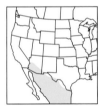

Habitat: Deserts with saguaro cacti, wooded streams, pine-oak woods.

Voice: High-pitched barks and chirps and a variety of other calls.

Conservation: TREND UNKNOWN. Almost gone from Calif. Reintroduction attempted; success uncertain. More common in rest of range.

Burrowing Owl

Speotyto cunicularia

Identification: 9″ Small; long legs; white throat; boldly spotted except for barred belly; yellow eyes; no ear tufts; **usually perched on ground.** Bows when approached.

Feeding: Eats insects, scorpions, crayfish, mice, ground squirrels, young prairie dogs, rabbits, amphibians, snakes, and, rarely, birds.

Nesting: Nests in small colonies, in deserted burrow of prairie dog, tortoise, armadillo, woodchuck, skunk, or other mammal. May dig own burrow, or enlarge another's; nest lined with horse or cow dung, grasses, weeds. Eggs: 6–11, white; I: 21–28 days; F: 28 days, altricial; B: 1.

Other Behavior: These endearing owls can often be seen standing on the raised mound at the entrance to their burrow, in habitats such as airport fields, highway shoulders, golf courses, and vacant lots, as well as their more traditional location, within prairie dog towns. They do not share a burrow with a prairie dog, but live in a deserted burrow. Rattlesnakes may live in prairie dog towns, and prey on owls and dogs. The owls are able to imitate the rattling sound of the rattlesnake as a defense against would-be predators.

Habitat: Open plains, grasslands, desert scrub.

Voice: A "coo-coo" given by male during courtship; a long chattering given during alarm.

Conservation: BBS: E ⇓ C ⇓ CBC: ↑ Declining in Calif.; increasing in Fla.

Barred Owl

Strix varia

Identification: 21" Besides the Barn Owl, our only **large eastern owl** with **dark eyes.** Chest barred; belly streaked; no ear tufts.

Feeding: Mice, rabbits, amphibians, reptiles, insects.

Nesting: Nests in tree cavity or abandoned hawk or crow nest, located 24–80 ft. high. Will use nest box with hole entrance diameter of 6 in. or greater. Eggs: 2–4, white; I: 28–33 days; F: 40–45 days, altricial; B: 1.

Other Behavior: Barred Owls are some of our most vocal owls and often call during the day. They have an amazing repertoire of sounds beyond the usual "who cooks for you?", including a spine-tingling scream. A pair may alternate calling back and forth. Average territory size is about 1 square mile. The territory may be expanded in winter, due to lack of food. Males may also leave territories in winter and feed elsewhere, often showing up in suburban areas or cities looking for food. They return in the early spring to their mate and territory.

Habitat: Woods, wooded swamps.

Voice: "Hoo — hoo — hoohoo," like "who cooks for you?" Female hoots higher-pitched. Also shrieks and monkeylike "haw haw ha ha ha."

Conservation:
BBS: E ⇑ C ⇑ CBC: ↑ Expanding range into northwestern U.S. and Can.

Great Gray Owl

Strix nebulosa

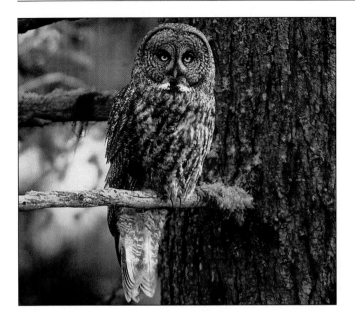

Identification: 29″ Our **largest owl; large facial disks** filled with concentric rings; **comparatively small yellow eyes;** 2 white marks below chin, like a **white bow tie;** tail relatively long; no ear tufts.

Feeding: Mostly voles, mice; also gophers, weasels, less usually birds and squirrels. In addition to pouncing on prey with talons, will occasionally plunge headfirst into snow in pursuit of vole. Daytime as well as nighttime hunter.

Nesting: Nests in abandoned hawk, crow, or raven nest, or on top of tree stump. Eggs: 1–5, white; I: 30 days; F: 20–28 days, altricial; B: 1.

Other Behavior: Rare and irregular winter visitor to areas outside its permanent range. Usually shows up in large, open, moist areas surrounded by woods, where it can be seen hunting for voles during the day.

Habitat: Northern coniferous and deciduous forests.

Voice: Slow series of deep hoots, evenly spaced.

Conservation: CBC: ↑

Long-eared Owl

Asio otus

Identification: 15" Slim owl; long close-set ear tufts; rufous facial disk; long wings that extend beyond tip of tail; yellow eyes; no white throat.

Feeding: Eats mostly voles, mice; also amphibians, reptiles, and insects.

Nesting: Sometimes loosely colonial. Nests in abandoned nest of crow, hawk, magpie, squirrel, or heron, or tree cavity. May add to nest with strips of bark or leaves, and feathers from female's breast. Eggs: 3–8, white; I: 21–28 days; F: 23–26 days, altricial; B: 1.

Other Behavior: At times, forms communal winter roosts of up to 50 or more birds, usually in dense conifers. It is important that bird watchers not disturb these through too much visiting. Has large vocal repertoire (although often silent), including catlike noises and canarylike twitterings when flying into nighttime roost before dawn. Feather tufts on head are not ears; they help the owl appear camouflaged when it elongates its body, looking like the ragged stub of a broken tree branch.

Habitat: Woods near open fields and marshes.

Voice: Single or double "hoo," given at a slow pace; barking sounds; high twittering calls; and a long tremulous "hoooo."

Conservation: CBC: ↓

Short-eared Owl

Asio flammeus

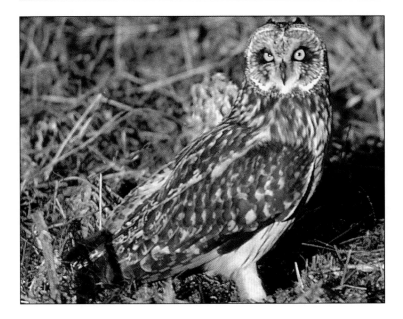

Identification: 15″ Medium-sized; often seen hunting at dusk over fields and marshes; **dark areas surround yellow eyes,** like sunglasses; **boldly streaked chest; light belly.** Although it has short ear tufts, these are rarely seen. **IN FLIGHT:** Often seen flying low over ground while hunting. Note **irregular floppy flight; pale buffy patches on upperwings;** and **dark wrist patches on underwings.**

Feeding: Feeds mostly on voles. When it has young to feed, it will also hunt songbirds and some gamebirds. Hunts mainly at dawn and dusk.

Nesting: Nests on the ground, in a depression concealed by surrounding reeds and grasses, lined with dried grasses and feathers from female's breast. Eggs: 4–14, white; I: 21–28 days; F: 31–36 days, altricial; B: 1.

Other Behavior: Irruptive species that varies in abundance from year to year. Will wander to locate good prey areas, then settle and breed. Has larger clutch sizes when there is ample prey. Forms winter communal roosts.

Habitat: Open fields, marshes, dunes, and grasslands.

Voice: Low-pitched "hoo" in a long series, given while perched or flying; also various snarls, squeals, and barking calls.

Conservation: BBS: E C ↑ CBC: ↓ Declining through much of range, due to habitat loss.

Boreal Owl
Northern Saw-whet Owl
Aegolius funereus   Aegolius acadicus

Boreal   Saw-whet

Identification: Boreal 10", Saw-whet 8"
BOREAL: Small; yellow eyes; no ear tufts; **facial
disk light gray bordered by black; forehead
black, covered with white spots;** bill pale. **SAW-
WHET: Small;** yellow eyes; no ear tufts; **facial disk
reddish brown with no dark border; forehead
brown with fine white streaks;** bill is dark.

Boreal   Saw-whet

Feeding: Boreal eats voles, lemmings, mice. Saw-whet
eats mice, voles, chipmunks, shrews, bats, insects.

Nesting: Boreal nests in tree cavity or old woodpecker
hole; may also use nest box. Eggs: 3–10, white; I:
25–30 days; F: 28–32 days, altricial; B: 1. Saw-whet
nests in tree cavity or old woodpecker hole; may use
nest box. Eggs: 4–7, white; I: 25–30 days; F: 28–35
days, altricial; B: 1.

Other Behavior: Saw-whet is sometimes incredibly tame.
Solely nocturnal. Roosts in dense evergreens in winter.
Boreal Owl is irruptive, often coinciding with irruptions
of Great Gray Owl and Northern Hawk Owl. Not easily
discovered, because it is strictly nocturnal and roosts
during the day in dense conifers.

Habitat: Coniferous
or mixed woods.

Voice: Boreal: 5–10
rapid whistled
"hoo"s, rising at
end. Saw-whet in
spring gives low
tooting whistle, 2
per second for long
periods; in fall, a
descending whistle.

Conservation:
Boreal:
CBC: ↓
Saw-whet:
CBC: ↑

Lesser Nighthawk
Common Nighthawk

Chordeiles acutipennis   *Chordeiles minor*

Lesser

Common

Common

Identification: Lesser 9", Common 10" Seen flying at dusk or dawn, sometimes during day. LESSER—IN FLIGHT: **Long, thin, rounded wings with conspicuous whitish bar across tips;** bar closer to tip than in Common. Flight tends to be low (10–20 ft. above ground), with rapid wingbeats. COMMON—IN FLIGHT: **Long, thin, pointed wings with conspicuous whitish bar across tips.** Flight tends to be high (over 40 ft.), with slower, deliberate wingbeats. In both species, male has white band near tail tip; female does not. ➤See Voice to recognize Antillean Nighthawk, *C. gundlachii,* which is in Fla. Keys.

Feeding: Both scoop flying insects into their large mouths while flying.

Nesting: Lesser nests on ground in arid lowlands, sides of canyons. Eggs: 2, grayish with dots; I: 18–19 days; F: 21 days, precocial, B: 1. Common nests on gravelly soil in fields or on gravel rooftops. Eggs: 2, olive with dark marks; I: 19–20 days; F: 21 days, precocial; B: 1.

Other Behavior: Common may feed near city lights.

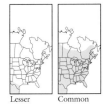

Lesser   Common

Habitat: Lesser: rivers, ponds, desert scrub. Common: forests, plains, urban areas.

Voice: Lesser gives soft trill; Common gives nasal "peent"; Antillean's call is "pity pit pit."

Conservation: Lesser: BBS: E C ⇑ CBC: ↑ Common: BBS: E ⇓ C ↓ CBC: ↓

245

Pauraque

Nyctidromus albicollis

Identification: 12" **Flies close to ground at dusk and dawn,** especially along roadsides, where it may also land. **In Flight: Long, thin, rounded wings with a conspicuous whitish bar across tip.** Distinguished from similar nighthawks by **long rounded (rather than notched) tail. Male:** White stripe along either side of tail. **Female:** White dots on either side of tail tip (hard to see in field).

Feeding: Flies low, catching insects in mouth. Can also hop or run after insects on ground.

Nesting: No nest, just lays eggs on flat bare ground, in open woodland, sometimes near canyon or river. Eggs: 2, pink with darker marks. I: ?; F: ?, precocial; B: 1, possibly more.

Other Behavior: Sometimes seen resting on road at night; detected when car headlights reflect off its eyes.

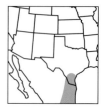

Habitat: Subtropical woodland edges, dense brush bordering open areas.

Voice: One to three short "pup" sounds, followed by a harsh descending whistle, like "gagawheeer."

Conservation:
BBS: E C ⇓ CBC: ↓

Common Poorwill
Whip-poor-will
Phalaenoptilus nuttallii   *Caprimulgus vociferus*

Common

Whip-poor-will

Identification: Common 8", Whip-poor-will 10"
**Both mostly heard calling in evening. See
Voice for main identification clues. COMMON—IN
FLIGHT: Small; short rounded wings; short
tail.** Sometimes seen at night along roads hunting
insects. **WHIP-POOR-WILL—IN FLIGHT: Larger;
dusky; rounded wings; relatively long tail.**

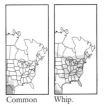

Common   Whip.

Feeding: Eat aerial insects, mostly night-flying moths;
also beetles, grasshoppers.

Nesting: Common's nest a scraped depression or none,
on gravelly ground or flat rock. Eggs: 2, whitish with
dark marks; I: ?; F: ?, altricial; B: 1. Whip-poor-will nests
on woodland floor. Eggs: 2, white with spots of gray or
brown; I: 19–20 days; F: 20 days, precocial; B: 1–2.

Other Behavior: Both nocturnal; rest during day. When
temperatures are cold, Common can lower body
temperature and enter state of torpor to conserve
energy.

Habitat: Open
woods, canyons,
dry, brushy areas.

Voice: Common:
"poorwill" or
"poorwillip," with
accent on "will."
Whip-poor-will:
"whip poorwill,"
with emphasis on
last syllable.

Conservation:
Common:
BBS: E C ⇑ CBC: ↓
Whip-poor-will:
BBS: E ↓ C ↑ CBC: ↓

247

Chuck-will's-widow

Caprimulgus carolinensis

Identification: 12" **Mostly heard calling in evening,** rarely seen. **IN FLIGHT: Rufous; rounded wings; long tail. MALE:** White along outer tail feathers. **FEMALE:** No white on tail. See Voice for other identification.

Feeding: Eats insects, which it catches in its large 2-in.-wide mouth.

Nesting: Nests on dead leaves on ground in forest. Eggs: 2, creamy with dark marks; I: 20 days; F: 17 days, precocial; B: 1.

Other Behavior: Nocturnal, feeding and calling at night.

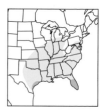

Habitat: Along edges of coniferous or mixed forests; often along rivers.

Voice: Call like name, with accent on 1st and 3rd syllables. Call given repeatedly at dusk.

Conservation: BBS: E ⇓ C ↑ CBC: ↑

Chimney Swift

Chaetura pelagica

Identification: 5½" IN FLIGHT: **Very rapid wingbeats with stiffly held wings, followed by gliding. Long, thin, pointed wings; short square tail; dark gray-brown above, paler below on throat and chest.**

Feeding: Feeds while flying, catching insects in its mouth.

Nesting: Nests in chimneys or around the eaves of old barns or buildings. While in flight, breaks dead twigs off trees with its feet, then carries them back to nest in its bill. Cements twigs onto vertical surface with sticky "saliva," to form nest cup. Eggs: 4–5, white; I: 19 days; F: 14–18 days, altricial; B: 1.

Other Behavior: The most common courtship flight display involves two birds flying together, one slightly above the other. The hind one abruptly lifts its wings into a V and glides; then the one in front does the same. Done between members of a pair throughout the breeding cycle. During migration, large flocks roost communally in chimneys or steeples. Will swirl around above the roost for over 45 minutes before entering at dusk.

Habitat: Rural or urban areas where there are chimneys; more rarely in hollow trees.

Voice: A rapidly repeated "chitter-chitter-chitter" and a quick series of separate "chip" calls.

Conservation: BBS: E ↓ C ↓

Buff-bellied Hummingbird

Amazilia yucatanensis

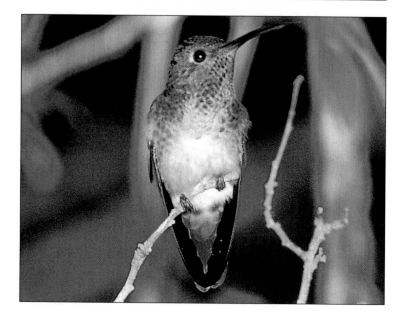

Identification: 4½" Throat iridescent green; belly pale buff; tail reddish brown; bill red with black tip. Sexes alike.

Feeding: Feeds on nectar from flowers, also eats insects. Comes to hummingbird feeders.

Nesting: Nest of downy plant material lined with plant down; held together with spider's silk and covered with lichens; placed in small tree or shrub. Eggs: 2, white; I:?; F: ?, altricial; B: 1 or possibly more.

Other Behavior: One of our largest hummingbirds Found where there is dense vegetation with lots of flowers in bloom. Occasionally winters along Gulf Coast to La. A resting hummingbird may take as many as 250 breaths per minute.

Habitat: Thickets, subtropical woods, suburbs.

Voice: Shrill metallic notes.

Conservation: CBC: ↓

Ruby-throated Hummingbird

Archilochus colubris

Male

Female

Identification: 3½" The only hummingbird in most of eastern N. America. **MALE: Upperparts green; throat iridescent red** (may appear black); **black patch from bill to below eye;** breast and central belly whitish. **FEMALE: Upperparts green; underparts whitish and unmarked.**

Feeding: Eats flower nectar, insects, spiders, sap from sapsucker-drilled holes. Comes to hummingbird feeders.

Nesting: Nest of plant down, bud scales, covered with lichens, bound with spider's silk, and placed on a small horizontal limb, 10–20 ft. high. Eggs: 2, white; I: 16 days; F: 30 days, altricial; B: 1–2.

Other Behavior: In spring, male defends territory of about ¼ acre. In dive displays, he flies in a U shape, rising 10–40 ft. on each side. In courtship or aggressive situations, male and female display by shuttling back and forth on horizontal plane and with tail spread. After mating, female builds nest and raises young alone. On migration, males and females will temporarily defend food source, such as your hummingbird feeder. Ruby-throats migrate 600 mi. across Gulf of Mexico, storing enough fat to make crossing. A male Ruby-throat weighs about the same as 2½ paper clips.

Habitat: Woods edges, streams, parks, gardens.

Voice: Varied chips and twitterings.

Conservation:
BBS: E ↑ C ↑ CBC: ↓

Black-chinned Hummingbird

Archilochus alexandri

Male

Female

Identification: 3½" MALE: **Black chin bordered by violet** (violet may appear black); **white collar;** chest and central belly white; back and sides green. FEMALE: **Green above; white below; throat clear to evenly and lightly streaked; repeatedly spreads and flips tail while feeding.** See Voice.

Feeding: Hovers and takes nectar from flowers. Eats small insects, spiders.

Nesting: Female constructs nest of plant down, gathered from willows or undersides of sycamore leaves; also uses feathers and tree flowers. Nest is bound with spider's silk; outside not coated with lichens; placed in tree or shrub 5–10 ft. high. Successive nests can be built on top of one another. Eggs: 1–3, white; I: 13–16 days; F: 21 days, altricial; B: 1–2.

Other Behavior: Has most extensive breeding range of any western hummingbird. Male and female defend separate territories, mate on neutral ground. Female rears young. Later in season, when breeding areas are too dry, they move into foothills or lower mountains where there are lush flowers.

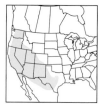

Habitat: Dry lowlands and foothills.

Voice: Call a distinctive descending "tyew."

Conservation: BBS: E C ↑ CBC: ↓ Planting nectar-rich flowers can provide additional feeding habitat.

Ringed Kingfisher

Ceryle torquata

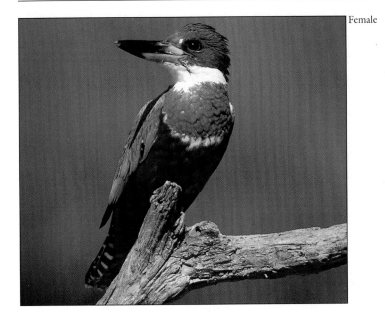
Female

Identification: 16" Limited to S. Tex. Our largest kingfisher. **Large bill; blue-gray head, wings, and back; white collar. MALE: Underparts all reddish brown. FEMALE: Breast blue-gray, belly all reddish brown; white breastband.**

Feeding: Dives from perch, or hovers and then plunges into water. Eats fish, frogs, small water reptiles.

Nesting: Nest is excavated tunnel, 5–8 ft. long, with hollowed chamber at end where eggs are laid; constructed in vertical banks. Eggs: 3–5, white; I: 22; F: 34–37 days, altricial; B: 1.

Other Behavior: Often shy and solitary. Has favorite hunting perches along streams. Prefers large open rivers or lakes with clear water.

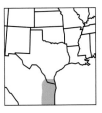

Habitat: Along rivers.

Voice: A loud low-pitched chattering; a "chack" call given in flight.

Conservation: CBC: ⇑

Belted Kingfisher

Ceryle alcyon

Female

Male

Identification: 13" Our only kingfisher outside Tex. **Large bill; blue-gray head, back, and wings; white collar.** MALE: **All-white belly.** FEMALE: **Reddish-brown belly band.**

Feeding: Hovers, then plunges into water, or dives from perch. Eats fish, amphibians, reptiles, and insects.

Nesting: Nest tunnel is excavated in a vertical bank. Entrance hole of 3–4 in. diameter is 1½ ft. down from top of bank. Tunnel is 3–15 ft. in length, with a spherical chamber at end where eggs are laid. Can be far from water. Eggs: 5–7, white; I: 22–26 days; F: 18–28 days, altricial; B: 1.

Other Behavior: Tunnel excavation is done with the bill. Birds alternate turns excavating, each one kicking out the earth excavated by the other when it enters tunnel, creating a spray of dirt coming out of the hole. Can dig about a foot of tunnel in a day. Kingfishers defend individual feeding territory during the nonbreeding season; size of territory averages about 500 yd. of stream length.

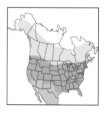

Habitat: Near water, such as rivers, lakes, coastal bays.

Voice: A continuous woody rattle; often given in flight. Very vocal.

Conservation:
BBS: E ↓ C ↓ CBC: ↑

Green Kingfisher

Chloroceryle americana

Male

Identification: 8" Limited to S. and central Tex. A **small** kingfisher with **proportionately large bill; dark green above; white collar.** MALE: **Reddish-brown breast.** FEMALE: **No reddish brown on breast; band of dark spots across breast.**

Feeding: From perch, dives into water after fish, amphibians, crustaceans, and insects.

Nesting: Male and female excavate tunnel 2–3 ft. long with nest chamber at end; in sandy bank, usually half-hidden behind vegetation. Eggs: 3–6, white; I: 19–21 days; F: 22–27 days, altricial; B: 1 or possibly more.

Other Behavior: Solitary or in pairs. Very territorial. Hunts from low perches, generally over shallow water.

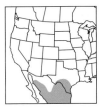

Habitat: Near lakes and clear streams.

Voice: Call a sharp "tick," often given in a series.

Conservation: CBC: ↓

Red-headed Woodpecker

Melanerpes erythrocephalus

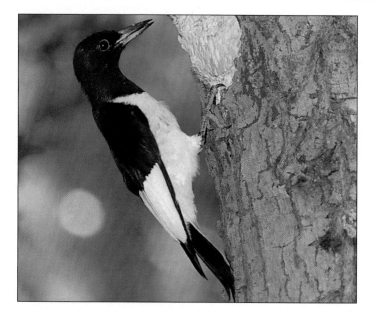

Identification: 8" Only woodpecker with an **all-red head; body and wings boldly patterned with black and white.** IN FLIGHT: Note white rump and white inner trailing half of wings. FALL JUV: Pattern similar to adult, but with brown head and back. Gradually molts into adult plumage in fall and winter.

Feeding: Feeds on acorns, beechnuts, and other nuts, insects, bird eggs and nestlings, sap from sapsucker holes, fruit, and berries.

Nesting: Both sexes excavate hole in live or dead tree or utility pole. Uses birdhouses. Eggs: 4–5, white; I: 12–13 days; F: 30 days, altricial; B: 1–2.

Other Behavior: Catches insects in midair, as well as foraging on leaves and on the ground. Caches pieces of nuts and acorns, also insects, in small cavities for use during nonbreeding season. Will even conceal the cache by closing it off with slivers of wet wood. Defends caches from other woodpeckers, jays, and crows. Northern populations are migratory and concentrate in woods with abundant acorns.

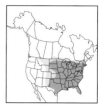

Habitat: Farmlands, open woodlands, suburbs, orchards.

Voice: Common call a loud "kweeer." Drums softly in short bursts.

Conservation:
BBS: E ⇓ C ↓ CBC: ↓ Declining due to woodlands being cut down and competition with starlings for nest sites.

Golden-fronted Woodpecker

Melanerpes aurifrons

Male

Female

Identification: 9″ Head and belly tan; yellow on forehead and nape; wings, back, and tail black barred with white. **MALE:** Small red patch on crown. **FEMALE:** No red.

Feeding: Eats a variety of insects, such as beetles, grasshoppers, ants; also grubs, berries, and fruit. Eats sunflower seed at feeders.

Nesting: Excavates a nest cavity in live trunk of large tree, usually mesquite, pecan, or oak, or in a dead limb; also uses fence posts and utility poles. May use nest box. Eggs: 4–5, white; I: 12–14 days; F: 25–30 days, altricial; B: 2–3.

Other Behavior: Noisy and conspicuous. Uses same cavity to nest in, year after year.

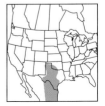

Habitat: Woodlands, parks, gardens.

Voice: Harsh "churr." Drums.

Conservation: BBS: E C ↓ CBC: ↑

Red-bellied Woodpecker

Melanerpes carolinus

Male

Female

Identification: 9" Head and belly tan; nape red; wings, back, and tail black barred with white. MALE: Red patch extends to forehead. FEMALE: Red just on nape.

Feeding: Feeds on trunks and limbs of trees, eating wood-boring and other insects; also fruit, berries, seeds. Comes to bird feeders, eating suet, nuts, seeds, fruit.

Nesting: Excavates in living trees, or ones that have recently died. Also uses abandoned hole in old stump, utility pole, or fence post. Nests in birdhouses. Eggs: 3–8, white; I: 12–14 days; F: 25–30 days, altricial; B: 2–3.

Other Behavior: As part of courtship, male and female mutually tap on tree, with one inside a potential nest hole, the other outside. Stores food by wedging it deeply in crevices. In late 1950s and early 1960s, began expanding range northward; now breeds in Northeast.

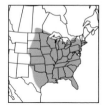

Habitat: Woodlands, parks, suburbs.

Voice: Harsh "churr" call. Drums in short bursts, only 1 second long.

Conservation: BBS: E ↑ C ↑ CBC: ↑

258

Yellow-bellied Sapsucker

Sphyrapicus varius

Male

Female

Identification: 8″ Black-and-white-streaked face; red patch on forehead; elongated white patch on shoulder of black wings; central belly yellowish. **MALE:** Red chin. **FEMALE:** White chin. **IN FLIGHT:** Note white rump and white shoulder patches. **FALL JUV:** Brownish overall, but with white wing patch like adult's. Gradually molts into adult plumage by spring.

Feeding: Drinks sap from trees and catches insects on the wing or on the ground. Also eats fruit, berries.

Nesting: Nests in a hole in live tree, often an aspen that is diseased by a tinder fungus that decays the heartwood but not the sapwood. Sapsucker easily excavates the softened heartwood but leaves tough sapwood, which remains as outer shell protecting the nest. Eggs: 5–6, white; I: 12–13 days; F: 25–29 days, altricial; B: 1.

Other Behavior: Drills horizontal rows of holes in trunks of many species of trees; when it finds abundant sap flow, it drills vertical rows of holes to take advantage of it. It then returns repeatedly to drink sap from holes. Other birds may also come to sap, such as titmice, nuthatches, and hummingbirds.

Habitat: Woods and orchards.

Voice: A "churr" call; a "weep weep" call. Drumming is short burst followed by irregular beats, like "tatatat tatat tatat."

Conservation: BBS: E ↓ C ⇑

Ladder-backed Woodpecker

Picoides scalaris

Male

Female

Identification: 7" Black-and-white-barred back; buffy-white face and underparts; black eye-stripe and black line off the base of the bill connect behind the cheek. **MALE:** Red from nape to forehead, wearing away over summer to black on forehead. **FEMALE:** No red.

Feeding: Eats fruit of cactus, and insects such as beetle larvae.

Nesting: Excavates nesting cavity in dead stub or dying branch of willow or mesquite, or in live saguaro cactus. Also excavates in agave, yucca, fence post, or utility pole. Eggs: 3–6, white; I: 13 days; F: ?, altricial; B: 1 or possibly more.

Other Behavior: During courtship, in spring, male and female do drumming on dry resonant tree limbs.

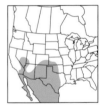

Habitat: Arid and semiarid brushlands, creeks, farms, and suburbs.

Voice: Call is a sharp "peek." Loud short bursts of drumming.

Conservation: BBS: E C ⇓ CBC: ↓

Downy Woodpecker
Hairy Woodpecker

Picoides pubescens   Picoides villosus

Female Downy

Female Hairy

Male Downy

Identification: Downy 6″, Hairy 9″ **Both species have a white back and white underparts;** white-spotted black wings; black-and-white-streaked faces. Males have red on nape; females have no red. **DOWNY: Bill is about half the length of the head;** white outer tail feathers with a few black bars. **HAIRY: Bill is almost as long as the head;** outer tail feathers all white.

Feeding: Both feed on a variety of insects, especially wood-boring insects. At feeders, suet, sunflower seeds.

Nesting: Downy excavates nest cavity in dead wood. Eggs: 4–5, white; I: 12 days; F: 21 days, altricial; B: 1–2. Hairy excavates nest cavity in live wood. Eggs: 4–6, white; I: 11–12 days; F: 28–30 days, altricial; B: 1. Both species only rarely accept a nest box.

Other Behavior: Both species do drumming — loud, continuous, very rapid pecking on resonant surfaces, such as dead tree stubs. This functions to announce territory and attract a mate during the breeding season. Sounds of pecking for food or nest-hole excavation are different; they are light taps in irregular rhythms.

Downy   Hairy

Habitat: Woods, farmland, suburbs.

Voice: Both have "teek" contact call. Downy: whinny call and a "queek queek" given during courtship. Hairy:"wickiwicki–wicki" during courtship.

Conservation:
Downy:
BBS: E ↑ C ↑ CBC: ↑
Hairy:
BBS: E ↑ C ↑ CBC: ↑

Red-cockaded Woodpecker
Picoides borealis

Male

Female

Identification: 8″ Black-and-white-barred back; conspicuous large white cheek. MALE: Very small red mark at upper edge of white cheek; hard to see. FEMALE: No red.

Feeding: Eats wood-boring and other insects, berries, nuts.

Nesting: Colonial. Excavates nest cavity in living pines 65–120 years old with rotting heartwood. Nest trees can be used for 40–50 years. Drills holes in bark and sapwood all around the nest cavity; resin flows from these and coats tree. This deters nest predators, especially tree-climbing snakes. Eggs: 2–5, white; I: 12–13 days; F: 22–29 days, altricial; B: 1.

Other Behavior: Lives in family groups of 2 breeding adults and their young. Male offspring from previous year may help raise young. Groups defend territories of 100–1,000 acres. The survival of this species is problematic. Its dependence on old pine forests makes it vulnerable, because this habitat is vanishing, reduced by 90% due to logging practices. Hurricane Hugo (1989) also destroyed vast numbers of nest trees. Total present population is now about 7,400 birds. Management plans may be inadequate.

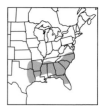

Habitat: Mature pine woods.

Voice: Harsh "shrip" call and a high-pitched "tsik."

Conservation: BBS: E ⇓ C ↑ CBC: ↓ Endangered in U.S. since 1970. Population is severely declining. A major conservation effort is under way.

Three-toed Woodpecker
Black-backed Woodpecker
Picoides tridactylus   Picoides arcticus

Female Three-toed

Male Black-backed

Identification: Three-toed 8", Black-backed 9". Both species have **black head with a fine white eye-stripe; wider white line off the base of the bill; barred flanks.** Males have yellow patch on crown; females have no yellow. THREE-TOED: **Black-and-white-barred back.** BLACK-BACKED: **Clear, glossy, black back.**

Three-toed   Black-backed

Feeding: Three-toed eats mostly insects, also berries, sap, nuts. Often forages on fire-killed trees. Black-backed eats larvae of wood-boring beetles and other insects, fruit, nuts.

Nesting: Three-toed is loosely colonial where food is abundant. Excavates nest cavity in dead, or sometimes live, tree, 2–15 ft. high; will also use utility pole. Eggs: 2–6, white; I: 12–14 days; F: 22–26 days, altricial; B: 1. Black-backed excavates nest cavity in live tree with rotting heartwood, 5–12 ft. high; may peel off bark around nest hole. Eggs: 2–6, white; I: 14 days; F: 25 days, altricial; B: 1.

Other Behavior: Both forage by scaling large patches of bark off dead trees. Black-backed more irruptive.

Habitat: Boreal coniferous forest.

Voice: Three-toed gives a "teek" contact call and short volleys of drumming. Black-backed gives a "kik" contact call and long volleys of drumming.

Conservation:
Three-toed:
CBC: ↑
Black-backed:
BBS: E ↓ C CBC: ↑

Northern Flicker

Colaptes auratus

Male "Red-shafted"

Male "Yellow-shafted"

Female "Yellow-shafted"

Identification: 13" Brown-and-black-barred back and wings; whitish or buffy breast with black spots; wide black necklace. IN FLIGHT: Conspicuous white rump. "YELLOW-SHAFTED" MORPH: Red patch on nape; gray crown; yellow undertail and underwings. MALE: Black line off base of bill. FEMALE: No line off base of bill. "RED-SHAFTED" MORPH: Lacks red patch on nape; brown crown; reddish undertail and underwings. MALE: Red line off base of bill. FEMALE: No line off base of bill.

Feeding: Feeds on ground, probing for ants, which are 45% of its diet; also catches insects in air and eats fruit, berries, seeds. Comes to bird feeders.

Nesting: Excavates nest cavity in tree, post, cactus. Uses nest box. Eggs: 7–9, white; I: 11–12 days; F: 14–21 days, altricial; B: 1–2.

Other Behavior: Head bobbing, accompanied by the "woikawoikawoika" call, is done by mated pairs as part of courtship. When done between birds of the same sex, it is usually competition for a mate or territory.

Habitat: Parks, suburbs, farmlands, woodlands.

Voice: Loud "kekekekeke" for territory advertisement; a "woika-woikawoika" during courtship. Soft muffled volleys of drumming.

Conservation:
BBS: E ⇓ C ⇓ CBC: ↓

Pileated Woodpecker

Dryocopus pileatus

Male

Female

Identification: 18" **Crow-sized; mostly black with a bright red crest.** MALE: Has red patch on black line off base of bill. FEMALE: All-black line off base of bill. IN FLIGHT: Note large size and striking white on linings of underwings.

Feeding: Eats large numbers of carpenter ants, especially in winter. Also eats beetles and other insects, seeds, fruit. Comes to bird feeders for suet mixes.

Nesting: Nest cavity is excavated in dead wood, 15–70 ft. high. The entrance hole is about 3½ in. in diameter, with a cavity depth of 10–24 in. Eggs: 3–5, white; I: 15–16 days; F: 28 or more days, altricial; B: 1.

Other Behavior: Territory size can be 150–200 acres. Signs of a Pileated's presence are chiseled-out, squarish, 3–6 in. holes in trees. These are feeding holes, where the bird has searched for, or obtained, carpenter ants that live in tunnels deep in the wood. Sometimes the Pileated will excavate a long gash in a tree to obtain ants. Drumming is done by unmated males to advertise for a female, or it can be done between mated pairs as part of courtship.

Habitat: Mature forests, suburbs.

Voice: Ten to fifteen "cuk" calls given between mates; "woika-woika" calls given during courtship or territorial interactions. Low-pitched drumming that trails off in speed and volume at the end.

Conservation:
BBS: E ⇑ C ↓ CBC: ↑

Flycatchers are a large family of birds that all share the habit of sitting on exposed perches and making short flights out to catch passing insects. A few North American flycatchers are brightly colored, but most are shades of gray, white, and olive-green.

One of the best ways to start identifying flycatchers is to learn to identify the distinctive groups within the family, such as phoebes, kingbirds, crested flycatchers, etc. The Learning Pages outline the characteristics of each group, list

the species in that group, and illustrate the most common representative of the group. Knowing this information will give you an excellent basis for learning the more difficult and/or less common species.

The few species not covered by these groups are distinctive and, in many cases, brightly colored. They include Northern Beardless-Tyrannulet (p. 268), Vermilion Flycatcher (p. 277), and Great Kiskadee (p. 281).

FLYCATCHER GROUPS

Pewees

Contopus spp. Medium-sized brownish-gray flycatchers that perch upright and have a small peak at the top of the head; may have faint wing bars.

Eastern Wood-Pewee, p. 270

Other species:

Olive-sided Flycatcher, p. 269

Phoebes

Sayornis spp. Medium-sized flycatchers that perch upright and have a habit of continuously bobbing the tail; wing bars faint or lacking. Often build nests on bridges or buildings.

Eastern Phoebe, p. 275

Other species:

Say's Phoebe, p. 276

Kingbirds

Tyrannus spp. Large flycatchers that perch at a diagonal. They have large bills, dark upperparts, and white or yellow bellies. They are often aggressive to other birds.

Crested Flycatchers

Myiarchus spp. Large flycatchers with a prominent rounded crest; many are brownish above, gray and yellow below, and have reddish brown on tail.

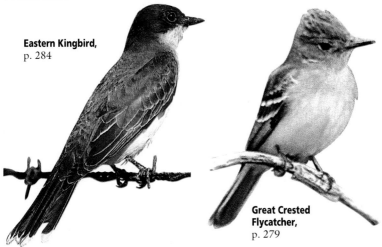

Eastern Kingbird,
p. 284

Great Crested Flycatcher,
p. 279

Other species:

Couch's Kingbird, p. 282
Western Kingbird, p. 283
Gray Kingbird, p. 285
Scissor-tailed Flycatcher, p. 286

Other species:

Ash-throated Flycatcher, p. 278
Brown-crested Flycatcher, p. 280

Empidonaxes

Empidonax spp. Small flycatchers with light eye-rings and wing bars; generally olive above and lighter below. Perch upright. Many species look so similar that even experts have trouble identifying them by sight and rely on song. Often referred to as "Empids."

Other species:

Yellow-bellied Flycatcher, p. 271
Acadian Flycatcher, p. 272
Alder Flycatcher, p. 273
Willow Flycatcher, p. 273

Least Flycatcher,
p. 274

Northern Beardless-Tyrannulet
Camptostoma imberbe

Identification: 4½" Limited to S.E. Ariz. and S. Tex. **Very small; bushy crest; 2 buffy wing bars;** grayish olive above; gray below; pale lower bill.

Feeding: Gleans insects from twigs, and eats small berries; sometimes hawks insects from air.

Nesting: Nest a globular collection of plant fibers, attached to pendant branches. Eggs: 2–3, white; I: ?; F: ?, altricial; B: 1 or possibly more.

Other Behavior: Nest often built in clump of mistletoe that is growing in a tree. The entrance is on the side.

Habitat: Subtropical woodlands, thickets, and riverside trees.

Voice: Song a loud descending series of "peer" notes; call is a loud "pee-yeerp."

Conservation: TREND UNKNOWN.

Olive-sided Flycatcher

Contopus borealis

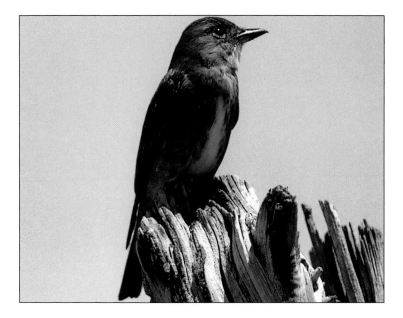

Identification: 7½" **Prominent peak at back of head; dark grayish olive overall** except for a **strip of white from chin to belly;** white patches on either side of lower back unique, but may be hidden by wings.

Feeding: Flies out from prominent perch to catch insects in the air.

Nesting: Nest of twigs and rootlets, lined with pine needles and moss, placed on a horizontal limb of deciduous or evergreen tree. Eggs: 3–4, whitish with darker marks; I: 14–17 days; F: 15–19, altricial; B: 1.

Other Behavior: More than most other flycatchers, this species has the habit of perching on high dead branches.

Habitat: Northern and mountainous coniferous forests.

Voice: An energetic "quick, three beers," with the 1st word quiet and 2nd accented. Also a repeated "pep-pep-pep."

Conservation: BBS: E ↓ C ⇓

269

Eastern Wood-Pewee

Contopus virens

Identification: 6″ **Prominent peak at back of head;** grayish olive above; **2 wing bars;** whitish throat; **grayish chest; whitish or yellowish belly.** **ADULT: Black upper bill, orange lower bill;** wing bars whitish. Distinguished from Western Wood-Pewee by range and song. **IMM:** Bill can be all dark; wing bars cinnamon or buffy. Imm. plumage kept into winter.

Feeding: Flies out from perch to catch aerial insects.

Nesting: Compact nest of plant fibers and downy materials, covered with silvery leaves or lichens, built over a horizontal limb or fork 8–40 ft. high. Eggs: 2–4, creamy white with darker marks at one end; I: 12–13 days; F: 14–18 days, altricial; B: 1.

Other Behavior: Male sings continuously through breeding season. In early part of breeding season, may occasionally fly to treetops to give a loud version of song. Dawn-song, a rapidly repeated version of song lasting up to a half hour, can be given early in the morning. Male may chase female as part of courtship; otherwise, very few displays seem to be associated with pairing. Territory is about 2–6 acres.

Habitat: Open woods.

Voice: High slurred whistles with long pauses, like "peeahwee peeoh." These phrases often given without pauses at dawn. Also a "chip" call.

Conservation: BBS: E ↓ C ⇓ CBC: ↓

Yellow-bellied Flycatcher

Empidonax flaviventris

Identification: 5½" A relatively large-headed short-tailed *Empidonax;* most common in E. Can. **Back green; throat yellow;** breast yellow with olive wash on sides; thin even-width eye-ring; conspicuous wing bars on dark wings. **See Voice.**

Feeding: Flies out from perch to catch aerial insects.

Nesting: Deep cup of mosses lined with finer material, placed on the ground under partial protection of tree roots, or among sphagnum moss. Eggs: 3–4, white with light markings; I: 12–13 days; F: 13–14 days, altricial; B: 1 or more.

Other Behavior: Our only flycatcher to regularly build its nest on the ground. Birds are quiet around nest, and male approaches only when feeding young. Female allows very close approach to nest and then flies off silently. Inconspicuous during migration, perching low in woods and thickets.

Habitat: Dense coniferous woods.

Voice: Song is a soft evenly stressed "cheluk," with the 2nd syllable lower-pitched; call is a whistled ascending "purweee" or just "preee."

Conservation:
BBS: E ⇑ C

Acadian Flycatcher

Empidonax virescens

Identification: 6″ A relatively **large-billed**, long-winged, broad-tailed *Empidonax;* most common in southeastern U.S. **Back very green; throat usually white; breast and belly pale yellow;** eye-ring clearly seen; wing bars buffy and contrast with dark wings. **See Voice.** Molts in late summer, before migrating and, at this time, imm. and adults may have yellow wash on throat, making them harder to distinguish from Yellow-bellied Flycatchers.

Feeding: Flies out from perch to catch aerial insects.

Nesting: Thin nest of long plant fibers, sometimes Spanish moss, partially suspended between 2 forks of a branch about 10 ft. high; long fibers usually hang off nest to 1–2 ft. below. Eggs: 2–4, whitish with slightly darker markings; I: 13–14 days; F: 13–15 days, altricial; B: 1.

Other Behavior: Even though this flycatcher looks very similar to several other species of flycatchers, such as the Willow and Alder Flycatchers, its nest is very distinct in being hammocklike and having long trailing streamers off the base.

Habitat: Mature deciduous forests; often near water.

Voice: Song is like the word "pizza"; call is a loud even-pitched "peet."

Conservation:
BBS: E ↑ C ⇓

Alder Flycatcher
Willow Flycatcher

Empidonax alnorum   *Empidonax traillii*

Alder

Willow

Identification: 6″ Relatively heavy-billed broad-tailed members of *Empidonax* genus that look identical and can be distinguished only by voice. During breeding, the Alder is most common in Can., the Willow is most common in U.S. south of Can. **Back olive-brown; throat white; breast pale olive; belly pale yellow;** eye-ring faint or lacking (sometimes bolder on Alder); wing bars dull white and do not stand out. **See Voice.**

Feeding: Fly out from low perch to catch insects.

Nesting: For both species, nest is firm thick-walled cup of plant fibers lined with plant down and cottony fibers, placed in shrub 2–6 ft. high. Eggs: 3–4, whitish with darker marks; I: 12–13 days; F: 12–14 days, altricial; B: 1 or possibly more.

Other Behavior: During migration, either species can be found in a wide variety of habitats.

Conservation:
Alder: BBS: E ↑ C ⇓
Willow: BBS: E ↑ C ⇑

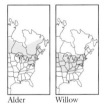

Alder   Willow

Habitat: Alder: Alder thickets at edge of lakes or swamps. Willow: Shrubby swamps.

Voice: Alder song a burry "rreebeet" or "rreebeea," accent on 2nd syllable; call is "peep." Willow song is "fitzbew," accent on 1st syllable; call is "wit."

273

Least Flycatcher
Empidonax minimus

Identification: 5ʺ The smallest *Empidonax;* has a relatively small bill; commonly seen throughout the East during migration. **Back brown-olive; throat whitish; breast washed with gray; belly pale yellow; eye-ring bold;** wing bars conspicuous. **See Voice.**

Feeding: Flies out from perch to catch aerial insects.

Nesting: Nest a compact cup of grasses, bark strips, and plant down, placed in the crotch of a limb. Eggs: 3–4, whitish; I: 14 days; F: 12–16 days, altricial; B: 1–2.

Other Behavior: Males chase females during courtship, frequently calling "chibek." Intruding males are chased out of the relatively small territory of 2–4 acres. Male may feed female on nest during incubation. Young are fed by parents for about 3 weeks after leaving the nest.

Habitat: Open woods, orchards, suburbs.

Voice: Song, given by both male and female, is an often-repeated "chibek," with accent on 2nd syllable; call a short "whit."

Conservation:
BBS: E ⇓ C ↓ CBC: ↑

Eastern Phoebe

Sayornis phoebe

Identification: 7" **Gray-brown above and whitish below; bill all dark; repeatedly bobs tail.** After molt in late summer, belly may be yellowish.

Feeding: Flies out from perch to catch aerial insects; also picks insects off ground.

Nesting: Nest a mounded cup of mud and moss, lined with fine grasses, placed on a ledge of building or bridge. Eggs: 4–5, white; I: 16 days; F: 18 days, altricial; B: 2–3.

Other Behavior: Males defend territories of several acres through chases and song. When female arrives, most singing stops, except for early in the morning when the pair get together briefly. Female builds nest and does all incubation. When she leaves nest to feed, male may come near nest; at other times the female will chase him away from the vicinity of the nest. Both parents feed the young. Once the young leave the nest, the female may start renovating nest for next brood, and male may renew singing for a short time. Twenty-five percent, or more, of phoebe nests are parasitized by cowbirds. This is the only flycatcher that winters in southeastern U.S.

Habitat: Woods, farmlands, suburbs; nests on bridges, outbuildings.

Voice: Song sounds like a hoarse rendition of name, like "feebee"; call is "chirp."

Conservation:
BBS: E ↑ C ↑ CBC: ↓

Say's Phoebe

Sayornis saya

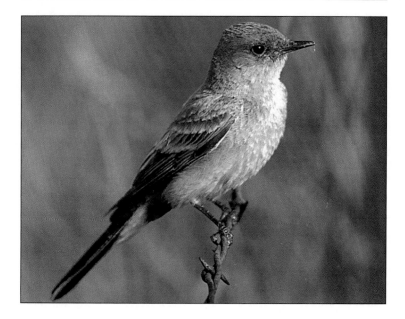

Identification: 8″ Brownish gray above; grayish throat and breast; cinnamon belly; repeatedly bobs blackish tail.

Feeding: Flies from perch to catch aerial insects; also hovers above grass to find insects.

Nesting: Nest a mounded cup of grasses, moss, cocoons, lined with hair or wool, placed most often in natural sheltered nook or in building or under bridge. Eggs: 4–5, white; I: 14 days; F: 14–16 days, altricial; B: 2–3.

Other Behavior: Nest reused in successive years. Unlike other phoebes, this species rarely uses mud in the construction of its nest.

Habitat: Arid open areas with sparse vegetation.

Voice: Song is repeated "pitseedar"; call a high-pitched downslurred "peeer."

Conservation:
BBS: E C ↑ CBC: ↑

Vermilion Flycatcher

Pyrocephalus rubinus

Male

Female

Identification: 6″ MALE: Scarlet crown and underparts; black back, wings, and tail. FEMALE: Gray-brown above; whitish breast lightly streaked with gray; **belly salmon-pink.** IMM—MALE: Crown and breast with varying amounts of red; belly salmon-pink; brown back, wings, and tail. FEMALE: Like adult female, but with light yellow belly. Imm. plumage kept 1 year.

Feeding: Flies from perch to catch aerial insects.

Nesting: Nest a shallow cup of twigs, weed stalks, grasses, bark, lined with downy materials, placed on horizontal branch of tree 8–55 ft. high. Eggs: 2–3, white with darker marks; I: 12 days; F: 14–16 days, altricial; B: 2.

Other Behavior: Watch for courtship display. With red belly and crest fluffed, male sings and rises with fluttery flight to 50 ft., then continues with level flight and drops down.

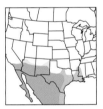

Habitat: Wooded or brushy areas near water.

Voice: Repeated "pit pitasee, pit pit pitasee," sometimes given in flight. Call a short "pitz."

Conservation:
BBS: E C ⇓ CBC: ⇓

Ash-throated Flycatcher
Myiarchus cinerascens

Identification: 8″ **Crested; grayish-brown upperparts; pale gray breast; pale yellow belly.** Very similar to Brown-crested Flycatcher, but smaller, with a shorter thinner bill and paler underparts. **See Voice.**

Feeding: Flies from perch to catch aerial insects.

Nesting: Nest a natural cavity, old woodpecker nest, or nest box lined with weed stems, rootlets, chips of manure, hair, and fur, and occasionally snakeskins. Eggs: 4–5, whitish with darker marks; I: 15 days; F: 14–16 days, altricial; B: 1.

Other Behavior: Will accept nest box with entrance hole 1½–2 in. in diameter. May nest in seemingly strange spots, such as mailbox, drainpipe, or fence post.

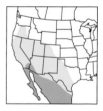

Habitat: Varied: open woods, wooded streams, arid brush.

Voice: Common calls include "prrrt" and burry "kabrik" and "kaweer."

Conservation:
BBS: E C ↑ CBC: ↓

Great Crested Flycatcher

Myiarchus crinitus

Identification: 8" Crested; **bright yellow belly; strongly reddish-brown tail.** Additional distinctions from other crested flycatchers: lower mandible yellow at base, and throat darker gray. The only crested flycatcher in the East, except for S. Tex. **See Voice.**

Feeding: Flies from perch to catch aerial insects; usually feeds high in treetops. Eats some berries.

Nesting: Nest in natural cavity, old woodpecker hole, or nest box lined with grass, fur, bits of paper, occasionally bits of snakeskin. Eggs: 5–6, whitish with darker marks; I: 12–15 days; F: 14–21 days, altricial; B: 1.

Other Behavior: Crest erected in alarm or curiosity. Aggressive displays involve showing the reddish-brown feathers of the wings and tail by fully spreading them. Will nest in nest box with a 1½–2½ in. diameter entrance hole, but often has to compete with starlings and flickers.

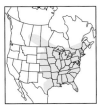

Habitat: Woods and wooded urban areas.

Voice: A loud strongly ascending "wheeep," and a burry "prreet."

Conservation:
BBS: E ↓ C ↓ CBC: ↓

Brown-crested Flycatcher
Myiarchus tyrannulus

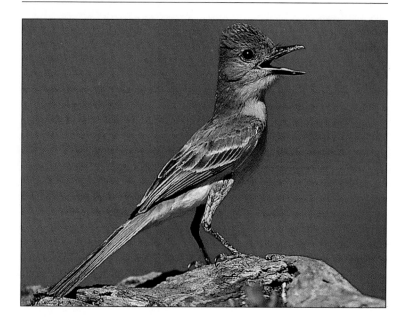

Identification: 8½" **Crested; relatively large bill;** upperparts gray-brown; throat gray; belly lemon-yellow; tail feathers edged with reddish brown down to tip. Voice helpful in distinguishing from other crested flycatchers. **See Voice.**

Feeding: Flies out from perch to catch aerial insects.

Nesting: Nest in natural wood cavity or old woodpecker hole lined with hair, fur, and other soft materials. Eggs: 3–5, whitish with darker marks; I: 13–15 days; F: 12–20 days, altricial; B: 1 or more.

Other Behavior: In Ariz., often nests in abandoned woodpecker holes in saguaro cactus — holes made by Gila Woodpeckers or Northern Flickers. Many species of birds in desert areas depend on these holes for nesting, and in some cases roosting, including Elf Owl, screech-owls, American Kestrel, Cactus Wren, Purple Martin, and Ash-throated Flycatcher.

Habitat: Arid or semiarid brush with saguaro cactus, streamsides, subtropical woodlands.

Voice: Song a repeated "weer per berg"; calls include a "whit" and "pureer."

Conservation:
BBS: E C ⇑ CBC: ↓

Great Kiskadee

Pitangus sulphuratus

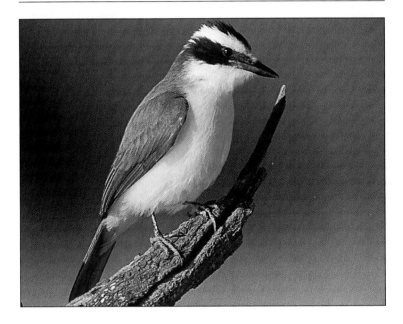

Identification: 10″ Limited to S. Tex. Conspicuous, with a **black-and-white-striped head** and **yellow belly.** Often noisy.

Feeding: Sits on perch and dives down to water or ground to catch prey, then flies back up to eat it. Eats fish, insects, lizards, fledgling birds, berries, and garbage.

Nesting: Large globular nest of twigs, grass, vines, moss, lined with softer material, placed high in a tree or on crossbar of telephone pole. Eggs: 3–4, whitish with light markings; I: ?; F: ?, altricial; B: 2–3.

Other Behavior: One of the earliest birds to call in the morning, and, while calling at dawn, may raise its crest and flap its wings. Very aggressive and drives away larger birds that come near the nest. Female incubates eggs, while male perches nearby. Both adults build nest and feed young.

Habitat: Woods near water; suburbs.

Voice: Call is a slow rendition of name "kis-ka-dee," which was originally from the French *Qu'est-ce qu'il dit?* (What did he say?). At dawn gives a longer "kayeer kayeer trrrrrr kweer."

Conservation:
BBS: E C ⇑ CBC: ↓

Couch's Kingbird
Tyrannus couchii

Identification: 9" Limited to S. Tex. **Large bill; light gray head with slightly darker ear patch; breast washed olive** (not gray as on Western Kingbird); **deeply notched tail brownish**.

Feeding: Flies out from perches to catch aerial insects; also eats some berries. May skim over water surface to drink water.

Nesting: Nest made of moss, bark strips, and plant down, placed on branch of tree 8–22 ft. high. Eggs: 3–4, whitish with darker marks; I: 15–16 days; F: 17–19 days, altricial; B: 1.

Other Behavior: Pairs often perch together and will attack larger birds that come near their nest. Even known to attack frigatebirds, hawks, and falcons.

Habitat: Scattered trees, open woodlands, suburbs.

Voice: Calls a "gweeer" and "kip."

Conservation: BBS: E C ⇑ CBC: ↓

Western Kingbird

Tyrannus verticalis

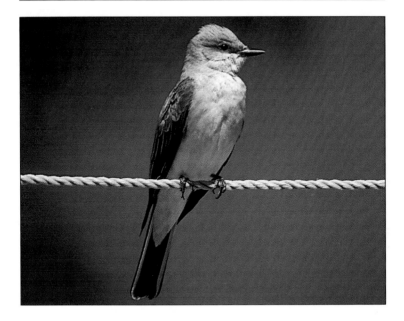

Identification: 9" Most widespread kingbird in West. Relatively **short bill; head, throat, and upper breast light gray;** belly bright yellow; **square-tipped tail black** with **thin white edges,** which are distinctive but sometimes hard to see.

Feeding: Eats mostly insects caught in midair; also some berries.

Nesting: Bulky nest of twigs, plant stems, rootlets, lined with finer materials, sometimes trash, placed in trees 8–40 ft. high. Eggs: 3–5, white with darker marks; I: 13–15 days; F: 16–18 days, altricial; B: 1 or possibly more.

Other Behavior: Has orange-red crown that is normally concealed, but exposed during aggressive encounters. Like other kingbirds, it is aggressive to large birds near the nest.

Habitat: Open areas with some trees or shrubs.

Voice: Call is "kit," sometimes extended to "kit kit kittledot."

Conservation: BBS: E ⇓ C ↑ CBC: ↓

Eastern Kingbird

Tyrannus tyrannus

Identification: 9″ **Black upperparts; white underparts;** conspicuous **white tip to black tail.**

Feeding: Sits on perches and flies out after insects, catching them in the air or off the ground.

Nesting: Somewhat disheveled nest of soft materials, such as weeds, moss, bark strips, feathers, cloth, and string, placed near the tip of a horizontal branch 10–20 ft. high. Eggs: 3–4, white with dark marks; I: 14–16 days; F: 14–17 days, altricial; B: 1.

Other Behavior: Male patrols territory of about an acre, in morning and afternoon, giving "zeer" and "kitter" calls. When the female first arrives on the territory, the male may chase her; after that, whenever they meet, they do a fluttering flight and give "kitter" call. Other kingbirds are allowed in the territory, if they do not get too close to the nest or try to mate with the female. Larger birds are chased out of the area, with the kingbirds diving onto their back and chasing them much farther than the territorial boundaries; a special aerial tumbling flight may occur after this. During incubation, the female may be aggressive toward the male in the vicinity of the nest. Once the young hatch, both parents feed them.

Habitat: Open areas with some trees.

Voice: Calls include "kitterkitterkitter," "kt'zee kt'zee," and "zeer."

Conservation: BBS: E ↓ C ↑ CBC: ↓

Gray Kingbird

Tyrannus dominicensis

Identification: 9 " Limited to coastal Fla. and coasts of adjacent states. **Pale gray head and back; black mask over eye; heavy black bill;** all-black tail; underparts whitish.

Feeding: Eats mostly insects caught in the air, but also some berries and a few seeds.

Nesting: Shallow nest of twigs lined with rootlets, placed on horizontal limb of tree or shrub. Eggs: 2, white with darker marks; I: 12–13 days; F: ?, altricial; B: 1 or possibly more.

Other Behavior: Displays may include spreading of wings and tail.

Habitat: Coastal areas with mangroves and hardwood hammocks; also suburbs.

Voice: A repeated shrill "chicheery."

Conservation: BBS: E ↓ C

Scissor-tailed Flycatcher

Tyrannus forficatus

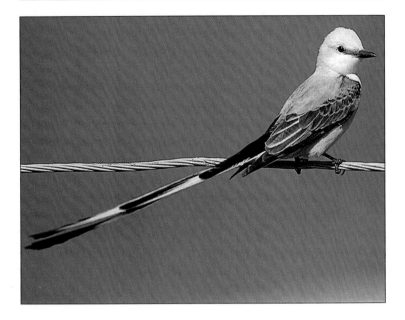

Identification: 14″ **Very long split tail;** pale gray body; **pinkish wash on flanks. IN FLIGHT:** Underwings bright pinkish orange. **IMM:** Tail long, but shorter than adult's; body paler with little or no pink on belly. Imm. plumage kept into winter.

Feeding: Flies from perch to catch insects on the ground or in the air.

Nesting: Nest a loose collection of soft natural and human-made materials, placed on horizontal limb or telephone pole. Eggs: 4–5, white with dark marks; I: 12–15 days; F: 14–16 days, altricial; B: 1.

Other Behavior: Courtship involves male doing spectacular flight to about 100 ft.; he then drops down in a series of shallow arcs, then may fly higher and somersault in midair before finally landing. Flights are accompanied by bill snapping and "kakweee" calls. From a few to 250 birds may roost together in trees at night; during breeding, female stays on eggs or with nestlings and does not go to roost.

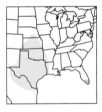

Habitat: Open areas with scattered trees.

Voice: Call a "kit" and, during display flight, a "kakweee kakweee."

Conservation: BBS: E C ↑ CBC: ↓

Rose-throated Becard

Pachyramphus aglaiae

Male

Identification: 6½" Limited to S. Ariz. and S. Tex. **Stocky, thick-necked, and short-tailed. MALE: Dark gray above, light below; rosy patch on throat. FEMALE: Gray cap; brown wings and tail;** light buffy underparts. **IMM:** Like adult female; imm. male has some rosy feathers on throat.

Feeding: Flies out from perch to catch insects in air or off leaves; eats some seeds.

Nesting: Long pendant nest of woven plant fibers, suspended from the end of a tree branch 30–50 ft. high. Eggs: 4–6, white with darker marks; I: ?; F: ?, altricial; B: 1.

Other Behavior: Often perches hidden in foliage; best located by call.

Habitat: Large trees along rivers or streams.

Voice: Rapid chattering followed by a descending "seeeoh."

Conservation:
TREND UNKNOWN.

Northern Shrike
Loggerhead Shrike

Lanius excubitor   Lanius ludovicianus

Northern adult

Northern immature

Loggerhead

Identification: Northern 10″ Loggerhead 9″ Northern Shrike breeds in Far North, generally only seen in winter; Loggerhead widespread in lower 48 states. **NORTHERN: Rounded forehead; long strongly hooked bill; thin black mask;** pale gray back blends with whitish breast. **IMM:** Mask may be faint; grayish-brown head and back; barring on breast and belly. Imm. plumage kept until spring. **LOGGERHEAD: Flattened forehead; relatively short, slightly hooked bill; thick black mask;** dark gray back contrasts with whitish breast. **IN FLIGHT:** White patches on wings and tail corners in both species.

Feeding: Both swoop on prey from perches. Prey on insects, small birds, and small animals.

Nesting: Nest of twigs, bark strips, placed in shrub or tree. Northern—Eggs: 2–9, gray with dark marks; I: 15–16 days; F: 20 days, altricial; B: ? Loggerhead—Eggs: 4–7, gray with dark marks; I: 10–17 days; F: 17–21 days, altricial; B: 2.

Other Behavior: Both store prey by impaling on thorns.

Northern   Loggerhead

Habitat: Open country with some shrubs and trees.

Voice: Song for both a series of whistles and calls; call a "chak chak."

Conservation: Northern: CBC: ↑ Loggerhead: BBS: E ⇓ C ⇓ CBC: ↓ Loggerhead endangered in Can. and on San Clemente Is., Calif.

White-eyed Vireo
Vireo griseus

Identification: 5″ Yellow lores and eye-ring ("spectacles"); white throat; whitish eyes; yellow flanks; conspicuous white wing bars. Young birds have all-dark eyes through their 1st winter; eyes turn white by Feb.

Feeding: Feeds in low thickets, eating mostly insects; also eats spiders, small lizards, snails, and wild berries.

Nesting: Nest of bark shreds, twigs, rootlets, grasses, and leaves, bound with spiderweb, lined with fine grasses and plant stems, decorated with lichens and pieces of paper, suspended from fork of small branch in tree or shrub 1–8 ft. above ground. Eggs: 3–5, white with brown spots; I: 12–16 days; F: ?, altricial; B: 1–2.

Other Behavior: Heard more than seen. Generally stays concealed in shrubbery. Males have a number of song types, generally singing one type over and over, then switching to another type. Males also incorporate into their songs fragments of the songs and calls of other birds, such as Gray Catbirds, Song Sparrows, Yellow-breasted Chats, and American Robins.

Habitat: Dense understory, thickets, hedgerows.

Voice: Song a series of rapid whistles that begins and ends with a sharp "chick," like "chick-adooweeoo-chick"; calls a "chick" and wrenlike scolding.

Conservation: BBS: E ↑ C ↓ CBC: ↑

289

Bell's Vireo

Vireo bellii

Identification: 4¾" Indistinct whitish eye-ring and lores ("spectacles"); 2 wing bars, the upper 1 faint or lacking; some birds may have a whitish eyebrow. **In East, birds are greenish above and yellowish below; in West, birds are grayish above and whitish below.** Plumage of this species varies in presence or absence of eye-ring, wing bars, spectacles, and eyebrow. Generally indistinct and hard to identify when not singing; song is distinctive among vireos.

Feeding: Very active. Forages low to ground in dense underbrush, shrubs. Eats insects, spiders, and fruits.

Nesting: Nest of bark, plant fibers, and cocoons lined with hair and fine grasses, suspended from fork of tree branch 1–10 ft. above ground. Eggs: 3–5, white with brown spots; I: 14 days; F: 11–12 days, altricial; B: 2.

Other Behavior: The Calif. subspecies is endangered due to loss of riparian habitat and the invasion of remaining habitat fragments by Brown-headed Cowbirds, which parasitize this vireo's nests. Restoration of habitat and local cowbird control may facilitate some recovery.

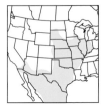

Habitat: Riparian brush, mesquite, thorny thickets.

Voice: Song a rapid series of harsh notes increasing in loudness, sometimes ending with an up or down inflection.

Conservation:
BBS: E ⇓ C ⇓ CBC: ↑ Calif. subspecies, Least Bell's Vireo (*V. b. pusillus*), is endangered in U.S.

Black-capped Vireo

Vireo atricapillus

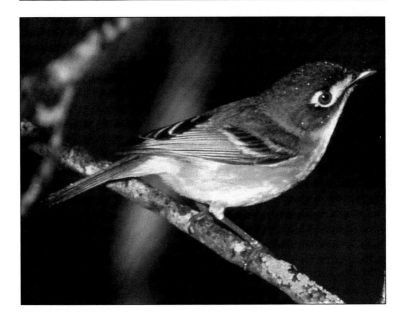

Identification: 4½" Small; dark cap and cheek; bold white eye-ring and lores ("spectacles"); 2 yellowish wing bars. **MALE:** Glossy black cap. **FEMALE:** Dark gray cap.

Feeding: Forages for food among low dwarf oaks and other thickets. Eats insects, spiders, and fruit.

Nesting: Nest of grasses, dried leaves, bark strips, catkins, and spider's cocoons, bound with spider's silk, lined with pine needles and fine grasses, suspended from fork of tree or shrub branch 1–15 ft. above the ground. Eggs: 3–5, white; I: 14–17 days; F: 10–12 days, altricial; B: 2.

Other Behavior: Very active. Most often seen in low brush. Populations are perilously declining due to habitat loss from housing development, brush clearance for range management, and sheep and goat grazing. There is also extremely heavy cowbird parasitism on this species. Despite some management attempts for recovery, the future survival of this species is in doubt.

Habitat: Shrubby hillside thickets, oak scrublands.

Voice: Song a rapid series of harsh 2–3 note phrases; call "chitit."

Conservation: TREND UNKNOWN. Endangered in U.S. Ninety percent of U.S population is under immediate threat from land development.

291

Solitary Vireo
Vireo solitarius

Eastern form

Identification: 5½" Gray head; bold white eye-ring and lores ("spectacles"); 2 bold white wing bars. Eastern birds have an olive back and yellowish flanks; Rocky Mountain and Great Basin birds (*V. s. plumbeus*) basically all gray and white; West Coast birds have grayish-green back.

Feeding: Forages for food in tree foliage, eating insects, spiders, and some fruit. Occasionally hawks for insects from perch.

Nesting: Nest of forbs, grasses, strips of inner bark, spiderweb, and rootlets lined with vine tendrils, pine needles, and decorated with lichens, suspended from fork of horizontal tree branch 3–30 ft. above ground. Eggs: 3–5, white with brown spots; I: 11–12 days; F: 14 days, altricial; B: 1–2.

Other Behavior: Moves about more sluggishly than the smaller vireos. Stays in treetops. Frequently parasitized by the Brown-headed Cowbird, which lays its eggs among the vireo's eggs.

Habitat: Mixed coniferous and deciduous woods.

Voice: Song is a short series of high-pitched whistled notes with long pauses between each series; call note a harsh "churr."

Conservation:
BBS: E ⇑ C ⇑ CBC: ↑

Yellow-throated Vireo

Vireo flavifrons

Identification: 5½" Bright yellow throat and breast; white belly; yellow eye-ring and lores, ("spectacles"); 2 bold white wing bars.

Feeding: Forages for food in tree foliage, eating insects and sometimes wild fruits.

Nesting: Nest of shredded bark, grasses, and forbs, bound with spiderweb and plant down, lined with fine grasses, decorated with lichens, suspended in fork of tree branch 3–60 ft. above the ground. Eggs: 3–5, white or pink-white with brown spots; I: 14–15 days; F: 14–15 days, altricial; B: ?

Other Behavior: The phrases in this vireo's song have longer pauses between them than those of the Red-eyed and Solitary Vireo. This vireo used to be more frequent in suburban areas, but it has been affected by the spraying of pesticides on shade trees.

Habitat: Mature deciduous forest canopy.

Voice: Song is a slow series of burry, 2–3 note, whistled phrases with long pauses between phrases, like "tweeoo, toowee, turway."

Conservation: BBS: E ↑ C ⇓ CBC: ↓

Warbling Vireo

Vireo gilvus

Eastern form

Identification: 5½" Whitish eyebrow; faint eyeline and pale lores; whitish underneath with variable amounts of yellow; yellow, if present, is brightest on flanks. Western birds slightly greener and yellower; eastern birds grayer.

Feeding: Gleans prey from tree foliage by both searching through and hovering above it. Eats insects and some berries.

Nesting: Nest of leaves, bark strips, grasses, and plant down, bound with spiderweb, lined with plant stems and horsehair, suspended in horizontal branch of tree 4–90 ft. above ground. Eggs: 3–5, white with brown spots; I: 12–14 days; F: 12–16 days, altricial; B: ?

Other Behavior: Best detected by its long, flowing, warbling song, which it sings throughout the day. Commonly parasitized by the Brown-headed Cowbird.

Habitat: Deciduous woods and streamside shrubs; aspen groves.

Voice: Song is an extended rambling series of slurred whistles.

Conservation: BBS: E ↓ C ↑ CBC: →

Philadelphia Vireo

Vireo philadelphicus

Identification: 5 " White eyebrow; dark eyeline and dark lores; variably yellowish underneath, with brightest yellow on the center of the throat and upper breast.

Feeding: Feeds at end of tree branches and in dense foliage, hovering before or hanging from twigs and branches. Eats insects, spiders, and fruit.

Nesting: Nest of lichens, birch bark, grasses, plant down, bound with spiderweb, lined with fine grasses and pine needles, suspended from horizontal branch of tree 10–90 ft. above the ground. Eggs: 3–5, white with brown spots; I: 14 days; F: 12–14 days, altricial; B: ?

Other Behavior: Its song resembles that of the Red-eyed Vireo but usually is higher, thinner, with the phrases slower.

Habitat: Open woods and streamside shrubs.

Voice: Song is short, high-pitched, whistled phrases with pauses between, like "teeyay, teeyee, teeyit."

Conservation:
BBS: E ↑ C CBC: →

Red-eyed Vireo

Vireo olivaceus

Identification: 6" Two eyebrows — a white one and a black one above it; dark eyeline; gray cap. Red eye visible from close up. **IMM:** Like adult, but with brown eyes; eyes change to red in spring. ▶The closely related Yellow-green Vireo, *V. flavoviridis,* has similar gray cap and eye patterns, but is otherwise yellowish overall. It lives in Mex. and only occasionally is seen in S. Tex. or coastal Calif.

Feeding: Forages in foliage of treetops, eating mostly insects. Also eats wild fruits and berries.

Nesting: Nest of fine grasses, rootlets, paper, grapevine bark, spiderweb, decorated with lichens, placed in horizontal tree or shrub branch 2–60 ft. above the ground. Eggs: 3–5, white with dark marks; I: 11–14 days; F: 10–12 days, altricial; B: 1–2.

Other Behavior: Female does all nest building and incubation. During incubation, the male sings faster, 50–60 phrases per minute. When he stops, the female comes off the nest and he feeds her, or they feed together. She then resumes incubating. This species is one of those most frequently parasitized by cowbirds.

Habitat: Deciduous woods, rural to suburban.

Voice: Short, medium-pitched, whistled phrases with space in between, like "eeyay, oolee, eeyup"; calls "nyaah" and "tjjjj."

Conservation:
BBS: E ↑ C ↓ CBC: ↓

Black-whiskered Vireo
Vireo altiloquus

Identification: 6" Limited to S. Fla. Similar to Red-eyed Vireo with **2 eyebrows — a white one and a black one above it; dark eyeline; gray cap;** and red eye visible from close up. Differs from Red-eyed Vireo in having a **larger bill** and a **black "whisker streak" off base of bill.**

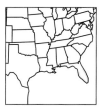

Feeding: Forages high in trees. Eats insects, wild berries, and some weed seeds.

Nesting: Nest of plant fibers, grasses, forbs, cocoons, spiderweb, lichens, lined with pine needles, palm threads, suspended from horizontal tree branches 3–20 ft. above the ground. Eggs: 2–3, white with brown spots; I: ?; F: ?, altricial; B: ?

Other Behavior: Sings throughout the day. Dense wet mangrove habitat may make it difficult to locate.

Habitat: Coastal mangroves.

Voice: Song a series of paired phrases, less continuous than those of Red-eyed Vireo.

Conservation: BBS: E ↑ C

Gray Jay
Perisoreus canadensis

Identification: 12" **White forehead; dark gray cap; short bill.** Varies geographically in darkness of gray upperparts and brightness of white underparts.

Feeding: Feeds on wide variety of items, including small rodents, invertebrates, the young and eggs of birds, berries, fruit, and human food scraps. Attracted to campsites, where it is unafraid of humans, takes handouts, and boldly steals food, even snatching it off plates.

Nesting: Nest of twigs, bark, mosses, lined with feathers and fur, placed on horizontal branch of tree, usually conifer, 6–28 ft. from ground. Eggs: 2–5, pale green or white with dark blotches; I: 16–18 days; F: 15 days, altricial; B: 1.

Other Behavior: Has special mucus-secreting glands inside bill, which allow it to use sticky saliva to form berries into balls. It stores these for future use by sticking them to tree branches or lichen clumps. Moves to lower elevations in winter. When food is scarce, large groups may move to areas outside their normal range.

Habitat: Mostly northern coniferous forests.

Voice: Often quiet; alarm call is a harsh "churrr"; many other calls given.

Conservation: BBS: E ↓ C ⇓ CBC: ⇑

Blue Jay
Cyanocitta cristata

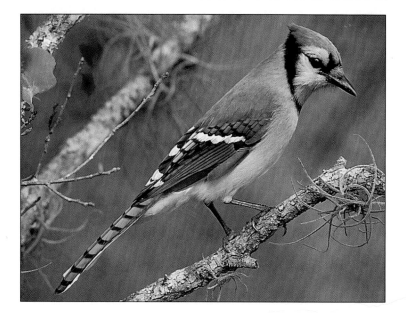

Identification: 12″ Crested; black collar and necklace; wings and tail spotted with white; blue above, grayish below.

Feeding: Eats acorns and other nuts; also fruit, insects, bird eggs and nestlings. Comes to bird feeders for sunflower seed and cracked corn, which it may cache.

Nesting: Nest of twigs, bark, leaves, and human-made objects, lined with fine rootlets, placed in a tree. May build preliminary nest of a loose platform of twigs that is not completed or used for breeding. Eggs: 4–5, greenish blue, spotted with brown; I: 17 days; F: 17–19 days, altricial; B: 1–2.

Other Behavior: In fall, forms large roaming feeding flocks that divide into smaller groups by midwinter. In spring, courtship flocks fly about in the mornings in a follow-the-leader fashion and give a variety of calls. These flocks are believed to be composed of 1 female and a number of males; the female is always in the lead as the birds take flight. After the flock lands, the males display with bobbing, raising and lowering their whole body repeatedly, while giving the "toolool" call. During breeding, the birds are quiet and inconspicuous. Blue Jays will mob and dive at hawks, giving "jaay" calls.

Habitat: Woods and suburbs.

Voice: A harsh "jaay, jaay," given in alarm and within flock; a liquid "toolool"; and a grating ratchetlike call. Also imitates hawk calls.

Conservation: BBS: E ↓ C ↓ CBC: ↑

Green Jay
Cyanocorax yncas

Identification: 12" Limited to S. Tex. **Crown a striking blue; back and belly green; tail green with yellow outer feathers;** bib and chin black.

Feeding: Eats nuts, beetles, crickets and other insects, earthworms, bird eggs, seeds, fruits, berries. Comes to feeders and eats sunflower seeds and cracked corn.

Nesting: Nest a twig platform lined with mosses, grasses, leaves, placed in small tree or shrub. Eggs: 3–5, pale gray or green with brown speckles; I: 17–19 days; F: 19–22 days, altricial; B: 1.

Other Behavior: After breeding, assembles into larger flocks, which can be inquisitive around humans. Young stay with parents for 1 year, and assist in territorial defense. Flocks mob predators.

Habitat: Subtropical woodland, dense brush.

Voice: Common call is "cheh cheh cheh"; also many other calls, and mimicry.

Conservation:
BBS: E C ↑ CBC: ↓

Florida Scrub-Jay

Aphelocoma coerulescens

Identification: 12″ Blue head, wings, and tail; no crest; throat streaked gray and white bordered by a bluish necklace; white eyebrow and whitish forehead; back grayish.

Feeding: Eats insects, acorns, pine seeds, invertebrates, eggs and nestlings of birds, frogs, berries, fruit. Caches food. Comes to bird feeders.

Nesting: Nest of twigs, grass, lined with fibers, rootlets, placed in shrub or bush. Eggs: 2–6, pale green or gray with marks of reddish brown; I: 16–19 days; F: 18 days, altricial; B: 1–2.

Other Behavior: Found in pairs or family groups that live throughout the year on a fixed territory. Has helpers at the nest — 1–3 young of previous year that help with territorial and nest defense and feeding of the nestlings. This assistance reduces nestling mortality due to predation. Population down 50% since 1900, due to loss of scrub-oak habitat to development.

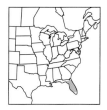

Habitat: Shrubby areas with some trees; may visit suburbs.

Voice: Calls vary locally. Common call a rasping "reeep." Mimics local birds, including hawks.

Conservation: BBS: E ⇓ C

American Crow
Fish Crow

Corvus brachyrhynchos Corvus ossifragus

American

Fish

Identification: American 18″, Fish 17″ **Large; all black;** tip of tail square or slightly rounded. **Best distinguished by calls. See Voice.**

Feeding: American Crow eats insects, nuts, seeds, corn, fruit, bird eggs and nestlings, carrion. Caches food. Comes to bird feeders. Fish Crow eats amphibians, crabs, fish, shrimps, seeds, fruit, eggs of birds, especially waterbirds.

Nesting: Nest of twigs, sticks, lined with bark, grass, moss, placed in trees. American — Eggs: 4–5, bluish green with brown marks; I: 18 days; F: 28–35 days, altricial; B: 1–2. Fish — Eggs: 4–5, bluish green with brown marks; I: 18 days; F: 21 or more days, altricial; B: 1.

Other Behavior: In East, American Crows live on territories year round in family groups of 2–10 birds, which include parents and young of previous years that help raise the newest brood. In Calif., only about one-third of the breeding pairs have additional helper, usually a yearling female, and pairs do not defend a territory. Fish Crows breed in small colonies. In winter, American Crows leave territories each evening and fly to large communal roosts that can include Fish Crows.

American   Fish

Habitat: American: varied habitats. Fish: coastal or inland along rivers.

Voice: American call a long, descending "caaaw"; Fish call a short nasal "ca." Both have a variety of other calls.

Conservation:
American:
BBS: E ↑ C ↑ CBC: ↑
Fish:
BBS: E ↑ C ⇑ CBC: ⇑

Common Raven
Chihuahuan Raven
Corvus corax   Corvus cryptoleucus

Common

Chihuahuan

Identification: Common 24", Chihuahuan 19"
Both are large, all black, with massive bill;
when flying, tip of tail is **wedge-shaped,** rather
than square or slightly rounded as in crows. Also
note range, habitat, and voice. **COMMON: Very
large; long shaggy feathers on the chin and
throat; often soars like a hawk. CHIHUAHUAN:
Smaller; less shaggy throat; less massive bill.**

Feeding: Both eat carrion, shellfish, rodents, insects,
seeds, fruit, food scraps, bird eggs and nestlings. Both
cache food.

Nesting: Nest is bulky mass of twigs, branches, earth,
lined with roots, moss, hair, placed on mostly cliffs, but
also trees and buildings. Eggs: 3–8, blue to greenish
with brown marks; I: 21 days; F: 35–42 days, altricial;
B: 1.

Other Behavior: Males have elaborate courtship flight
maneuvers, including steep dives, tumbles, and barrel
rolls. Both have large communal roosts in fall and
winter, generally consisting of nonbreeding birds.
Breeding pairs tend to stay on their territories year
round. Featured in many Native American myths.

Common   Chihuahuan

Habitat: Common:
mountains, forests,
canyons, deserts;
coast. Chihuahuan:
arid areas.

Voice: Common
call a very low
"gronk";
Chihuahuan call a
higher-pitched
"kraak."

Conservation:
Common:
BBS: E ⇑ C ⇑ CBC: ⇑
Chihuahuan:
BBS: E C ⇓ CBC: ⇓

303

Horned Lark

Eremophila alpestris

Identification: 8″ **Distinctive black facial marks** — black forehead with black "horns" (more prominent on males); black line from bill to eye and down cheek; and black bib. Other areas on **face, throat, and belly vary from whitish to deep yellow** based on subspecies. IN FLIGHT: Note **light underwings; black tail with white outer feathers.**

Feeding: Feeds on ground, eating weed seeds and grain, insects, spiders.

Nesting: Nest a depression in ground lined with grasses, placed near a grass clump or clod of manure. Eggs: 3–5, gray, sometimes spotted with brown; I: 11 days; F: 9–12 days, altricial; B: 1–3.

Other Behavior: Male does spectacular courtship flight up to 800 ft. high, circling and singing at the top, then dives down quietly. Male also raises "horns" and walks stiffly in front of female during courtship. Female starts 2nd brood about a week after young leave nest. Forms large flocks during migration and in winter. Has expanded range in East.

Habitat: Open ground with low vegetation.

Voice: Song a light twittering, given during display flight; call "tsee-titi" or "zeet."

Conservation:
BBS: E ↑ C ↓ CBC: ↓

Purple Martin
Progne subis

Immature male,
1st summer

Male (l.), female (r.)

Identification: 8″ **MALE: All dark purple** with black wings and tail. Purple areas are shiny. **FEMALE:** Gray chest; **whitish belly; dull purple back;** black wings and tail. **IMM:** Female is like adult female. Male, in first fall, is also like adult female. The next spring and summer, he resembles adult female, but has more shiny purple on back and is slightly darker on the belly. Imm. plumage kept 1 year.

Feeding: Feeds on the wing, eating insects.

Nesting: Colonial nester in East, primarily in man-made birdhouses consisting of many individual compartments. In West, tends to nest singly, in natural cavities in trees and in holes in saguaro cactus. Nest composed of mud, sticks, twigs, feathers, bark, paper; fresh green leaves added during incubation. Eggs: 5–6, white; I: 15–16 days; F: 27–35 days, altricial; B: 1.

Other Behavior: Native Americans were the first to put out hollow gourds for breeding martins. Now, thousands of people put out martin nest boxes. After nesting, young and adults gather in premigratory roosts of many thousands.

Habitat: Open areas, often near water.

Voice: Song is pairs of notes followed by guttural warble, given during pair interactions. "Cher cher" call given near nest.

Conservation: BBS: E ↓ C ↑ CBC: ↑

Tree Swallow

Tachycineta bicolor

Adult

Immature female

Identification: 6″ **Upperparts iridescent blue; underparts bright white; dark on head encloses eye.** In fall, iridescent upperparts may appear greenish. Adult females may have a brownish forehead. **IMM:** Male like adult male. Female has mostly brown upperparts, mixed with varying amounts of iridescent blue; over 2 years, this plumage gradually becomes like adult's.

Feeding: Eats insects while flying. Before migration, will land in bayberry shrubs and eat berries.

Nesting: Often in loose colony. Grass nest lined with feathers, placed in tree cavity, old woodpecker hole, or nest box. Eggs: 5–6, white; I: 14–15 days; F: 21 days, altricial; B: 1–2.

Other Behavior: The Tree Swallow is the only N. American passerine with an imm.-plumaged female in the 1st (and sometimes 2nd) year. This imm. plumage allows them to approach breeding adults and their nests without being chased away. This, in turn, lets them monitor breeding pairs and be ready to replace any adult female that dies during the nesting season.

Habitat: Open areas near woods and water.

Voice: Song, given by male, is 3 descending notes, followed by warble. "Cheedeep" call is given during alarm.

Conservation: BBS: E ↑ C ↑ CBC: ↓ Competes for nest sites with starlings, House Sparrows, House Wrens, and bluebirds.

Northern Rough-winged Swallow

Stelgidopteryx serripennis

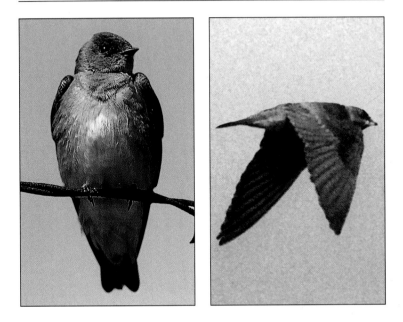

Identification: 5 " **Upperparts grayish brown; chin, breast, and flanks grayish;** belly white. Slower deeper wingbeat than similar Bank Swallow.

Feeding: Eats insects while flying.

Nesting: Alone or in small scattered groups. Sometimes a few pairs will nest on the periphery of Bank Swallow colonies. Nest of grass, leaves, twigs, moss, straw, placed in cavity or crevice, such as cave, old tunnel of Bank Swallows, drainpipe; rarely uses tree hole. Eggs: 4–8, white; I: 16–18 days; F: 18–21 days, altricial; B: 1.

Other Behavior: After the breeding season, forms large flocks that roost together in marshes, mangrove islands, sugar cane fields.

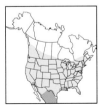

Habitat: Open areas, especially near water and cutaway banks.

Voice: A harsh "brrrt" given during alarm and aggressive encounters.

Conservation: BBS: E ↑ C ↓ CBC: ⇓

Bank Swallow

Riparia riparia

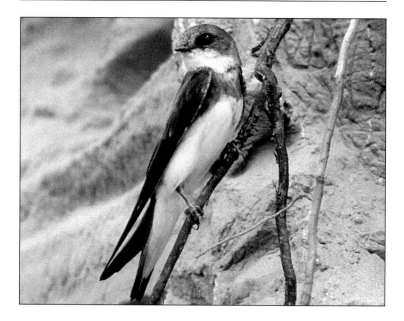

Identification: 5″ **Upperparts dark brown, underparts white except for brown breastband.** Rapid shallow wingbeat.

Feeding: Eats a wide variety of insects.

Nesting: Highly colonial. Nest of grasses, weeds, lined with feathers, placed in a tunnel in vertical sandy river bank, coastal cliff, gravel quarry; nests may be as close as 1 ft. apart. Bird excavates nest tunnel; it is about 20–40 in. long, slopes upward, and ends in a wider chamber, where nest is placed. Eggs: 3–6, white; I: 12–26 days; F: 22 days, altricial; B: 1–2.

Other Behavior: Older birds return to nest sites well before 1st-year birds, and they choose nest sites higher on the bank. Bank Swallows are not as site-tenacious as some other swallows with more stable nest sites. After breeding, hundreds or thousands may form flocks that feed and roost together. Nests are often placed in stream banks and gravel quarries where development and quarry operations destroy them.

Habitat: Open areas near water with cutaway banks.

Voice: Contact call between pair is a harsh "tchrrt tchrrt"; a long twittering may be given during courtship; also a rapid buzzy chatter.

Conservation: BBS: E ↓ C ↓ CBC: ↓

Cliff Swallow

Hirundo pyrrhonota

Identification: 6" **Buffy rump; whitish forehead; dark reddish-brown throat.** Also, belly is white; back has white streaking; **tip of tail is square.**

Feeding: Feeds in close-knit flocks. Eats mainly insects; rarely berries.

Nesting: Colonial, sometimes in enormous colonies. Nest a spherical cavity with narrow entrance tunnel, built of mud pellets mixed with a little grass, and lined with grass and feathers. Nests are sometimes built on cliffs, but usually under bridges, in culverts, and on buildings. Eggs: 2–5, white with brown blotches; I: 12–15 days; F: 24 days, altricial; B: 1–3.

Other Behavior: Birds within a colony breed synchronously. May reuse old nesting sites, but can switch sites from year to year, possibly to avoid nest parasites, such as fleas and lice, present in old nests. At colony, birds try to steal grass and mud from each other's nests. Females may lay their eggs in other female's nest, or even carry them there from their own nest. Males may copulate with females who are not their mates.

Habitat: Open areas near cliffs, bridges, outbuildings.

Voice: An extended, harsh twittering, given by male; a "churr" call, given between a pair; and a nasal "nyew" call, given during alarm.

Conservation: BBS: E ↑ C ↑ CBC: ↓ Has begun to adapt to nesting on built structures, to its advantage.

Cave Swallow

Hirundo fulva

Identification: 6″ **Buffy rump; reddish-brown forehead; buffy throat.** Also, belly is white; back has white streaking; **tip of tail is square.**

Feeding: Feeds in small flocks, sometimes in mixed flocks with Cliff and Barn Swallows.

Nesting: In colonies. Nest is open half-bowl made of mud pellets or guano lined with fibers, grass, feathers, placed in cave, culvert, bridge, wall, or building. Old nests may be repaired and reused. Eggs: 3–5, white with reddish-brown speckles; I: 15–16 days; F: 22–26 days, altricial, B. 1–3.

Other Behavior: Less synchronous breeder than Cliff Swallow. First bred in the U.S. in 1914; at first in caves, more recently in highway culverts and buildings. Sometimes nests in association with Barn Swallows. May hybridize with Barn Swallows.

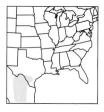

Habitat: Open areas near caves, culverts, and bridges.

Voice: An extended song of squeaks, followed by a warble; a "choo," given during alarm; a "chuweet," given within flock.

Conservation:
BBS: E C ⇑
Use of culverts for nesting has allowed for range expansion.

Barn Swallow

Hirundo rustica

Identification: 7" **Long forked tail; upperparts blue-black; breast buffy;** chin and throat reddish brown.

Feeding: Eats insects. Feeds in pairs while egg-laying, in loose flocks at other times. Feeds in flight, and can skim over water to pick up floating insects.

Nesting: Singly or in colonies. Nest a deep bowl of mud pellets and grass lined with feathers, placed on beam or some projection in barn, under bridge, in culvert, mine shaft, cave. Eggs: 2–7, white with reddish-brown speckles; I: 14–16 days; F: 18–23 days, altricial; B: 1–3.

Other Behavior: Both male and female build nest, usually in the morning, and can make up to 1,000 trips to collect mud. Usually monogamous, but rarely males will pair with 2 females. In colonies males may copulate with females other than their mate. Paired male aggressively defends small area around nest, and guards his mate from intruding males that might attempt to copulate with her.

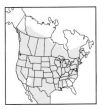

Habitat: Open country near barns or open outbuildings, bridges, culverts.

Voice: Both sexes give song of continuous twitter interspersed by grating sounds; during feeding or alarm, call "chitchit."

Conservation: BBS: E ↓ C ↑ CBC: ↑

Black-capped Chickadee
Carolina Chickadee

Parus atricapillus   Parus carolinensis

Black-capped

Carolina

Identification: Black-capped 5¼", Carolina 4¾" Both birds have **black cap and bib; white cheek. Best distinguished by range and song. BLACK-CAPPED:** Feathers on **shoulder of folded wing (greater coverts) have white edges** (worn down in late summer); lower edge of bib ragged; see Voice. **CAROLINA: Feathers on shoulder all gray;** lower edge of bib clean-cut; see Voice. Hybrids exist where ranges overlap.

Feeding: Both acrobatically move through tree branches searching for insects; also eat seeds and berries. Commonly seen at bird feeders. Favor sunflower seed, which they hold in feet, then crack open.

Nesting: Both excavate cavity in rotted wood, or use birdhouse or natural cavity. Nest materials are mosses, wood chips. Black-capped—Eggs: 6–8, white with speckles; I: 12 days; F: 16 days, altricial; B: 1–2. Carolina—Eggs: 6, white with reddish speckles; I: 11–12 days; F: 13–17 days, altricial; B: 1–2.

Other Behavior: Both form stable winter flocks. In spring, the flocks disperse into breeding pairs. Males sing, and each pair defends a breeding territory.

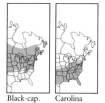

Black-cap.   Carolina

Habitat: Woods, farmland, suburbs.

Voice: Song of Black-capped is 2 whistled notes, the 1st slightly higher than the 2nd; song of Carolina is 4 notes, the 1st and 3rd much higher than the others.

Conservation:
Black-capped:
BBS: E ⇑ C ↑ CBC: ⇑
Carolina:
BBS: E ↓ C ↓ CBC: ↑

Boreal Chickadee

Parus hudsonicus

Identification: 5¼" **Brown cap; black bib; limited white on cheek; flanks strongly reddish brown.** In general, appears plumper, and brown rather than gray as in other chickadees; worn, late summer plumage quite dull.

Feeding: Acrobatically clings to branches, searching for insects. Also eats seeds. Comes to bird feeders for sunflower seed and suet.

Nesting: Nest of mosses, lichens, plant down, hair, fur, placed in a natural or excavated tree cavity, or abandoned woodpecker hole. May also use nest box. Eggs: 4–9, white with brown speckles; I: 11–16 days; F: 18 days, altricial; B: 1.

Other Behavior: Rather shy. Common in spruce-fir forests. Forms winter flocks. Sometimes wanders south of range in winter.

Habitat: Northern coniferous woods; spruce bogs.

Voice: Calls and song wheezy and more drawn out than those of Black-capped Chickadee.

Conservation: BBS: E ⇓ C CBC: →

Tufted Titmouse

Parus bicolor

Gray-crested morph

Black-crested morph

Identification: 5″ Small gray bird; black on forehead or crest; flanks usually buffy. Black-crested morph has whitish forehead and lives in S., C., and W. Tex.; gray-crested morph has black forehead and lives in rest of range.

Feeding: Eats insects, seeds, berries. Common at bird feeders, where it prefers sunflower seed and suet.

Nesting: Nest of mosses, hair, grasses, leaves, cotton, bark strips, placed in natural cavity or birdhouse. Eggs: 4–8, white with small brown speckles, I. 13–14 days, F. 17–18 days, altricial; B: 1–2.

Other Behavior: In late winter or early spring, family flocks break up and the male starts singing and defending breeding territory of 2–5 acres. Rival males come together at territorial boundaries and sing back and forth. As part of courtship, the male feeds the female while she quivers her wings and gives high-pitched notes. This mate-feeding continues through nest-building and incubation phases. The female does almost all of the nest building and often collects large amounts of moss or bark.

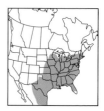

Habitat: Woods and suburbs.

Voice. Song is a downslurred whistle, like "peter peter peter." Calls include a scolding "jweejweejwee" and "tseejwee"; a contact note of "tseet"; and a series of extremely high-pitched whistles.

Conservation: BBS: E ↑ C ↑ CBC: ↑

Verdin

Auriparus flaviceps

Identification: 4¼" **Tiny and gray; yellow head.** Small reddish-brown patch on shoulder may be visible. **Juv:** Dull gray-brown overall; its shorter tail and longer, straight bill help distinguish it from the similar-looking Bushtit.

Feeding: Feeds by gleaning insects from trees and shrubs. Also eats seeds and berries.

Nesting: Conspicuous spherical nest of thorny twigs, grasses, and spider's silk lined with feathers and plant down, placed at end of low branch in shrub, cactus, or tree, especially mesquite. Eggs: 3–6, pale greenish white with dark marks; I: 10 days; F: 21 days, altricial; B: 2.

Other Behavior: Several nests are built by male, then female chooses one for breeding. Smaller nests are built for winter roosting.

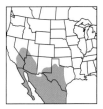

Habitat: Brushy desert and semi-desert areas.

Voice: Song is 3 notes with 2nd higher, like "tee tsee tee"; calls include loud "chip" and "tzee."

Conservation:
BBS: E C ⇩ CBC: ↑

Bushtit

Psaltriparus minimus

Coastal

Interior

Identification: 3½" **Tiny and gray; tiny beak** (top of upper mandible strongly curved); **long tail.** Coastal birds are light with gray-brown cap; interior birds are dark with a brownish cheek; southwest males or juveniles may have black cheek patch. In all morphs, males have dark eyes, females light yellow eyes.

Feeding: Acrobatically feeds, gleaning aphids, bugs, beetles, and other insects from outer branches of trees or shrubs. Also eats seeds and fruits. Comes to feeders.

Nesting: Gourd-shaped nest of mosses, rootlets, lichens, and leaves lined with plant down, hair, and feathers is attached by spider's silk to twigs of tree or bush 4–25 ft. above ground. Eggs: 5–7, white; I: 12 days; F: 14–15 days, altricial; B: 1–2.

Other Behavior: In winter, moves about in animated flocks of 6–30 or more birds that give an ongoing chatter of soft contact calls. At night flocks roost huddled together, possibly for warmth.

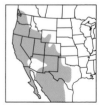

Habitat: Open woods, chaparral, suburbs, parks, gardens.

Voice: Song is a high-pitched trill; calls include short "tseep" and "tsip," possibly given as contact notes when the flock moves about.

Conservation: BBS: E C ⇑ CBC: ⇑

Red-breasted Nuthatch

Sitta canadensis

Male

Identification: 4½" White eyebrow separates dark cap from black eyeline; rusty underparts. MALE: Black cap with richly colored underparts. FEMALE: Gray cap with more lightly colored underparts.

Feeding: Creeps headfirst down trunks of trees searching for insects. Eats the seeds of conifers. Will come to bird feeders for sunflower seed and suet.

Nesting: Nest of rootlets, grasses, mosses, and shredded bark, placed in excavated hole, birdhouse, or abandoned woodpecker hole 5–120 ft. above ground. Smears pitch around the entrance of nest cavity to deter predators. Eggs: 5–7, white or slightly pink with brown speckles; I: 12 days; F: 16–21 days, altricial; B: 1–2.

Other Behavior: Has periodic irruptions south in winter in years when there is a failure of cone crop in northern regions. Birds must therefore move south to find food and often become more abundant at bird feeders in those years. Has breeding territory of 20–30 acres. Uses birdhouses and tree cavities to roost in, as well as for breeding.

Habitat: Coniferous woods.

Voice: Common call is a nasal "nyeep nyeep," also a short "tsip."

Conservation:
BBS: E ⇑ C ⇑ CBC: ⇑

White-breasted Nuthatch

Sitta carolinensis

Male

Female

Identification: 6" **Dark crown and nape; white face; gray back.** Varying amounts of reddish brown on rump and flanks. Sexes differ in color of crown and back, except in Southeast, where they cannot be reliably distinguished by plumage. **MALE: Glossy black crown and nape; blue-gray back. FEMALE: Gray or dull black crown and nape; gray back.**

Feeding: Creeps headfirst down tree trunks. Eats nuts, acorns, and insects. Comes to bird feeders for suet and sunflower seed.

Nesting: Nest of twigs, bark shreds, fur, and hair, placed in natural cavity, birdhouse, or abandoned woodpecker hole 15–50 ft. above ground. Eggs: 3–10, white with dark marks; I: 12 days; F: 14 days, altricial; B: 1–2.

Other Behavior: Nuthatches are best known for their habit of storing food in bark crevices and their ability to move headfirst down trees, enabling them to find food that "right-side up" birds, like woodpeckers, might miss. Courtship begins in late winter with the male singing. He does mate-feeding — presenting female with food — through the incubation phase.

Habitat: Deciduous and mixed woods.

Voice: Song is "werwerwerwer"; calls include contact notes of "ip" and "ank ank," the latter given in a rapid series during aggressive encounters.

Conservation: BBS: E ↑ C ↑ CBC: ↑

318

Brown-headed Nuthatch

Sitta pusilla

Identification: 4½" **Tiny; dull brown cap bordered by dark eyeline; gray back; dull buffy underparts.** White patch on nape visible from close up.

Feeding: Creeps over branches, trunks, utility posts, and buildings, looking for insects, spiders, and pine seeds. Comes to feeders.

Nesting: Nest of bark strips, grasses, hair, feathers, and cotton, placed in birdhouse or excavated cavity in tree, post, stump, 2–50 ft. above ground. Eggs: 3–9, white with brownish spots; I: 14 days; F: 18–19 days, altricial; B: 1.

Other Behavior: Known for "tool use." Uses a piece of bark to pry off other pieces of bark in its search for insects. Breeding pairs sometimes have a nest "helper," an unmated male that assists with all aspects of nesting.

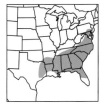

Habitat: Pine forests.

Voice: A distinctive squeaky "jeejay jeejay" and a rapidly repeated "kikikiki."

Conservation: BBS: E ↓ C ⇑ CBC: ↓ Depends on older pines for food and nesting habitat; declining in areas where these are cut down or logged.

Brown Creeper

Certhia americana

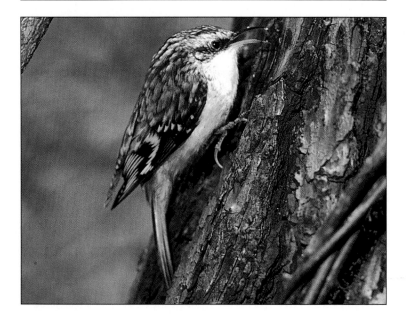

Identification: 5½" Small brown bird that hitches up tree trunks; brown-streaked above; whitish below; relatively long downcurved bill; long pointed tail feathers.

Feeding: Has distinctive habit of feeding by creeping up tree trunk then dropping down to base of next tree and starting up again. Probes bark for insects and larvae. Sometimes visits bird feeders for chopped nuts and suet.

Nesting: Hammocklike crescent-shaped nest of bark, twigs, mosses, lined with feathers, placed behind loose piece of bark of dead tree, or in natural cavity 5–15 ft. above the ground. Eggs: 5–6, white with dark spots; I: 14–16 days; F: 13–15 days, altricial; B: ?

Other Behavior: Usually located first by its distinctive song or high-pitched call. Looks very camouflaged against tree trunks. When alarmed, will flatten itself and remain motionless against trunk, becoming even more inconspicuous.

Habitat: Woods.

Voice: Song is a series of high-pitched whistles like "see wee see tu wee." Call is a high "tseee."

Conservation:
BBS: E ↑ C CBC: ↑

Cactus Wren

Campylorhynchus brunneicapillus

Identification: 8" Our **largest wren. Dark crown; wide white eyebrow; heavily spotted breast; barred wings.** Long tail prominently barred black and white underneath.

Feeding: Forages on ground. Eats insects, spiders, small lizards, berries, and seeds. May visit bird feeders for bread, seeds, and pieces of fruit.

Nesting: Large football-shaped nest of plant stems and grasses has side entrance leading through small passage to inner chamber lined with fur, feathers. Nest is placed in cholla or prickly pear cactus, tree yucca, or other thorny plant. Eggs: 3–7, pinkish white with dark marks; I: 16 days; F: 19–23 days, altricial; B: 2–3.

Other Behavior: Female selects nest site. When female is almost through incubating, male builds another nest to use for 2nd brood or as a roost. Old nests are used as winter roosts.

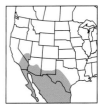

Habitat: Deserts and semideserts with cactus, such as prickly pear, cholla.

Voice: Song is a low-pitched "cha cha cha cha" or "choo choo choo choo."

Conservation: BBS: E C ⇓ CBC: ↓ Coastal Calif. pop. in jeopardy due to clearing for grazing land, vineyards, and development.

Rock Wren

Salpinctes obsoletus

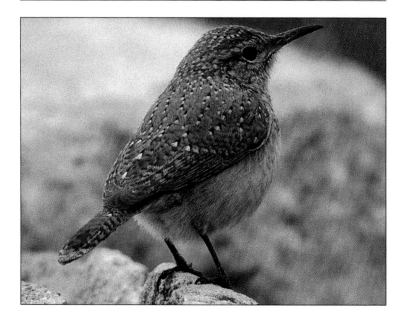

Identification: 5½" Upperparts grayish brown with fine white spotting; breast and belly pale. IN FLIGHT: Note **cinnamon rump; buffy corners of tail.**

Feeding: Forages on the ground, eating insects and spiders.

Nesting: Nest of rootlets, grasses, and plant stems lined with wool, spider's silk, and feathers, placed in crevice of rocky slope or abandoned gopher burrows. Entrance to nest is paved with small pebbles and pieces of rock. Eggs: 4–6, white with brown marks; I: 12–14 days; F: 14–16 days, altricial; B: 1–2.

Other Behavior: Often bobs its head, especially when frightened. When nest sites are reused in subsequent years, more pebbles are added to entrance. In one case, there were more than 750 pebbles and bits of stone in front of the nest.

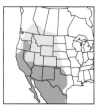

Habitat: Sparsely vegetated rocky areas, including talus slopes and road cutaways.

Voice: Song is repeated 2-part phrase, like "tawee tawee tawee tawee"; calls include a sharp "tikeer" and a high trill.

Conservation: BBS: E C ⇓ CBC: ↑

Canyon Wren

Catherpes mexicanus

Identification: 5½" Bill very long; throat and breast white; belly rich brown; crown dark gray; rest of upperparts brown, all with fine whitish spotting.

Feeding: Creeps mouselike over rocky areas, and probes for insects and spiders.

Nesting: Nest of twigs and mosses lined with spider's silk, feathers, fur, and plant down, placed in crevice of canyon, rock wall, or building. Eggs: 5–6, white with light marks; I: ?; F: ?, altricial; B: ?

Other Behavior: Little is known about its breeding biology. Needs more study.

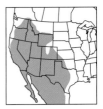

Habitat: Canyon walls, cliffs, mesas, boulders, stone homes.

Voice: Spectacular song is a loud series of downslurred whistles, like "tew tew tew tew tew tew," often amplified by its habitat; call is a harsh "jeet."

Conservation: BBS: E C ⇓ CBC: ↑

Carolina Wren

Thryothorus ludovicianus

Identification: 6 " **Warm brown above; rich buff below; prominent white eyebrow;** no streaking on back or white barring on tail edges.

Feeding: Forages on the ground and on the bark and foliage of trees, eating insects, tree frogs, and some vegetable matter. May come to bird feeders.

Nesting: Nest of twigs, mosses, rootlets, bark, and sometimes snakeskin lined with fine materials, placed in natural cavity or a host of other places, including birdhouse, pail, brushpile, mailbox. Eggs: 4–8, creamy or pink-white with brown marks; I: 12–14 days; F: 12–14 days, altricial; B: 2–3.

Other Behavior: Expands population northward in years with mild winters. Males can sing up to 40 versions of song and sing throughout the year. Expanding range in Northeast.

Habitat: Forest understory, vines, and woodlands in rural or suburban areas.

Voice: A loud, repeated, 3-part phrase, like "tea kettle, tea kettle, tea kettle"; calls include a piping alarm note, a raspy buzz, and a harsh descending "teeer."

Conservation: BBS: E ↑ C ↑ CBC: ↑

Bewick's Wren

Thryomanes bewickii

Identification: 5½" A sleek wren with a **white eyebrow; long tail marked with black and white underneath.** Underparts pale gray; upperparts grayer in West, browner in East. Tail often flicked from side to side, showing white outer tips.

Feeding: Feeds on the ground and in trees and bushes, eating insects and spiders.

Nesting: Nest of twigs, hair, leaves, and grasses lined with feathers and grasses, placed in a variety of cavities. Eggs: 4–11, white with dark spots; I: 14 days; F: 14 days, altricial; B: ?

Other Behavior: Carries tail cocked upward. Explores every crevice. Has been known to nest in wide variety of places, such as mailbox, fence post, tin can, clothing hung in outbuilding, crevice in wall. May also use nest box.

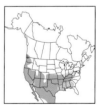

Habitat: Thickets, brush, and open woodlands in rural or suburban areas.

Voice: Song a complex jumble of thin notes and trills (similar to that of Song Sparrow); call a "chip."

Conservation: BBS: E ⇓ C ↓ CBC: ↑ The Appalachian Bewick's Wren, a subspecies, has declined extensively.

325

House Wren

Troglodytes aedon

Identification: 5″ **Plump little bird with short tail often cocked; upperparts unstreaked and grayish brown; faint buffy eyebrow; underparts grayish white with some buffy barring on flanks.** Our dullest-colored wren, with no prominent field marks.

Feeding: Forages on the ground and in foliage for insects.

Nesting: Nest of twigs lined with grass, rootlets, feathers, and hair, placed in a wide variety of cavities, including birdhouse or tree hole 4–30 ft. above ground. Eggs: 5–6, white with brown marks; I: 12–15 days; F: 16–17 days, altricial; B: 1–2.

Other Behavior: In spring, male establishes a small breeding territory by singing from exposed perches and putting stick foundations in prospective nest holes. When female enters his territory, his song becomes very high and squeaky and he vibrates his wings. After pairing with him, the female chooses one of the nests, adds a lining of soft material, and lays eggs. Male brings food to female while she incubates. House Wrens can be aggressive to other hole-nesting species and even destroy their eggs and young.

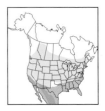

Habitat: Woods edges in rural or suburban areas; also mountain forests and clearings, and aspen groves.

Voice: Song a descending warble lasting 2–3 seconds; calls include a series of short buzzes and a rattlelike "churr."

Conservation: BBS: E ↑ C ↑ CBC: ↓

Winter Wren

Troglodytes troglodytes

Identification: 4" Very small; extremely short tail; chocolate brown above; buffy brown below; dark barring on belly and undertail coverts.

Feeding: Forages on the ground near rotting logs and brush and in tree foliage, eating insects and spiders.

Nesting: Nests near water. Nest of mosses, grasses, and twigs lined with hair and feathers, placed under roots, in rock crevice, in stump, stream bank, or other natural cavity. Eggs: 4–7, white with brown spots; I: 14–16 days; F: 19 days, altricial; B: ?

Other Behavior: Rather secretive. Bobs head. Known to be polygynous.

Habitat: Summers along rocky woodland streams, especially in coniferous forests; winters in woods, wood piles, and tangles.

Voice: Song is a beautiful long series of tinkling twitters and trills; call is "chip-chip."

Conservation:
BBS: E ⇑ C ⇑ CBC: ↑

Sedge Wren

Cistothorus platensis

Identification: 4½" Small; upperparts brown; fine white streaks on crown and upper back; underparts buffy; indistinct buffy eyebrow.

Feeding: Forages in foliage, eating insects and spiders.

Nesting: Spherical nest of dried and green grasses, reeds, and sedges lined with down, feathers, and catkins woven into grass and sedges 1–3 ft. above the ground or shallow water. Eggs: 4–8, white; I: 12–15 days; F: 12–14 days, altricial; B: 2.

Other Behavior: Formerly known as Short-billed Marsh Wren. May not return to former breeding site, since it shifts breeding areas from year to year.

Habitat: Summers in wet grasslands, often with sedges; winters also in coastal marshes.

Voice: Song is a few short staccato notes followed by a long chatter, like "chip chip chip churrrrr."

Conservation: BBS: E ⇑ C ↑ CBC: ↑

Marsh Wren

Cistothorus palustris

Identification: 5 " Warm brown above; usually shows white streaks on upper back; dark brown unstreaked crown; white eyebrow; white throat and breast; pale belly. Secretive.

Feeding: Forages on the ground and in dense foliage. Eats aquatic insects and sometimes bird eggs.

Nesting: Spherical nest of soaked reeds, grass, and cattails lined with plant down and feathers is lashed to marsh grasses 1–3 ft. above the ground. Eggs: 3–8, cinnamon brown with dark spots; I: 13–15 days; F: 14–16 days, altricial; B: 1–2.

Other Behavior: In spring, the male frequently does a flight display over his small territory. He flies up, then flutters gradually down, giving his dry rattling song. He also builds about 5 or 6 "courting nests," consisting of an outer shell of woven cattails. After the female arrives and pairs with the male, she selects 1 of these nests and adds a lining, or she may build a new nest herself. She then lays and incubates the eggs. Marsh wrens are often polygynous, with 2 or 3 females paired with 1 male. Polygyny can be advantageous to females when male territories are especially rich in food, making it easier to raise young.

Habitat: Marshy areas, especially with tall cattails and rushes.

Voice: Song is a dry rattling warble; call a single "chek," sometimes rapidly repeated in a chatter.

Conservation:
BBS: E ⇓ C ↑ CBC: ⇑

Golden-crowned Kinglet

Regulus satrapa

Female

Identification: 3½" **Very small; black cap with yellow or orange patch in center; white eyebrow; 2** white wing bars. **MALE:** Yellow crown with orange center. **FEMALE:** Yellow crown.

Feeding: Gleans food from the bark of trees, eating insects, spiders, fruit, and seeds. Drinks tree sap.

Nesting: Globular nest of moss, lichens, and spiderweb lined with inner bark, rootlets, and feathers, hung from branches 4–60 ft. above ground. Eggs: 8–11, creamy white with dark marks; I: 14–15 days; F: 14–19 days, altricial; B: 2.

Other Behavior: Kinglets have a habit of nervously flicking their wings when hopping about from limb to limb. Often found in mixed-species flocks with chickadees, nuthatches, woodpeckers, Brown Creepers, and Ruby-crowned Kinglets.

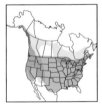

Habitat: Summers in coniferous woods; winters also in mixed and deciduous forests.

Voice: Song several high notes ending in a chatter; call is very high and like "tsee tsee tsee."

Conservation:
BBS: E ⇑ C CBC: ⇑

Ruby-crowned Kinglet

Regulus calendula

Male

Identification: 4¼" **Very small; grayish green above; white eye-ring; no white eyebrow; 2 white wing bars.** MALE: Red patch on crown, usually concealed. FEMALE: No patch on crown.

Feeding: Feeds at the tips of branches by hovering and gleaning from leaves. Eats insects, spiders, and some fruit and seeds. Drinks tree sap.

Nesting: Nest of mosses, twigs, and lichens lined with fur and other fine materials, hung from branch 2–100 ft. above the ground. Eggs: 5–11, creamy white with brown marks; I: 12 days; F: 12 days, altricial; B: ?

Other Behavior: Flicks wings and chatters as it moves about. Found in winter in mixed-species flocks with chickadees, titmice, woodpeckers, warblers, Golden-crowned Kinglets.

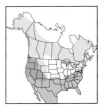

Habitat: Summers in coniferous woods; winters in woods and brushy edges.

Voice: Song a series of descending high notes followed by 3-part phrases, like the words "see see see you you you look-at-me, look-at-me, look-at-me."

Conservation: BBS: E ↓ C ⇑ CBC: ↑

Blue-gray Gnatcatcher

Polioptila caerulea

Male

Male

Identification: 4½" Slim; **upperparts bluish gray; long tail black above, mostly white below, white eye-ring.** Tail often cocked or flicked from side to side, like a miniature mockingbird. **MALE:** Black eyebrow during breeding. **FEMALE:** No black eyebrow. ➤The Black-capped Gnatcatcher, *P. nigriceps,* is a Mexican species that is rarely seen in S.E. Ariz. It is similar in most respects to the Blue-gray Gnatcatcher, except that its call is a descending "mew," it has a noticeably longer bill, and, in breeding plumage, the male has an entirely black cap.

Feeding: Actively searches trees and crevices for insects, their eggs and larvae, and spiders.

Nesting: Tiny cup nest of plant fibers, down, and spider-web lined with finer materials and covered with bits of lichen, saddled on horizontal branch or in fork of tree 2–80 ft. above the ground. Eggs: 3–6, pale blue with dark spots; I: 13 days; F: 10–12 days, altricial; B: 1–2.

Other Behavior: Darts out to catch flies and gnats in midair.

Habitat: Woods, swamps, and shrubby areas.

Voice: Song is a series of buzzy grasshopper-like notes; call is a thin peevish "zeeeee."

Conservation:
BBS: E ↑ C ↓ CBC: ↑

Northern Wheatear

Oenanthe oenanthe

Male

Female

Identification: 6" **White rump; dark wings; black band at tail tip.** Eastern birds are more cinnamon below; western birds are more whitish below. SUMMER—MALE: **Black mask; black wings.** FEMALE: **No black mask; brown wings.** WINTER: Male similar to female except for **black lores** (in female, lores are brown) **and black wings; female is same as in summer.**

Feeding: Feeds on ground, eating insects, snails, earthworms.

Nesting: Nest of rootlets, mosses, and grasses lined with rootlets, grasses, wool, hair, and feathers, placed in a cavity or under a group of rocks or other sheltered location. Eggs: 3–8, light blue with reddish marks; I: 14 days; F: 15–16 days, altricial; B: ?

Other Behavior: Actively flits about as it feeds, often fanning tail and constantly bobbing. During courtship, male also fans tail and exposes white rump during flight displays and while hopping about the female on the ground. Western birds migrate to Siberia and eastern birds migrate through Europe and into Africa, but a few migrants are regularly seen along the Atlantic Coast.

Habitat: Summers in rocky tundra; winters in plowed fields and sparsely vegetated fields.

Voice: Alarm call is "chak"; song is a series of musical notes interspersed with the "chak" call and mimicry of other birds.

Conservation: TREND UNKNOWN.

Eastern Bluebird

Sialia sialis

Male

Female

Identification: 6½" MALE: Brilliant blue head, back, wings, and tail; brick-red throat and breast. FEMALE: Rich buffy throat and breast; grayish-blue head and back; light blue wings and tail; white eye-ring. Color on upperparts of female varies from almost as deep blue as on male to grayish brown.

Feeding: Feeds from perches, dropping down to the ground to catch insects. May come to bird feeders for peanut butter mixes, berries, mealworms, raisins.

Nesting: Nest of grasses, plant stems, pine needles, lined with hair, feathers, and fine grasses, placed in birdhouse, natural tree cavity, or abandoned woodpecker hole 3–20 ft. above the ground. Eggs: 3 6, pale blue; I: 12 18 days; F: 16–21 days, altricial; B: 2–3.

Other Behavior: Bluebird populations severely declined up until the 1970s due to loss of nesting cavities and nest competition from House Sparrows and European Starlings. In 1978, the North American Bluebird Society was formed. This society, along with many others, has placed bluebird nesting boxes all across the country. This is helping bluebird populations recover.

Habitat: Farmland and rural yards; open woodlands.

Voice: Song a series of downslurred whistles, like "cheer cheerful charmer"; call a mellow "turwee."

Conservation:
BBS: E ⇑ C ⇑ CBC: ⇑

Veery
Catharus fuscescens

Identification: 7½" Uniformly reddish brown above; blurry spotting and buffy wash on upper breast; gray flanks; no conspicuous eyering. • Eastern subspecies (*C. f. fuscescens*) is cinnamon above; western subspecies (*C. f. salicicolus*) is darker brown above and has more spotting on breast.

Feeding: Gleans food from the forest floor and the bark of trees, often overturning leaves on the ground with bill in search of food. Eats insects, larvae, spiders, snails, earthworms, and wild fruit.

Nesting: Nest of weed stems, twigs, and mosses lined with grasses, inner bark, and rootlets, on top of foundation of dead leaves. Placed on or very near the ground. Eggs: 3–5, light blue; I: 10–12 days; F: 10 days, altricial; B: 1–2.

Other Behavior: The male Veery often sings his beautiful song from a perch at dusk. Although commonly heard, this bird frequently stays hidden in dense woods, making it a challenge to observe. Much more needs to be learned about its behavior.

Habitat: Moist deciduous woods, especially along streams.

Voice: Song is a descending spiral of flutelike notes, like "tureeooreeoo-reeooreeoo"; call is a loud descending "veeer," also a querulous snarl.

Conservation:
BBS: E ↓ C ⇓ CBC: ↓

Gray-cheeked Thrush
Bicknell's Thrush

Catharus minimus   Catharus bicknelli

Gray-cheeked

Bicknell's

Identification: 8″ Both species have **bold spotting on all of breast; gray cheek; indistinct eye-ring; no buff on face.** Breeding ranges do not overlap. **GRAY-CHEEKED:** Slightly larger than Bicknell's; back and tail both gray-brown; base of lower mandible pinkish. See Voice. **BICKNELL'S:** Slightly smaller than Gray-cheeked; chestnut tail contrasts with olive-brown back; base of lower mandible yellow.

Feeding: Feed mostly on the ground, eating insects, spiders, crayfish, caterpillars, earthworms, and berries.

Nesting: Nest of twigs, moss, grass, some mud, and decayed leaves lined with rootlets, fine grasses, and sometimes lichen, built in tree 1–20 ft. above the ground. Eggs: 3–5, pale blue with faint marks; I: 13–14 days; F: 11–13 days, altricial; B: 1–2.

Other Behavior: Rather shy. During migration may be seen in a variety of habitats.

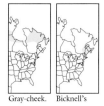

Gray-cheek.   Bicknell's

Habitat: Coniferous woods at tree line, tall shrubby areas.

Voice: Gray-cheeked song ends with a descending whistle; Bicknell's song ends on same pitch or rises. Calls are a downslurred "weeoh."

Conservation: Gray-cheeked: BBS: E ↓ C CBC: ↓ Bicknell's: TREND UNKNOWN.

Swainson's Thrush

Catharus ustulatus

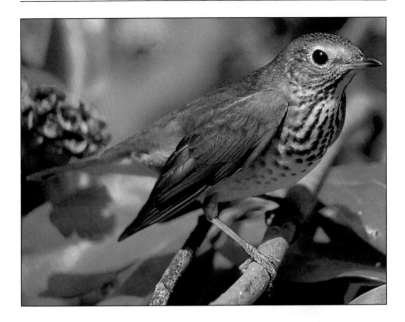

Identification: 7½" **Conspicuous buffy eye-ring; buffy lores and breast;** spotting on all of breast. Upperparts uniformly grayish brown in East, dark reddish brown in West. See Voice for further help in distinguishing from other thrushes.

Feeding: Feeds on the ground and in foliage, eating all kinds of insects, spiders, cherries, and berries.

Nesting: Nest of twigs, barks, mosses, grasses, and plant fibers lined with skeletonized leaves, lichens, and fine materials, placed on horizontal branch of tree 2–20 ft. above the ground. Eggs: 3–5, light blue with brown spots; I: 11–14 days; F: 10–14 days, altricial; B: ?

Other Behavior: Sings a lot. On migration is often found with flocks of warblers, feeding in the tree canopy.

Habitat: Coniferous and mixed woods, shrub thickets along streams.

Voice: Song is a series of rising whistles; calls a short "whit" and a Spring Peeper–like "heep."

Conservation: BBS: E ↓ C ⇓ CBC: ↓

Hermit Thrush

Catharus guttatus

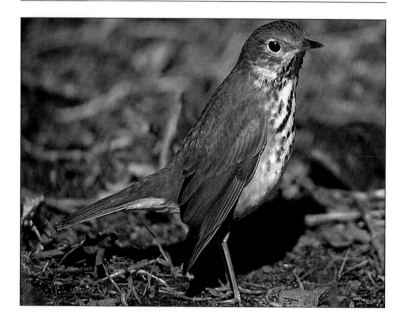

Identification: 7½" **Brown head, back, and wings; reddish-brown tail; spotting on all of breast; thin whitish eye-ring.** See Voice for further help in distinguishing from other thrushes.

Feeding: Feeds mostly on the ground, eating insects, spiders, earthworms, snails, and wild fruits and berries.

Nesting: Nest of mosses, grasses, and rotted wood lined with rootlets, bark strips, and other fine materials, built on the ground or 2–8 ft. above it in a bush or tree. Eggs: 3–6, light blue or blue-green; I: 12–13 days; F: 12 days, altricial; B: 2.

Other Behavior: After alighting on a perch, this thrush has a habit of slightly raising and lowering its tail, an action often accompanied by a "chuck" note. Also frequently flicks wings. Sings on migration.

Habitat: Coniferous and mixed woods; shrub thickets.

Voice: One long whistle followed by 3–4 higher and differently pitched whistles; calls a soft "chuck" and a whining "tweee."

Conservation: BBS: E ↑ C ↑ CBC: ↑

Wood Thrush

Hylocichla mustelina

Identification: 8″ **Bright reddish-brown head; brown back, wings, and tail; large spots on breast and upper belly; thin white eye-ring.** See Voice for further help in distinguishing from other thrushes.

Feeding: Gleans food from the ground and occasionally from the foliage of trees.

Nesting: Nest of mosses, dead leaves, weed stalks, paper, string, with a middle layer of mud, lined with rootlets. Placed on a horizontal limb where there is a fork of branches 5–20 ft. above the ground. Eggs: 2–5, blue-green; I: 12–13 days; F: 12–14 days, altricial; B: 1–2.

Other Behavior: Males sing frequently, especially in the morning and early evening. Females give shorter versions of song when there is a disturbance near the nest. Both give the "bweebeebeeb" call when they are alarmed, and a softer version is used as a contact note between the pair.

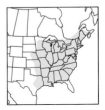

Habitat: Deciduous woods in rural to urban areas.

Voice: Flutelike notes preceded by lower repeated notes, like "bupbup eecohlay, bupbup aholee"; calls a "bweebeebeeb" and a loud "pit pit pit."

Conservation:
BBS: E ↓ C ↓ CBC: ↓

339

American Robin

Turdus migratorius

Male

Identification: 10" **Dark gray above; brick-red below; yellow bill;** white undertail coverts; white eye crescents. **MALE: Black head and dark red breast. FEMALE: Dark gray head and pale reddish breast.** JUV: Similar to adult, but heavily spotted on breast.

Feeding: Hops about on lawns, meadows, and golf courses looking for earthworms. Also eats insects, fruit, berries. Occasionally comes to feeders for fruit.

Nesting: Nest of grasses and middle layer of mud, lined with fine grasses, placed on horizontal limb of shrub, tree, or on building ledge 5–20 ft. above the ground. Eggs: 3–7, light blue; I: 12–14 days; F: 14–16 days, altricial; B: 2–3.

Other Behavior: The song of male birds usually functions to advertise territory or attract a mate, but with robins it is not strongly associated with either. Robins sing most just before the young hatch. During nest building the female may have mud across her breast due to pressing it against the muddy lining as she forms the inner cup. After the breeding season, robins flock together and go to large communal roosts at night; this continues from fall through winter.

Habitat: In many environments, from woods to open lawns and plains to timberline.

Voice: Song a ringing whistle, like "cheeryup cheerily"; calls a "teeek" or "tuk tuk tuk" and a "tseeep" given in overhead flight.

Conservation:
BBS: E ↑ C ⇑ CBC: ↑

340

Gray Catbird

Dumetella carolinensis

Identification: 9" **All gray with a black cap;** inconspicuous reddish-brown patch under base of tail.

Feeding: Feeds on the ground and in foliage, eating various insects, as well as spiders, wild grapes, and berries.

Nesting: Nest of twigs, leaves, grasses, and grapevine bark lined with rootlets, pine needles, and horsehair, placed in shrub, vine, or small tree 2–10 ft. above the ground. Eggs: 2–6, dark blue-green; I: 12–14 days; F: 10–13 days, altricial; B: 1–2.

Other Behavior: When the male catbird arrives on the breeding ground, he soon begins to sing within his chosen territory. When the female arrives, the male does several courtship displays, including fluffing out the body feathers, high squeaky singing, and prolonged chases of the female within the territory. Both sexes give the "meeow" call in situations of alarm.

Habitat: Shrubs, tangled thickets, woods edges; rural to suburban.

Voice: Song mimics other birds', each version given only once; calls include catlike "meeow" and "kwut."

Conservation: BBS: E ↓ C ↓ CBC: ↓

Northern Mockingbird

Mimus polyglottos

Identification: 11" Gray above; whitish below; white outer feathers on long tail; small white patch on lower edge of folded wing. IN FLIGHT: Bold white patches on wings.

Feeding: Feeds on the ground and in foliage, eating various insects, spiders, snails, crayfish, lizards, small snakes, and wild fruits and berries. May occasionally come to bird feeders for raisins, other fruit, bread, and suet.

Nesting: Nest of twigs, plant stems, mosses, cloth, string, and dry leaves lined with rootlets and grasses, placed in shrub, vine tangle, cactus, or tree 3–10 ft. above the ground. Eggs: 2–6, blue-green with brown marks; I: 12–13 days; F: 10–13 days, altricial; B: 1–3.

Other Behavior: Mockingbirds form territories of about 1–2 acres, 2 times a year. In spring, the male sings and defends a breeding territory against other mockingbirds, cats, snakes, people, large birds, and any other potential predator. In fall, both male and female sing and defend a feeding territory centered around a good source of berries. They will chase out other mockingbirds, robins, jays, and starlings. Mockingbirds often sing at night.

Habitat: Open areas with shrubs, gardens, parks,

Voice: Song mimics other birds', each version repeated 3 or more times; calls include a raspy "chjjj" and a loud "chewk."

Conservation: BBS: E ↓ C ↓ CBC: ↓

Sage Thrasher

Oreoscoptes montanus

Identification: 8½" For a thrasher, relatively short tail; relatively short straight bill; gray upperparts; heavily streaked breast and flanks; outer tips of tail white; 2 white wing bars. In late summer, wing bars and much of streaking on breast can be worn away.

Feeding: Feeds by running around on the ground, picking up and eating various insects and spiders. Often comes to cultivated gardens of grapes and berries in summer and fall, to eat the fruit.

Nesting: Bulky nest of twigs, grasses, leaf shreds, and bark lined with rootlets, horsehair, and fur, placed on the ground or in low bush, especially sage, up to 3 ft. above ground. Eggs: 1–7, deep green-blue with brown spots; I: 13–17 days; F: 11–14 days, altricial; B: ?

Other Behavior: Sage Thrashers spend most of their time on the ground, but it is common to see and hear males singing from prominent elevated perches. One of the few birds found in the Great Basin sage deserts and valleys, but here typical and common.

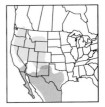

Habitat: Summers in sage; winters in desert scrub.

Voice: Song is warbled notes, sometimes repeated; call is "chuck."

Conservation:
BBS: E C ⇑ CBC: →

Brown Thrasher

Toxostoma rufum

Identification: 11″ **Long downcurved bill;
reddish-brown upperparts; heavily streaked
breast and belly; long tail; pale eye.** Only
thrasher throughout most of East.

Feeding: Feeds on the ground, using its bill to toss aside
leaves in search of food. Occasionally jumps into the air
to catch its prey. Eats insects, lizards, snakes, tree frogs,
and various wild berries.

Nesting: Nest of twigs, grass, dead leaves, grapevine,
and paper lined with grasses and rootlets, placed on the
ground or in bush, vine tangle, or tree up to 15 ft.
above the ground. Eggs: 2–6, light blue with fine dark
marks; I: 12–14 days; F: 9–12 days, altricial; B: 2.

Other Behavior: In their attempt to attract females, male
Brown Thrashers often sing loudly from prominent
perches when they first arrive on their breeding grounds
in spring. Brown Thrashers, along with Northern
Mockingbirds and Gray Catbirds, share the feature of
endlessly improvising their song, mimicking the songs
and calls of other birds. A good way to tell these birds
apart is to remember that, in general, catbirds repeat
phrases once, Brown Thrashers twice, and mockingbirds
3 or more times.

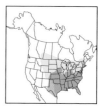

Habitat: Thickets
and shrubs in open
areas or at woods
edges.

Voice: Song a loud
series of twice-
repeated phrases,
mimicking other
birds; call a loud
"smack."

Conservation:
BBS: E ↓ C ↓ CBC: ⇓

344

Long-billed Thrasher

Toxostoma longirostre

Identification: 11″ Limited to S. Tex. Very similar to Brown Thrasher. Differences include: **gray on face and sides of neck; longer downcurved bill; dull brown head and back; reddish-brown tail;** pale eye.

Feeding: Feeds on the ground and in foliage, eating insects, spiders, and wild berries.

Nesting: Nest of dead leaves, thorny twigs, and grasses lined with rootlets, grasses, and straw, placed in shrub, thorny bush, or tree 4–10 ft. above the ground. Eggs: 2–5, light green or blue-green with fine dots; I: 13–14 days; F: 12–14 days, altricial; B: 2.

Other Behavior: In spring, male Long-billed Thrashers can be seen and heard singing from high prominent perches. Defends a feeding territory in winter.

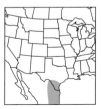

Habitat: Dense thickets, brush, subtropical woodlands.

Voice: Song is loud series of repeated phrases, often mimicking other birds; call is a loud "smack."

Conservation:
BBS: E C ⇑ CBC: ⇑

Curve-billed Thrasher
Toxostoma curvirostre

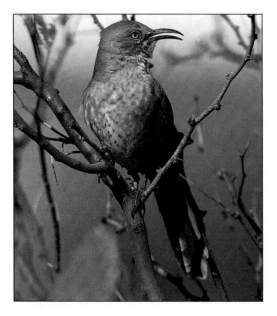

Identification: 10½" Large, blurry, rounded spotting on upper breast; long noticeably downcurved bill; orangish eye.

Feeding: Forages on the ground for insects. Also eats seeds, berries, and often comes to bird feeders for fruit, and to birdbaths.

Nesting: Nest of twigs, grasses, and leaves lined with horsehair, grass, and rootlets, placed in cholla cactus, thorny bush, or small tree 2–15 ft. above the ground. Eggs: 1–5, light green-blue with brown spots; I: 12–15 days; F: 12–18 days, altricial; B: 2–3.

Other Behavior: The most common and widespread thrasher in Texas. Usually stays within brush, but can be located by its song and common "whit-weet" call.

Habitat: Semidesert scrub and suburban parks and yards

Voice: Song is whistled phrases; common call is "whit-weet," with 2nd syllable higher.

Conservation:
BBS: E C ⇓ CBC: ↓

American Pipit
Sprague's Pipit
Anthus rubescens   Anthus spragueii

Summer American

Winter American

Sprague's

Identification: 6½" **AMERICAN—SUMMER: Bobs tail as it feeds. Grayish brown above; buffy breast and belly; buffy eyebrow above dark cheek; legs usually black or dark brown. WINTER:** Like summer, but **brownish above and buff below; breast heavily streaked. SPRAGUE'S: Does not bob noticeably short tail while feeding. Brown above with scaled look on back; buffy face; lightly streaked breast with whitish belly; legs yellow to pale brown. IN Flight:** Both show white outer tail feathers.

Feeding: Both feed on the ground, eating insects and the seeds of grasses and weeds. American also eats crustaceans and mollusks from tidal flats.

Nesting: Nest of grasses, twigs, lined with fine materials, placed on the ground. American—Eggs: 3–7, gray-white with dark marks; I: 14 days; F: 13–15 days, altricial; B: 1. Sprague's—Eggs: 3–7, gray-white with dark marks; I: ?; F: 10–11 days, altricial; B: ?

Other Behavior: American is seen in pairs or small flocks. Sprague's is more secretive and most often seen alone.

American   Sprague's

Habitat: American: tundra, open fields. Sprague's: short-grass fields.

Voice: American song is a repeated "chiwee"; call a short "peet-peet." Sprague's song descending notes; call "sweep sweep."

Conservation: American: CBC: ⇓ Sprague's: BBS: E C ↓ CBC: ↑

Bohemian Waxwing
Cedar Waxwing
Bombycilla garrulus   Bombycilla cedrorum

Bohemian

Cedar

Identification: Bohemian 8", Cedar 7" Both are sleek crested birds; black eye-stripe; yellow tip to tail. **BOHEMIAN:** Grayish above; gray belly and reddish-brown undertail coverts; red, yellow, and white spots on wing. **CEDAR:** Brownish above; yellow belly and white undertail coverts; only red spots on wings. **JUV:** Both species similar to adult, but with blurry streaking on breast.

Feeding: Both eat insects and a large variety of wild fruits and berries.

Nesting: Nest of grasses, twigs, and mosses lined with rootlets and fine materials, placed in fork or branch of tree 4–50 ft. above ground. Bohemian—Eggs: 2–6, pale blue with dark marks; I: 14 days; F: 13–15 days, altricial; B: 1. Cedar—Eggs: 2–6, pale with dark marks; I: 12–16 days; F: 14–18 days, altricial; B: 1–2.

Other Behavior: Both of these waxwings are almost always found in large flocks that visit scattered locations and feast on berries and small fruits. Even during nesting season, they will leave their territory and join a flock to feed. Bohemian irrupts to South some winters.

Bohemian   Cedar

Habitat: Bohemian: coniferous woods. Cedar: open rural or suburban areas.

Voice: Bohemian call is a repeated, high-pitched, buzzy trill. Cedar call is a very high-pitched thin "seee."

Conservation: Bohemian: CBC: ↓ Cedar: BBS: E ⇑ C ⇑ CBC: ⇑

European Starling

Sturnus vulgaris

Summer

Winter

Identification: 8ʺ Short-tailed stocky "blackbird." SUMMER: **Glossy purple-black overall; long yellow bill.** Juveniles, which are commonly seen in large flocks during summer, are uniformly grayish brown and have dark bills. WINTER: **Black body speckled overall with white and gold; black bill.**

Feeding: Forages on ground for insects, spiders, earthworms, garbage, salamanders, snails, weed seeds, and berries. Comes to feeders for seed and suet.

Nesting: Nest of twigs, grasses, feathers, tree flowers, and cloth, placed in natural tree cavity, abandoned woodpecker hole, birdhouse, or any other cavity 2–60 ft. above ground. Eggs: 2–8, light blue with dark marks; I: 12–14 days; F: 18–21 days, altricial; B: 1–3.

Other Behavior: In 1890, starlings were introduced into New York City from Europe. Since then they have spread all across North America. Starlings aggressively compete with native species of birds for nesting cavities. To reduce competition from starlings for birdhouses, make sure the entrance hole is 1½ inches or less in diameter, since this is too small for starlings to enter.

Habitat: Urban and suburban areas.

Voice: Song is a running stream of squeals, squawks, and imitations of other birds; flight call a short "chjjj."

Conservation: BBS: E ↓ C ↑ CBC: ⇑

Learning Pages WARBLERS

Warblers are small songbirds that eat insects. They are a challenge to identify because they move very quickly and are often obscured by tree or shrub foliage. Many warblers are primarily seen during spring and fall migration, en route between their northern breeding grounds and wintering grounds in the Caribbean, Central and South America, and southern U.S.

Good places to find migrating warblers are coastal thickets, edges of lakes, river valleys, and parks.

Identifying Warblers

In spring, warblers are relatively easy to identify, because males sing and have brightly colored patterns and females generally have similar,

though more subtle, patterns.

In fall, identifying warblers can be more difficult. While the fall plumage of most adults is very similar to the spring plumage, in some cases it is significantly different.

In addition, the patterns of many immature warblers are quite dull. This is especially true of immature females, which can be very obscurely patterned and may look similar to the immature females of other warbler species.

For help in identifying fall warblers, start by familiarizing yourself with the warblers shown on these Learning Pages. They are the ones you will most commonly see. Complete descriptions of them are in their main accounts.

Common Widespread Breeding Warblers

Two warblers are commonly seen in summer, for they breed throughout most of North America and nest in areas people frequent.

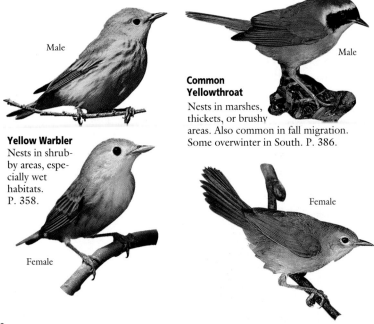

Male

Common Yellowthroat
Nests in marshes, thickets, or brushy areas. Also common in fall migration. Some overwinter in South. P. 386.

Male

Yellow Warbler
Nests in shrubby areas, especially wet habitats. P. 358.

Female

Female

Yellow-rumped Warbler: The Most Abundant Fall Migrant

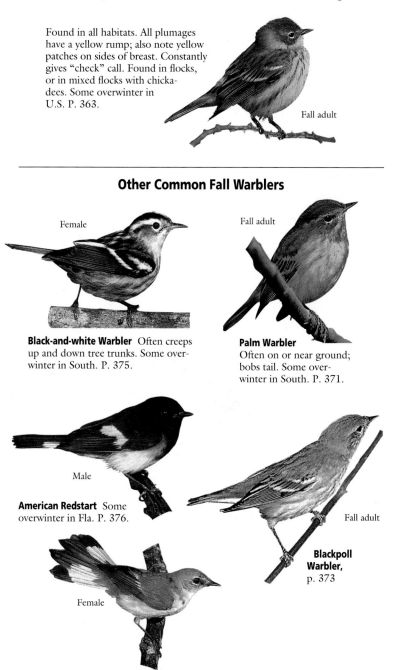

Found in all habitats. All plumages have a yellow rump; also note yellow patches on sides of breast. Constantly gives "check" call. Found in flocks, or in mixed flocks with chickadees. Some overwinter in U.S. P. 363.

Fall adult

Other Common Fall Warblers

Female

Fall adult

Black-and-white Warbler Often creeps up and down tree trunks. Some overwinter in South. P. 375.

Palm Warbler Often on or near ground; bobs tail. Some overwinter in South. P. 371.

Male

American Redstart Some overwinter in Fla. P. 376.

Fall adult

Blackpoll Warbler, p. 373

Female

Blue-winged Warbler

Vermivora pinus

Male

Female

"Brewster's"

Identification: 4¾" **MALE:** Bright yellow crown, face, and underparts; black eyeline; 2 white wing bars; blue-gray wings. **FEMALE AND IMM:** Paler than male, not as much yellow on crown. Hybridizes with Golden-winged Warbler.

Feeding: Eats insects and spiders.

Nesting: Cuplike nest of leaves, grasses, and grapevine bark is concealed in vines and tangles near ground. Eggs: 4–7, white with brown spots; I: 10–11 days; F: 9–10 days; altricial; B: 1.

Other Behavior: Hybridizes with Golden-winged Warbler and the hybrids intergrade in color of body plumage. A single gene controls face pattern. The genetically dominant and more common hybrid, "Brewster's Warbler," has the facial pattern of the Blue-winged Warbler. The recessive and rarer hybrid, "Lawrence's Warbler," has the facial pattern and black throat of the Golden-winged Warbler. First-generation hybrids always have the pattern of the "Brewster's Warbler." Subsequent hybrids can have either facial pattern. Hybrids sing the song of either or both parents. Blue-winged expanding range to the North. Replaces Golden-winged within 50 years of contact.

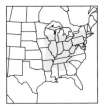

Habitat: Second-growth forests, brushy fields.

Voice: Song is 2 buzzy low-pitched notes, with 1st higher than the 2nd. Almost sounds like words "blue-winged."

Conservation:
BBS: E ↑ C ⇑

Golden-winged Warbler

Vermivora chrysoptera

Male

Identification: 4¾" MALE: **Yellow wing patch; black throat and ear patch;** yellow crown; white underparts. FEMALE: **Paler, with gray throat and ear patch;** underparts washed with gray. IMM: Yellowish-green back; pale yellow underparts.

Feeding: Eats insects, spiders.

Nesting: Cup nest of leaves, grass, and grapevine is hidden in vegetation on ground. Eggs: 3–6, creamy white with densely clustered brown marks at large end; I: 10–11 days; F: 9–10 days, altricial; B: 1.

Other Behavior: Hybridizes with Blue-winged Warbler and the hybrids intergrade in color of body plumage. A single gene controls face pattern. The genetically dominant and more common hybrid, "Brewster's Warbler," has the facial pattern of the Blue-winged Warbler. The recessive and rarer hybrid, "Lawrence's Warbler," has the facial pattern and black throat of the Golden-winged Warbler. First-generation hybrids always have the pattern of the "Brewster's Warbler." Subsequent hybrids can have either facial pattern. Hybrids sing the song of either or both parents.

Habitat: Forest openings or edges, overgrown fields. Requires drier and earlier successional areas than Blue-winged Warbler.

Voice: Song is a buzzy "zee bee bee" or "zee bee bee bee." Call is a sweet "chip."

Conservation: BBS: E ↓ C

Tennessee Warbler

Vermivora peregrina

Spring male

Fall adult

Immature

Identification: 4¾" SPRING—MALE: Greenish above with gray crown; white eyebrow; dark eyeline; white undertail coverts; relatively shorter tail and long straight bill. FEMALE: Similar, but head olive-gray; throat, breast, and eyebrow lightly washed with yellow. FALL—ADULT AND IMM: Olive-green above; yellow eyebrow; variable amounts of yellow on breast and belly; usually hint of a wing bar. Distinguished from Orange-crowned Warbler by white undertail coverts, more distinct eyeline and eyebrow, and no breast streaks.

Feeding: Eats insects, spiders, fruit.

Nesting: Grassy cup nest on ground, concealed by vegetation, often in damp area. Eggs: 4–7, white with reddish-brown marks; I: 11–12 days; F: ?, altricial; B: 1.

Other Behavior: Male's loud song, given from high prominent perch, makes him conspicuous during breeding season. Female is very secretive. Population increases during major outbreaks of Spruce Budworm caterpillars.

Habitat: Deciduous, mixed, or coniferous woods, forest clearings.

Voice: Song is 2–3 phrases of loud repeated notes, the last phrase fastest, like "tsit tsit tsit tsit, tsut tsut tsut tsut, tee tee tee tee tee tee." Call is a sweet "chip."

Conservation:
BBS: E ⇑ C ⇓ CBC: ↑

354

Orange-crowned Warbler

Vermivora celata

Eastern form

Identification: 5 " Very drab. Best identified by its lack of field marks. **Dull olive-green upperparts; pale olive-yellow below; yellow undertail coverts; faint blurred streaks on sides of breast.** Imm: Grayish wash overall; pale yellow undertail coverts. •West Coast birds are more yellow overall; eastern birds are grayer. More common in the West. Orange crown patch is seldom visible in the field.

Feeding: Eats insects, berries. Can be seen foraging low in weeds. In winter comes to bird feeding stations for nuts, suet.

Nesting: Cuplike nest of bark strips and grasses, placed on ground or in shrub. Eggs: 3–6, creamy white with reddish-brown markings; I: 12–14 days; F: 8–10 days, altricial; B: 1.

Other Behavior: The scientific name of this species, *celata*, means concealed. It refers to the orange crown patch, which is almost always hidden under the olive head feathers, except when the bird's crest is raised. Some females and imm. lack this patch.

Habitat: Dense thickets, forest edges, brushy fields.

Voice: Song is a high-pitched chipping trill, trailing off at end. Call is a metallic "chet."

Conservation: BBS: E ⇓ C CBC: ↓

Nashville Warbler

Vermivora ruficapilla

Male

Immature

Identification: 5″ Wags tail. MALE: Gray head with semivisible rufous crown patch; bold white eye-ring; yellow throat; yellow breast and undertail coverts are separated by patch of white on lower belly; olive-green upperparts. Duller overall in fall. FEMALE AND IMM: Buffy eye-ring and duller overall, especially imm. female, which has grayish-olive head with no rufous; whitish throat. •Told from Connecticut Warbler by smaller size, dark legs, and yellow throat.

Feeding: Eats insects, including tent caterpillars, gypsy moths, and grasshoppers.

Nesting: Cuplike nest of pine needles, mosses, fur, hair, placed on ground, often at base of shrub. Eggs: 4–5, white with brown dots; I: 11–12 days; F: 11 days, altricial; B: 1.

Other Behavior: Rufous crown patch is partly concealed by other feathers. Can be exposed when bird raises crest, such as when alarmed or displaying to another bird.

Habitat: Open second-growth woods, thickets, woodland edges.

Voice: Song is a repeated 1st phrase followed by a shorter lower trill, like "see-it see-it see-it, tititi." Call is a metallic "chink."

Conservation: BBS: E ↑ C ⇑ CBC: ↑

Northern Parula

Parula americana

Male

Female

Identification: 4½" Very small; short tail. MALE: Upperparts blue-gray with greenish-yellow patch on back; band of black and rufous across breast; yellow throat and breast; 2 white wing bars; white eye crescents. FEMALE: Similar to male, but chestbands absent. IMM: Similar to respective adults, but duller, more greenish tinged. Imm. male has less distinct breastband.
➤A similar species, the Tropical Parula, *P. pitiayumi*, is rare resident in far southern Tex. It lacks white eye crescents and has more yellow on underparts. Male has black mask; orangish breast. Female is similar but duller.

Feeding: Eats insects, also spiders.

Nesting: Nest is lined with grasses and plant down, built within Old-Man's-Beard (*Usnea*) lichens in North, or Spanish moss in South. Can also be an open nest built in clusters of conifer twigs. Eggs: 3–7, white with brown dots; I: 12–14 days; F: ?, altricial; B: ?

Other Behavior: Can hang upside down, chickadee-like, while searching for insects in leaf clusters.

Habitat: Deciduous and coniferous forests, usually near water.

Voice: Song is a buzzy trill that rises in pitch and usually, but not always, ends with a lower note, like "zeeeeeeeeee-yup." Call is musical "chip."

Conservation:
BBS: E ↑ C ⇓ CBC: →

357

Yellow Warbler

Dendroica petechia

Male

Female

Identification: 5″ In all plumages, has yellow tail spots. MALE: All yellow with reddish streaks on breast. FEMALE AND IMM: Duller yellow, with breast streaks fainter or absent. Imm. females do not have breast stripes and are buffy olive with much less yellow in plumage.
• There are a number of subspecies of this warbler. Alaskan birds are smaller and dull olive-green; Southwestern birds are paler; birds in Florida Keys are bright gold.

Feeding: Eats caterpillars, cankerworms, gypsy moths, beetles, aphids, and other insects.

Nesting: Nest of milkweed stem fibers, grasses, down from willow seeds, and spider's silk, placed in upright fork of shrub or small tree 3–12 ft. high. Eggs: 4–6, white with blotches at end; I: 10 days; F: 9–11 days, altricial; B: 1.

Other Behavior: Begins southward movement in July.

Habitat: Shrubby areas, especially near water with willows and alder; yards, gardens.

Voice: Song sounds like "sweet sweet sweet I'm so sweet," with last note accented. Also has unaccented song version. Call is a musical "chip."

Conservation: BBS: E ↑ C ↓ CBC: →

Chestnut-sided Warbler

Dendroica pensylvanica

Spring male

Fall male

Identification: 5″ **SPRING—MALE: Chestnut on sides and flanks; lemon-yellow crown; black eye-stripe and moustache;** streaked back; 2 pale yellow wing bars. **FEMALE: Similar, with less chestnut on sides; less black on face. FALL— ADULT AND IMM: Lime-green above; bold white eye-ring;** gray face; whitish below; yellowish wing bars. Adult male has distinct chestnut on sides; female and imm. male often show small amount of chestnut on sides; imm. female never has chestnut sides.

Feeding: Eats insects, spiders, seeds, and berries.

Nesting: Nest of weeds, grapevine bark, and plant down, placed in fork of shrub, small tree, or brambles. Eggs: 3–5, whitish with darker blotches; I: 12–14 days; F: 10–12 days, altricial; B: 1.

Other Behavior: Characteristically cocks tail and droops wings. Shrubby areas are its preferred breeding habitat.

Habitat: Undergrowth in cutover woods, shrubby regrowth, roadside thickets.

Voice: Song is like "pleased, pleased, pleased to meet you," with the last 2 syllables accented; also has unaccented version. Call is a musical "chip."

Conservation: BBS: E ↓ C ⇓ CBC: ↑

Magnolia Warbler

Dendroica magnolia

Spring male

Spring female

Immature

Identification: 5″ In all plumages has large white spots midway on tail. SPRING—MALE: Yellow underparts, with heavy black streaks radiating down breast; black face with broad white eyebrow; 2 wing bars join to form a white patch; yellow rump; white undertail coverts. FEMALE: Similar, with finer streaking on breast; 2 white wing bars; grayer eyebrow and face. FALL—ADULT AND IMM: Narrow gray band across upper breast; white undertail coverts; thin eye-ring; olive back.

Feeding: Eats insects and spiders, foraging at low to middle levels in trees and understory.

Nesting: Nest of twigs and grasses, placed on conifer limb. Eggs: 3–5, white with brown spots; I: 11–13 days; F: 8–10 days, altricial; B: 1.

Other Behavior: Often fans tail, revealing white spots, as it moves about branches foraging.

Habitat: Woodlands and coniferous forests, especially thickets of spruce, hemlock, balsam fir. Most abundant in earlier-growth habitats.

Voice: Song is a series of short musical notes, like "weety, weety, weety, wee." Call is a longish "clenk."

Conservation: BBS: E ↑ C ⇓ CBC: ↓

Cape May Warbler
Dendroica tigrina

Spring male

Spring female

Immature female

Identification: 5″ Birds in all plumages have yellow or olive-yellow rumps and are streaked below. SPRING—MALE: Chestnut-orange ear patch surrounded by yellow; black streaks on yellow underparts; white wing patch; short tail. FEMALE: Yellow patch on neck below ear patch; 2 narrow white wing bars; paler yellow below with faint streaks. FALL—MALE: Duller than spring male, but still has white wing patch; at least some chestnut on ear patch. FEMALE: Duller than spring female with still a tinge of yellow on neck and underparts. IMM—MALE: Ear patch lacks chestnut; wing patch smaller than spring male's. FEMALE: Very drab, often lacking any yellow except on rump.

Feeding: Eats insects. Hovers at tips of branches.

Nesting: Bulky cup of moss, twigs, placed in spruce or fir. Eggs: 4–9, cream, marked; I: ?; F: ?, altricial; B: ?

Other Behavior: Population increases when there is Spruce Budworm outbreak.

Habitat: Spruce forests; in migration, woodlands.

Voice: Song is a very high-pitched "seet, seet, seet, seet." Call is a very high "tsee."

Conservation: BBS: E ↑ C CBC: ↑

Black-throated Blue Warbler

Dendroica caerulescens

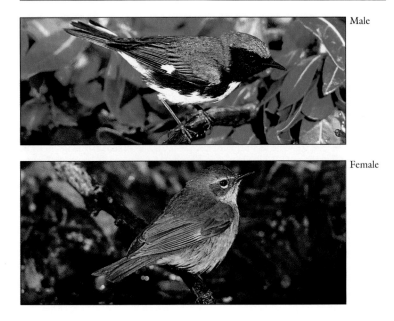

Male

Female

Identification: 5¼" White patch at base of primary feathers in almost all plumages. **MALE: Black throat, upper breast, and flanks; blue above.** In Appalachians, male is darker and brighter. **FEMALE: Quite different from male; brownish olive above; buffy below; pale eyebrow. IMM:** Similar to respective adults, but imm. female's wing patch may be absent.

Feeding: Eats insects, seeds, fruits.

Nesting: Bulky nest with rough exterior covered by bark strips, wood fibers, and birch bark, lined with finer material, placed low in fir or spruce tree, shrub, rhododendron. Eggs: 3–5, cream with marks; I: 12 days; F: 10 days, altricial; B: 1.

Other Behavior: Usually forages and stays low in the understory or sometimes on the ground.

Habitat: Mature mixed woodlands with well-developed under story, cutover areas.

Voice: Song is 3 or 4 drawn-out notes, the last usually upslurred, like "I am so lazy." Call note is a flat "tip."

Conservation: BBS: E ↑ C CBC: ↓

Yellow-rumped Warbler

Dendroica coronata

Spring male "Myrtle"

Fall adult "Myrtle"

Identification: 5½" Formerly considered 2 species, the northern and eastern "Myrtle Warbler" and western "Audubon's Warbler." Now considered 1 species. **Birds in all plumages have a yellow rump and a yellow patch on side, in front of each wing.** SPRING—MALE: "Myrtle Warbler" has yellow crown patch, white throat; "Audubon's Warbler" similar, with yellow throat. SPRING FEMALE, FALL ADULTS AND IMM: Same basic pattern as breeding males, but duller, with more brown in plumage. Some imm. females may lack yellow crown and side patch.

Feeding: Eats insects, and berries, especially in winter. Comes to bird feeders for suet and fruit.

Nesting: Cup of twigs, grasses, rootlets, placed 5–50 ft. up in conifer. Eggs: 4–5, cream with brown marks; I: 12–13 days; F: 12–14 days, altricial; B: 2.

Other Behavior: Most abundant warbler across U.S. Commonly seen on fall migration, sometimes in flocks. Regularly winters in U.S.

Habitat: Coniferous or mixed forests. In winter, brushy thickets of bayberry and wax myrtle.

Voice: "Myrtle's" song is musical trill, often in 2-note phrases. Call is sharp "check." "Audubon's" song is slow warble. Call is like "whip."

Conservation:
BBS: E ↑ C ↑ CBC: ↑

Black-throated Green Warbler

Dendroica virens

Male

Female

Immature female

Identification: 5" **MALE:** Olive-green above; black throat and upper breast; yellow face; olive line through eye; olive ear patch surrounded by yellow. **FEMALE:** Similar, but has pale yellow throat with much less black on it. **IMM—MALE:** In nonbreeding, practically identical to adult female. **FEMALE:** Paler, with pale throat and breast and faint dusky streaks on sides. • In all plumages, has yellow wash on vent area.

Feeding: Eats insects and berries. Forages at medium to high levels in trees.

Nesting: Cup of grass and bark shreds is lined with feathers, hair, placed high in conifer. Eggs: 4–5, whitish with marks; I: 12 days; F: 8–10 days, altricial; B: 1.

Other Behavior: Different warbler species have varying numbers of songs, and these are sung in different contexts. The male Black-throated Green Warbler has 2 song types, 1 with an accented and 1 with an unaccented ending. Accented-ending song is given when near females, low in vegetation, or foraging. Unaccented-ending song is given from exposed perches when advertising territory or when close to other males.

Habitat: Open coniferous and mixed deciduous forests, second growth.

Voice: Song has several variants: accented "zee zee zee zoo zee"; or unaccented "zoo zee zoo zoo zee." Call is a non-musical "tick."

Conservation: BBS: E ↓ C ⇓ CBC: ↑

Golden-cheeked Warbler

Dendroica chrysoparia

Male

Identification: 5½" Breeds in Edwards Plateau in C. Tex. MALE: **Golden yellow face with black eyeline; black upperparts, crown, throat, and upper breast; white underparts with bold streaks.** FEMALE: **Similar, but crown and upperparts are greener; throat white or yellowish; black mottling on breast.** IMM: Similar to adult female; imm. female dullest, but eyeline is still noticeable.

Feeding: Eats insects, which it gleans or flycatches at medium to high levels in trees.

Nesting: Female uses strips solely from the inner bark of mature Ashe Juniper tree for nest building. Strips are woven with grasses and spider's silk; lining is hair. Nest is placed in Ashe Juniper tree. Eggs: 3–5, white with brown marks; I: 12 days; F: 9 days, altricial; B: 1.

Other Behavior: Population was 15,000–17,000 in 1974, but in 1990 was 2,200–4,600 and is still declining due to habitat loss and severe parasitism by cowbirds.

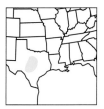

Habitat: Open woodlands with stands of Ashe Juniper trees.

Voice: Song is a buzzy whistled "zee dee sidee-zee." Call is a medium-loud "chup."

Conservation:
BBS: E C ⇓
Endangered in U.S.

Blackburnian Warbler
Dendroica fusca

Male

Female

Identification: 5" MALE: Fiery orange throat, eyebrow, and crown patch; dark ear patch; large white wing patch; black back with white lines; streaked flanks. FEMALE, FALL ADULT, AND IMM: Same basic pattern as breeding male, but the orange is replaced by orange-yellow or, on imm. female, peachy buff; 2 wide white wing bars.

Feeding: Feeds on insects and occasionally berries.

Nesting: Nest of twigs, grasses, plant down, and spider's silk, placed far out on horizontal limb of conifer or deciduous tree up to 84 ft. high. Eggs: 4–5, greenish white with dark spots; I: 11–13 days; F: ?, altricial; B: ?

Other Behavior: Usually stays high in upper canopy. Breeding biology needs more study.

Habitat: Mature coniferous woods, especially with hemlocks; also deciduous woods.

Voice: Song is a series of thin high-pitched notes with last note very high, like "tsip, tsip, tsip, titi, tzeeeee." Call is a nonmusical "tick."

Conservation: BBS: E ↑ C ⇓ CBC: ↑

Yellow-throated Warbler

Dendroica dominica

Male

Identification: 5½" **MALE: Bright yellow throat and upper breast; black face bordered by yellowish or white eyebrow; white patch on neck; plain gray back;** white below with streaked sides. **FEMALE AND IMM:** Similar to adult male, but duller, especially imm. female. •The race *D. d. albilora*, which breeds from Appalachians west, has an all-white eyebrow. All other races usually have yellow on the eyebrow in front of the eye. "Sutton's Warbler," a rare hybrid of Northern Parula and Yellow-throated Warbler, has no streaks on sides and a greenish back.

Feeding: Eats spiders and insects, including caterpillars, moths, grasshoppers. Comes to bird feeders.

Nesting: Nest of grasses, plant down, and spider's silk, placed on tree limb of pine or in Spanish moss. Eggs: 4–5, greenish gray; I: 12–13 days; F: ?, altricial; B: 1–2.

Other Behavior: Creeps along branches and trunks of trees, picking insects from bark crevices. Sings from canopy.

Habitat: Live oak woodland, pine forest, sycamore-cypress swamps, floodplain forest.

Voice: Song is a descending series of whistled notes that ends with a higher note. Call is a loud "chirp."

Conservation: BBS: E ↑ C ↑ CBC: ↓

Pine Warbler

Dendroica pinus

Male

Immature female

Identification: 5½" Birds in all plumages have plain unstreaked upperparts; white wing bars; white undertail coverts; black legs; white spots on corner of tail; comparatively large bill. **MALE:** Yellow throat and breast; indistinct black streaks on breast sides; bright olive-green above. **FEMALE:** Similar, but paler, with a buffy-yellow breast; grayish tinge on upperparts, especially on the nape of the neck. **IMM—MALE:** Similar to adult female, but browner above and yellower on breast. **FEMALE:** Very dull; grayish brown above; pale buff to whitish below.

Feeding: Flycatches, or creeps along branches, searching for insects. Eats insects, spiders; in winter, fruits, berries, pine seeds. Comes to bird feeders for sunflower seeds and suet.

Nesting: Cup of pine needles, weeds, bark, placed far out on limb of pine tree. Eggs: 3–5, whitish with brown speckles; I: 10 days; F: 10 days, altricial; B: ?

Other Behavior: Usually seen in pines.

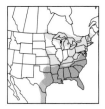

Habitat: Pine or mixed woodlands.

Voice: Song is a trill similar to Chipping Sparrow's, but more musical. Call is a sweet "chip."

Conservation:
BBS: E ↑ C ↑ CBC: ⇑

Kirtland's Warbler

Dendroica kirtlandii

Male

Identification: 5¾" Limited to northeastern lower peninsula of Mich. Wags tail frequently. **MALE:** Blue-gray upperparts with black streaks; yellow below, with black streaking confined to sides; white eye-ring; 2 white wing bars. **FEMALE AND IMM:** Duller overall; brown wash on upperparts; less distinct flank streaks.

Feeding: Eats insects, blueberries.

Nesting: Nest of grass and leaves, placed on ground in grassy opening or under the branches of young tree. Eggs: 3–5, creamy with brown marks; I: 13–16 days; F: 9 days, altricial; B: 1–2.

Other Behavior: Requires highly specialized nesting habitat of dense young Jack Pine stands of 320 acres or more with trees 6–18 ft. high. These trees need intense heat from forest fires to release seeds from their cones. Protection of Kirtland's Warbler involves a management plan that includes some controlled burning of trees; logging mature trees and replanting several million seedlings each year; habitat protection; and continual trapping and removal of the Brown-headed Cowbird, a severe nest parasite.

Habitat: Young Jack Pine stands.

Voice: Song is loud series of low-pitched notes followed by 2–3 higher-pitched whistles. Call note is a loud "tsip."

Conservation: Endangered in U.S. Population was counted at 765 singing males in 1995.

Prairie Warbler

Dendroica discolor

Male

Female

Immature female

Identification: 4¾" Wags or pumps tail. MALE: Yellow face with black line through eye; yellow patch below eye bordered by black; yellow underparts; black streaks on sides; olive above with chestnut streaks on back, which are often concealed; 2 white or yellowish wing bars. FEMALE AND IMM: Paler overall, with streaking and face pattern less discernible, especially on imm. female, which has gray cheek and grayish wash on head.

Feeding: Eats insects, which it gleans off leaves or catches in the air.

Nesting: May nest in loose colonies. Nests of grasses, plant down, lined with feathers, hair, placed in bush or small tree. Eggs: 3–5, whitish with brown marks; I: 10–14 days; F: 8–10 days, altricial; B: 1–2.

Other Behavior: Males sometimes polygynous.

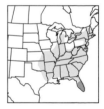

Habitat: Dry brushy areas, old fields, young pine plantations, mangrove swamps.

Voice: Song is a series of buzzy notes that continually rise. Call is a musical "tsup."

Conservation: BBS: E ⇓ C ⇓ CBC: ↓

370

Palm Warbler

Dendroica palmarum

Spring adult (eastern)

Fall

Spring adult (western)

Identification: 5½" In all plumages: constantly bobs tail; yellow undertail coverts; often forages on ground. SPRING ADULT: Sexes similar. Chestnut crown; yellow eyebrow and throat; underparts streaked with chestnut; rump olive-yellow. Eastern birds have yellowish underparts; western birds have grayish-white underparts. FALL ADULT AND IMM: Similar, but duller and browner overall, including crown.

Feeding: Eats insects, which it picks off the ground. Hops rather than walks.

Nesting: Nests in spruce bogs or dry plains of pines. Grassy cup lined with feathers, fine grasses, placed on ground near spruce trunk or low in shrub or low branches of conifer. Eggs: 4–5, creamy with wreath of brown marks; I: 12 days; F: 12 days, altricial; B: 1–2.

Other Behavior: One of the commonest warblers in S. Fla. throughout winter. Birds that breed in the East winter on the Gulf Coast from W. Fla. to N.E. Mex. Birds that breed in the West winter in S. Fla., the W. Indies, and occasionally on Atlantic Coast to Va.

Habitat: Spruce bogs. On migration and in winter, grassy fields, brushy areas, beaches, lawns.

Voice: Song is a buzzy trill that may rise. Call is a musical sharp "sup."

Conservation: BBS: E ⇑ C CBC: ⇓

Bay-breasted Warbler

Dendroica castanea

Spring male

Fall adult

Identification: 5½" **All plumages have dark gray legs.** SPRING—MALE: **Chestnut (i.e., bay) crown, throat, upper breast, and sides;** black face; pinky-buff patch on side of neck; 2 white wing bars. FEMALE: **Paler, with less chestnut on head and sides.** FALL ADULT AND IMM: Yellowish olive above with some streaking; underparts buffy white, with trace of chestnut or warm buff on flanks; buff undertail coverts. Imm. female lacks chestnut or buff on flanks. •The similar imm. Blackpoll Warbler has straw-colored feet and legs (which often have dark sides) and white undertail coverts; it is yellowish green below, with faint streaks on sides. The similar imm. Pine Warbler has an unstreaked back and is more gray-brown.

Feeding: Feeds on insects, which it gleans from leaves.

Nesting: Grass and twig nest in conifer. Eggs: 4–7, white with marks; I: 12–13 days; F: 11–12 days, altricial; B: 1.

Other Behavior: Fall migration is earlier than Blackpoll's.

Habitat: Coniferous forests.

Voice: Song is a series of high-pitched doubled notes, like "seetzy, seetzy, seetzy." Call is a high-pitched "see."

Conservation: BBS: E ↓ C ↓ CBC: ↓

Blackpoll Warbler

Dendroica striata

Spring male

Spring female

Fall adult

Identification: 5½" All plumages tend to have yellowish or yellowish-pink legs; yellow soles of feet; white wing bars; some streaking on sides. SPRING—MALE: Chickadee-like face pattern of black cap and white cheeks; white below; black streaks on sides and back. FEMALE: Olive-gray streaked cap and upperparts; underparts whitish or yellowish, with fine streaking on sides. FALL ADULT AND IMM: Olive-green above; sides of legs may be dark brown; throat and breast greenish yellow; fine streaking on sides; belly and long undertail coverts white. Distinguished from fall Pine and Bay-breasted Warblers by leg color (usually), white undertail coverts, and lower belly contrasting with greenish-yellow breast; faint streaks on sides; pale eyebrow.

Feeding: Eats insects, spiders, a few seeds and berries.

Nesting: Grassy nest in spruce. Eggs: 4–5, white with brown dots; I: 11 days; F: 11–12 days, altricial; B: 1–2.

Other Behavior: Abundant fall migrant.

Habitat: Spruce-fir forests. In migration, other woodlands.

Voice: Song is series of extremely high "seet" notes, loudest in middle. Call is loud "chip."

Conservation:
BBS: E ↑ C

Cerulean Warbler

Dendroica cerulea

Immature female

Male

Female

Identification: 4¾" In all plumages, appears short-tailed. MALE: "Cerulean" blue upperparts with black streaks; white wing bars; white below, with black breastband and streaking on sides. FEMALE: Turquoise-blue upperparts; metallic-bluish crown; yellowish-white eyebrow, throat, and upper breast; faint streaks on sides; white wing bars. IMM—MALE: Duller than adult male, with greener tinge; faint streaks on back and sides, yellowish tinge to underparts. FEMALE: Duller than adult female, but olive-green above with extensive yellowish below.

Feeding: Feeds on insects high in treetops. Gleans or flycatches.

Nesting: Nest of bark and weeds is placed 21–60 ft. high in deciduous tree. Eggs: 3–5, greenish with variable brown marks; I: 12–13 days; F: ?, altricial; B: ?

Other Behavior: Usually stays high in tree canopy.

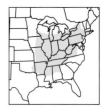

Habitat: Mature deciduous trees, especially near swampy areas and streams.

Voice: Song is series of rapid buzzy notes on 1 pitch, ending with a higher note, like "zray zray zray zree." Call is a sharp "chip."

Conservation: BBS: E ⇓ C ⇓

Black-and-white Warbler

Mniotilta varia

Male

Female

Identification: 5¼" Creeps down tree trunks like a nuthatch. MALE: Black-and-white-striped crown, upperparts, and underparts; black throat and ear patch much reduced or lost in winter. FEMALE: Similar, but has gray ear patch; white throat; grayish streaking on underparts. IMM—MALE: Similar to adult female, but has blacker streaking on sides and undertail coverts. FEMALE: Ear patch, flanks, and undertail coverts are buffy.

Feeding: Relatively long bill enables it to get insects from under the bark of tree trunks and limbs.

Nesting: Grassy cup with leaves, moss, placed on ground, concealed near base of tree or under fallen branch. Eggs: 4–5, creamy, circled with brown marks; I: 10–13 days; F: 8–12 days, altricial; B: 1–2.

Other Behavior: One of the earliest migrants in spring, often before trees have leafed out.

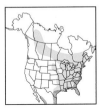

Habitat: Deciduous and mixed woodlands, especially damp woods.

Voice: Song is high-pitched "wee-see wee-see wee-see." Calls are a soft "tseet" and a sharp "pit."

Conservation:
BBS: E ↑ C ↓ CBC: ↑

375

American Redstart
Setophaga ruticilla

Male

Female

Identification: 5¼" **Constantly flits about with tail fanned, exposing bright orange tail patches on male and yellow tail patches on female and imm. MALE:** Black upperparts and chest; orange patches on wings and sides. **FEMALE AND IMM:** Olive-gray upperparts; yellow patches on wings and sides. Imm. female lacks, or shows much reduced, wing patches. Imm. male, in spring, shows some black body or head feathers; salmon on wing, tail, and side patches.

Feeding: Frequently flycatches, also gleans. Eats insects, occasionally seeds and berries on migration.

Nesting: Cup of grasses, bark, and spider's silk, placed in crotch of small tree or shrub. Eggs: 2–5, whitish with brown marks; I: 12 days; F: 8–9 days, altricial; B: ?

Other Behavior: Very active. Adult males breed in more preferred habitat than 1st-year males.

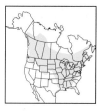

Habitat: Deciduous and mixed woodlands, thickets.

Voice: Song is a quite variable series of high notes, ending with a downslurred note. Call is a sweet "chip."

Conservation:
BBS: E ↓ C ↓ CBC: ↑

Prothonotary Warbler

Protonotaria citrea

Male

Identification: 5½" Relatively long bill; large dark eyes. MALE: Bright golden-yellow head and underparts; blue-gray wings; extensive white in tail and undertail coverts. FEMALE AND IMM: Yellow head and underparts; olive tinge on crown, nape, and back; gray wings.

Feeding: Searches crevices in logs and tree trunks for insects and spiders.

Nesting: Nest of twigs, mosses, grasses, placed in natural cavity, birdhouse, or old woodpecker hole, especially that of Downy Woodpecker. Height of nest is usually 4–6 ft. Eggs: 4–6, white with irregular brown spots; I: 12–14 days; F: 11 days, altricial; B: 1–2.

Other Behavior: Seventy-five percent of the time the nest tree is at the edge of or in water.

Habitat: Wooded swamps, floodplain forests.

Voice: Song is series of loud "zweet" notes on 1 pitch. Call is a loud "tink."

Conservation:
BBS: E ↓ C ⇓ CBC: ↓

Worm-eating Warbler

Helmitheros vermivorus

Identification: 5½" Warm buff head and underparts; 2 black lines on crown; black line through eye; long pointed bill.

Feeding: Eats insects, such as grasshoppers, beetles, smooth caterpillars. Hops on ground or acrobatically forages in trees, grabbing and poking into curled dead leaves for insects.

Nesting: Nest of dead leaves, stems of hair-cap mosses, concealed on ground on shaded hillside or bank. Eggs: 3–6, white with brown speckles; I: 12 days; F: 10 days, altricial; B: 1.

Other Behavior: Misnamed, since it does not eat earthworms, only insects.

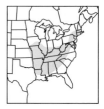

Habitat: Wooded hillsides and ravines.

Voice: Song is a dry trill on 1 pitch with a sewing-machinelike quality. Similar to song of Chipping Sparrow. Call is a sharp "chip."

Conservation: BBS: E ↓ C ↓ CBC: ↓

Swainson's Warbler

Limnothlypis swainsonii

Identification: 5½" Warm brown crown; pale eyebrow; narrow brown eyeline; long tapered bill; pale tan below.

Feeding: Walks on ground looking for insects, overturning leaves, or probing into earth.

Nesting: Cuplike nest of pine needles, moss, leaves, placed in bush, canes, tangles. Eggs: 3–5, white; I: 14–15 days; F: 12 days, altricial; B: 1–2.

Other Behavior: Secretive; stays on ground or low in vegetation. May nest semicolonially in good breeding habitat.

Habitat: Swamps, canebrakes; also rhododendron thickets in southern Appalachians.

Voice: Song is 3–4 loud whistles, followed by warbling notes that often end in "teeu." Call is a loud "tsip."

Conservation:
BBS: E ↓ C ↓

Ovenbird

Seiurus aurocapillus

Identification: 6" **Orange crown bordered by 2 dark brown stripes; white eye-ring;** olive-brown back; white below, with heavy dark stripes composed of elongated spots on breast and flanks.

Feeding: Eats insects, worms, spiders. Pokes under leaves.

Nesting: Nest of grasses and rootlets, placed on ground, is always roofed over with branches, leaves. The entrance is a small slit. Eggs: 3–6, white with brown and gray marks; I: 11–14 days; F: 8–11 days, altricial; B: 1–2.

Other Behavior: Heard more than seen. Song often has a ventriloquial quality. The Ovenbird's name comes from the fact that its domed-over nest looks like a Dutch oven. Walks on ground and fallen branches, frequently "teeters."

Habitat: Mature deciduous or mixed forests.

Voice: Song is a ringing series of notes that increase in loudness, like "teacher teacher teacher." Call is a sharp "chip."

Conservation: BBS: E ↑ C ⇓ CBC: ↓

380

Northern Waterthrush

Seiurus noveboracensis

Eastern

Western

Identification: 5¾" Eyebrow, of even width or tapering behind eye, is yellowish buff (eastern birds) or whitish (western birds); uniformly colored underparts are pale yellowish buff in eastern birds and whitish in western birds; heavily streaked with brown from chin to breast and along flanks; flesh-colored legs.

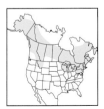

Feeding: Searches under leaves and on fallen logs. Wades in water. Eats insects, mollusks, crustaceans, small minnows, smaller prey than Louisiana Waterthrush.

Nesting: Nest of mosses, leaves, and grasses is concealed in roots of upturned tree or under the overhang of a bank near standing water. Eggs: 3–6, white with variable brown or purplish marks; I: 12 days; F: 10 days, altricial; B: ?

Other Behavior: Bobs tail while walking.

Habitat: Wooded ponds, swamps, willow thickets, lake shores, beside still water or slow-moving rivers.

Voice: Song is a loud series of notes with a downslurred ending. Call is a metallic "chink."

Conservation: BBS: E ↑ C ⇑ CBC: ↓

Louisiana Waterthrush

Seiurus motacilla

Identification: 6″ Eyebrow is wider, especially behind eye, and more extensive than that of similar Northern Waterthrush; eyebrow tinged with pale buff in front of eye, becomes bright white behind eye; heavily streaked whitish underparts contrast with buff flanks and unstreaked belly and undertail coverts; throat usually white; chin unstreaked; pinkish legs.

Feeding: Walks along searching under leaves, or wades in water. Eats insects, mollusks, crustaceans, small fish.

Nesting: Nest of mosses, leaves, and grasses is concealed amid roots of upturned tree or under the overhang of a bank a few feet from running water. A constructed walkway of leaves leads from nest to water. Eggs: 4–6, white with variable brown or purple marks; I: 12–14 days; F: 9–10 days, altricial; B: ?

Other Behavior: Bobs tail and whole rear end while walking. Has long narrow breeding territory along a stream.

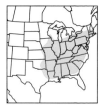

Habitat: Wooded ravines near mountain brooks and streams.

Voice: Three or 4 slurred notes followed by a warbling twitter. Call is a sharp "chink."

Conservation:
BBS: E ↑ C ↑ CBC: ↓

Kentucky Warbler

Oporornis formosus

Female

Identification: 5¼" Bold yellow "spectacles" **stand out;** yellow underparts; unmarked olive-green upperparts; male darker on crown, under eye area, and on sides of neck than female and imm.

Feeding: Turns over leaves and twigs, or forages in low bushes. Eats insects, spiders.

Nesting: Nest of leaves, weed stems, and grasses, placed under log or in low bush in dense undergrowth. Eggs: 3–6, creamy with brown marks; I: 12–13 days; F: 9–10 days, altricial; B: ?

Other Behavior: Shy, skulking. Mostly seen on the ground.

Habitat: Ravines and bottomlands of moist deciduous or mixed woodlands.

Voice: Song is a rolling series of 2-syllable notes, like "chur-ree, chur-ree, chur-ree." Similar to Carolina Wren's, but not as melodic. Call is low rich "chuck."

Conservation:
BBS: E ↓ C ⇓ CBC: ↓

Connecticut Warbler

Oporornis agilis

Male

Identification: 5¾" In all plumages: complete bold white or whitish eye-ring; brown or gray hood; yellow underparts; short-tailed appearance created by long undertail coverts reaching more than halfway to tip of tail; long legs. **MALE:** Gray hood. **FEMALE AND IMM:** Paler underparts; browner hood; paler throat.

Feeding: Feeds on the ground or on fallen logs, searching for insects, spiders.

Nesting: Nest of leaves, grasses, plant fibers, placed on the ground, usually at the base of a shrub or sapling. Eggs: 3–5, white with brown marks; I: ?; F: ?, altricial; B: ?

Other Behavior: Generally more rare than Mourning or MacGillivray's Warbler. Skulks in undergrowth. Bobs head while walking with elevated tail. Breeding biology needs more study.

Habitat: Spruce and tamarack bogs, open poplar woods, willow scrub, young Jack Pine stands.

Voice: Song is loud repetitive notes, like "wee cher cher wee cher cher." Call is metallic "chink."

Conservation: BBS: E ↑ C ⇑

Mourning Warbler

Oporornis philadelphia

Male

Female

Immature

Identification: 5¼" MALE: Gray hood; lacks eye-ring; black mottled patch on upper breast. FEMALE: Paler gray hood; very faint, broken, whitish eye-ring, which may occasionally be complete; pale throat; no black on breast. IMM: Has thin broken eye-ring; yellowish throat breaks through lower part of hood and connects to yellow underparts; hood browner, less evident than that of imm. MacGillivray's Warbler; imm. male may have some black feathers on sides of upper breast.

Feeding: Feeds on the ground or gleans from understory. Eats insects and spiders.

Nesting: Bulky cuplike nest of dead leaves and grasses, placed on ground at base of shrub, or low in tangle. Eggs: 3–5, white with variable brown marks; I: 12 days; F: 7–9 days, altricial; B: 1.

Other Behavior: Hops on ground, while Connecticut Warbler walks. Generally skulks in dense undergrowth.

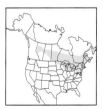

Habitat: Dense undergrowth of moist woods, brushy areas, swamps, and bogs.

Voice: Song is loud series of 2-note phrases with the 2nd part lower-pitched. Call is a loud "check."

Conservation:
BBS: E ↓ C ↑

Common Yellowthroat

Geothlypis trichas

Male

Female

Immature male

Identification: 5″ **MALE:** Yellow throat and upper breast; black mask with grayish-white border; buff flanks; yellow undertail coverts. **FEMALE:** Yellow throat and breast; olive-brown face and upperparts; whitish eye-ring; suggestion of eyebrow; brown wash on forehead. **IMM—MALE:** Partly developed mask often obscured by pale feather tips. **FEMALE:** Paler than adult female, with buffy-yellow throat; no brown on forehead. •There is much geographical variation in this species. Northern and eastern birds have whitish belly and yellow undertail coverts; southwestern birds have solid yellow underparts.

Feeding: Eats insects, spiders, and seeds gleaned from the ground or shrubs.

Nesting: Nest of coarse grasses, dead leaves, lined with fine grasses or hair, placed 1–2 ft. high in shrubbery. Eggs: 3–4, creamy white with brown marks; I: 12 days; F: 8–9 days, altricial; B: 1–2.

Other Behavior: Very abundant species.

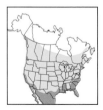

Habitat: Dense brushy habitats near wet areas, drier habitats with dense understory.

Voice: Song sounds like "witchity, witchity, witchity," or "your money, your money, your money." Call is sharp "tchat, tchat."

Conservation:
BBS: E ↓ C ↓ CBC: →

Hooded Warbler

Wilsonia citrina

Male

Immature female

Identification: 5¼" In all plumages, has large dark eye and frequently flicks tail, revealing white on tail feathers. **MALE: Black hood that surrounds yellow face;** yellow below; greenish olive above. **FEMALE: Similar to male; shows variation in amount of black in hood; some have almost as much black as male. IMM— MALE:** Like adult male. **FEMALE:** Does not have black on head.

Feeding: Frequently flycatches, darting out from a low perch to capture prey. Eats insects, spiders.

Nesting: Nest is a cup of dead leaves, plant fibers, and bark strips, placed in fork of a shrub. Eggs: 3–5, whitish with brown marks; I: 12 days; F: 8 days, altricial; B: 1.

Other Behavior: Spends most of its time in dense understory. Male is most conspicuous when singing.

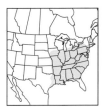

Habitat: Dense shrubbery in mature deciduous woodlands, especially near streams.

Voice: Song is loud, musical, paired notes, like "wee-ta, wee-ta, wee-tee-yo." Call is a metallic "chink."

Conservation: BBS: E ⇑ C ⇓ CBC: ↑

Wilson's Warbler

Wilsonia pusilla

Male

Female

Identification: 4¾" **MALE:** Black cap; yellow below; olive-green above. **FEMALE:** Has some black on crown, occasionally extensive. **IMM— MALE:** Like adult male, but sometimes duller. **FEMALE:** Does not have any black on crown. •Western birds are brighter yellow on face and underparts than eastern birds.

Feeding: Actively flycatches. Eats insects, berries.

Nesting: May be loosely colonial in ideal habitat. Nest of grasses, leaves, mosses, placed on the ground, usually at base of shrub. Eggs: 4–6, white with brown marks; I: 11–13 days; F: 8–10 days, altricial; B: 1.

Other Behavior: Frequently twitches tail and flicks wings. Stays low in undergrowth. More common in the West than the East.

Habitat: Willow and alder thickets near water, moist woodlands.

Voice: Song is a chattering trill that drops in pitch. Call is a flat low "chet."

Conservation: BBS: E ↑ C CBC: ↑

Canada Warbler

Wilsonia canadensis

Male

Immature female

Identification: 5¼" MALE: Necklace of black streaks across yellow breast; yellow "spectacles"; unmarked dark blue-gray back; white undertail coverts. FEMALE: Necklace is blurred and more subtle, especially on imm. female.

Feeding: Often flycatches. Feeds at low to middle levels in vegetation. Eats insects, spiders.

Nesting: Nest of weeds, leaves, and grasses, placed in tree stump or in roots of upturned tree, or sphagnum hummock. Eggs: 3–5, cream with brown marks; I: ?; F: ?, altricial; B: ?

Other Behavior: Frequently twitches tail. Breeding biology needs more study.

Habitat: Dense understory of mature deciduous or mixed woodlands, shrubby areas near streams and swamps.

Voice: Song is a musical warble that starts with a "chip" note. Call is a loud "chit."

Conservation: BBS: E ↓ C

Yellow-breasted Chat
Icteria virens

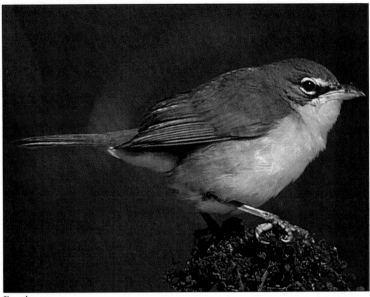

Female

Identification: 7½" The largest warbler. MALE: White spectacles; black lores; white moustache stripe; yellow throat and breast; long tail; thick bill. FEMALE: Similar, with gray lores.

Feeding: Eats insects, berries, wild grapes, and other fruit. Forages low in shrubbery.

Nesting: Can be loosely colonial. Nest is a bulky cup of dead leaves, straw, weeds, and shredded bark lined with fine grasses, placed in shrub or small tree. Eggs: 3–5, white with brown marks; I: 11–12 days; F: 8–12 days, altricial; B: 2.

Other Behavior: Heard more than seen. Song is more reminiscent of a mockingbird's than a warbler's. In spring, males perform song flights.

Habitat: Dense thickets and brushy edges in dry or moist areas.

Voice: Song is an amazing assortment of whistles, rattles, squeaks, scolds, mews. Call is a grating "chack."

Conservation: BBS: E ↓ C ↓ CBC: ↓

Summer Tanager
Piranga rubra

Male

Female

Immature male

Identification: 7½" **MALE: Uniformly bright rose-red head and body; darker red wings and tail. FEMALE: Yellowish below; slightly darker above; no gray cheek patch or white wing bars. IMM—MALE: Patches of red and green over body. FEMALE: Like adult female. Imm. plumage kept 1 year.**

Feeding: May catch insect prey in midair. Fond of eating bees and wasps, and will raid their nests. Eats fruit and berries. Sometimes comes to bird feeders for fruit, bread crumbs, and peanut butter mixtures.

Nesting: Nest of weed stems, bark, and coarse grasses lined with finer materials, placed on horizontal branch of tree 10–35 ft. above the ground. Eggs: 3–5, pale bluish green with dark marks; I: 12 days; F: ?, altricial; B: ?

Other Behavior: Usually concealed in tree foliage. More easily detected by song. Range in the East is diminishing. Where range overlaps with Scarlet Tanager's, these 2 species are aggressive to each other.

Habitat: Pine-oak woods, willows and cottonwoods along streams.

Voice: Song is a string of varied whistles; call is a rapid harsh "chchbit."

Conservation:
BBS: E ↓ C ↓ CBC: ↑

Scarlet Tanager

Piranga olivacea

Male

Female

Immature male

Identification: 7″ **MALE:** Scarlet-red body with black wings and black tail. **FEMALE:** Yellowish below; greenish above; wings grayish brown. Differs from similar female Summer Tanager by smaller overall size and smaller bill. **IMM—MALE:** Body with patches of red and yellow; wings and tail dark brown. **FEMALE:** Like adult female. Imm. plumage kept 1 year.

Feeding: Feeds on the ground and in foliage, eating insects and some wild berries.

Nesting: Nest of twigs, grasses, rootlets, placed on horizontal limb of tree 5–75 ft. above the ground. Eggs: 2–5, pale blue-green with irregular dots of brown; I: 12–14 days; F: 9–10 days, altricial; B: 1.

Other Behavior: Despite the brilliant red of the male, he is often hard to spot in the forest canopy. The best clue to his presence is his singing. Both sexes can also be detected by their frequent "chip-burr" call note. When the female arrives on the breeding territory, the male sings less and follows her about, displaying to her from a lower perch by drooping his wings, revealing his red back. Frequently parasitized by cowbirds.

Habitat: Mature deciduous forests.

Voice: A well-spaced series of burry 2-part whistles, like "zureet zeeyeer zeeroo"; call a distinctive "chip-burr."

Conservation: BBS: E ↑ C ↓

Northern Cardinal

Cardinalis cardinalis

Male

Female

Identification: 8½" MALE: **All bright red with black around base of bill; large crest;** reddish bill. FEMALE: **Buffy below; grayish brown above; reddish bill,** crest, wings, and tail. Juveniles look like adult female but have dark bill.

Feeding: Feeds by hopping around on ground, gleaning food from low shrubbery and trees. Eats insects, spiders, wild fruits and berries, weed seeds. A favorite at bird feeders, where it prefers sunflower seed, safflower seed, cracked corn.

Nesting: Nest of twigs, bark strips, vines, leaves, rootlets, and paper lined with fine grass and hair, placed in dense shrubbery or among branches of small tree 1–15 ft. above ground. Eggs: 2–5, buff-white with dark marks; I: 12–13 days; F: 9–11 days, altricial; B: 1–4.

Other Behavior: At your bird feeder you may see mate-feeding, a highlight of the relationship between a pair of breeding cardinals that can occur as often as 4 times a minute. In this, the male picks up a seed, hops over to the female, and the two momentarily touch beaks as she takes the food. Mate-feeding will continue through the egg-laying and incubation phases of breeding. Both male and female sing.

Habitat: Shrubs near open areas, woods, suburban yards.

Voice: Song a series of clear repeated whistles that vary, like "whoit whoit whoit, cheer cheer cheer"; call a metallic "chip."

Conservation:
BBS: E ↓ C ↑ CBC: ↓

Pyrrhuloxia
Cardinalis sinuatus

Male

Female

Identification: 8" **MALE: Gray with rose-red on face and central underparts, wings, and tail; long red-tipped crest;** stubby bill orangish yellow. **FEMALE: Gray with long red-tipped crest; some red on face, wings, and tail;** stubby bill yellowish.

Feeding: Forages on the ground, eating weed and grass seeds, catkins, cactus fruit, mesquite beans, and insects. May come to bird feeders for sunflower seeds and fruit.

Nesting: Nest of thorny twigs, inner bark, coarse grass, and spiderweb lined with plant fibers, fine grass, horsehair, and rootlets, placed among the branches of mesquite or other thickets 5–20 ft. above the ground. Eggs: 2–5, gray-white or green-white with brown spots; I: 14 days; F: 10 days, altricial; B: 1.

Other Behavior: Male feeds female as part of courtship activities. During winter, found in small flocks and may wander to locate good food sources.

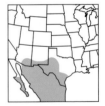

Habitat: Arid and semiarid areas with thorny shrubs and woodlands

Voice: Song a series of clear repeated whistles that vary; call a metallic "chip."

Conservation: BBS: E C ↓ CBC: ↓

Rose-breasted Grosbeak

Pheucticus ludovicianus

Female

Summer male

Immature male

Identification: 8 " SUMMER—MALE: **Black head and back; red triangle on breast;** white belly. **In flight, shows white patches on wings; rose-red "armpits"; white rump.** FEMALE: **Large pale bill; white eyebrow; heavy streaking on whitish breast; 2 white wing bars.** Yellow "armpits" in flight. Plumage similar in winter and on imm. WINTER—MALE: Similar to summer, but with brown edges to head and back feathers. IMM: Male looks similar to adult female, but with rosy triangle on buffy breast and reddish "armpits" (seen in flight). Imm. plumage kept until spring.

Feeding: Gleans food from tree foliage. Eats insects, seeds, tree buds, and some fruit. Comes to feeders for sunflower seed.

Nesting: Nest of coarse and fine twigs lined with horsehair, rootlets, and grasses, placed on branch of tree 5–25 ft. above the ground. Eggs: 3–6, pale blue with irregular brown spots; I: 12–14 days; F: 9–12 days, altricial; B: 1–2.

Other Behavior: Both male and female sing.

Habitat: Deciduous woods, mixed shrubs and trees.

Voice: Song a rapid series of melodious whistles, referred to as "a robin in a hurry"; call a distinctive squeak, like a sneaker on a gym floor.

Conservation:
BBS: E ↓ C ↓ CBC: ↑

Blue Grosbeak
Guiraca caerulea

Male

Immature in fall

Female

Immature male, 1st spring

Identification: 7" **MALE: Dark blue overall, with 2 reddish-brown wing bars,** the upper 1 broader; large silvery bill; black feathers around base of bill. **FEMALE: Plain brown overall; dark wings and tail; 2 buffy-brown wing bars; large, gray, conical bill. IMM:** Fall male and female resemble adult female, but may be a more reddish brown. In spring, male gains some blue patches on body feathers. Imm. plumage kept 1 year.

Feeding: Forages on the ground, hopping about in search of insects; also gleans foliage. Eats spiders, seeds, and wild fruits.

Nesting: Nest of rootlets, grasses, twigs, snakeskins, cotton, and bark strips lined with rootlets, grasses, and tendrils, placed in shrub, vine tangle, or tree 3–12 ft. above the ground. Eggs: 2–5, pale blue; I: 11–12 days; F: 9–13 days, altricial; B: 2.

Other Behavior: Often twitches and rapidly spreads tail when agitated. On migration, can be found in association with buntings.

Habitat: Open areas with some shrubbery, such as roadsides, hedgerows, farmlands, prairies.

Voice: Song a warbled phrase of musical notes; call a loud "chink."

Conservation: BBS: E ↑ C ↓ CBC: ↓

Indigo Bunting
Passerina cyanea

Summer male

Female

Immature male, 1st spring

Identification: 5½" SUMMER—MALE: Deep blue overall; dark gray conical bill. FEMALE: Extremely plain brown, with faint wing bars and faint streaking; short, gray, conical bill. Keeps same plumage all year. WINTER—MALE: Brownish, with some blue on underparts, wings, and rump. IMM: Female like adult female. Male like adult female through winter, then a mixture of brown and blue feathers on body. Imm. plumage kept 1 year.

Feeding: Forages on the ground and in low foliage for insects, weed seeds, wild berries, and grains.

Nesting: Nest of dead leaves, weed stems, grasses, lined with finer grasses and downy material, placed in the fork of branch of shrub, tangle, or tree 2–10 ft. above the ground. Eggs: 2–6, white; I: 12 days; F: 10–12, altricial; B: 1–2.

Other Behavior: Male conspicuously sings from tops of trees and shrubs. Female can be very secretive. If you are anywhere near the nest, the birds will give "spit" call, do tail-flick, and be reluctant to approach the nest. Sometimes hybridizes with Lazuli Bunting.

Habitat: Brush and low trees near open areas like overgrown fields.

Voice: A short rapid series of whistles, many paired, like "tsee tsee tew tew teer teer"; call a short "spit."

Conservation: BBS: E ↓ C ↓ CBC: ⇓

Varied Bunting

Passerina versicolor

Male

Female

Identification: 5ʺ **MALE:** Dark blue face; reddish-brown nape; blue rump; rest of body appears black in most lights, even though it includes blues and purples. **FEMALE:** Strongly curved top to upper mandible; dull grayish-olive upperparts; gray-brown underparts; bluish-gray rump; 2 narrow buff wing bars. **IMM:** Similar to adult female. Imm. plumage kept 1 year.

Feeding: Forages on the ground and in low foliage. Eats insects and seeds.

Nesting: Nest of stems, dried grasses, paper, and sometimes snakeskin lined with fine grasses, rootlets, and hair, placed in low foliage of bush, tangle, or tree 2–10 ft. above the ground. Eggs: 3–5, light blue; I: 12 days; F: ?, altricial; B: ?

Other Behavior: Breeding biology needs more study.

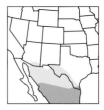

Habitat: Arid areas with thorny brush, such as dry washes.

Voice: Song a short warbled phrase; call a "tsink."

Conservation:
BBS: E C ⇑

Painted Bunting
Passerina ciris

Male

Female

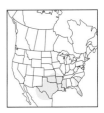
Immature male, 1st spring

Identification: 5½" **MALE:** Brilliantly colored with **blue head, red underparts, and a light green back and wings. FEMALE: Very plain; leaf-green above; lighter green below; conical gray bill. IMM:** Male in winter is like adult female and in spring may acquire some blue and red feathers. Imm. female is like adult female. Imm. plumage kept 1 year.

Feeding: Forages on the ground and in low foliage for the seeds of grasses and insects. May come to bird feeders for sunflower seeds and other seed mixes.

Nesting: Nest of forb stems, grasses, and leaves lined with hair, fine grasses, rootlets, and occasionally bits of snakeskin, placed in low foliage of tree or shrub 3–25 ft. above the ground. Eggs: 3–5, light blue-white or gray-white with brown spots; I: 11–12 days; F: 12–14 days, altricial; B: 2–4.

Other Behavior: Males are sometimes polygynous.

Habitat: Brush, clearcuts, mesquite, rangeland, thickets.

Voice: Song a musical warble; call a short "chit."

Conservation:
BBS: E ⇓ C ⇓ CBC: ⇓

Dickcissel

Spiza americana

Summer male

Summer female

Immature

Identification: 6½" **SUMMER—MALE:** Yellow breast with triangular black bib; yellow eyebrow; reddish-brown shoulder. **FEMALE:** Similar to male, but lacks the black bib. Keeps same plumage all year. **WINTER—MALE:** Same as summer, but yellow tips to feathers on breast cover much of the black bib. **IMM:** Fine streaking on breast, with little or no yellow; brown crown with fine, dark streaks; dusky line off base of bill. Imm. plumage kept until spring.

Feeding: Forages for food on the ground, eating insects and all kinds of weed seeds and grain.

Nesting: Nest of weed stems, grasses, leaves, and occasionally cornstalk lined with rootlets, fine grasses, and hair, placed in tree or hedge 2–14 ft. above the ground. Eggs: 2–6, light blue; I: 12–13 days; F: 7–10 days, altricial; B: 1.

Other Behavior: Found in large flocks during migration and winter. During nesting season, many nests are destroyed by mowing machines; Dickcissel nests are also frequently parasitized by the Brown-headed Cowbird. Sings persistently during breeding.

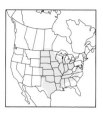

Habitat: Prairies, weedy fields, grain fields.

Voice: Song is 2 short notes followed by buzzy notes, like "dick dick dickzizzel"; call is short "zzzt."

Conservation:
BBS: E ⇓ C ↓ CBC: ↓

Olive Sparrow

Arremonops rufivirgatus

Identification: 5½" Limited to S. Tex. **Dull olive upperparts; 2 brown stripes on crown; thin brown eyeline; yellowish edgings to wing and tail feathers;** underparts clear grayish white.

Feeding: Forages on the ground, scratching within the underbrush for insects and seeds.

Nesting: Domed nest of dried forbs, grass, straws, weed stems, twigs, and leaves lined with hair and other fine materials, placed in the dense foliage of bush or cactus 2–5 ft. above the ground. Eggs: 2–5, white; I: ?; F: ?, altricial; B: 2.

Other Behavior: Very little known of life history. Needs more study.

Habitat: Understory of dense subtropical woodlands, thick brush.

Voice: Song is series of "chips," speeding up at the end; call a short "chip."

Conservation: BBS: E C ⇑ CBC: ↓

Green-tailed Towhee

Pipilo chlorurus

Identification: 6½" Gray face; reddish-brown cap; white chin; unmarked back, wings, and tail are greenish.

Feeding: Forages on the ground by scratching under brush. Eats weed seeds, wild berries, insects, and may come to bird feeders for seed.

Nesting: Nest of twigs, grasses, bark, and stems lined with horsehair, rootlets, fine plant stems, placed on or near the ground under the cover of brush. Eggs: 2–5, white and heavily spotted; I: ?; F: ?, altricial; B: 2.

Other Behavior: May include notes of other birds in its song. When alarmed during breeding, will run with its tail raised high, drawing attention to itself and away from its nest.

Habitat: Dense shrubs, chaparral slopes, sage brush, manzanita. Summers in mountains; winters in lowlands and foothills.

Voice: Song 2–3 whistled notes followed by harsh trill, like "weeteer chrrrrrr"; call a catlike "meew."

Conservation: BBS: E C ↓ CBC: →

Eastern Towhee

Pipilo erythrophthalmus

Male

Female

Identification: 8" Dark hood and back contrast with reddish-brown flanks and white belly. MALE: Upperparts black. FEMALE: Upperparts reddish brown in the East, dark brown in the West. •White-eyed form in Fla.

Feeding: Hops backward, raking up leaf litter. Eats insects, spiders, lizards, snakes, weed and grass seeds, and wild berries. Comes to feeders for seed on ground.

Nesting: Nest of leaves, strips of bark, grasses, lined with fine grasses, placed on or near the ground in a scratched depression under brush. Eggs: 2–6, creamy with brown spots; I: 12–13 days; F: 10–12 days, altricial; B: 1–3.

Other Behavior: The distinctive "chewink" or "chwee" call note of both sexes is a good clue to their presence. In the spring, the male starts continually singing and countersinging with neighboring males. He courts the female with song and by displaying with wings and tail spread. During egg laying and incubation, the male rarely comes near the nest and the female is quite secretive. Both parents feed the nestlings.

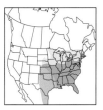

Habitat: Shrubby edges or open woods with shrub understory.

Voice: Song is 2 whistles followed by a high trill, like "drink your teeee"; call "chewink" or "chweee."

Conservation: BBS: E ⇓ C ↓

Learning Pages

Sparrows are a group of small generally brown-streaked birds that are often found in grassy, weedy, or brushy areas. To some people, they may all look alike and seem hard to identify, but there are several things you can do to distinguish among them.

First, learn the most common species, which are shown on these Learning Pages. Knowing these will enable you to identify most of the sparrows that you see and give you a base from which you can begin to identify others. To learn more about these common species, see their full accounts.

Another aid to identification is to become familiar with some of the more obvious clues that just a few species have. These include breast dots (on clear or streaked breasts), eye-rings, and white on the outer tail feathers (seen in flight).

Sparrows with Central Breast Dots

- **Always have dot on streaked breast:**
  Fox Sparrow, p. 423
  Song Sparrow, p. 424
- **Sometimes have dot on streaked breast:**
  Vesper Sparrow, p. 413
  Savannah Sparrow, p. 417
- **Always have dot on clear breast:**
  American Tree Sparrow, p. 409
  Lark Sparrow, p. 414

Sparrows with White Eye-rings

  Rufous-crowned Sparrow, p. 408
  Field Sparrow, p. 412
  Vesper Sparrow, p. 413
  Grasshopper Sparrow, p. 418

Sparrows with White on Outer Tail Feathers

  Cassin's Sparrow, p. 407
  Vesper Sparrow, p. 413
  Lark Sparrow, p. 414
  Dark-eyed Junco, p. 430

Other Common Birds That Look Like Sparrows

Several frequently seen birds resemble sparrows but are not related to them. The most common of these is the House Sparrow, which lives in cities, in suburbs, and on farms. It is a member of the Weaver Finch family.

Another is the female House Finch. One way to identify her is by her close association with the male, which has red on its head, breast, and rump. Both species come to bird feeders.

Male

House Sparrow, p. 460

Female

Female

House Finch, p. 453

MOST COMMONLY SEEN SPARROWS

Three of these sparrows, the Dark-eyed Junco, White-throated Sparrow, and American Tree Sparrow, breed in the north or at higher elevations and are seen by most people only in winter, often at their feeders. The other two, the Song Sparrow and Chipping Sparrow, are common in most areas in summer, but may move south in winter. They also come to bird feeders.

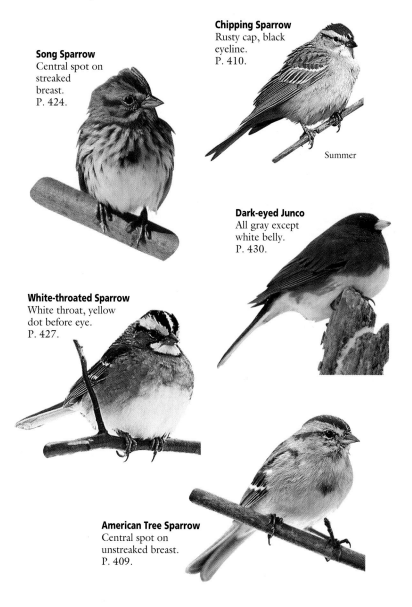

Chipping Sparrow
Rusty cap, black eyeline.
P. 410.

Song Sparrow
Central spot on streaked breast.
P. 424.

Summer

Dark-eyed Junco
All gray except white belly.
P. 430.

White-throated Sparrow
White throat, yellow dot before eye.
P. 427.

American Tree Sparrow
Central spot on unstreaked breast.
P. 409.

Bachman's Sparrow

Aimophila aestivalis

Identification: 5½" **Large gray bill; flat forehead; thin dark line behind eye; unstreaked buffy-gray breast; heavy reddish-brown streaking on back.** Subspecies vary: reddish brown in western part of range; grayish brown in southern part of range. **Secretive; best located and identified by song.** See Voice.

Feeding: Feeds on the ground, eating weed seeds and insects.

Nesting: Cuplike or domed nest of grasses lined with hair and other fine materials, placed on the ground among grasses. Eggs: 3–5, white; I: 12–14 days; F: 10–11 days, altricial; B: 1–2.

Other Behavior: When disturbed from the nest, adults have been seen to do a distraction display in which they feign injury as they flutter away. Singing from the male is beautiful and can be heard through much of the summer. When singing, the bird may be perched atop trees or shrubs or well concealed among lower branches.

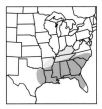

Habitat: Open pine or oak woods, brushy fields.

Voice: Song a clear whistled note followed by a sweet trill; calls include a hissing note.

Conservation: BBS: E ⇓ C ↓ CBC: ↓ Decline due to loss of old-growth pine woods from development and logging. Historic range reduced.

Botteri's Sparrow
Cassin's Sparrow

Aimophila botterii   Aimophila cassinii

Botteri's

Cassin's

Identification: Botteri's 6", Cassin's 5½" Both have flat head, long rounded tail. **BOTTERI'S: Clear buffy breast; reddish-brown back** (grayer in S. Tex.) **with black streaks.** Lacks wing bars, white corners of tail, and flank streaking of Cassin's. **Best located and identified by song.** See Voice. **CASSIN'S: Clear pale breast; gray back with black marks; slight streaking along flanks; whitish wing bars on fresher fall through spring plumage.** In flight, note **white corners of tail.** Song differs from Botteri's. See Voice.

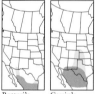

Botteri's   Cassin's

Feeding: Both species feed on the ground, eating insects and weed seeds. Cassin's occasionally eats flowers.

Nesting: Cassin's—Cuplike nest of grass lined with rootlets and hair, placed on ground or to 1 ft. high in shrub or cactus. Eggs: 3–5, white; I: ?; F: ?, altricial; B: ? Botteri's—Breeding biology needs more study.

Other Behavior: Both seen briefly flying above grass tops, then dropping down. Cassin's does song in flight as it rises up, then flutters down; courtship chases with "tzee tzee" call. Both secretive when not breeding.

Habitat: Tallgrass areas with shrubs.

Voice: Botteri's song accelerating notes, "tsp tsp tsptsp tstststs." Cassin's song short trill with 1–2 short notes at start and end, "tup tup trrrrr tew tew."

Conservation: Botteri's: TREND UNKNOWN. Cassin's: BBS: E C ⇓ CBC: ↑

Rufous-crowned Sparrow

Aimophila ruficeps

Identification: 5½" Clear gray breast; whitish throat; gray face; thin rufous eyeline; rufous crown. One black whisker mark off base of bill; thin eyeline starts behind eye; conspicuous whitish eye-ring.

Feeding: Eats insects and seeds on ground.

Nesting: Cuplike nest of grasses, twigs, and bark lined with hair and fine grasses, placed on ground or in tree or shrub 1–3 ft. high. Eggs: 3–4, white; I: ?; F: ?, altricial; B: 1–2.

Other Behavior: Males sing from the tops of small shrubs during territory formation. Often, several pairs in same general area. Usually shy and retiring.

Habitat: Dry rocky or grassy hillsides.

Voice: Song a bubbling jumble of notes; call "deer."

Conservation:
BBS: E C ⇓ CBC: ↑

American Tree Sparrow

Spizella arborea

Identification: 6" Clear gray breast with central black dot; gray face; thin rufous eyeline; rufous crown; white wing bars; 2-toned bill — upper bill dark, lower bill yellow. In winter, gray edges to crown feathers may slightly obscure rufous color.

Feeding: Feeds mostly on ground, eating weed seeds, but may also eat seeds on shrubs and trees. At feeders, eats seed scattered on ground or on a tray.

Nesting: Cuplike nest of grasses and bark strips lined with softer materials, placed on ground or in shrub 1 ft. high. Eggs: 3–5, pale greenish or bluish white; I: 12–13 days; F: 9–10 days, altricial; B: 1.

Other Behavior: Most often seen in winter, when the birds migrate south and gather into small flocks as they feed. Females tend to winter farther south than males. Groups of 30–50 birds remain on fairly fixed winter territories, breaking up into smaller flocks within that area.

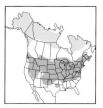

Habitat: Summers in subarctic scrub; winters in weedy fields, brushy edges, open woodlands, gardens.

Voice: Main winter sound is a 3-note call, "tseedle-eet."

Conservation: BBS: E ⇓ C CBC: ⇓

Chipping Sparrow
Spizella passerina

Summer

Winter

Juvenile

Identification: 5½" SUMMER: Clear gray breast; bright rufous crown; whitish eyebrow; strong black eyeline; black bill. WINTER: Head is buffier and less distinctly colored; brown crown with fine black streaks; buffy eyebrow; indistinct eyeline; grayish bill; gray rump. JUV: Finely streaked breast; finely streaked crown; buffy face. Late-brood birds may partially arrest molt into adult winter plumage, creating plumages intermediate between juvenal and winter adult.

Feeding: Eats insects and seeds on ground. May hawk insects in air. Sometimes comes to feeders.

Nesting: Cuplike nest of grasses, placed on branch of tree 3–10 ft. high. Eggs: 3–4, pale blue with dark blotches; I: 11–12 days; F: 7–10 days, altricial; B: 2.

Other Behavior: Male arrives first on territory and sings from exposed perches. Territories are about ½ acre. When the female arrives, mating is often seen, as is nest building, which is done by the female as the male follows her to and from the nest.

Habitat: Grassy areas, open woods, lawns, parks.

Voice: Song a continuous rapid trill, 2–3 seconds long.

Conservation:
BBS: E ↑ C ↑ CBC: ↑

Clay-colored Sparrow

Spizella pallida

Identification: 5½" Clear light gray breast; brown crown with fine black streaks and whitish central stripe; whitish eyebrow; buffy cheek patch outlined above and below with black; gray collar; long notched tail; faint whisker stripe; unstreaked buffy rump. **IMM:** Like adult, but with buffy eyebrow and buffy band across breast. Imm. plumage kept through winter.

Feeding: Feeds mostly on the ground, eating weed seeds, insects, and some flowers.

Nesting: Cuplike nest of grasses and weed stems lined with finer grasses and hair, placed on ground or in shrub up to 5 ft. high. Eggs: 3–5, pale aqua with dark marks; I: 11–14 days; F: 7–9 days, altricial; B: 1–2.

Other Behavior: Males advertise small territories of slightly less than an acre by singing from exposed perches. Range expanding eastward.

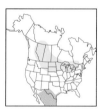

Habitat: Summers in open brushy areas, often near water. In winter, also in weedy fields.

Voice: Song is 2–5 buzzes, given relatively slowly.

Conservation: BBS: E ↓ C ↓ CBC: ⇓

Field Sparrow

Spizella pusilla

Identification: 5½" Clear buffy to light gray breast; bright pink bill; rufous crown; conspicuous white eye-ring; grayish face with rufous eyeline and variably sized rufous ear patch.

Feeding: Feeds on the ground, eating mostly insects in summer and weed seeds the rest of the year. May come to feeders where seed is scattered on the ground.

Nesting: Cuplike nest of grasses, placed on ground or up to 5 ft. high in shrub or small tree. Eggs: 3–4, pale blue with dark markings; I: 10–11 days; F: 8 days, altricial; B: 1–3.

Other Behavior: Each male has his own distinct and consistent version of song. In a field with several males, you can then recognize individuals and watch as they outline territories by singing from several prominent perches. Territories are about 2–6 acres. You can tell when females arrive on the territories, for male singing drops off markedly. Watch for the female as she builds the nest. Nest failures due to storms and predation are frequent, but the birds usually just renest in the same area.

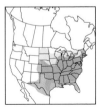

Habitat: Open areas with scattered shrubs and small trees.

Voice: Song a series of downslurred whistles that gradually increase in speed, like a bouncing ball. Calls are "chip" and a trill.

Conservation: BBS: E ⇓ C ⇓ CBC: ⇓

Vesper Sparrow

Pooecetes gramineus

Identification: 6" Finely streaked breast with no central dot; white eye-ring; small chestnut shoulder patch that is not always visible; medium-length notched tail. **IN FLIGHT: Note white outer tail feathers.**

Feeding: Feeds on the ground, eating insects, weed seeds, and grain.

Nesting: Cuplike nest of grasses and rootlets, placed on the ground in a slight depression. Eggs: 3–5, creamy to greenish white with darker marks; I: 11–13 days; F: 7–12 days, altricial; B: 2.

Other Behavior: Male sings from highest perches within territory, such as fence posts, shrubs, or tree limbs; often sings at dusk. Territory size is 1–2 acres. The male may do flight song over the territory during courtship. Frequently seen dust bathing.

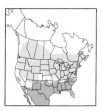

Habitat: Dry fields with sparse vegetation, occasionally beach grass, sagebrush, forest clearings, or agricultural fields.

Voice: Song is 2 pairs of slurred whistles, the 2nd pair higher-pitched, followed by trills.

Conservation: BBS: E ⇓ C ↑ CBC: ↓

413

Lark Sparrow

Chondestes grammacus

Identification: 6½" Easily recognized by its striking **red-brown cheek patch and crown stripes; clear gray breast with central dot. IN FLIGHT: Note long rounded tail with white corners. JUV:** Juvenal plumage sometimes kept into fall. Face and tail pattern resemble adult, but breast and crown streaked.

Feeding: Feeds on ground, eating mostly weed seeds and some insects. May be seen feeding in small flocks during summer and large flocks during winter.

Nesting: Cuplike nest of grasses lined with finer grasses and rootlets, placed usually on ground. Eggs: 4–5, white with dark marks; I: 11–12 days; F: 9–10 days, altricial; B: 1.

Other Behavior: Males defend immediate area around nest, but leave territory to feed with other Lark Sparrows. In courtship, male struts around female with wings half-open and fluttering and bill pointed up. Song may be given from the ground, from perches, or in flight. Also known to sing at night.

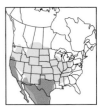

Habitat: Open woods, farmland, roadsides, open residential areas.

Voice: Complex song of trills, clear notes, and buzzes; call a sharp "tsip," sometimes given in a series.

Conservation:
BBS: E ⇓ C ⇓ CBC: ⇓

Black-throated Sparrow

Amphispiza bilineata

Adult

Immature

Identification: 5″ **Black throat and breast; gray crown and ear patch; bright white eyebrow and malar streak. In Flight: Note black tail with white outer feathers. Imm:** Like adult, but chin and throat white; upper breast finely streaked with black. Imm. plumage kept 1 year.

Feeding: Feeds mostly on the ground, eating insects, weed and grass seeds, and some green vegetation.

Nesting: Loose cuplike nest of grasses and weed stems lined with hair, placed 1–3 ft. high in shrub or cactus. Eggs: 3–4, pale bluish white; I: ?; F: ?, altricial; B: ?

Other Behavior: Males may defend territories against Sage Sparrows as well as other Black-throated Sparrows. After breeding and throughout winter, look for Black-throated Sparrows in small flocks of 5–20 birds, often feeding with other species of sparrows such as Brewer's, Chipping, Sage, and White-crowned.

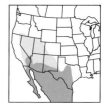

Habitat: Arid and semiarid regions with sage, cactus, creosote, or mesquite.

Voice: Song varies, but often is a few clear whistles followed by trills.

Conservation:
BBS: E C ⇓ CBC: ↓

Lark Bunting
Calamospiza melanocorys

Summer male

Winter male

Female

Identification: 7″ SUMMER—MALE: **All black with large white wing patch;** conical blue-gray bill. FEMALE: **Brown-streaked breast; conical blue-gray bill; long white patch on brown wings.** Looks similar in winter. WINTER—MALE: **Similar to summer female, but with black chin and white patch on black wings.** IN FLIGHT: **Large white wing patches obvious.**

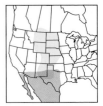

Feeding: Feeds on the ground, eating seeds and insects.

Nesting: Loose cup of grasses and weed stems lined with down, placed on ground near clump of grass. Eggs: 3–6, pale blue-green with darker marks; I: 12 days; F: 8–9 days, altricial; B: 1–2.

Other Behavior: Male does flight song over territory, rising to 20–30 feet, circling, and then slowly descending. Territories are small and many males may be seen displaying at the same time and fairly close to each other. These birds gather into large flocks during migration and reach wintering grounds by late summer. Loss of prairie habitat has reduced their range in northern and eastern portions.

Habitat: Prairies, sparsely vegetated areas with some shrubs, feedlots, plowed fields.

Voice: Song is a mixture of trills and whistles; call is a whistled "toohee."

Conservation: BBS: E C ↓ CBC: ⇓

Savannah Sparrow

Passerculus sandwichensis

"Ipswich Sparrow"

Identification: 5½" **Streaked breast; variable yellowish eyebrow; thin white central stripe in brown crown; short notched tail.** Streaking on breast may form a central dot. •Varies geographically. *P. s. princeps,* "Ipswich Sparrow," in Northeast is one of the palest.

Feeding: Feeds on ground, eating mostly seeds but also insects, spiders, and snails in summer. Sometimes jumps backward to scrape away ground debris and uncover food.

Nesting: Small cuplike nest of grasses and moss lined with hair or finer grasses, placed on the ground. Eggs: 4–5, blue-green or white with dark marks; I: 12 days; F: 14 days, altricial; B: 1–2.

Other Behavior: Males at times may have more than one mate. Females may also lay eggs in other pairs' nests. This sparrow runs along the ground like a small vole to avoid possible danger and, when flying, stays close to grass tops.

Habitat: A variety of moist tallgrass areas — meadows, beaches, lake and river edges; varied habitats in winter.

Voice: Song is several short notes followed by 2 rapid, high-pitched, buzzy trills, the 2nd one lower-pitched, like "tsit tsit tsit zeee zaaay."

Conservation: BBS: E ↓ C ↓ CBC: ↓

417

Grasshopper Sparrow

Ammodramus savannarum

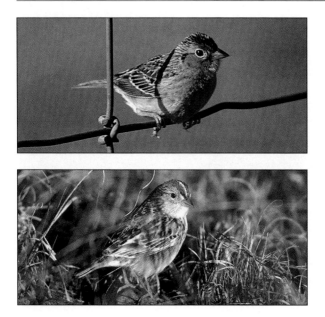

Identification: 5″ **Clear buffy breast and flanks; brown crown with thin whitish central stripe; whitish eye-ring; usually an orange-yellow spot before eye.** Varies geographically; darkest subspecies in Fla.

Feeding: Eats many insects, including grasshoppers. Also eats weed and grass seeds.

Nesting: Cuplike, slightly covered-over nest of grasses lined with hair, placed on ground at the base of a grass clump. Eggs: 4–5, creamy white with dark speckles; I: 11–12 days; F: 9 days, altricial; B: 2.

Other Behavior: Look for male singing from weed tops or fence posts. Song may occur during day or night and female often answers with her own trill. Male occasionally chases female in courtship. Several pairs may nest together in a loose colony.

Habitat: Prairie, dry weedy fields, old pastures, hayfields.

Voice: Song a very high-pitched buzz with 1 or more introductory notes, like "tik-zzzzzzz."

Conservation:
BBS: E ⇓ C ⇓ CBC: ↓ Florida subspecies, *A. s. floridanus,* is endangered.

Henslow's Sparrow

Ammodramus henslowii

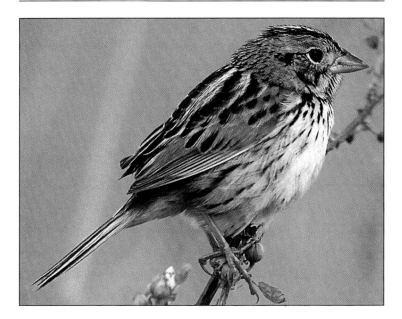

Identification: 5" Olive-green head and neck; reddish-brown wings; upper breast has necklace of fine streaks; broad dark streaks on back. Flat head, large bill, and short tail typical of the genus. Secretive and is often best located by hearing song.

Feeding: Feeds on ground, eating insects, especially small crickets, and weed and grass seeds.

Nesting: Cuplike nest of grasses lined with finer grasses and hair, placed on the ground in a slight depression near a grass clump. Eggs: 3–5, creamy or light green with dark marks; I: 11 days; F: 9–10 days, altricial; B: 1–2.

Other Behavior: Males defend territories of 1–2 acres by singing from exposed perches. Pairs tend to nest near each other in loose colonies.

Habitat: Damp fields and meadows with some shrubs.

Voice: Song is quiet "tselik" or "tsetselik."

Conservation:
BBS: E ⇓ C ↑ CBC: ↓

Le Conte's Sparrow

Ammodramus leconteii

Identification: 5" Dark crown with a white central stripe; reddish-brown streaks on gray nape; buffy upper breast and flanks with dark streaks, especially on sides of breast and flanks; orange to buffy-orange face surrounding a gray ear patch. Flat head and short tail typical of the genus. Fine streaking on upper breast of juveniles may be retained on adults into winter.

Feeding: Feeds on the ground, eating grass and weed seeds, as well as insects.

Nesting: Cuplike nest of grasses, placed on or just above the ground. Eggs: 3–5, light gray with darker marks; I: 12–13 days; F: 8–10 days, altricial; B: 2.

Other Behavior: May sing during day or night. Often runs through grasses, rather than flying over them, to avoid danger.

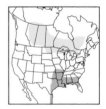

Habitat: Marshes, wet meadows, weedy fields.

Voice: Song a high-pitched buzz with accents at start and end, like "tika-zzzzzz-tzt."

Conservation:
BBS: E ↑ C ↓ CBC: ↑

Salt Marsh Sharp-tailed Sparrow
Nelson's Sharp-tailed Sparrow

Ammodramus caudacutus   *Ammodramus nelsoni*

Salt Marsh

Nelson's

Identification: 5″ Both species have a **dark back with white stripes; breast and flanks buffy with streaking on flanks; dark crown with a gray central stripe that widens into a gray, unstreaked nape;** white belly. Flat head and short tail typical of the genus. SALT MARSH: **Dark orange face surrounds dark gray ear patch; sharp streaking on flanks and breast;** chin usually white. Canadian subspecies, *A. c. subvirgatus* has dull buff on face and flanks; grayish streaks on back. NELSON'S: **Bright buffy face surrounds diffuse light gray ear patch; blurry streaking on flanks and little or none on breast;** chin usually light buff.

Feeding: Feed on the ground, eating grass and weed seeds, as well as insects.

Nesting: Both have loosely woven nest of grasses, placed on ground or in dense grasses. Eggs: 3–7, light green with dark marks; I: 11 days; F: 10 days, altricial; B: 1–2.

Other Behavior: Threats to populations include filling of marshes and spraying of pesticides to kill mosquitoes.

Salt Marsh   Nelson's

Habitat: Salt and fresh-water marshes, wet meadows, lakeshores.

Voice: Song of both a faint, raspy trill with a soft introductory note, like "cata-tseeeee."

Conservation:
Salt Marsh:
BBS: E ↓ C
Nelson's:
BBS: E C ↑

421

Seaside Sparrow

Ammodramus maritimus

Identification: 6" Very dark grayish sparrow; dark gray head, with yellow dash above and before the eye; white throat; blurry gray streaks cover breast. Relatively long bill.

Feeding: Feeds on the ground, eating small crabs and other seaside animals, as well as insects. May even wade through shallow water.

Nesting: Cuplike nest of grasses, placed on the ground. Eggs: 3–5, white with dark marks; I: 12–13 days; F: 8–9 days, altricial; B: 1–2.

Other Behavior: Look for the male in early spring singing from grass tops or singing as he flies up about 20 ft. high, advertising his territory. Males return to the same territories each year, and the territories of several pairs may be grouped together, forming a small colony. Loss of coastal marshes to development threatens its limited habitat.

Habitat: Coastal marshes.

Voice: Song is several short soft introductory notes followed by a loud buzzing, like "catazheeeeee"; like song of Red-winged Blackbird.

Conservation: BBS: E ⇑ C ⇑ CBC: ↑ Fla. subspecies, *A. m. mirabilis,* is endangered.

Fox Sparrow
Passerella iliaca

Identification: 7" Large sparrow; rufous streaking on gray head and back; whitish underparts boldly streaked with brown or rufous and with an irregular central dot on breast; reddish-brown rump and tail.

Feeding: Feeds on the ground, eating seeds, fruits, and insects. Often jumps forward and back, pulling aside ground debris to uncover food items beneath. May come to feeders where seed is scattered on the ground.

Nesting: Cuplike nest of grasses, lichens, and leaves lined with hair, fur, and rootlets, placed on ground under small tree or shrub. Eggs: 4–6, light blue-green with darker marks; I: 11–14 days; F: 7–12 days, altricial; B: 1–2.

Other Behavior: Males may have 1–3 versions of their song which are distinctive to each male. Males with more than 1 version tend to go through their complete repertoire before repeating any version.

Habitat: Deciduous or coniferous woods, brushy areas, woods edges.

Voice: Song is a short series of clear melodious whistles; more melodic than that of most other sparrows.

Conservation:
BBS: E ⇑ C CBC: ↓

Song Sparrow

Melospiza melodia

Identification: 6" Whitish breast with brown streaks and a dark central dot; reddish-brown crown with a gray central stripe; gray eyebrow; white throat bordered by heavy brown marks off the base of the bill; long rounded tail.
•Varies geographically, with paler subspecies in the Southwest and darker subspecies along the West Coast.

Feeding: Feeds on ground, eating seeds, insects, and some fruit. May come to feeders with seed scattered on the ground.

Nesting: Cuplike nest of grasses and occasionally leaves, placed on ground or in shrub or weeds 1–4 ft. high. Eggs: 3–5, greenish white with dark marks; I: 12–13 days; F: 10 days, altricial; B: 2–3.

Other Behavior: Males define territories of ½–1½ acres by giving song from prominent perches. Male chases female when she first arrives on territory, and reduces amount of his singing. Later courtship involves male diving at female and her giving a trill-like call.

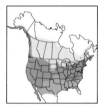

Habitat: Dense shrubs at the edge of open areas such as fields, lawns, or streams.

Voice: Song is a few repeated notes followed by a rich and varied warble. Calls include "tsip" and "tchump."

Conservation:
BBS: E ↓ C ↑ CBC: ↓

Lincoln's Sparrow

Melospiza lincolnii

Identification: 5½" Buffy wash across upper breast and flanks is finely streaked with black; clear white belly; reddish-brown crown with thin gray central stripe; broad gray eyebrow; buffy lines off base of bill; distinct buffy eye-ring.

Feeding: Feeds on ground, scratching backwards with both feet to uncover seeds and insects.

Nesting: Cuplike nest of grasses lined with hair or feathers, placed on ground at the base of a grass clump or shrub. Eggs: 4–5, pale green with darker marks; I: 11–12 days; F: 9–12 days, altricial; B: 1–2.

Other Behavior: Males sing from perches and defend territories of about 1–2 acres. Females may give a "zeezeezee" call, and this stimulates the male to dive at her and may lead to mating. Males sometimes do flight songs over their territories. Generally secretive, especially on wintering grounds.

Habitat: Summers in bogs and wet meadows; winters in weedy fields and shrub edges.

Voice: Song a mixture of musical trills and buzzy notes; somewhat like a House Wren's. Calls include "tsup" and "zeee."

Conservation:
BBS: E ↑ C ⇑ CBC: ↓

Swamp Sparrow

Melospiza georgiana

Winter

Summer

Immature

Identification: 5½" SUMMER: **Rich reddish-brown wings with no wing bars; reddish-brown crown,** sometimes with fine black streaks and thin lighter central stripe; **white throat and belly; gray breast,** sometimes with indistinct streaking; buffy flanks; gray eyebrow and nape. WINTER: Like summer, but **crown heavily streaked with brown and black and with a gray central stripe; flanks darker brownish buff.** IMM: Like winter adult, but buffy (rather than gray) eyebrow and nape, and indistinct streaking on breast. Imm. plumage kept until spring.

Feeding: Feeds on the ground, often in shallow water, eating insects and weed and grass seeds.

Nesting: Bulky cuplike nest of grasses, placed in cattails or shrub to 2 ft. high. Eggs: 4–5, pale green with dark marks; I: 12–15 days; F: 10–13 days, altricial; B: 1–2.

Other Behavior: Male Swamp Sparrows may sing at night as well as during the day. Also, after a few weeks of quiet in late summer, they can be heard again singing in fall.

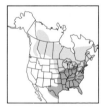

Habitat: Summers in freshwater marshes, swamps, bogs, winters also in damp fields with tall grass.

Voice: Song is a slow musical trill on 1 pitch; calls include a sharp "chip."

Conservation:
BBS: E ↑ C ↑ CBC: ↑

426

White-throated Sparrow

Zonotrichia albicollis

White morph

Tan morph

Identification: 6½" **Dark crown with buff or white central stripe; eyebrow white or tan with yellow mark at front; throat white; breast gray with a few faint streaks.** There are two morphs of this species: white and tan, based on the color of their eyebrows. Female may have less bold pattern on head, duller yellow before eye, grayer throat, and more streaking on breast. **IMM:** Indistinguishable from adult female in the field. Imm. plumage kept through winter.

Feeding: Feeds on the ground, eating weed seeds, grain, fruit, and insects. At feeders, eats cracked corn, sunflower seed, and millet from trays or scattered on the ground.

Nesting: Cuplike nest of grasses lined with hair and rootlets, placed on ground under small tree or shrub. Eggs: 4–6, light blue-green with dark marks; I: 11–14 days; F: 7–12 days, altricial; B: 1–2.

Other Behavior: Breeding pair usually contains 1 bird from each morph, either a tan female and a white male, or a white female and a tan male.

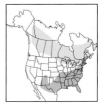

Habitat: Coniferous and mixed woods, brushy areas.

Voice: Song is 2 long whistled notes followed by 3–4 higher, quavering notes, like phrase "sweet sweet Canada Canada Canada." Calls are "tseeet" when birds are in flocks and "pink" in alarm.

Conservation:
BBS: E ↓ C ⇓ CBC: ↓

427

White-crowned Sparrow
Zonotrichia leucophrys

Adult *Z. l. gambelli*

Adult *Z. l. leucophrys*   Immature

Identification: 7″ **Boldly black-and-white-streaked head; no yellow dot before eye;** pink-orange bill; gray face and nape; clear gray breast; whitish throat. **IMM:** Head pattern similar to adult, but colors of streaks are reddish brown and grayish brown instead of black and white. Imm. plumage kept through winter. •Several subspecies: *Z. l. gambelli* has a gray breast and whitish lores; *Z. l. leucophrys* has black lores.

Feeding: Feeds on ground, scratching back leaf debris with both feet as it looks for seeds and insects. Occasionally hawks insects. Comes to feeders with seed scattered on the ground.

Nesting: Bulky nest of grasses, twigs, plant stems, lined with finer grasses, hair, and feathers, placed on ground or in small tree or shrub. Eggs: 3–5, pale blue or green with darker spots; I: 11–15 days; F: 10 days, altricial; B: 1–4.

Other Behavior: In winter, often in flocks of 10–20 birds which often stay in the same area for many weeks. Often nests in residential areas. Has been expanding its winter range into the Northeast since about 1950.

Habitat: Varied; includes wet meadows, shrubby borders, woods, gardens, parks.

Voice: Song variable geographically. Often whistled notes and a trill; calls include a sharp "pink."

Conservation: BBS: E ⇓ C ↓ CBC: ↓

Harris' Sparrow
Zonotrichia querula

Summer

Winter

Immature

Identification: 7½" Our largest sparrow.
SUMMER: **Black on crown, surrounding bill, and on chin and throat; gray face; pink-orange bill; white belly with streaking on flanks.** WINTER: Like summer, but **lighter flecks in black on head; light brown face.** IMM: Similar to winter adult, but with little or no black on face; flecks of black on brown crown; chin and throat mostly white. Imm. plumage kept through winter.

Feeding: Feeds on the ground, eating mostly weed and grass seeds, grain, and small fruits. Also eats some insects. At feeders, eats seed scattered on the ground or on trays.

Nesting: Cuplike nest of mosses, grasses, weed stems, lined with finer grasses, placed in depression in ground. Eggs: 3–5, whitish with darker marks; I: 13 days; F: ?, altricial; B: 1.

Other Behavior: Harris' Sparrows breed far to the north and are mostly seen in winter in south-central states.

Habitat: Summers in the coniferous forest-tundra; winters in woods edges, brushy thickets.

Voice: Song is 3–4 quavering whistles, first on 1 pitch, then on another.

Conservation: CBC: ⇓

Dark-eyed Junco
Junco hyemalis

"Slate-colored" race

"Pink-sided" race

"Oregon" race

"Gray-headed" race

Identification: 6" In all plumages: **pale bill; dark eye; whitish belly; tail dark with conspicuous white outer feathers.** •Varies geographically. Eastern "Slate-colored" race is uniform dark gray (male) or brownish gray (female); western "Oregon" race has black (male) or gray (female) hood and brown back; western "Pink-sided" race has gray head and pinkish sides; "Gray-headed" race of the southern Rockies and Southwest is light gray with a reddish-brown back; "White-winged" race of north-central states has extensive white on tail and usually white wing bars.

Feeding: Feeds mostly on ground, eating weed and grass seeds. At feeders, eats seed on ground or on trays.

Nesting: Cuplike nest of grasses, moss, pine needles, lined with rootlets, placed in depression in ground near tall vegetation. Eggs: 3–6, gray or pale bluish with dark blotches; I: 12–13 days; F: 9–13 days, altricial; B: 1–2.

Other Behavior: Flocks return to same areas each winter. They are fixed in membership and have a hierarchy. Aggression at feeders is expression of dominance.

Habitat: Summers in woods, woods edges, bogs, mountains above tree level; winters in woods edges, brush.

Voice: Song is a short trill or series of trills on 1 or more pitches; calls include "tsip," "zeet," and "kew kew."

Conservation:
BBS: E ↓ C ⇑ CBC: ↓

McCown's Longspur

Calcarius mccownii

Summer male

Summer female

Identification: 6" In all plumages, note **dark central tail feathers and dark band at tail tip forming a T; reddish-brown shoulder patch, sometimes hidden; large bill.** Tips of folded wings extend over halfway down tail. SUMMER—MALE: **Gray head; black cap and whisker mark; black bib on upper breast.** FEMALE: **Brownish, with dark streaks on crown and back; may be a suggestion of black bib.** WINTER—MALE: **Like summer female, but with more black on bib.** FEMALE: **As in summer, but with pale breast and belly.**

Feeding: Feeds on ground, eating seeds and insects.

Nesting: Nest of grasses lined with finer grasses, placed in shallow depression in ground near grass clump or small plant. Eggs: 3–6, pale pink or pale green with darker spots; I: 12 days; F: 12 days, altricial; B: 1–2.

Other Behavior: Male does flight song on territory, rising up to 30 ft. and then gliding down with wings and tail spread and legs hanging down. Birds form large flocks during migration and in winter.

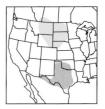

Habitat: Summers in short-grass plains; winters in plowed agricultural fields, dry lake beds.

Voice: Song is a series of short musical warbles. Call a "chitup chitup."

Conservation:
BBS: E C ⇑ CBC: ⇑

Lapland Longspur

Calcarius lapponicus

Summer male

Summer female

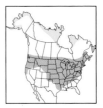

Winter female

Identification: 6″ Our most widespread longspur in winter. Although outer tail feathers are partially white, **in all plumages tail appears mostly dark, even in flight. SUMMER—MALE: Black crown, face, throat, and bib; reddish-brown nape; yellow bill. FEMALE: Brownish; dark streaks on crown and back; pale, streaked, chestnut collar; brown ear patch has dark outline on back edge; black flecking in area of bib. WINTER—MALE: Like summer female. FEMALE:** Like summer, but lacks chestnut collar and dark area of bib; may show substantial rufous on wings.

Feeding: Feeds on ground, eating seeds, insects, and spiders.

Nesting: Cuplike nest of grasses lined with finer grasses, hair, and feathers, placed in shallow depression in ground scraped out by birds. Eggs: 3–7, pale green to buff with dark marks; I: 12–13 days; F: 10–12 days, altricial; B: 1.

Other Behavior: Male does flight song display on territory.

Habitat: Summers in wet grassy areas of tundra; winters in open grassy areas, plowed agricultural lands, airports, occasionally beaches.

Voice: Song a rich warbling given during flight display. Calls a dry "tikerik tikerik" and a rich "tew."

Conservation: CBC: ⇑

432

Smith's Longspur

Calcarius pictus

Summer male

Winter

Identification: 6″ In all plumages, outer tail feathers white and no band at tip of tail. SUMMER—MALE: Black-and-white "helmet"; buffy-orange throat, nape, and breast. FEMALE: Brownish; dark streaks on crown and back; small white shoulder, sometimes hidden. WINTER: Both sexes like summer female.

Feeding: Feeds on ground, eating seeds, insects, and spiders.

Nesting: Cuplike nest of grasses lined with finer grasses, hair, and feathers, placed in shallow depression in ground scraped out by birds. Eggs: 4–6, grayish with dark dots; I: 11–12 days; F: ?, altricial; B: 1.

Other Behavior: Often winters in wide-open short-grass areas, such as airport fields and pastures. Can be approached closely before it flies. Usually remains separate from other longspurs.

Habitat: Summers in grassy tundra; winters in open areas with short grass.

Voice: Song a series of warbles ending with phrase "wee-tew." Call a short dry clicking sound.

Conservation: CBC: ↑

Chestnut-collared Longspur

Calcarius ornatus

Summer male

Female

Identification: 5½" In all plumages, note triangular black area at base of mostly white tail. SUMMER—MALE: Black crown; buffy face and throat; chestnut collar; black breast and upper belly. FEMALE: Brown-streaked; best distinguishing characteristic is black triangle on tail. WINTER—MALE: Buffy edgings to feathers make summer pattern indistinct, but buffy throat and hint of black belly and chestnut crown are still visible. FEMALE: As in summer.

Feeding: Feeds on ground, eating seeds and some insects.

Nesting: Cuplike nest of grasses lined with finer grasses, hair, and feathers, placed in shallow depression in ground scraped out by birds. Eggs: 3–6, creamy with dark marks; I: 11–13 days; F: 10–12 days, altricial; B: 2.

Other Behavior: Male does flight display over territory while singing; glides down exposing white on fanned wings and tail.

Habitat: Short-grass prairies and cultivated fields.

Voice: Song is a musical twittering. Call is "tilip tilip."

Conservation:
BBS: E C ↓ CBC: ⇑

Snow Bunting

Plectrophenax nivalis

Summer female

Summer male

Winter male

Identification: 7" SUMMER—MALE: **Strikingly marked with white on head and body; black on back, wings, and tail; bill black.** FEMALE: Subtler version of male coloration. **Head is grayish white; dark areas on back, wings, and tail are brownish gray.** WINTER: **Crown black (male) or buffy (female); back streaked with buff and black; buffy ear patch; white belly; flanks and breast washed with buff; bill yellow-orange.** IN FLIGHT: **Note long white wings with black outer portions.**

Feeding: Feeds on ground, eating seeds, leaf buds, and insects.

Nesting: Nest of moss, grasses, and earth, placed on ground in rocky area. Eggs: 3–9, creamy blue or gray; I: 10–16 days; F: 10–17 days, altricial; B: 1–2.

Other Behavior: In winter, can be seen bathing in snow. May burrow into snow to keep warm. Stays in large flocks throughout winter, roosting on ground or perching on telephone wires.

Habitat: Summers in arctic tundra and rocky shores; winters in open fields, roadsides, beaches.

Voice: Song is a musical warble. Calls include a short whistled "tew" and soft buzzy notes.

Conservation: CBC: ⇓

Bobolink

Dolichonyx oryzivorus

Summer female

Winter

Summer male

Identification: 7" SUMMER—MALE: Black head and black body with bold buffy-white nape. In flight note white rump. FEMALE: Buffy, with brown streaks on back and flanks; dark streaks on crown; dark eyeline behind eye. WINTER: Both sexes like summer female, but buffier. In all plumages, note sharply pointed tail feathers.

Feeding: Feeds on the ground, eating insects, weed and grass seeds. Also eats cultivated rice crops in the South.

Nesting: Nest of coarse grass and sedge lined with finer material, placed on the ground. Eggs: 4–6, cinnamon with brown blotches; I: 12 days; F: 10–14 days, altricial; B: 1.

Other Behavior: Loss of hayfield breeding habitat is due to urban development, reforestation, and loss of dairy farms. Studies show that early cutting of hayfields, before Bobolinks fledge, can kill more than 80% of young. When hayfields are on conservation lands, conservation commissions can help by setting a policy to delay cutting until after Bobolink young have adequately fledged. Studies in North recommend this cutting be after July 20 or in August.

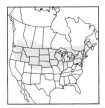

Habitat: Hayfields and grasslands.

Voice: Song is a long bubbling sound given by male in flight; call a "pink."

Conservation:
BBS: E ↓ C ⇓ CBC: ↓ Populations have declined due to loss of grassland breeding habitat and hunting during the last century to protect rice crops.

Red-winged Blackbird

Agelaius phoeniceus

Male

Female

Identification: 8½" **MALE: All black with a red shoulder patch bordered by yellow.** Males in central Calif. have no yellow on shoulder patch; they are sometimes called Bicolored Blackbirds. **FEMALE: Brown above and heavily streaked brown below; sharp-pointed bill; buffy-to-whitish eyebrow. IMM—MALE:** Similar to adult female, but darker and with an orangish shoulder patch bordered by white. **FEMALE:** Like adult female. Imm. plumage kept 1 year.

Feeding: Eats insects, weed seeds. Comes to bird feeders singly or in large flocks for cracked corn, seed mixes.

Nesting: Nest of reeds and grasses lined with finer material, placed in reeds and grasses or shrubs 3–8 ft. high. Eggs: 3–5, pale greenish blue with dark marks; I: 11 days; F: 11 days, altricial; B: 2–3.

Other Behavior: Males hold territories of ⅛–¼ acre, which they defend by singing from perches with wings spread open and red shoulder patches exposed. They can also conceal the red patch, showing only the yellow border. Males are polygynous, averaging 3 mates per breeding season. Huge communal roosts in winter.

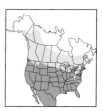

Habitat: Marshes and meadows.

Voice: Song a loud "okaleee"; calls include "check," "tseert," and, given only by female, a "ch'ch'ch'chee chee chee."

Conservation: BBS: E ↓ C ↓ CBC: ↑

Eastern Meadowlark
Western Meadowlark
Sturnella magna   Sturnella neglecta

Eastern

Western

Identification: 9" Both species are **brownish above and yellow below with a black V on breast. Best distinguished by voice.** See Voice. **IN FLIGHT: Note white outer tail feathers and quick flutters followed by short glides.** Mostly indistinguishable in the field, except by song and range. In the Western Meadowlark, the yellow on the throat extends slightly up onto the cheek; in the Eastern, it does not. Hybrids occur in Midwest.

Feeding: Both feed on the ground, eating insects, grain, and weed seeds.

Nesting: Both have a domed nest of coarse grass lined with finer grass, placed in natural or scraped depression on the ground. Eggs: 3–7, white with dark marks; I: 13–15 days; F: 11–12 days, altricial; B: 1–2.

Other Behavior: Occasionally hybridize where ranges overlap. Both form winter flocks of up to 100 or more birds that feed and roost together. Western is expanding range in Northeast. Eastern is declining because of loss of breeding habitat as grasslands become converted to suburbs. Also, mowing of fields destroys many nests.

Eastern   Western

Habitat: Meadows, grasslands.

Voice: Eastern song 2–8 high-pitched whistles, "seeoo seeyeer"; call a "dzeert." Western song a short phrase of lower-pitched flutelike notes; call is low "chup."

Conservation:
Eastern:
BBS: E ⇓ C ↓ CBC: ⇓
Western:
BBS: E ⇓ C ↓ CBC: ⇓

438

Yellow-headed Blackbird

Xanthocephalus xanthocephalus

Male

Female

Identification: 9½" **MALE:** Bright yellow hood; black body; white patch on wing shows in perched and flying bird. **FEMALE:** Grayish brown overall, except for yellow chin and breast; white streaks on upper belly. **IMM—MALE:** Like adult female, except: more orangish yellow on breast; no white streaking on belly; and, in flight, shows thin white patches on upperwings. **FEMALE:** Like adult female. Imm. plumage kept 1 year.

Feeding: Feeds on the ground, eating insects, grass and weed seeds. Forages in fields, agricultural areas, meadows, ranches, farms.

Nesting: Nest of water-soaked reeds and grasses lined with softer material, placed in vegetation up to 7 ft. above water. Eggs: 3–5, pale greenish gray with dark marks; I: 11–13 days; F: 9–12 days, altricial; B: 2.

Other Behavior: In fall and winter, joins with other blackbirds, European Starlings, and Brown-headed Cowbirds in large mixed flocks that roost in marshes.

Habitat: Summers in marshes; winters in grain fields.

Voice: Song is short choked notes, interspersed with a long buzz; call is a low "krrt."

Conservation:
BBS: E ↑ C ↑ CBC: ⇓

Rusty Blackbird

Euphagus carolinus

Summer male

Summer female

Winter male

Winter female

Identification: 9″ SUMMER—MALE: Appears dull black overall; pale yellow eye; slightly shorter tail and longer bill than similar male Brewer's Blackbird. FEMALE: Dark grayish to black; pale yellow eye; may have brown edges to wing feathers. WINTER—MALE: Like summer, but feathers edged with rusty brown on head, back, and wings; black rump. FEMALE: Buffy underparts; buffy eyebrow; rusty back; gray rump. Birds of both sexes in their first fall tend to be rustier and buffier than in following years. Summer plumage acquired by wearing off of lighter tips to feathers.

Feeding: Feeds on the ground and in very shallow water, eating insects, crustaceans, fish, grain, and weed seeds.

Nesting: Nest of grass, moss, and mud lined with finer material, placed in shrub or tree 2–20 ft. above the ground. Eggs: 4–5, pale greenish with dark marks; I: 14 days; F: 11–14 days, altricial; B: ?

Other Behavior: Forms huge winter flocks with other blackbirds and starlings.

Habitat: Summers in spruce bogs, wet woods; winters in woods and fields near water.

Voice: Song a squeaky "chugalasqueeek"; call a "chek."

Conservation: BBS: E ⇓ C CBC: ⇓

Brewer's Blackbird
Euphagus cyanocephalus

Male

Female

Identification: 9" MALE: Black, with purplish gloss on head and greenish gloss on body; pale yellow eye; slightly longer tail and shorter bill than similar male Rusty Blackbird. May have minimal brownish-gray edges to body feathers in fall. FEMALE: Grayish brown; dark eye.

Feeding: Feeds on the ground, eating grain, weed seeds, fruit, and insects.

Nesting: Nest of twigs, grass, and a matrix of mud or cow dung lined with finer material, placed on or just above the ground in vegetation. Eggs: 3–7, pale gray with dark marks; I: 12–14 days; F: 13–14 days, altricial; B: 1–2.

Other Behavior: In fall and winter, forms huge flocks often mixed with other blackbirds, starlings, and Brown-headed Cowbirds. These flocks forage during the day in agricultural areas. Communal roosts in marshes may number in the tens of millions.

Habitat: Wet meadows, rivers, stream margins bordered by dense shrubs, cultivated areas, parks, desert oases, urban areas, roadsides.

Voice: Song is a squeaky "kasqueek"; call a "chick."

Conservation: BBS: E ↑ C ↑ CBC: ↓

441

Great-tailed Grackle

Quiscalus mexicanus

Male

Female

Identification: 18" MALE: Large all-black bird with purplish gloss on flattish head and on back; long tail is folded up on the sides; bright yellow eye. FEMALE: Buffy brown below; darker above, with slight greenish iridescence; yellow eye; 2–4" shorter than male. IMM— MALE: Lacks gloss of adult; tail flat rather than folded; eye is dark, changing to yellow by spring. FEMALE: Paler than adult; may have more contrast on face, with light eyebrow and dark eyeline; eye is dark, changing to yellow by spring. Imm. plumage kept 1 year. •In S. Calif. and W. Ariz., birds much smaller; female breast very pale.

Feeding: Eats insects, grain, fruit, crustaceans, fish, bird eggs. Visits bird feeders for seed and grain.

Nesting: Nest of grasses, reeds, and mud or cow dung lined with finer material, placed in marsh plant or tree. Eggs: 3–4, bluish green with dark marks; I: 13–14 days; F: 20–23 days, altricial; B: 1–2.

Other Behavior: Nests colonially, sometimes in the thousands. Forms huge winter roosts.

Habitat: Open land with some trees; parks, ranches, urban areas.

Voice: Song a spectacular series of whistles, hisses, and ratchety sounds.

Conservation: BBS: E C ⇑

Boat-tailed Grackle

Quiscalus major

Male, yellow-eyed

Male, dark-eyed

Female, dark-eyed

Identification: 16″ MALE: Large all-black bird; bluish-green gloss on rounded head and on back; long tail folded up on the sides. FEMALE: Buffy-brown below; darker above with no iridescence; 2–3″ shorter than male. IMM— MALE: Lacks gloss of adult; tail flat; eye dark. FEMALE: Paler than adult; eye is dark. Imm. plumage kept 1 year. •Adult eye color varies: it is bright yellow on Atlantic Coast; dark in Florida and western Gulf Coast (where range overlaps with Great-tailed Grackle, which has a yellow eye and flatter head); brown with yellow outer edge in central Gulf Coast.

Feeding: Eats insects, grain, crustaceans, fish, and nestlings. Picks insects off backs of cattle. May steal fish from herons and Glossy Ibises. Visits bird feeders.

Nesting: Nest of grass and mud or cow dung lined with finer materials, placed in shrub or tree 3–12 ft. high. Eggs: 3–5, pale blue-gray with dark marks; I: 13–15 days; F: 20–23 days, altricial; B: 2–3.

Other Behavior: Expanding range to West and North.

Habitat: Salt marshes, parks, lakes.

Voice: Song a series of harsh high-pitched notes, like "jeeb jeeb jeeb jeeb"; calls include a "chuck" and various squeaks.

Conservation: BBS: E ↑ C ⇑

443

Common Grackle

Quiscalus quiscula

Male, purple

Male, bronze

Identification: 12″ MALE: **Black with iridescence on head, back, and belly; tail folded up at edges mostly during breeding; yellow eye.** Iridescence on body is purplish on birds from Southeast to S. New England, bronze on birds elsewhere. Smaller, shorter tail and smaller bill than similar Boat-tailed and Great-tailed Grackles. FEMALE: **Similar to male, but with shorter flat tail and less iridescence.**

Feeding: Feeds mostly on ground, eating insects, weed seeds, grains, minnows, small crayfish, rodents, and birds. Comes to bird feeder for seed and cracked corn.

Nesting: Nest of grass, twigs, reeds, and mud lined with finer materials, placed in shrub or tree 3–30 ft. above the ground or water. Eggs: 4–7, pale greenish brown with dark marks; I: 13–14 days; F: 12–16 days, altricial; B: 1.

Other Behavior: During courtship, male flies with tail held in V. Forms huge winter roosts, often mixed with Red-winged Blackbirds and cowbirds, that can number in tens of millions of birds and be a nuisance if located near urban areas. Large flocks may damage grain crops.

Habitat: Open areas with some trees; city parks, urban yards, farmland.

Voice: Song a short series of harsh sounds ending in a squeak, like "grideleeek"; calls a "chaack" and "chaaah."

Conservation: BBS: E ↓ C ↓ CBC: ↑

Bronzed Cowbird

Molothrus aeneus

Male

Female, Texas subspecies

Identification: 8ʺ MALE: Black overall, with bluish iridescence on wings and tail; long, dark, conical bill; flat forehead; red eye. FEMALE: Similar bill, profile, and eye color; subspecies in Southwest grayish brown overall; in Tex., dull black overall.

Feeding: Feeds mostly on the ground, eating insects, grains, and weed seeds. Can also be seen on the backs of cattle, picking off ticks and other parasites.

Nesting: No nest. Eggs: Usually 1 per host nest, pale greenish blue; I: 10–13 days; F: 11 days, altricial; B: ?

Other Behavior: Female lays usually 1 egg per nest in the nests of other bird species, especially orioles. She usually removes 1 of the eggs of the host species, replacing it with her own egg. The cowbird egg hatches 1 day earlier than the others. The cowbird nestling is larger than the young of the host, gets more of the food, and may crowd the other young out of the nest. In most cases, some of the host young do fledge, although cowbird parasitism reduces their number. Some birds deal with cowbird parasitism by ejecting or destroying cowbird eggs, abandoning their nest, or building over the eggs and starting a new clutch.

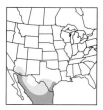

Habitat: Urban lawns, agricultural fields, parks, open woods.

Voice: Song a series of squeaks; call a low "chuck."

Conservation: BBS: E C ⇑ CBC: ⇑

Brown-headed Cowbird

Molothrus ater

Male

Female

Identification: 7″ **MALE: Dark brown head; glossy black body;** dark gray conical bill. **FEMALE: Grayish brown overall with very little distinct marking; dark gray conical bill;** faint streaking on breast.

Feeding: Feeds on the ground, eating grain, grass and weed seeds, and insects. Visits bird feeders.

Nesting: No nest. Eggs: Usually 1 per host nest, white with dark marks; I: 10–13 days; F: 9–11 days, altricial; B: ?

Other Behavior: See Bronzed Cowbird account for more information. Although 97% of cowbird eggs and nestlings fail to reach adulthood, the average cowbird pair replaces itself with 1.2 pairs, enough to keep the cowbird population expanding. Cowbird parasitism reduces the breeding success of many species and, in some cases, poses a severe threat to their survival. This is the case with Kirtland's Warbler, Golden-cheeked Warbler, Black-capped Vireo, and the Calif. subspecies of Bell's Vireo. Cowbirds have been recorded as successfully parasitizing 144 species. The fragmentation of forests, due to suburban development, gives cowbirds new access to many forest species.

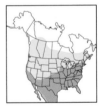

Habitat: Pastures, woods edges, urban lawns, forest clearings.

Voice: Song is a liquid "bublucom-seee"; call is high "pseeeseee" and "ch'ch'ch'ch."

Conservation: BBS: E ⇓ C ↓ CBC: ⇓

Orchard Oriole
Icterus spurius

Female

Male

Immature male, 1st spring

Identification: 7″ MALE: **Black hood, wings, and tail; reddish-brown belly and rump.** FEMALE: **Olive-green above; yellow below; 2 thin white wing bars.** IMM—MALE: In fall, similar to adult female. In next spring and summer, like adult female, but with black throat and upper breast, sometimes with a few reddish-brown feathers mixed in. FEMALE: Like adult female. Imm. plumage kept 1 year.

Feeding: Feeds in trees and shrubs, eating insects and fruit, tree blossoms. May come to hummingbird feeders.

Nesting: Shallow pouchlike nest of woven grass blades lined with finer materials, suspended from fork in branch of tree 6–20 ft. above the ground. Eggs: 3–7, pale grayish blue with dark marks; I: 12–14 days; F: 11–14 days, altricial; B: 1.

Other Behavior: Nests singly or in loose colonies. Males sing from trees. Often hidden in foliage, but not usually shy. Adults and young stay together until time for southward migration. Common cowbird host.

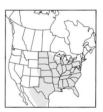

Habitat: Orchards, open woods, shade trees in towns, wetlands, parks, streamside groves.

Voice: Song a rapid series of whistled notes; call a short "chuk."

Conservation: BBS: E ↓ C ⇓ CBC: → Population is declining due to loss of tropical forests on wintering grounds.

Hooded Oriole
Spot-breasted Oriole
Icterus cucullatus   Icterus pectoralis

Hooded male

Immature Hooded male, 1st spring

Hooded female

Spot-breasted

Identification: Hooded 7½", Spot-breasted 8½"
HOODED—MALE: **Orange-to-yellow body**
(depending on subspecies; **black face and
throat; long, thin, slightly downcurved bill.**
FEMALE: **Uniformly greenish yellow below;
long, thin, slightly downcurved bill.** IMM—
MALE: In fall, like adult female; next spring and
summer, like adult male, but with gray-brown
wings. FEMALE: Like adult female. SPOT-
BREASTED: **Black throat; spots on breast;
orange shoulder patch.** IMM: Has same orange
shoulder patch, but lacks black throat; breast spots
may be missing.

Feeding: Both feed in foliage, eating insects, berries, and
nectar from flowers. May come to sugar-water solutions.

Nesting: Both have nests woven of grasses and plant
fibers lined with finer material, suspended from branch.
Hooded—Eggs: 3–5, pale with marks; I: 12–14 days;
F: 14 days, altricial; B: 2–3. Spot-breasted — Eggs: 3–5,
pale blue with marks; I: ?; F: ?, altricial; B: 2.

Other Behavior: Spot-breasted is introduced from Mex.
species, now resident in Fla.

Hooded   Spot-breasted

Habitat: Hooded:
urban or rural areas
with palms. Spot-
breasted: parks.

Voice: Hooded
song is a varied
series of whistles;
call "weeet." Spot-
breasted song is
loud whistles; call
"check."

Conservation:
Hooded:
BBS: E C ⇑ CBC: ↓
Spot-breasted:
TREND UNKNOWN.

Altamira Oriole
Audubon's Oriole

Icterus gularis   Icterus graduacauda

Altamira

Audubon's

Identification: Altamira 10" Audubon's 9½"
Both species limited to S. Tex. **ALTAMIRA:**
Orange head; black face and throat; orange
shoulder patch; relatively short thick-based
bill. IMM: Yellowish orange overall; black face and
throat; yellow shoulder patch; relatively short
thick-based bill. Imm. plumage kept 1 yr.
AUDUBON'S: Black hood; greenish-yellow back
and belly. IMM: Similar to adult, but lacks black
on head and has brown wings. Imm. plumage
kept 1 yr.

Feeding: Altamira forages in trees, shrubs; Audubon's
closer to the ground. Both eat insects and berries.

Nesting: Both have nests of coarse grasses and plant
fibers lined with finer material. Altamira—Nest up to 2
ft. long, suspended from branch tips 30–80 ft. above
the ground. Eggs: 3–4, white with dark marks; I: ?; F: ?,
altricial; B: 2. Audubon's—Nest suspended from
mesquite tree or other bush 6–14 ft. above the ground.
Eggs: 3–5, pale blue or gray-white with dark marks; I: ?;
F: ?, altricial; B: ?

Altamira   Audubon's

Habitat: Both live
in open subtropical
woodland, brush,
streamside willows.

Voice: Altamira
song is series of
whistles mixed with
low notes; call low
"ryk." Audubon's
song a few low
musical whistles.

Conservation:
Altamira:
BBS: E C ⇩
Audubon's:
BBS: E C ⇧

Baltimore Oriole
Bullock's Oriole
Icterus galbula   Icterus bullockii

Baltimore male

Baltimore female

Bullock's male

Bullock's female

Identification: 8½" Baltimore is mostly eastern, Bullock's is mostly western. BALTIMORE—MALE: Black hood and back; orange body. FEMALE: Olive-yellow on rump; orange-yellow below; head and back mottled with black; throat variably blotched with black. IMM: Female like adult. Male like adult female, but with orange-tipped lesser coverts. BULLOCK'S—MALE: Orange face; black eyeline; large white wing patch. FEMALE: Yellowish head and breast; whitish belly. IMM: Female like adult. Fall male yellowish with black throat and eyeline; spring male like adult male, but lacks white wing patch.

Feeding: Eats insects, fruits, flower nectar. Comes to bird feeders for orange halves and sugar solutions.

Nesting: Both use hanging nest of plant fibers suspended from branch 6–60 ft. high. Eggs: 4–6, pale bluish white with dark marks; I: 12–14 days; F: 12–14 days, altricial; B: 1.

Other Behavior: Male and female sing in both species.

Baltimore   Bullock's

Habitat: Deciduous trees near openings, such as parks, gardens, roads.

Voice: Song is 4–8 medium-pitched whistled notes; calls a 2-note "teetoo" and a rapid chatter, "ch'ch'ch'ch'ch."

Conservation:
Baltimore:
BBS: E ↓ C ↓
Bullock's:
BBS: E C ↓

Pine Grosbeak

Pinicola enucleator

Male

Female

Identification: 9″ **MALE:** Rose-red head, chest, and back; gray belly; black wing with 2 white wing bars; stubby black bill. **FEMALE:** Similar to male, but colored areas olive-yellow and restricted to head and rump. **IMM—MALE:** Like adult female, but head and rump orangish. **FEMALE:** Similar to adult female. Imm. plumage kept 1 year.

Feeding: Forages on ground and in foliage for the seeds, nuts, buds, and fruits of many trees, such as crabapples, maples, ashes, pines. Also eats insects. At bird feeders prefers sunflower seed.

Nesting: Nest of mosses, twigs, roots, lichens, and grasses lined with rootlets, fur, lichens, placed in shrub or tree 2–30 ft. above the ground. Eggs: 2–6, blue-green with dark marks; I: 13–15 days; F: 13–20 days, altricial; B: 1.

Other Behavior: Irruptive species; in some winters moves south of normal range in great numbers, generally when populations are high and food sources in North are scarce. May associate with Bohemian Waxwing flocks.

Habitat: Summers in coniferous woods, high montane forests; winters near fruit and seed trees.

Voice: Song a musical warble; call a 3-note whistle, with middle note highest, like "teeweetee."

Conservation: BBS: E ↓ C CBC: ↑

451

Purple Finch
Carpodacus purpureus

Male

Female

Identification: 6″ MALE: Upperparts, breast, and flanks raspberry red (brightest in summer); head uniformly covered with red; little or no brown streaking on breast or flanks. FEMALE: Well-defined pattern on face of broad white eyebrow, brown eyeline, and white cheek; broad, blurry, brown streaking underneath; no streaking on undertail coverts. IMM: Male and female like adult female. Male may sing and breed in this plumage. Imm. plumage kept 1 year. See Voice for distinctive flight call.

Feeding: Forages on the ground and above in foliage for seeds and buds of trees and weeds, berries, and insects. Comes to bird feeders for sunflower seed and millet.

Nesting: Nest of twigs, grasses, rootlets, moss, bits of snakeskin, and string lined with horsehair, moss, and rootlets, placed on branch of tree 5–60 ft. high. Eggs: 3–6, light green-blue with dark marks; I: 13 days; F: 14 days, altricial; B: 1–2.

Other Behavior: Irruptive in some winters.

Habitat: Mixed woods, coniferous forests, lower mountain slopes, suburban yards.

Voice: Song an extended musical warble; call in flight a short "pik."

Conservation: BBS: E ↓ C ⇓ CBC: ↑

House Finch
Carpodacus mexicanus

Male   Yellowish male

Female

Identification: 5½" MALE: **Red on head and upper breast; broad brown streaking on lower breast and flanks.** In some regions, red replaced with yellow or orange. FEMALE: **Uniformly brown-streaked head; broad brown streaking on breast and belly;** white undertail coverts usually unstreaked. Short bill helps distinguish from much larger-billed Cassin's Finch.

Feeding: Forages on ground and in trees, eating weed seeds, blossoms, fruits, and buds. Can monopolize bird feeders, where it prefers sunflower seed.

Nesting: Nest of twigs, grasses, leaves, and debris, placed in variety of artificial and natural cavities, such as foundation plantings, vines, hanging planters, and occasionally birdhouses. Eggs: 2–6, bluish white with speckles; I: 12–16 days; F: 11–19 days, altricial; B: 1–3.

Other Behavior: Forms winter flocks. Native to western states. Was introduced to the East in New York City area in 1940 when pet dealers, being arrested for illegally selling House Finches as "Hollywood Finches," released the birds. Has since spread throughout much of East. Range still expanding.

Habitat: Urban areas, suburbs, parks, canyons, semidry brush country.

Voice: Song a musical warble often ending with a harsh downslurred "jeeer." Female and male both sing.

Conservation:
BBS: E ⇑ C ⇑ CBC: ↑

Red Crossbill
White-winged Crossbill
Loxia curvirostra   Loxia leucoptera

Red male

White-winged male

Red female

White-winged female

Identification: 6″ Both species have **long bills with tips crossed.** RED—MALE: Red-to-orange body; black wings and tail; no white wing bars. FEMALE: Grayish with olive tinge; no wing bars. WHITE-WINGED—MALE: Pinkish-red body; black wings with 2 white wing bars. FEMALE: Grayish with olive tinges on head and back; yellowish on breast and rump; black wings with 2 white wingbars; some streaking on back and flanks.

Feeding: Both extract conifer seeds by forcing scales of cones apart with bills and lifting out seeds with tongue. They also eat other seeds, insects, and road salt, often resulting in traffic casualties. Occasionally at feeders.

Nesting: Both have nests of twigs, rootlets, grasses, moss, bark, lichens, placed in tree branch 6–40 ft. (Red) or 3–70 ft. (White-winged) above the ground. Eggs: 2–5, greenish white or bluish white with dark marks. Red—I: 12–18 days; F: 15–20 days, altricial; B: 1–2. White-winged—I: 12–14 days; F: ?, altricial; B: ?

Other Behavior: Irruptive species, making large migrations beyond normal range in some winters.

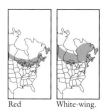
Red   White-wing.

Habitat: Coniferous woods. Red prefers pines; White-winged uses spruce and pines.

Voice: Songs a rapid warble. Red flight call a "jip jip jip"; White-winged flight call a "chif-chif."

Conservation:
Red:
BBS: E ⇑ C ↑ CBC: ↑
White-winged:
BBS: E ⇓ C ⇑ CBC: ↓

Common Redpoll
Hoary Redpoll

Carduelis flammea   Carduelis hornemanni

Common male

Hoary

Common female

Hoary

Identification: 5½" Both species recognized by their **red forecrown and black chin. COMMON— MALE: Brown streaking on flanks and on pale rump; rose limited to central breast in winter, on breast and cheeks in summer. FEMALE: Lacks red on breast, but has brown streaks on sides of upper breast. HOARY—MALE: Whitish overall; little or no streaking on underparts, nape, or rump; rose on breast absent or faint. FEMALE: Similar to male, but with no rose tinge on breast.** •Vast majority of redpolls seen south of Can. are Common Redpolls.

Feeding: Both eat seeds and buds of trees, grasses, weeds, and insects. Come to bird feeders for sunflower seed and thistle (niger) seed.

Nesting: Both have nests of twigs and grasses, placed in bush or on ground. Common—Eggs: 4–7, pale green or blue with dark marks; I: 10–11 days; F: 12 days, altricial; B: 1–2. Hoary—Eggs: 3–7, pale green or blue with dark marks; I: 11 days; F: 9–14 days, altricial; B: 1.

Other Behavior: Both are irruptive species.

Common   Hoary

Habitat: Summer in tundra; winter in brushy areas.

Voice: For both, song is a mixture of trills and buzzes; calls include a "chit chit" and a rising "sweeyeet."

Conservation: Common: BBS: E ⇓ C CBC: ↓ Hoary: CBC: ↓

Pine Siskin

Carduelis pinus

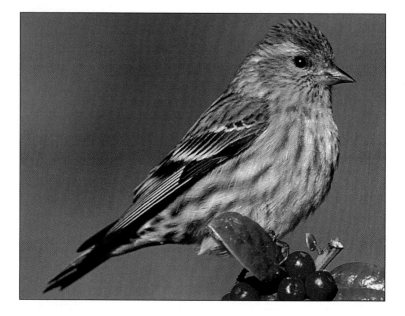

Identification: 5" **Brown above, light below; brown-streaked overall; long pointed bill; yellow on the wings and base of tail,** not always immediately visible in perched birds. **IN FLIGHT:** Yellow stripe down length of wing.

Feeding: Forages on the ground and in foliage for conifer cone seeds, weed seeds, insects, flower buds, and nectar. Comes to bird feeders, sometimes in large numbers, for sunflower and thistle (niger) seed.

Nesting: Nest of grasses, twigs, rootlets, bark strips, and lichens lined with feathers, fur, and rootlets, placed in tree branch 3–50 ft. above the ground. Eggs: 1–5, light green-blue with dark marks; I: 13 days; F: 14–15 days, altricial; B: 1–2.

Other Behavior: Irruptive species. Seen in large numbers in some years. Often found with goldfinches. Listen for buzzy "zrreeeee" call, a good clue to its presence.

Habitat: Coniferous or mixed woods, shrub thickets, suburban yards.

Voice: Song a mixture of trills and rapid warbles; calls include a "sweeyeet" and a buzzy, ascending "zrreeeee."

Conservation:
BBS: E ↑ C ↓ CBC: ⇑

Lesser Goldfinch

Carduelis psaltria

Male (eastern portion of range)

Male (western portion of range)

Female

Identification: 4½" **MALE:** Comes in 2 forms. In western half of range has a **black cap, green back, yellow belly, and white patch on wings.** In the eastern half of range is **black above, yellow below, and has a whitish patch on the wings. FEMALE:** Greenish above; yellow below; yellow undertail coverts; black wings have a white patch seen in flight. **IMM:** Female like adult female. Male has mixed green-and-black cap. Imm. plumage kept 1 year.

Feeding: Eats wide variety of seeds from trees, weeds, grasses, also flower buds and berries. Comes to bird feeders for sunflower and thistle (niger) seed.

Nesting: Nest of bark, moss, and plant stems lined with feathers, cotton, and plant down, placed in shrub or tree 2–30 ft. above the ground. Eggs: 3–6, light blue or blue-white; I: 12 days; F: ?, altricial; B: ?

Other Behavior: Found in small to large flocks in winter, often along with other goldfinches, Pine Siskins, and Dickcissels. Drawn to habitats that include a good water source.

Habitat: Woods edges, roadsides, gardens, parks.

Voice: Song a rapid series of repeated phrases from other birds' songs; call a "peeyeet."

Conservation: BBS: E C ⇓ CBC: ↓

American Goldfinch
Carduelis tristis

Summer male

Summer female

Winter

Identification: 5" SUMMER—MALE: Yellow body; black cap, wings, and tail. FEMALE: Yellowish green overall, with black wings and tail. WINTER—MALE: Yellowish brown, with yellow wash on face and chin; black wings with white wing bars. FEMALE: Grayish brown, with little yellow; dark brown wings with white wing bars.

Feeding: Feeds on the ground, on weed stalks and foliage, eating seeds, insects, berries. At bird feeders, prefers hulled sunflower and thistle (niger) seeds.

Nesting: Nest of strands from weeds and vines, downy filaments from wind-dispersed seeds, such as thistles, bound with caterpillar webbing, placed in shrub or tree 4–20 ft. above the ground. Eggs: 3–7, light blue; I: 12–14 days; F: 11–15 days, altricial; B: 1–2.

Other Behavior: During breeding, male does deep loop flight, an exaggeration of the normal looping flight of goldfinches, with the "perchicoree" call. Often done while circling his territory. Female builds nest and may start 2nd nest while fledged young are fed by male. In winter, found in flocks that wander in search of food.

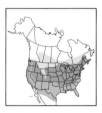

Habitat: Open areas with some shrubs and trees, farms, suburban yards, gardens.

Voice: Two songs: a long canarylike song, and a short forceful warble; calls include "sweeyeet," "beerbee," and "perchicoree" flight call.

Conservation: BBS: E ↓ C ↓ CBC: ↑

Evening Grosbeak

Coccothraustes vespertinus

Male, winter

Female, winter

Identification: 8" MALE: **Yellow body; darker head with a bright yellow eyebrow; black-and-white wings.** Bill is yellow in winter, pale green during summer. FEMALE: **Brownish gray overall, with yellow on nape; black-and-white wings.** Bill is same as male's.

Feeding: Feeds mainly on seeds of trees such as box elder, sugar maples, pines, tulip poplars. Also eats fruit, buds, nuts, insects, tree sap, and road salt. At bird feeders prefers sunflower seed.

Nesting: Nest of lichens, twigs, roots, and mosses lined with rootlets and finer materials, placed at the end of a tree branch 20–100 ft. above the ground. Eggs: 2–5, blue or bluish green with dark marks; I: 11–14 days; F: 13–14 days, altricial; B: 2.

Other Behavior: Breeding range has expanded. Irruptive species, occurring in large numbers in some years. At those times, it is common at bird feeders, flocks devouring large quantities of sunflower seed. In spring, beak turns from yellow to light green and courtship begins. Watch for the male feeding female sunflower seeds.

Habitat: Summers in northern mixed and coniferous woods; winters in open areas with trees and shrubs, suburban yards.

Voice: Song a halting warble; call is a ringing "peeer" and when given by a flock is reminiscent of sleighbells.

Conservation: BBS: E ↓ C CBC: ⇑

House Sparrow

Passer domesticus

Female

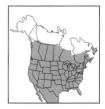
Summer male · Fall male

Identification: 6" MALE: Black bib; gray crown and cheek; rich brown back and nape. After molt in fall, gray feather tips obscure the black bib. FEMALE: Grayish-brown breast; brown crown; buffy eyebrow.

Feeding: Forages on the ground and in foliage for insects, spiders, small fruit, weed seeds, waste grain, and crumbs. Comes to feeders.

Nesting: Nest of straw, weeds, trash, grass, lined with feathers and hair, placed in any natural or constructed crevice or cavity, such as birdhouse, under eaves of house, in signs or nooks of commercial buildings. Eggs: 3–7, white, light green, or light blue with dark marks; I: 10–14 days; F: 14–17 days, altricial; B: 2–3.

Other Behavior: Roosts in groups at night in fall and winter, and also during midday, when birds gather at fixed spot and chirp noisily for up to an hour. Also called English Sparrow because was introduced from England to N. America in middle of 19th century. Aggressively competes with our native cavity-nesting species of birds for nest spots. Will kill adult birds, nestlings, and eggs of other species in order to take over a birdhouse or cavity.

Habitat: Urban areas, parks, open farmland.

Voice: Song a repeated "chirup chireep chirup"; call "chilup."

Conservation: BBS: E ⇓ C ↓ CBC: ↓

Eurasian Tree Sparrow
Passer montanus

Identification: 5½" Brown cap; small black bib; white cheek with a black spot in the center.

Feeding: Eats grains, weed seeds, and insects. Comes to bird feeders.

Nesting: Nest of grasses, straw, feathers, hay, and weed stems lined with feathers, placed in natural or artificial cavity, including birdhouse. Eggs: 2–8, white or light gray with dark marks; I: 12–14 days; F: 12–14 days, altricial; B: 2–3.

Other Behavior: Old World species introduced at St. Louis, Mo., in 1870 and 1879. Lives in suburbs, parks, and farmland there and in nearby western Ill. These sparrows are often seen in flocks of 25–100 birds, sometimes mixed with House Sparrows. More retiring than House Sparrow and generally seen more in trees and less around buildings when House Sparrows are present.

Habitat: Farms and urban areas.

Voice: Song a high-pitched repeated "chirup chireep chirup"; call "cheeleep."

Conservation:
BBS: E ⇑ C CBC: ⇑

Glossary

Accipiter — A genus of hawks with generally short wings and long tails; they catch other birds in the air.

Air sac — A membrane that extends from the lungs and in grouse and prairie-chickens is often inflated during breeding displays.

Altricial — A pattern of development in which young birds are featherless and dependent upon the parents for food and warmth for the first few weeks of their life.

Breastband — A dark band of feathers across the breast of a bird.

Breeding range — The geographical area where a species regularly breeds.

Brood — All young from a single clutch of eggs.

Buteo — A genus of hawks with long broad wings and short tails; they catch mostly rodents.

Call — A short instinctive vocalization.

Cap — A darker area of feathers on the top of the head.

Cere — A raised fleshy area at the base of the upper mandible on hawks, eagles, falcons, and their relatives.

Chevrons — Small V-shaped dots on the underparts of some birds.

Clutch — A complete set of eggs laid for one brood.

Colonial — A term used to describe many pairs of birds nesting very close together.

Coverts — Small feathers that overlap the bases of larger feathers on the wings and tail.

Crest — Slightly longer feathers on the top of the head which, when raised, form a peak.

Ear patch — Darker feathers located just behind and below the eye around the area of the ear.

Ear tuft — Longer feathers on either side of the top of the head. These usually can be raised and lowered.

Eclipse plumage — A briefly held nonbreeding plumage of male ducks which resembles that of the female. It usually occurs in mid-summer.

Eyebrow — A stripe above the eye.

Eye comb — A brightly colored fleshy area over the eye; most common in grouse and prairie-chickens and used in their displays.

Eye crescent — An arc of lighter color above and/or below the eye.

Eye-ring — A lighter area encircling the eye.

Eye-stripe — A stripe on the head from the base of the bill to the eye and on behind the eye.

Facial disk — Feathers that radiate out from the eyes, especially in owls.

Flank — The side of the belly just below the wing.

Flight feathers — The largest feathers of the wings; called primaries and secondaries.

Gorget — The area of the throat on hummingbirds that is often iridescent on the males.

Hood — A plumage pattern in which the head of a bird is all dark and contrasts with lighter feathers on the body.

Hybrid — The result of two species interbreeding.

Immature — A young bird in between juvenile and adult stages.

Inner wing — The portion of the wing closest to the body.

Irruption — A rapid increase in population of a species.

Introduced — Term used to describe a species that was brought by humans to a geographical area outside its normal range.

Juvenal plumage — The first full set of feathers of a young bird after it loses its natal down.

Juvenile — A young bird in juvenal plumage.

Leading edge — The front edge; term often used when describing plumage on wings.

Lore — The area between the eye and the base of the bill.

Mandible — The upper or lower half of the bill.

Mirror — Term used in relation to gulls to refer to the small white dots at the tips of the wings.

Molt — A complete or partial shedding of feathers.

Morph — A regularly occurring color variation within a species that is not related to the sex, age, or seasonal plumage of the bird.

Moustache — Dark streaks on either side of the base of the bill along the sides of the throat.

Nape — The back of the head and neck.

Neck-ring — A darker area of feathering that encircles the throat.

Plumage — The complete set of a bird's feathers at a certain time.

Polyandrous — Pairing and mating with more than one male.

Polygynous — Pairing and mating with more than one female.

Precocial — A pattern of development in which young birds hatch with feathers and are able to move and feed themselves.

Primaries — The longest flight feathers; they are located on the outer half of the wing.

Rump — The top of the base of the tail.

Secondaries — Flight feathers located on the inner half of the wing; they are about half as long as the primaries.

Sideburn — A dark vertical mark behind the eye, especially on falcons.

Song — An extended complex vocalization that is in part learned.

Spectacles — Light eye-rings and lores, making the bird look like it is wearing a pair of glasses.

Speculum — A colored patch on the inner wing of ducks.

Territory — A defended area.

Trailing edge — The back edge; term often used when describing plumage on wings.

Underparts — The area of the body below the wings, including the belly, breast, and throat.

Upperparts — The area above the wings, including the back, nape, and top of the head.

Uppertail coverts — The small feathers that cover the top of the base of the tail.

Undertail coverts — The small feathers that cover the underside of the base of the tail.

Vent — The anal and reproductive opening.

Wattle — A fleshy bumpy area on the face of a bird; often hangs down, as in the wattle of a Wild Turkey.

Window — A lighter area of translucence in a wing, often at the base of the primaries.

Wing bar — A continuous lighter area at the tips of wing coverts.

Wing lining — The coverts of the underwing.

Wing-stripe — A lengthwise stripe on the upper surface of the wing.

Winter plumage — The plumage held during the winter months.

Winter range — The geographical range of the bird during winter.

Wrist — The point of the first bend in the wing.

Photo Credits

The letter or letters immediately following each page number refer to the position of the photograph on the page (T = top; B = bottom; L = left; C = center; R = right). A second number in parentheses after a credit indicates that the photograph also appears as a small silhouette in the Learning Pages or in the Quick Guide to the Most Common Birds. For example, 261L (xxiv) identifies the photo of the male Downy Woodpecker, shown in the Species Accounts on page 261 and in the Quick Guide on page xxiv.

Steve Bentsen: 6, 55R, 118R, 139BR, 161L, 178R, 206L, 207BR, 215, 224 (xxiv), 227, 229R, 232R, 245TR, 253, 254R, 255, 257R, 260L, 260R, 280, 281, 314R, 321, 382, 394L, 396TL, 396TR, 398R, 399L, 399TR, 399BR, 407R, 415L, 415R, 418T, 437R (xxi), 442R, 449R, 457L.

Rick and Nora Bowers: 291, 309L, 310R, 346, 347B, 398L, 428BL, 439L, 439R, 443R (xxii).

Lysle R. Brinker: 216T, 219B, 374BR, 392BR, 435BR, 455TL, 455BL, 455TR, 455BR.

Kathleen and Lindsey Brown: 86B, 111R, 264L (xxiv), 314L (xxiii), 317 (xxiii), 318L (xxiii), 318R, 334L, 334R, 349L (xxii), 349R (xxii), 393L (xix), 393R (xix), 409 (405), 417L, 424BR (xx) (405), 427R (xx), 458TR (xviii), 458L (xviii).

Bill Burt: 133, 134.

William S. Clark: 104BL, 111BL, 118TL (93), 119TL.

Cornell Laboratory of Ornithology: L. Page Brown — 107R; Linda Drake — 352BR; Bill Dyer — 354BR, 369; Lang Elliott — 308; Mike Hopiak — 249L; O. S. Pettingill — 199TL (192); Mary Tremaine — 120T, Fred K. Truslow — 273L; Lawrence Wales — 135B.

Rob Curtis: 228L, 228R, 275R, 277L, 277R, 278, 286, 287, 292, 311T, 315, 322, 327, 331T, 331B, 335, 338, 352T, 354BL, 363T, 371BR, 373L (351), 381B, 384, 385L, 389T, 392L, 406, 423, 424TR, 426TR, 426BR, 429BR, 432BR.

Dave Czaplak: 210BL.

Mike Danzenbaker: 3B, 8B, 10T, 10B, 12L, 12TR, 12BR, 16, 17, 45R, 49L, 54, 57T, 64B, 68T, 68B, 71T, 74T, 74B, 81T, 83B, 89TL, 89BL, 129, 137, 146BL (145), 155 (145), 157R, 166R, 171T, 188L, 188R, 189R, 198TL (192),

201TR, 202BL, 202BR, 204TL, 208TR, 208L, 211TR, 212TL, 212BL, 217TL, 245L, 249R, 273R, 275L (266), 276, 282, 285, 288R, 304, 309R, 311B, 312B (xxiii), 323, 332T, 347TR, 348R, 368T, 371L (351), 390, 396BR, 402, 414, 417TR, 418B, 420L, 420R, 421L, 425, 433B, 434B, 435TR, 436BR, 448TR, 457BR, 459T (xviii).

Larry R. Ditto: 45L, 59T, 61B, 73B, 123L, 130, 143, 223B, 235, 243, 244R, 319, 345, 394R, 416BL, 440BL, 440BR.

Steven D. Faccio: 326 (xx), 336B.

Kenneth W. Fink: 39, 53B, 61T, 69B, 76BR, 78R, 86B, 140B, 171BL, 185BL, 194BL, 195TR, 196T, 199BR, 202TL, 204BL, 213TR, 225, 242, 303L, 432TR, 440TL, 441L, 445L, 450BL, 451L, 451R.

Sam Fried: 189L, 193TR, 196BL, 200T, 201TL, 203TR, 204BR, 205L, 211TL, 214BR, 232L, 237, 263R, 268, 279 (267), 307L, 307R, 310L, 431B, 433T, 438R, 443TL.

Gary K. Froehlich: 25TL, 25R, 27L, 28L, 28R, 66T, 66B, 83T, 99L (90), 100TR (92), 160L, 160BR, 183, 193TL (192), 231, 283, 442L.

W. Edward Harper: 124R, 128B, 197TR.

James R. Hill, III: 305L, 305R, 306R.

Joseph R. Jehl, Jr.: 186BR, 187BR, 194BR.

Kevin T. Karlson: 4T, 9T, 77BL, 77T, 79T, 126T, 126BL, 126BR, 169BL (144), 174T, 174B, 178L, 179L, 186T, 187T, 251L (xix), 357B, 361BR, 363B (351), 372R.

Peter LaTourrette: 195BL.

Harold and Kathy Lindstrom: 366R.

Stephen G. Maka: 41L, 94L (92), 172BL (144), 262L, 262R, 341 (xxiv).

Maslowski Photograph: 29L, 52, 53T, 116R, 131, 184, 186BL, 187BL, 213L, 236L, 240, 254L, 256, 271, 284 (267), 293, 295, 296, 320, 324 (xx), 328, 329, 330, 337, 339, 356B, 358B (350), 359B, 377, 389B, 400T, 426L, 427L (xx) (405), 432L, 435L, 460BR (404).

Arthur Morris/Birds as Art: 11T, 11B, 24L, 26L, 27R, 29R, 32, 33R, 38R, 38BL, 40T, 40B, 41R, 42L, 44L, 44R, 46, 47L, 51, 60B, 62, 64T, 65B, 72T, 72B, 73T, 75T, 84T, 84B, 85T, 135T, 138T, 141, 146BR, 147R, 148, 151L, 152, 154, 156T, 156B, 157L, 158R, 163 (145), 164, 165T, 165BR, 168T, 168B, 170T, 170BL (144), 170BR, 172T, 172BR, 173T, 173BL, 175B, 177BL (144), 177TR, 177BR, 181TL, 181TR,

181BR, 182L, 182TR (145), 182BR, 185BR, 193BR, 194TR, 195BR, 197BR, 199BL (192), 200BL, 201BL, 201BR, 206BR, 209T, 210BR, 213BR, 217TR, 270 (266), 299 (xxiii), 332B, 347TL, 355, 358T (350), 359T, 361T, 364T, 364BR, 366L, 370L, 371TR, 375T, 385BR, 391TR, 395L, 410L (xx) (405), 416T, 422, 443BL (xxii).

Blair Nikula: 22R, 23T, 23B, 173BR, 209BR, 211BL, 211BR, 212TR, 218R, 348L.

Rod Norden: 20.

Wayne R. Petersen: 15, 19, 26R, 417BR, 431T.

B. "Moose" Peterson: 88B.

Photo/Nats: Don Johnston — 124L; Barbara Magnuson — 76T; Stephen Maka —203BL; John F. O'Connor — 60T.

B. J. Rose: 198BR, 448BR.

Ray Schwarz: 119R, 119BL.

Leroy Simon: 35R, 138B.

Arnold Small: 4B, 77BR, 78L, 79BR, 80B, 81B, 82B, 87T, 87B, 88T, 181BL, 185T, 195TL, 217BR, 222, 269.

Brian E. Small: 85B, 160TR (145), 174BR, 214TR, 229R, 230, 248, 250, 252R, 272, 288TL, 289, 294, 297, 300, 302T (xxiii), 316L, 336T, 340 (xix), 343, 354T, 357T, 360T, 360BL, 361BL, 362T, 362B, 367, 370TL, 373TR, 373BR, 376T (351), 376B (351), 380, 385TR, 386T (350), 386BL (350), 387T, 387B, 388T, 388B, 395BR, 397L, 397BR, 400BR, 407L, 410TR, 410BR, 411, 413, 421R, 428T, 440TR, 446L (xxi), 457TR.

Hugh P. Smith, Jr.: 24R, 70, 101R, 102R, 139TR, 198BL (192), 245BR, 252L, 259R, 316R, 325, 342 (xxiv), 430BR, 441R, 448TL, 448BL, 450BR, 453TL (xix), 453TR, 456 (xx), 458BR (xviii), 460L (xx).

Barbara Spencer: 13.

Lillian and Don Stokes: 7R, 25BL, 33L, 34, 36, 38TL, 42R, 43L, 43R, 47B, 55L, 56, 58, 94R, 139L, 140T, 142, 149R, 161R, 167B, 175T, 261L, 261TR, 261BR (xxiv), 306L (xxiv), 453B (xix) (404).

John L. Tveten: 21B, 31, 37, 121, 123R, 149L, 151R, 162, 166L, 193BL (192), 198TR, 199TR, 202TR, 204TR, 207T, 214L, 221R, 437L (xxi), 444T (xxii).

Richard R. Veit: 14, 69T, 200BR, 203BR.

Tom Vezo: 35L, 57B, 59B, 71B, 76BL, 79BL, 80T, 82T, 103BL, 125T, 125B, 146TR, 147L, 150T (144), 167T (144), 169T, 169BR, 176, 179R, 196BR, 207BL, 210TR, 247B, 257L, 259L, 274 (267), 360BR, 370BL, 381T, 386BR.

VIREO: S. Bahrt — 313; Rick and Nora Bowers — 132, 247T; John Cancalosi — 153, 223T; A. and S. Carey — 122, 234; R. J. Chandler — 180R, 333L, 333R; H. Clarke — 356T; A. Cruickshank, 100BR; H. Cruickshank — 194TL, 205L, 206TR, 220, 416BR, 434T, 445R; Rob Curtis — 238, 303R, 401, 408; T. Davis — 150B; J. Dunning — 159; Sam Fried — 165BL, 268; W. Greene — 67, 127, 236R, 251R, 265L, 312T (xxiii), 459B (xviii); V. Hasselblad — 461; B. Henry — 444B, 454TL, 454BL, 454TR, 454BR; D. R. Herr — 103R; J. Hoffman — 290; M. P. Kahl — 209BL; Kevin T. Karlson — 3T, 5B, 9B; S. J. Lang — 5T, 136, 258R, 436L, 436TR, 568L (xxi); G. Lasley — 365; J. Maron — 180L; Arthur Morris/Birds as Art — 7L, 50, 75B, 89R, 146TL, 197BL, 203TL (192), 210TL, 212BR, 288BL, 298L, 302B, 368B, 391L, 424L, 428BR, 438L, 449L; O. S. Pettingill, Jr. — 452L (xix); R. L. Pitman — 18, 21T, 22L; D. Roby and K. Brink — 216B; F. K. Schleicher — 158L (145), 352BL, 430TL (xxiii) (405); B. Schorre — 344, 353, 364BL, 372L, 374TR, 374L, 375B (351), 378, 383, 391BR, 392TR, 395TR, 396BL, 397TR, 400BL, 447L, 447TR, 447BR, 450TL (xviii), 450TR (xviii); Johann Schumacher — 63, 264BR, 446R (xxi); T. J. Ulrich — 218L, 219T, 226, 258L (xxiv), 301, 429L, 430BL, 430TR, 452R (xix); R. Villani — 177TL, 263L, 460TR (xx) (404); A. Walther — 197TL; Doug Wechsler — 30R, 65T, 221L (xxiv), 246, 298R, 379; Brian K. Wheeler — 98BL, 100L, 102BL, 105TR, 106L (91), 110BR, 112R, 116BL (93), 120L, 120R; J. R. Woodward — 8T, 568R (xxi); D. and M. Zimmerman — 264TR, 429TR.

Brian K. Wheeler: 48L (91), 48R, 49R (91), 95 (93), 96L (93), 96R, 97L, 97R, 98TL (93), 98R, 99C, 99R, 101TL (92), 101BL, 102TL (92), 103TL (92), 104TL, 104R, 105L, 105BR, 106C, 106R, 107L (91), 107C, 108L, 108R, 109L, 109C, 109R, 110L, 110TR, 111TL (91), 112L, 113R, 113TL (91), 113BL, 114L (90), 114TR, 114BR, 115L, 115R, 116TL, 117L (93), 117R, 118BL, 120L, 120R.

Art Wolfe: 217BL, 233, 239, 241, 244L.

Index

Color Tab Index to Bird Groups

Quick Guide to the Most Common Birds

Seabirds — Loons, Grebes, Shearwaters, Pelicans, Cormorants

Heronlike Birds — Bitterns, Herons, Egrets, Ibises

Swans, Geese, Ducks — Whistling-Ducks, Swans, Geese, Ducks

Hawklike Birds — Osprey, Kites, Eagles, Hawks, Falcons

Chickenlike Birds — Pheasant, Grouse, Turkey, Quail

Marsh Birds — Rails, Gallinule, Moorhen, Coot, plus Cranes

Shorebirds — Plovers, Stilt, Avocet, Sandpipers, Dowitchers, Phalaropes

Gull-like Birds — Jaegers, Gulls, Terns, Skimmer, plus Alcids

Pigeonlike Birds — Pigeon, Doves

Owls and Other Nocturnal Birds — Owls, Nighthawks, Whip-poor-will

Swift, Hummingbirds — Swift, Hummingbirds, plus Kingfishers

Woodpeckers — Woodpeckers, Sapsucker, Flicker

Flycatchers — Flycatchers, Phoebes, Kingbirds

Shrikes, Vireos — Shrikes, Vireos

Jays, Crows — Jays, Crows, Ravens

Swallows — Martin, Swallows

Chickadees, Nuthatches, Wrens — Chickadees, Titmice, Nuthatches, Wrens

Thrushes, Mimics — Bluebird, Thrushes, Robin, Catbird, Mockingbird, Thrashers

Warblers — Warblers, Parula, Redstart, Ovenbird, Waterthrushes, Chat

Tanagers, Grosbeaks, Buntings — Tanagers, Cardinal, Grosbeaks, Buntings

Sparrows — Towhees, Sparrows, Junco, Longspurs

Blackbirds, Orioles — Blackbirds, Grackles, Cowbirds, Orioles

Finches — Finches, Crossbills, Redpolls, Goldfinches